WORDS AND THE
FIRST WORLD WAR

ALSO AVAILABLE FROM BLOOMSBURY

Linguanomics, Gabrielle Hogan-Brun
The Language of War Monuments, David Machin and Gill Abousnnouga
Wordcrime, John Olsson

WORDS AND THE FIRST WORLD WAR

Language, Memory, Vocabulary

Julian Walker

Bloomsbury Academic
An imprint of Bloomsbury Publishing Plc

B L O O M S B U R Y
LONDON · OXFORD · NEW YORK · NEW DELHI · SYDNEY

Bloomsbury Academic

An imprint of Bloomsbury Publishing Plc

50 Bedford Square	1385 Broadway
London	New York
WC1B 3DP	NY 10018
UK	USA

www.bloomsbury.com

BLOOMSBURY and the Diana logo are trademarks of Bloomsbury Publishing Plc

First published 2017

British Library Cataloguing-in-Publication Data

A catalogue record for this book is available from the British Library.

ISBN:	HB:	978-1-3500-0193-0
	PB:	978-1-3500-0192-3
	ePDF:	978-1-3500-0195-4
	ePub:	978-1-3500-1274-5

Library of Congress Cataloging-in-Publication Data

A catalog record for this book is available from the Library of Congress.

Cover design by Irene Martinez Costa
Cover image: First World War letter from a schoolboy to his father
© IWM / Soldier reading newspaper. Image from the private collection of the author.

Typeset by RefineCatch Limited, Bungay, Suffolk
Printed and bound in Great Britain

To find out more about our authors and books visit www.bloomsbury.com. Here you will find extracts, author interviews, details of forthcoming events and the option to sign up for our newsletters.

To my grandparents, who went through it

To my grandparents, who went through it all

CONTENTS

ACKNOWLEDGEMENTS

Many people have given support to this research and writing through conversations and suggestions in person or through the internet; thanks particularly to Alistair Martin, Jonathon Green, Lynda Mugglestone and Rob Schäfer. I wish to thank Christophe Declercq and Peter Doyle, for their encouragement and assistance; the editorial and design team at Bloomsbury for bringing it to realisation, and Sara Bryant for her copy editing; my family for their support; and my parents, from whom I learned the love of words.

ILLUSTRATIONS

ABBREVIATIONS

AEF	American Expeditionary Force
AIF	Australian Imperial Force
ANZAC	Australian and New Zealand Army Corps
ASC	Army Service Corps
BEF	British Expeditionary Corps
CLC	Chinese Labour Corps
DORA	Defence of the Realm Act
FSP	Field Service Postcard
GHQ	General Headquarters
ILP	Independent Labour Party
NCO	Non-Commissioned Officer
PBI	Poor bloody infantry
PoW	Prisoner of War
RAF	Royal Air Force
RAMC	Royal Army Medical Corps
RFA	Royal Field Artillery
RFC	Royal Flying Corps
RNAS	Royal Naval Air Service
RSM	Regimental Sergeant Major
UPS	University and Public School
VAD	Voluntary Aid Detachment
WREN	Women's Royal Naval Service

PREFACE

n 1914 my grandfather was living in east London, was working as a clerk, and was an enthusiastic performer of comic songs. Pre-war photographs show him in evening dress, with top hat and monocle, slicked-back hair and a performer's smile. A programme for a charity concert in October 1914 shows him singing four songs: 'Now are we all here?', 'Tally Ho', 'As far as it goes', and 'I followed her here, and I followed her there'. In 1915 he attested under the Derby Scheme, which involved enlisting, but returning to work until called for; at some stage he was either wounded or declared unfit, as he was on garrison duty in late 1916. There is a sudden change in 1918, seen in his diary, with entries only from the autumn, which show him at the Front, temporarily blinded in a gas attack, on burial parties, learning to use a Lewis gun. The spare pages at back and front have a few addresses and the lyrics for a comic song, which I assume was his own composition.

I was six when my grandfather died, so I have few memories, but those I have are of him performing, singing either to me or on stage. He was one of those hundreds of thousands who 'never spoke about the war'. My memories are of a gentle-mannered old man; these were also the memories of those I knew who knew him. How could I reconcile these with the knowledge both that he had been trained to use a Lewis gun, had in some capacity been involved in the fighting, and possibly had killed; but also that, from the evidence of the diary, a single letter to my grandmother, and another programme from February 1919, he had been thinking about dressing up in a Pierrot costume and singing songs with silly, harmless and naïve lyrics? This is a question that I cannot answer. How did people switch between the extremely harmless and the ultimately harmful? How did they manoeuvre between the creative and the destructive, and what can their surviving words tell us about this?

'Fritz has made a mess of this place', my grandfather wrote in the one surviving letter; the war made a mess of people, people's bodies and minds, so much so that many – perhaps most – of the soldiers who survived tried to close the doors on that period of their lives. Yet through this bewilderingly horrific period of history, people talked, wrote and read; some record of their spoken words survives, and we look through the written record for evidence of how they talked to each other. There are so many fields of language that indicate how people managed: journalism, soldiers' postcards, memoirs, official reports, poster slogans, song lyrics, graffiti, politicians' speeches. All of them can take us some way to understanding how words got people into this situation, how words helped them get through it, and how words helped them deal with it afterwards.

R. H. Mottram has a charming description of British soldiers doing little domestic services in a Flemish farmhouse, with 'elaborate Sunday-school politeness, ... tittering slightly at anything not quite nice, and singing, not so often the vulgar music-hall numbers, as the more sentimental "Christmas successes" from the pantomimes'. I can easily imagine my grandfather there, not so far from the nice front rooms of lower middle-class terraced houses in east London, and the household that he grew up in; it was an environment where words mattered – where his 'best girl', my grandmother, who was in service, learned that the choice of one word rather than another showed you to be slightly more refined. Yet the lyrics of the song in my grandfather's diary have an edge, a sharpness, an acceptance of violence, that make for uneasy reading. Time and again, while researching and writing this book, I have found myself discomfited by the polarity of the simple, sometimes silly, almost childish, use of words, in the same environment as the most cynical, callous and inhumane actions; I find myself repeating the question – how can this have been? If this study does not provide an answer, I hope it helps to formulate the question.

INTRODUCTION

We have become accustomed to think of the First World War as affecting everyone by loss, with terms such as 'the Fallen' and 'the lost generation' focusing on death and grieving. But the period saw great creativity in the English language: changes in how words were used to persuade and inform people, incentives to find ways of expressing the apparently inexpressible, and the development of ways to control communication. Slang became an object of fascination, with competing claims over meanings, forms and origins, a diversion from the usual disapproval of new forms of language; English-speakers were exposed to languages that were new to them, and temporarily adopted or created terms from those languages; and their own language separated people at the Front from those at home.

As well as changing in use and meaning as terms moved between different groups, some terms changed during the course of the war, as part of the normal process of language change, possibly accelerated through extreme circumstances. The spelling 'Gerry' largely disappeared and was replaced by 'Jerry',[1] 'I am going on fine' began to be superseded by 'I am getting on fine'. 'Wanky' changed to 'wonky' during the course of the war,[2] and, as a result of soldiers' contact with French, some words in longstanding use were edged out by French replacements. Certain regional variants became dominant within some groups, technical jargon became widespread, and the precursor of 'politically correct language' emerged; wordplay and irony became prevalent, and, while a tension developed between verbal expression and verbal retention, as the war dragged on verbal humour became more important. Charles Wilson, Lord Moran, writing long after the war, noted how monotony had become a serious problem in the trenches from 1916, as few soldiers read, apart from the repeated reading of letters from home, evidenced by the constant requests for a letter; as Moran saw it, apathy and 'doing nothing' were only relieved by humour.[3]

At this point it is necessary to establish the subject, to determine how to answer the question – what is the language of the First World War? There are many types of language to be examined. If we look at just postcards sent home by soldiers – and these are among the nearest formats to people speaking freely to each other that have survived – we would have to consider the following: the postcard message, the text printed on the postcard, the officially authorised postcard (Field Service Postcard), family slang and colloquialisms within the message, the use of French expressions which might not be understood at home, the awareness of what cannot be written, the relationship between what is written and what would have been spoken, and the language of the censor. This range of different types of language would apply across several fields of linguistic activity, from the words chalked on a shell to the wording of an official citation for bravery. A corpus study of the period would have to study every accessible utterance in order to make a satisfactory statistical analysis, but would effectively create itself, a linguistic one-to-one map of the world. The present study has of necessity been based on selectivity, a working selectivity based on extensive reading across the spectrum, but with the awareness that everybody was affected by the language of the war. From this focuses emerge, focuses that are very much influenced by the way we now look at the conflict, dominated in the twentieth-century mind by 'the trench'. Dan Todman has proposed that since the post-war period 'culture came to focus on the soldier in the trench as the iconic experience of the real war',[4] though Richard S. Grayson's study of the time spent in various activities by all the sections of the military indicates that less time than might be expected was actually spent in the trenches.[5]

The 'man in the trench' as the icon of the war has maintained an unchallengeable position down to the present, through mediations such as the BBC series *The Trench* (2002), the market for fragments of shrapnel, the number of books focusing on the soldiers' gear, clothing or journeys to the Front. The front line occupies a place in the public consciousness of the war as being more important than any other place or activity – the 'business end' of the war, the most dangerous part. It is inevitable that this should be so, because this was, it is supposed, where the most extreme experiences happened – it makes up the majority of what is remembered, and what is thought of as documented. In fact it was not just the frontline trench that was a locus of extreme danger; communication trenches were under heavy artillery fire, and intersection points behind the fire trench were frequently 'taped' by snipers and machine-gunners, resulting in high casualties. But the front line and its close merging, through saps (listening posts), into no man's land, has remained more iconic than the naval patrol, the home area under Zeppelin raid, the hospital ten miles behind the lines, and countless other sites and experiences.

This was not just a post-war perception. During the war the military, emotional, and political movement was towards the trenches at the Front. Specimen trenches were dug in parks as fundraisers, children and unattached ladies sent letters to soldiers 'in the trenches', and prospective soldiers were advised to 'Learn to use your entrenching tool, and to make the most of it'.[6]

The most basic awareness of the war includes a line of trenches stretching from the North Sea to Switzerland; the basic chronological icons – the Christmas Truce, The Somme, The Armistice – are located there, as is the iconic imagery of the soldier carrying his wounded comrade on his shoulders, the section going over the parapet, or the sentry pressed against the side of the trench peering over the edge; *Pearson's Weekly* on 17 April 1915 reckoned that '"Trench" is at present the commonest word in the English language' (p. 921). The frequency of use of the term 'in the trenches', and its value as both very specific and not

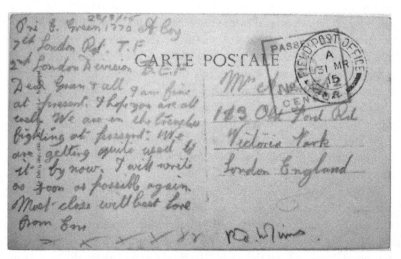

FIGURE 0.1 1915 postcard sent 'On Active Service'. The writer notes that 'we are in the trenches fighting at present', and has, against regulations, given details of his unit.

a problem to the censors, shows how much it mattered; 'in the trenches' particularly embraced more than one concept – for the people at home it was a place, while for the soldier it was place, experience, a nemesis, a set period of time, an ordeal and, if survived, an achievement.

But the experience of the war was just as much a round of petty tasks, training, sleeping, being bored, fantasising about home leave, repair, amusement, convalescence, sentry duty and drill. It was an experience that included veterans too old to fight, and people at home, both of which sections of the populace found themselves linguistically at odds with the men at the Front: 'old soldiers' felt that the slang of the new armies was poor stuff compared to the slang of the pre-war professional army, and those at home found their vocabulary enriched by terms such as 'over the top' – which by the time it was being used in Britain had acquired a different meaning at the Front – or 'toot the sweet', which was considered passé at the Front when it was 'the new language' at home.

All fields of activity to do with the war produced new terms, many of them involving picking up terms from other languages, or parodying official expressions. The linguistic phenomena of the period emerged from the relationships between groups of people, the rank-and-file soldier struggling with the staff officers, the home press struggling with the desire of their readership to know as much as possible and the desire of the authorities to tell them as little as possible, the relationship based on what could not be said by the soldier to his family. All those who had a voice, and some who did not, should be taken into account. And the phenomenon did not stop at 11 o'clock on 11 November 1918; indeed some of its most interesting aspects involve how people recorded the language of the war afterwards, how people abandoned war terms, and the kinds of memoirs that emerged into the public domain in the decades after 1918. This should surely include the language of war memorials, post-war expressions such as 'the lost generation' and 'lions led by donkeys', and the survival of First World War slang a hundred years after the event.

It is tempting to assume that the further in time we are from the event the more likely it is that memories are diluted; selectivity is manifested by the need to tell a good story, or the relationship between speaker/writer and listener/reader. This is always so, not only when removed at a temporal distance from the event. The legal frameworks at the beginning of the twentieth century constraining the printing of taboo words, and the near uniformity with which soldiers' postcards are limited to talking about the weather, cigarettes, cake, the writer's health, and the irregularity of receipt of letters from home show that not all that was in the writer's head or mouth went down on paper. The size of the available medium of communication necessarily influenced the text: apparently terse comments in pocket diaries were constrained by the size of the page. Different micro-discourses emerge, and all merit consideration, including where their absence is noticeable. Some discourses emerge more strongly than others: soldiers' and sailors' correspondence to home has survived much more than correspondence in the other direction – there has been more documentation of soldiers' letters and postcards, more research and infinitely more publishing. Letters from home were read and reread, stored in conditions of stress, and are documented as being strewn across the battlefields after attacks.[7] We may surmise that after the war there was no need for former servicemen to keep them, or that they were reminders of distress for the recipient, even that there was a general perception that they were no longer needed; while correspondence from troops to their families would always carry emotions of gratitude for the writer's survival, or remembrance in case of loss.

From the various discourses of the period emerge a range of voices creating texts which either repeat terms, or initiate terms which are later repeated, or, in situations where certain terms might be expected, use other terms which are not encountered again. A new weapon is used, gas for example: people encounter it, and 'are gassed'; they try to hide the fact that they are using it and call their own weapon 'the accessory', 'roger', and other names; they become so familiar with it and its effects that they feel it is acceptable to re-use an existing metaphor for being drunk ('gassed'); a particular kind of gas, from its colour, becomes 'mustard gas', while protection against it becomes, not an 'anti-gas mask', but a 'gas-mask'. In this situation calling it a 'goggle-eyed bugger with a tit' stands out as an idiolect or a sociolect; we could investigate where, among whom, and for how long the term lasted, and certainly even if there was no mention of it elsewhere, or until Robert Graves published *Goodbye to All That* in 1929, and it would still require to be considered as an example of 'the language of the First World War'. The more frequently a term is used the more likely there are to be variants, even contradictory variants: was 'a Blighty touch' a wound received in combat that would be welcomed for its assurance of a return to Blighty, or a wound self-inflicted with the same intention? There is documentation for both usages.[8]

However, problematic areas remain, especially where documentation and literature overlap: how do we deal with the subject of 'authenticity' which came under question during the war itself, how do we treat fiction drawn from fact? Descriptions of combat, such as those in Charles Edmonds' *A Subaltern's War* (1929) or Lord Moran's *Anatomy of Courage* (1945) seem far more authentic than Ian Hay's *The First Hundred Thousand* (1915/16), but Lancelot Spicer's letter home on 3 December 1915 stated that Hay's work was 'exceedingly true to life'.[9] Evaluations have to weigh up Edmonds' edge of fear and Moran's use of the present tense in describing a trench raid with Sidney de Loghe's claim at the beginning of *The Straits Impregnable* (1917): 'This book, written in Australia, Egypt and Gallipoli, is true'.

As an example of how complex are questions of authenticity within fiction it is useful to examine some sound recordings of dramatisations of trench scenes, which were the subject of study by Paul Fussell;[10] it is also essential to consider the gap between composed speech and documented speech. These recordings were published on disc by Parlophone, with titles such as *The Attack/The Estaminet*, the artists being named as 'Some of The Boys'.[11] Clearly recorded in the studio, they feature a range of sound effects best described as 'suggestive of artillery', but the sound-acting is strong and reasonably natural. A range of regional and class accents is noticeable. Fussell describes *The Attack* as being 'played absolutely straight, with great attention to "realism"'. The script is full of words and phrases that act as markers, both of the place and experience, such as calls for stretcher-bearers, observations of the need to cut the wire; and there are markers, such as 'Jerry's got the wind up' and 'clean out that big boche dug-out', which use vocabulary that has come to be associated with the period. But there are more subtle markers, the regional slang: 'lumme', ''ark at that bird' and 'I couldn't 'arf do with a cup of char'; and what would have seemed most authenticating to veterans: the opening noise, of birdsong.

The sequence of activity is accelerated from calm to preparation to the point where the soldiers go over the top; Fussell's view is that 'the suspense is well managed, and the effect is surprisingly exciting', but essentially it is theatrical, 'a sort of folk-memoir'. It is thus a mix of the authentic – the accents and dialect phrases, seldom documented elsewhere, plus the birdsong – and the inauthentic, that is, something made with the intention that the home listeners would be informed, stimulated and to a certain extent entertained.

This can be contrasted with a similar recording, directed by Major A. E. Rees, issued in 1917 as *In the Trenches*, one of a six-part series in which Privates Ginger and Tippy progress from 'Leaving for the Front' to 'Back Home in Blighty'. In *In the Trenches* Privates Ginger and Tippy have a bet on whether a whizz-bang is a dud or not, Tippy is found to be learning French ('Oui-oui – that's yus, yus'), and Tippy unasked goes out to rescue a wounded comrade in no man's land. Ginger keeps up a commentary on his actions:

Bravo Tippy, my boy, I'm covering yer. Go it laddie. Gently does it. They've spotted yer. That's it, lie still a bit. Ah, the perishers, they've turned the machine-gun on him, he's down. They've done 'im in. Oh, no, he's creeping forward again. Good boy, good boy. That's it, Tippy, get 'im on yer back. That's the idea. Hello, what's that, a sniper? I saw him move. You touch my pal if you dare. Ah you would, would yer? Take that (shoots), and that (shoots). Got him, the dirty Hun. Come on Tippy my boy, that's it. Let me give you a hand.

After this Tippy (introducing himself as Reginald Winter to the visiting officer who rather suddenly appears) looks set to get a medal. This mix of melodrama and plausibly accurate observation may not have employed the exact terminology of the trenches – 'perishers' and 'done him in' are seldom documented for this context – but there is much about this to corroborate claims for authenticity, particularly the voice of its author. Major A. E. Rees was a serving soldier who had been at Gallipoli and, from 1915, was acting as a recruiting officer in Britain, his work including writing and directing this material for Columbia records. Though the speech given above is a difficult one to act, especially given the time constraints, it is preceded with what appears to be entirely natural male conversation:

Ginger: Here's old Tippy learning to say 'yes' and 'good morning' to the French girls.
Tippy: Non comprenez – that's 'I don't understand'.
Ginger: Not half you don't. Garn – narpoo to you.[12]

If this sounds very authentic, beneath this layer of speech-authenticity is another layer, which would not have been noticed by most of the non-veteran listeners, typified by the statement, 'Here comes a whizz-bang' –

these shells were so called because the whizz of the shell passing was heard before the bang of the gun's report, so in no way could anyone see them coming; thus, again, this is a mix of degrees and kinds of authenticity.

Tim Cook's study of these productions proposes that 'the tendency for superficial and cartoon style treatment is sometimes diluted with touches of realism' and that 'the script continues to link sentimental dialogue with an ever-present truth that the next sequence of action could be their last'.[13] So within this 'theatre' there is realism and truth present, the truth of the situation, and the realism, which, since it cannot come from the recording situation or the sound effects, must come from the words and/ or their presentation.

The question of authenticity is effectively rhetorical; it requires us to evaluate our own criteria as well as those of people nearer the time who evaluated the language of the war. Frequently Fraser and Gibbons in 1925, and Brophy and Partridge from 1930, label terms as 'a newspaper coined expression' or 'journalese', comments easy to interpret as implying 'less authentic' or 'secondary'. How do we deal with 'Arf a Mo Kaiser', a caption to an image of a soldier smoking, which has all the feeling of true First World War language? It was initiated by Bert Thomas a cartoonist, before he became a soldier, and publicised and promoted by the press, but is scarcely documented as being used by soldiers. Whereas 'Are we downhearted?' was around long before the war, was parodied mercilessly by soldiers, and was pushed into extended use throughout the Home Front (for example, into bachelor fear of babies), but remains a strong linguistic marker for the war.

1 LANGUAGE, DIALECT AND THE NEED TO COMMUNICATE

Slang, dialect and status

The growth of education in Britain in the second half of the nineteenth century involved the meeting of different linguistic cultures in the classroom, especially in urban areas, where the concept of 'bad English' became associated with failure. John Walker's *A Critical Pronouncing Dictionary of the English Language* (1791) and his lecture tours had provided the aspirational middle classes with a model for social improvement, and editions[1] fifty years after the first publication were still offering 'Rules to be observed by the Natives of Ireland in order to obtain a just Pronunciation of English', and similarly for 'Natives of Scotland' and 'the Londoners'. For Londoners in particular four 'faults' were proscribed, including not sounding 'h' after 'w', and not sounding 'h' where it ought to be sounded, and sounding it where it should not be heard – both of which are frequently transcribed in documentation of the war period as 'wot 'e said'. Walker recommended a 'cultured' London accent, compared to which the 'vulgar pronunciation of London' was 'a thousand times more offensive and disgusting'.[2] As middle-class accents took on more characteristics of the 'cultured London accent' with the growth of the railways, working class accents grew with the spread of conurbations in the North and the Midlands. As children were taught to pronounce, and to write, in school in a way that was distinct from their home environments, a two-tier system developed, seen in the operation of state funding for schools, by which children's failures in tests were punished by cuts in funding to schools. The concept arose then of a sense of language failure, which was exacerbated by the status of slang. Henry Alford, whose *A Plea for the Queen's English* is for the most part a sensible plea for clear communication, recommends 'Avoid likewise all *slang* words. There is no greater nuisance in society than a talker of slang. It is only fit (when innocent, which it seldom is) for raw schoolboys, and one-term freshmen, to astonish their sisters with.'[3] The very presentation of so many slang dictionaries in the course of the nineteenth century cemented the position of this aspect of the language as something separate, not mainstream. This sense of language being susceptible to value judgements has been retained to the 21st century, with GCSE examination boards reminding students that their work will be marked according to their use of 'good English.'[4] Despite public support for slang during the war, after the war standard English, effectively middle-class speech, continued to be the aspiration in education, and was the benchmark for success or failure in the use of language. The Newbolt Report (1921) offered a model of what was to be avoided; 'The great difficulty of teachers in Elementary Schools in many districts is that they have to fight against the powerful influence of evil habits of speech contracted in home and street. The teachers' struggle is thus not with ignorance but with a perverted power.'[5] Though there had been a fascination with army language during the years 1914 to 1918, and though sociolinguists at an academic level found it worthy of collection and study, what the Newbolt Report did was to formalise a default stratification of quality within the English language. In the same year George Sampson's *English for the English*, while maintaining Newbolt's stance on the value of plain non-obfuscating English, claimed that, 'Much of the failure in elementary and even in secondary education is due to the fact that the children do not possess language, and are treated as if they did, ... Boys from bad homes come to school with their speech in a state of disease, ...'.[6]

Many of the British troops during the war are shown as having had very little education: 'A few of them [ASC men] were men with a certain amount of education, but the bulk were of the genus Gor Blimey';[7] Richard Holmes' comment in *Tommy*, 'units such as 23/Royal Fusiliers or 6/ Camerons, with their high proportion of educated men serving in the ranks' indicates that generally this was not the case.[8] Arthur Heath, 2nd Lt, reckoned that it was no use encouraging his men to 'remember Waterloo' because most of them would think he was referring to the railway station.[9] Occasional spelling queries indicate a view of the value of correct English: Rifleman William Taffs was concerned about how to spell 'bandeau',[10] but the contrast is most noticeable in the assumption of a higher level of education among Germans, who were expected at least to know other languages: 'It was a huge disappointment to all that the [captured] German could speak no English'.[11] German levels of elementary education were higher than those in England and Wales, and Germans frequently commented on 'how stupid and ill-informed British prisoners were'.[12] In the French Army literacy levels were a problem, with one writer claiming that in some regiments there was an 'inability to understand any orders, either verbal or written'.[13]

Slang then should be seen in a context that evaluated different kinds of English within an educational structure, and the written and printed presentation of it frequently reinforced its apartness. Occasionally its impending use was highlighted with the term 'langwidge', usually shown within inverted commas. 'Language' had been a code-word for 'bad language' since the early 19th century, but the spelling 'langwidge', in use from mid-century, specifically located it in the field of poor literacy and transcription of working-class accents.[14] The relationship between standard English and slang is seen in the use of inverted commas in documentation, as a marker of a range of ways to understand the enclosed text. Inverted commas had evolved as part of the formulation of punctuation towards the end of the nineteenth century to indicate direct speech, glosses, technical terms, titles and special meanings, in all cases creating a notice of otherness from the main text. In some cases there would be an overlap between senses; it is seen in the advertisement for Onoto Pens in *Punch* 'Unless you are a "neutral"',[15] with the implication that this is an untruth; for 'neutral' read 'not really neutral'. Foreign words were regularly placed in inverted commas – 'by this time there is a regular "strafe" on',[16] or 'I have not been "dans les tranchées" for about a fortnight now'.[17] An immediately post-war advertisement for clothing uses inverted commas to emulate speech – '"The" house for mufti dress and service kit',[18] clearly indicating the stress on the first syllable.

Inverted commas around slang can indicate the expression as either new to the English language generally, expected to be new to the reader, or new to the writer. Thus there are inverted commas round 'No-man's-land';[19] 'The "Tanks" seem to be Fritz's pet aversion',[20] 'Suggestions for "Sammy"',[21] 'we should have been shot thirty seconds ago if the "Jerries" could shoot',[22] 'Perennial duel between "Archies" and Skycraft',[23] 'Black Marias or "coal boxes"'.[24] Though the terms may have been in use for a few years, their quasi-unofficial status may be marked by inverted commas.

For the benefit of his readers John Crofts uses inverted commas to advertise unfamiliar terms; 'stunt', 'pill-box', 'going over',[25] 'they had "taken us in"', writes Walter Brindle;[26] 'the "dixies" were filled with water'.[27] Curious usages might be emphasised, involving new terms, slang or jargon: 'helping to ward off "war panic"';[28] 'Don't "War-Scare" the Children!'[29] 'An early morning "Soviet" gathered', 'it was usually a "hot shop"';[30] 'the continual "plonks" outside are very irksome',[31] 'we jocularly said that the "morning hate" was a little worse',[32] 'twelve unfortunate brethren are "told off" to don the gum-boots'.[33] Inverted commas might indicate a teaching act, an explanation: '"no man's land"– that is the land between our trenches and the Germans',[34] and though an explanation may not be given, children are clearly being introduced to adult language, and a stoically British viewpoint, in 'our men "stuck it"'.[35] Slang or vocabulary new or strange to the writer is marked as a curiosity: Emma Duffin marks 'swing the lead', 'blighty', 'cushy job'; there may also be a sense of enjoying the new expression in 'Sister Rankin "straffed" me on the top of her voice',[36] the unfamiliarity given away by her idiosyncratic spelling. Ethel Bilbrough wrote in her diary that 'only the other day they were "shelling out" for the French red cross day';[37] Aubrey Smith notes that 'in December they started to "ear-mark" twenty-five men from each company';[38] '[I was] quite "jiggered"';[39] and Edward Stuart wrote home 'After dinner we put the "cap on" our rest (why so called I do not know) by having a route march for two hours'.[40]

Insider slang is signalled by inverted commas indicating a code, a euphemism, something not intelligible to the non-initiate. Ian Hay talks about German artillery 'distributing coal' ('coal-boxes' – 5.9″ shells),[41] 'we've been "in" since the 8th',[42] 'we had two "short arm" inspections';[43] and the ubiquitous 'somewhere in France' at the top of many On Active Service postcards, often shortened to 'somewhere', the tacit acknowledgement that the writer was being censored. Being part of the group was a useful commercial tool, and the advertiser's claim could be highlighted by the use of inverted commas: 'In the trenches – Symingtons Soups are easy to "fix up"';[44] Ivelcon is 'truly miraculous in its "bucking up" effect';[45] and 'Somewhere in France' begins Craven A's advertisement using the story of Sir John French.[46] It was not necessary that it should be actual soldiers' slang, as the mere fact of using something identifiable as slang linked the product to the military experience. The educational drive may explain the use of inverted commas round slang expressions – 'badly "smashed-up"'; 'Jerry'; 'chatting' – in "Frank Honywood, Private",[47] by Eric Partridge, the twentieth century's expert on

English slang. Partridge explains slang expressions unobtrusively: 'delousing ("chatting" was the army phrase) always remained distasteful'; 'a pleasant sight, all those "Diggers" (as the Australian soldiers were already called) sitting in the mellow sunlight.'[48] The writer might indicate a learning experience for himself, as in 'that piece of land which lies between the British and German trenches, and which is known as "no mans land", and rightly so too.'[49]

This use of inverted commas exploited inclusion, but strong class sociolects meant that some people wished to distance themselves from slang, while still claiming membership of the group identified by it. 'And that put (in vulgar phrase) the tin hat on it'[50] does this, while Coningsby Dawson uses inverted commas: 'My sergeant is waiting, so, as the men say, "I must ring off"'.[51] There is an association here with the idea of 'the men' making mistakes with language – Emma Duffin twice points out the incorrect usage in 'albumin water called "aluminium water" by the troops', and '"aluminium water" as they always call it'.[52] Newspapers and magazines that were aimed at the better off might use inverted commas around slang to help their readers keep a safe social class distance from anything undesirable – the *Daily Mail* was still using inverted commas round 'Tommies' in May 1915. The punctuation here points out slang's role – the bomb called a 'Jack Johnson' or a 'Black Maria'[53] – and conveys a combination of awareness of class difference, pointing out a mistake or a simulacrum, and fascination with a safe aspect of the working class: and this could be combined with supporting the army by sending them, through a newspaper-based charity, 'the "smokes" that help to keep our heroes smiling'[54] so that they should not have to share 'one "Fag-end" among six';[55] The *Weekly Dispatch* famously marketed its Tobacco Fund campaign with the slogan ''Arf a 'mo, Kaiser', always presented as a soldier's quote. There is also a connection with the function of the inverted commas to apologise, to provide a safe place for the not quite polite, such as the headline 'Two Women Who "Swanked" As Captains',[56] or a letter from a 48th Infantry Regiment soldier, Erwin, to Ben, Freda and Ruth saying 'we had another "blow-out" the other evening'.[57]

The progress of abandoning inverted commas shows the gradual acceptance of terms that were previously marked as not mainstream. The *Illustrated London News* was using the form 'Tommy' in early October 1914, and though it dropped the inverted commas the following month, they were resumed in February 1915, dropped in an advertisement that appeared in May and June 1916, then resumed until October 1916; after January 1918 there were no inverted commas round the word. The

Birmingham Daily Post used inverted commas round 'Jack Johnson' (as the slang name for the shell) consistently from September 1914 until September 1915, after which it omitted inverted commas slightly more often than using them; the use of the term tailed off altogether through most of 1917, with an appearance with inverted commas in October, and without in November. Articles and letters in the *Manchester Guardian* omitted inverted commas round 'Blighty' only when it was in a quotation, until January 1917, after which there were more or less equal numbers of incidences with and without inverted commas. *The Times* began to use the word 'cushy' without inverted commas only after the Armistice. Emma Duffin's treatment of 'Blighty' moves from 'home or "Blighty" as they called it' (before May 1916), to 'wait till I get to "blighty"' (1915/16), to 'the others were up and talking of going to Blighty' (autumn 1917).[58]

In terms of the management of the Allied campaigns it is useful to see this relationship between different registers of one language in terms of a wider linguistic perception of status between languages, which was highlighted by the war. Differences in sociolects seem to have brought the soldiers in the anglophone armies for the most part closer together, and there seem to have been no cases where misunderstandings through dialect or accent caused any operational difficulties. British soldiers came into contact with French soldiers to the south and Belgian soldiers to the north, but there are only rare occurrences of realisation that in both these armies languages other than French were spoken. In these armies there were clear status relationships between languages; British forces do not seem to have been aware of the range of languages in use in the French army, but there is evidence of an awareness of Flemish spoken by civilians. The Belgian army held the line, mostly fighting a defensive campaign, between the British army north of Ypres and the coast, a distance which over the period ranged from 11 to 38 kilometres,[59] much of it marshy or flooded, creating unhealthy conditions which added to Belgian casualties.

The Belgian army was not officially an ally of the British army or the French army, due to Belgium's neutrality, but was in effect fighting its own campaign against the German invasion. The army reflected the social and linguistic structure of Belgium, where French was the language of administration, law and education, with the officer class speaking French and the administration of the army being in French; however, over two-thirds of the soldiers were Flemish-speaking, and many supported the campaign for greater recognition of the Flemish language and culture (also supported by the German army of occupation as *Flamenpolitik*).

The French army, besides its colonial soldiers from Algeria, Senegal and elsewhere, had soldiers from mainland France whose first language was Breton, Flemish, Gallo or Occitan; in the case of Breton soldiers, for many Breton was their only language. The position of Breton-speaking soldiers was highlighted by memories of the Franco-Prussian War (1870–1) in which they had suffered both militarily, reflecting doubts as regards their loyalty, and as a result of the conditions in which they were maintained by the military and political authorities. Breton soldiers suffered proportionately twice the number of casualties as other sections of the French army during the First World War, and there were several claims that Breton-speaking soldiers had died unnecessarily through not understanding orders.[60] Marc Bloch, telling the story of a Breton soldier who in effect died through not being able to understand or make himself understood, describes the situation in his section after the arrival of fresh troops: 'recruitment had taken them from the four corners of Brittany so effectively that each spoke a different dialect, and those amongst them who knew a little French could barely serve as interpreters for the others'.[61] Louis Barthas, from Languedoc, gives the story of a fellow-poilu who tellingly flings back a comment in Occitan rather than standard French as he deserts – *Béni mé querré* (*viens me chercher* – come and get me).[62]

The position of French–Canadian soldiers was also conflicted. The French–Canadian community's allegiance was to itself rather than to France, and particularly not to Britain. The effect of years of struggle as a minority language group rendered enlistment from this group constrained, and there were claims that they were pressurised into not enlisting;[63] their language skills were not particularly widely exploited in interpreting, and the small proportion of French used in the 1 January 1916 issue of *The Growler*, trench journal of the Royal Montreal Regiment – three out of four columns on one page of a twelve-page journal – indicates the small proportion of the language accommodation for them. Francophone Canadian soldiers tended to get a better deal from the locals in France, often involving greater access to alcohol, which did not impress the military authorities;[64] a Canadian War Record Office report stated that 'The population applauded us. The people rushed to the doors of their houses to offer us fruits and wine.... Gradually it dawned on these people that among the strange soldiers from across the ocean were men speaking their mother tongue, not the French of modern Brittany and Normandy, but French none the less'.[65] Where anglophones could speak French, their French might be of no avail when confronted with a local dialect or accent, let alone the local dialects of Flemish; R. H. Mottram met a boy who spoke Flemish but said no one locally could read a Flemish inscription on a windmill, because it was 'Vlamsch ... of another commune'.[66] Masefield tells in a letter of not being able to understand 'a cruelly different patois',[67] and Douie failed to converse with a woodman who used 'a flood of patois which I could not understand'.[68]

The need to communicate

The lowest level of literacy among the British troops was usually sufficient to allow for letter-writing and reading, and the facilities provided encouraged this – the YMCA provided free writing paper and envelopes for soldiers' letters.[69] Combined with the newly available telephone, cheap printing, and the logistics of managing huge numbers of people, there quickly developed a huge and diverse culture of verbal and written communication. To see this in context, in 1910 nearly one person in ten purchased a national daily newspaper, and at the outbreak of war the postal service in Britain was such that any conurbation was receiving up to twelve postal deliveries daily. In the eighteen months from March 1916 to August 1917 approximately 8.5 million bags of mail were received by the BEF (British Expeditionary Force) in France, an average of 15,500 bags per day; the maximum strength of the Army Postal Service with the BEF, at 18 December 1918, was 3,031.[70] In the French army four million letters were exchanged daily between the Front and home,[71] with a quarter of a million parcels sorted in Paris daily.[72]

The expectation of mail from home is one of the most repeated messages in soldiers' letters and postcards, comments such as 'I have not heard from you today' indicating the hope, almost the expectation, of daily news from home. In April 1915 John Masefield followed the custom in the French army of writing to his family nearly every day, twice a day sometimes. Up to 20,000 letters a week were sent home by Indian soldiers – their deep desire for communication with home is expressed in a letter from Raja Khan to Mohamed Fazl, sent on 17 October 1917: 'Be good enough to tell my father to write every week. If it is too much trouble to write at length it will do if he simply makes his thumb impression on a sheet of paper and sends it ... if I get no letter from India I have no appetite at all and feel useless for my work'.[73] For another Indian soldier the need to write was so strong that he had to break a frozen pot of ink, and melt the ink to be able to write.[74] John Masefield, working as a nurse with the French army in March 1915, watched a soldier die on his ward before the man's wife could get there: 'all his marching & fighting & narrow escapes came to nothing, & all his letters that he wrote with a stub of pencil in the trenches will be all the poor woman has'.[75] From the distance of a hundred years, the soldiers are most present in their names and in their surviving words; there is a possibility that they had some idea of this, in that editors of *The Pow-Wow*, issue 23 April 1915, suggested that readers should keep a copy of the journal for posterity.

In the correspondence of British soldiers the overwhelming realisation is that the fact of the letter or card sent from or to the Front was as important as its content.

So many soldiers' postcards say very little beyond the fact that the writer is well, that a letter or card or parcel has or has not been received, and the state of the weather, though Indian soldiers' letters tended to be less restricted by the desire not to worry families at home. In the correspondence of British soldiers the overwhelming realisation is that the fact of the letter or card sent from or to the Front was as important as its content: just as the very act of a communication from the Front meant that the soldier was alive, the soldiers needed the constant reminders and reassurance of home. The Field Service Postcard, available from 1914, in Urdu as well as English, was a pragmatic combination of the rigid censorship needs of the army, the authorities' awareness that the main value of a card was the fact of its being written rather than its content, and the realisation that many soldiers would not know what to write. It annoyed some with its limitations, and quickly gave rise to pastiches, many in trench journals, which referenced idealised or bizarre situations at home and at the Front, and offered suggestions for answering postcards; pastiches of the Field Service Postcard published in trench journals tended to be heavily referential of army life. Bureaucracy spawned acres of paper, memoranda from HQ quickly referred to as 'Comic Cuts' by officers, and generally as 'bumf' (bum fodder). Officers in the trenches were exasperated by the form-filling and record-keeping required of them: Lancelot Spicer complained about fatuous reports requiring him to

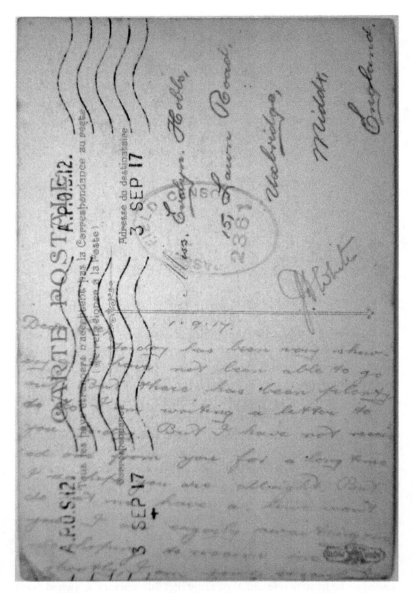

FIGURE 1.1 A postcard sent 'On Active Service' with the common complaint 'I am writing a letter to you today. But I have not received one from you for a long time'.

let HQ know 'the number of men who have not cut their toenails for the last fortnight (giving reasons)'.[76] The war saw the fast development of many forms of communication; runners, dogs and carrier pigeons used in 1914 were supplemented and replaced by telephone wires, necessitating constant repairs and the reburying of exposed cables. The American Signal Corps created their own telephone network in France using 250,000 kilometres of cabling to enable 150,000 local and 4,000 long-distance calls daily at the end of the war, while hand-signalling by aviators and flag-signalling and morse in the Navy were supplemented by electron-tube radio by 1919.[77] But at the same time that newspapers and magazines were exciting their readers with information about science in the service of the military campaigns, they were publishing morale-boosting photographs of shells carrying hand-chalked messages 'To Fritz', 'To Willie with Compliments', or 'To Captain Fryatt's Murderers';[78] Louis Barthas noted in 1914 'How many bellicose, bragging inscriptions scrawled in chalk on the railway cars!',[79] and the tunnels below Arras are a mass of messages, names and regimental insignia carved into the chalk walls. The open celebration of verbal communication in such destructive circumstances is seen in the culture of the trench-name, with all its references to home and safety, as well as the alphabetical structure by which names could be cross-referenced to corps maps; the trench names may have started as chalked words on a spare plank, but by 1917 the Royal Engineers were using sign-writers to make them.

The communicative imperative did not stop at the parapet, for there are countless instances of communication of many kinds between the frontline trenches. Graves noted 'a daily exchange of courtesies between our machine-guns and the Germans' at stand-to; by removing cartridges from the ammunition belt one could rap out the rhythm of the former prostitutes' call: 'MEET ME DOWN IN PIC-A-DILL-Y', to which the Germans would reply ... : 'YES, with-OUT my DRAWERS ON!'[80] The simplest form of cross-no-man's-land communication was the shouted message, sometimes challenging, sometimes friendly or just acknowledging the other's existence. One Bavarian cornet-player responded positively to a request from British soldiers opposite.[81] The 'live and let live' attitude or the desire to maintain a quiet sector encouraged low-level conversation to retain a calm atmosphere. Tony Ashworth gives several examples of German soldiers sending messages either in defused grenades or tied to stones, and of informal truces, up to as late as May 1918;[82] the breaking of one truce provoked a German

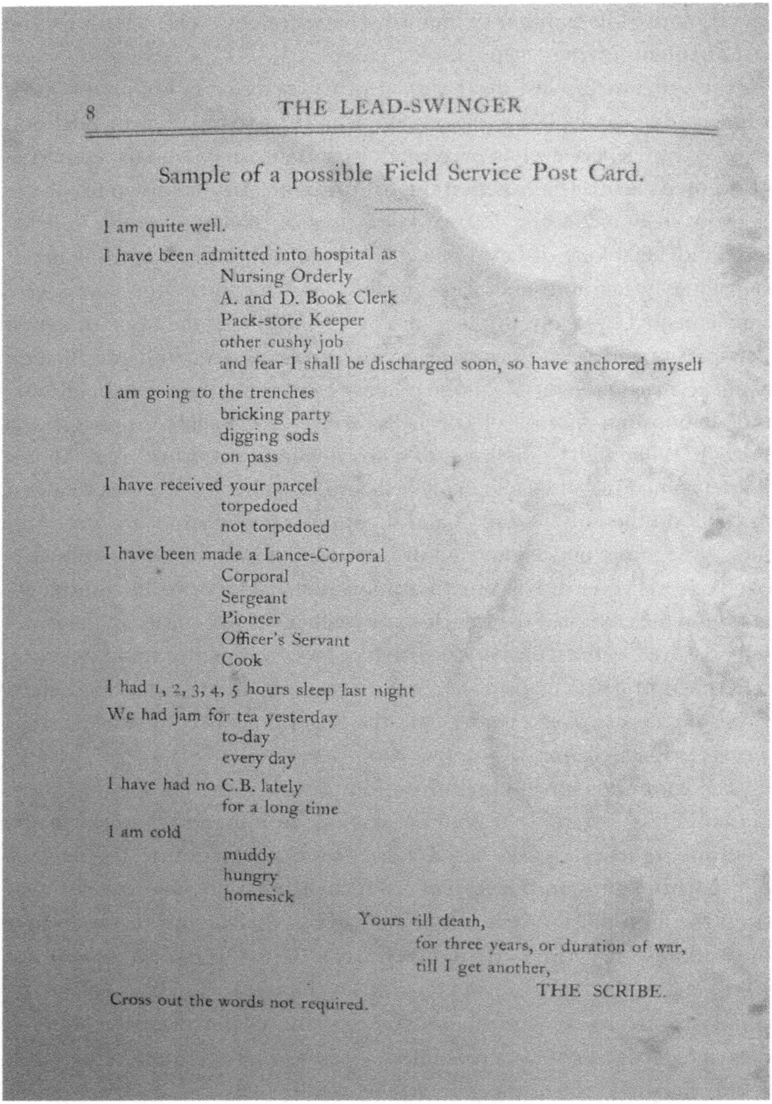

Sample of a possible Field Service Post Card.

I am quite well.
I have been admitted into hospital as
       Nursing Orderly
       A. and D. Book Clerk
       Pack-store Keeper
       other cushy job
       and fear I shall be discharged soon, so have anchored myself
I am going to the trenches
       bricking party
       digging sods
       on pass
I have received your parcel
       torpedoed
       not torpedoed
I have been made a Lance-Corporal
       Corporal
       Sergeant
       Pioneer
       Officer's Servant
       Cook
I had 1, 2, 3, 4, 5 hours sleep last night
We had jam for tea yesterday
       to-day
       every day
I have had no C.B. lately
       for a long time
I am cold
       muddy
       hungry
       homesick

                 Yours till death,
                    for three years, or duration of war,
                    till I get another,
                            THE SCRIBE.
Cross out the words not required.

FIGURE 1.2 Variations on the Field Service Postcard: an original FSP sent in January 1918; a pastiche sent from training camp; a pastiche published in *The Lead-swinger* 16 Oct 1915, p. 8, (Issues September – December, published 1916); a multiple-choice holiday card, 1920s.

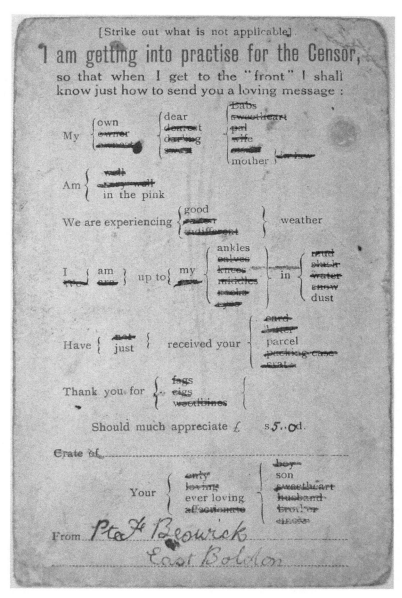

FIGURE 1.2 *Continued*

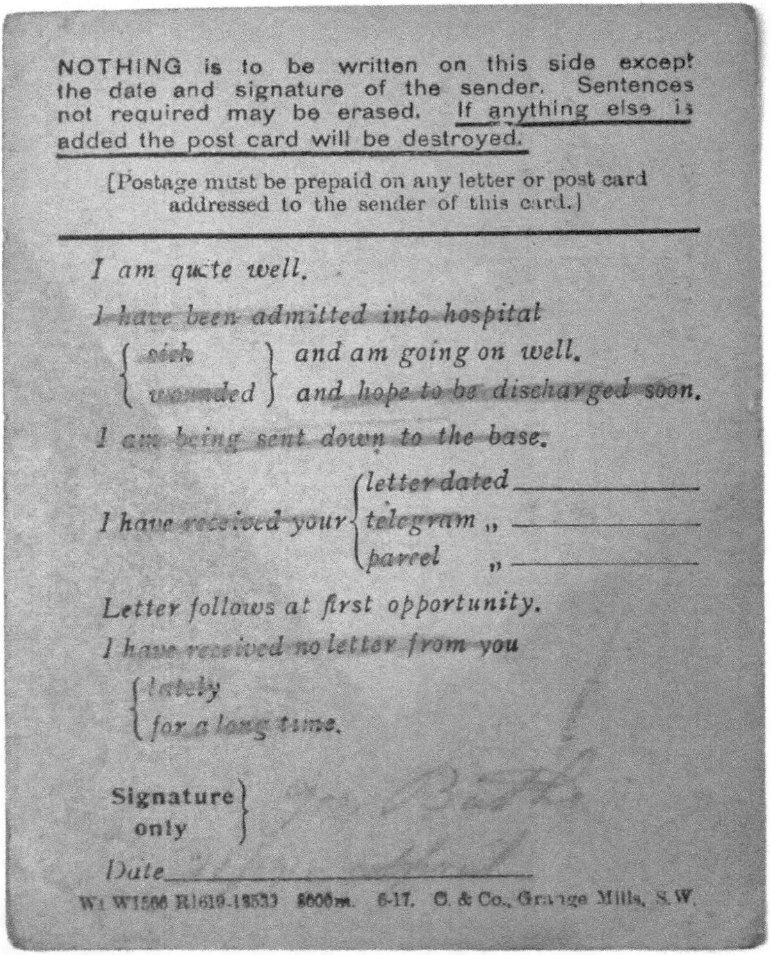

NOTHING is to be written on this side except
the date and signature of the sender. Sentences
not required may be erased. If anything else is
added the post card will be destroyed.

[Postage must be prepaid on any letter or post card
addressed to the sender of this card.]

I am quite well.

I have been admitted into hospital

{ *sick* } *and am going on well.*
{ *wounded* } *and hope to be discharged soon.*

I am being sent down to the base.

I have received your { *letter dated* _____
*telegram ,, _____
*parcel ,, _____

Letter follows at first opportunity.

I have received no letter from you

{ *lately*
{ *for a long time.*

Signature
only }

Date _____

W₁ W1566 R1619-19533 8600m.   6-17.   O. & Co., Grange Mills, S.W.

FIGURE 1.2 *Continued*

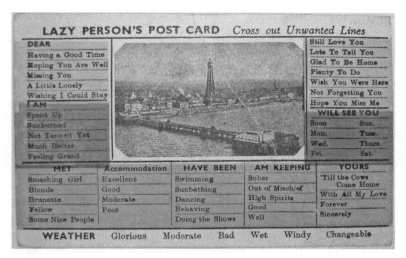

LAZY PERSON'S POST CARD *Cross out Unwanted Lines*

DEAR				Still Love You
Having a Good Time				Lots To Tell You
Hoping You Are Well				Glad To Be Home
Missing You				Plenty To Do
A Little Lonely				Wish You Were Here
Wishing I Could Stay				Not Forgetting You
I AM				Hope You Miss Me
Spent Up				WILL SEE YOU
Sunburned				Soon Sun.
Not Tanned Yet				Mon. Tues.
Much Better				Wed. Thurs.
Feeling Grand				Fri. Sat.

MET	Accommodation	HAVE BEEN	AM KEEPING	YOURS
Smashing Girl	Excellent	Swimming	Sober	'Till the Cows Come Home
Blonde	Good	Sunbathing	Out of Mischief	
Brunette	Moderate	Dancing	High Spirits	With All My Love
Fellow	Poor	Behaving	Good	Forever
Some Nice People		Doing the Shows	Well	Sincerely

WEATHER	Glorious	Moderate	Bad	Wet	Windy	Changeable

FIGURE 1.2 *Continued*

placard to be put up telling the British to 'Chuck It'.[83] Despite the appalling death toll on both sides in the early months of the war there were curious anecdotes of communication across no man's land; one case involved the Germans sending newspapers to the French via a horse,[84] though these did carry news of German successes, while the same article reported a singing contest, and an attempt to exchange news via a goat, which unfortunately could not be made to return to the German trench it had been sent from. Unsurprisingly for an agricultural area which, at least in the early months of the war, continued to be farmed, animals were involved incidentally in the business of warfare: one angry Belgian farmer appeared in front of a British trench and accused, through an interpreter, the British troops of killing a pig; when the charge was denied he strode off across no man's land to harangue the trench opposite.[85] Truces involving fraternisation in no man's land between anglophone and German troops inevitably were conducted in English: Archie Stanley, during the 1914 Christmas Truce, heard a German soldier say 'Cor blimey, mate, I was in a London hotel when the war broke out'.[86] Areas where the front lines were close together seemed to almost encourage conversation, and Lancelot Spicer described while out on patrol having a conversation with German soldiers in their trench.[87] Aubrey Herbert in Gallipoli used French to 'make speeches' across no man's land assuring that those Turks who surrendered would not be killed.[88] Sometimes the conversation was tactical – trying to get the enemy to speak in order to identify a regional accent, to identify the speaker's regiment; Lancelot Spicer tells how this attempt failed on one occasion because the German soldier was determined to speak English.[89] In a more sinister way German soldiers would creep up to the British parapet at night and 'converse in slang English' and 'ask for "a fag"' in order to get into British trenches unseen,[90] though the live-and-let-live spirit is seen in the anecdote of a British soldier who lost his way in no man's land and asked over a parapet, 'Are you the Scottish?', to receive the polite reply, 'No, we are the Bavarians. The Scottish are opposite'.[91] The use of trench mortars, which allowed little chance of protection or avoidance, pushed any negotiation through conversation aside: one trench mortar attack on the German lines provoked the shouted response, 'You bloody Welsh murderers!'[92]

Placards put up facing enemy troops tended to be more challenging than conciliatory: in May 1916 placards were put up facing Irish troops which stated that 'English guns are firing on your wives and children', and telling about the surrender at Kut-el-Amara.[93] *The War Illustrated* 3 June 1916 claimed that this had infuriated the Munster Regiment so much that they mounted a raid and 'brought back the placard in triumph'. Less successfully provocative, and less accurate, was one which appeared to read 'Kitchener has been drowned in the Devon'; under better light the words were seen to be 'Kitchener has been taken by the Devil'.[94] Stephen Hewett suspected that one placard announcing the fall of Kut-el-Amara might have a machine-gun trained on it or be a mined lure to attract outraged British soldiers; taunts have always been part of warfare – at the Somme Australian soldiers shot to pieces a placard directed at them saying 'Advance Australia – If You Can!'[95] A conversation by various means in 1915 was reported by 2nd Lt Arthur Heath: the conversation was started by a sergeant shouting through a megaphone that 'Fritz your navy is destroyed', with a placard listing the ships destroyed (with the addition of 'Hoch!'). This brought the response 'Schwein' and a placard listing Germany and Austro-Hungary's successes against Russia.[96] Masefield somehow heard in May 1917 of an exchange of information on the Eastern Front, with both the Germans and the Russians claiming success in the fall of the Tsar.[97] On occasions there were no doubt misunderstandings, from badly translated English or from lack of understanding of other theatres of war: 'Skeen told us that when the Turks stuck up a placard saying Warsaw had fallen, the Australians gave three hearty cheers'.[98] There was scope for humour too, as a wiring party in no man's land responded to a German placard announcing 'Gott mit uns' with one of their own saying 'Don't swank – we've got mittens too'.[99] As the Germans withdrew to the Hindenburg Line in 1917 a more literary mind set up a large placard on the ruins of the town hall at Péronne with Goethe's words '*Nicht ärgen, nur wundern!*' (do not be angry, be amazed). The placard survived the war.

The canonical idea of 'The Poetry of the First World War' sometimes masks the fact that thousands of people wrote, and published, verse during the conflict; Vivien Noakes in her introduction to her anthology proposes that 'no war in history has produced so much poetry as did the First World War'.[100] These poems found their homes not in slim volumes, but in trench journals, autograph books, magazines and newspapers, collections published in support of a particular cause, and YMCA hut visitors' books. E. B. Osborn's anthology *The Muse in Arms* (1917), reprinted three times within a year, had as its object 'to show what passes in the British warrior's soul when … he has glimpses of the ultimate significance of warfare'; its authority was claimed by the title page's note that these were 'war poems' and that they were for the most part written by those who were serving or had served in the war.[101] The presence of works by Sassoon, Gurney and Brooke as well as less successful poems such as the imitation of Masefield by 'Imtarfa' ('Let me back to the guns again, I hear them calling me') and 'The Death of the Zeppelin' by 'O.' ('At last! At last the wingéd Worm draws near, / The vulture-ship that dare not voyage by day') indicate that the authenticity of having served in the forces was the prime determinant of inclusion. The writing of poetry, whether limerick, doggerel, ballad pastiche or sonnet, provided a medium for exploring unselfconscious patriotism, celebration of the group, and affirmation of continuity through narrative, as well as the familiar outrage of the canonical poets. But most of the presentation of poetry was not that of the isolated individual, but of people contextualised by the regiment, the army, the war: of the wartime anthologies which provided poems for Vivien Noakes' book, over two-thirds had titles which referred specifically to the war – they are 'war poems', belonging to the experience of the group, and part of the communicating of the war.

A group mindset drove the trench journals, particularly avoiding the individual in favour of the group experience. Ranging from single sheets to multipage magazines, with methods that included individual handwritten sheets produced in a trench, and professionally designed and set runs produced in Britain or America, these publications depended on the shared experience of the military unit, expressed through a shared voice. Though the voice may be identifiable by class, education, degree of deference to military authority, it is almost always the unidentifiable voice of the soldier rather than the named journalist, for though Roberts and Pearson are now well known as the editors of the *Wipers Times*, their names did not feature at the time, the magazine always being 'published by Sherwood, Forester & Co'. Individuals did stand out – the poet 'F.W.H.' (Will Harvey) of the *Fifth Gloucester Gazette*, Philip Harris, editor of *Aussie* – but trench journals thrived on providing a recognisably familiar, if unnamed voice. For material they required shared experience, identifiably distinct from peacetime and non-army life, as the first British trench journals appeared far from the frontline trenches, in the training camps in Britain – *The Pow-Wow*, the journal of the University and Public School Battalions, first appeared in November 1914. As the war progressed and the units moved to France, Flanders and Gallipoli, the journals moved with them, being written, edited and sometimes printed within the sound of the guns – *The Gasper* proudly, though perhaps opaquely, proclaimed that it was 'edited from the trenches'. The tone of the journals has been recognised as essentially humorous, balancing a support for the prosecution of the war while maintaining a constant barrage of complaint against its details – poor food, vermin, excessive paperwork, poor support at home, the claims of journalists, the absence of women. The attitude towards the enemy is more of annoyance than hatred, but Graham Seal's assessment is that the journals were primarily a negotiation of compromise between the soldier and the authority that sent him out to risk his life; the conflict appeared more in terms of dying than of killing, and the trench journal, in demanding that the voice of the soldier exist on record, in effect makes the statement that 'you may have my body, but not my mind', echoing comments that the army took a soldier's body but not his soul (see p. 246). It is the fulfilment of the idea that the British soldier will do anything if you let him have his grouse. Columns such as 'We Know But We Shan't Say' set up a paradigm for 'us and them' in which there was a tacit acknowledgement that anyone other than the private soldier could be the target of satire; for Graham Seal this goes towards the creation of the trench journal as a 'democratic cultural republic',[102] but this goes only for the more daring journals. Declarations that others were published 'by permission' or edited by a high-ranking officer[103] indicate that the negotiation was not all from the soldiers' side. Trench journals flourished: there were over 100 titles published in English, and twice this number in French; Robert Nelson proposes that every German soldier would have read trench journals regularly.[104] The British Museum received copies of trench journals for archiving as part of the Legal Deposit process, but the diligence with which very flimsy material was acquired indicates a sense at the time of its importance; journal editors perhaps realised the worth of the papers too, suggesting that readers should buy two copies, one to send home. They were also constantly testing the boundaries of what was permissible. When in 1916 some journals started to claim that they had been passed by the censor, nobody was really sure whether this was so or whether this was another push at authority.[105]

> Where the body was obliterated or lost, the name on the unignorable architectural structure made some compensation for the absence of the body, the word thus becoming the most permanent communication across time, monumentalised in the phrase 'their name liveth for evermore'.

The desire of the British Museum to preserve the verbal culture of the war is just one of many aspects of the preservation of words through and after the conflict. Of these the most fundamental was the preservation of the names of soldiers who died, attaching the name to a place, a monument or a tombstone. In the French army bottles functioned as receptacles for preserving the names of soldiers, the names written on paper and placed in bottles on the soldiers' graves 'that they may not be obliterated by snow and rain'.[106] Where the body was obliterated or lost, the name on the unignorable architectural structure made some compensation for the absence of the body, the word thus becoming the most permanent communication across time, monumentalised in the phrase 'their name liveth for evermore'. *Home Chat* as early as October 1914 proposed that 'every parish should . . . have its list of heroes to be engraved on brass or stone after the war'.[107] Winter and Walter describe the phenomenon of family members touching the names of lost loved ones on memorials,[108] where the word functions as a metonym for the person and the loss. This continuity of communication through the word indicates a continuity of the impulse towards communication during the war, as the fixing and repetition of names provides a model for commemoration to the present.

An article in the *South Shields Daily Gazette* indicates the sense that somehow or other people would manage to communicate with each other: 'An English Lieutenant writes from Salonica: "A characteristic Salonica incident on the way to camp. The man with whom I was a Serbian Jew attached to the Zadruga Bank. We met two Tommies in language difficulties with two men, the one of whom spoke Russian and the other Greek. So the Tommies talked English to me; I talked German to my friend, who talked Serbian to the Russian (who replied in his own language), who talked Greek to the other fellow."[109]

Managing languages

The variety of theatres of conflict and the range of languages involved meant that the war was fought in a multilingual environment. Though the British Army in 1914 already had a term, 'bolo the bat', from Hindi, meaning to speak the (local) language, the First World War extended the experience beyond anything that had gone before. R. H. Mottram, finding himself an interpreter in Flanders, was under the command of staff officers who were able to speak other languages, but these were the languages used in administering the British Army in India. *The King's Regulations* of 1912, which in paragraph 900 encouraged the study of French and German 'at certain large military centres', and in paragraph 901 proposed the secondment of officers to Russia, Japan and China, for the purposes of language study, had recognised the need for competence in other languages, but the early losses to the officer corps had probably undone much of the preparation that had come from this.

Aubrey Herbert at Gallipoli met a Serbian who had been learning Italian specifically to aid his ambition of stabbing a Cretan,[110] while Emma Duffin nursing soldiers in France found herself tending Portuguese officers, one of whom was 'very keen to learn English and asked me the English name of everything in the book'.[111] The administrators of Flemish-speaking refugees in Britain were bewildered by what they saw as 'the Shakespearean tendency of the Flemish peasant to spell his surname differently on any occasion that arose for spelling it',[112] while those in Wales suggested helping the situation by 'the distribution of French, Flemish and English glossaries'.[113] It was not uncommon for soldiers to use Field Service Postcards or picture postcards printed in languages other than their own, to send home; a German *Feldpostkarte* was sent to Manchester in September 1918 by a British soldier.[114]

Gallipoli particularly was a multilingual environment, with many Turks able to speak French, which became a de facto lingua franca and language of negotiation for temporary truces, though Aubrey Herbert's ability to speak Turkish as well as French meant he was much in demand.[115] The changes of control over trenches on the Western Front, between allies and enemies, led to changes of language for the names of the trenches,[116] and required transliteration into non-Latin scripts. The war in Africa involved 100,000 soldiers from several language groups, and British troops also encountered as allies speakers of Japanese, Chinese, Portuguese, Greek, Serbian, Russian, Arabic and Italian.

The changes brought about by so much cross-language communication were seen as ultimately beneficial by one writer to the *Daily Express* in June 1918, who felt that 'we were too insular before the war'; the British soldier had pragmatically abandoned 'the pen of my grandmother' in favour of 'Whisky nahpoo', but, rather than an eventual multilingual world, what he envisages is a situation where 'we shall hear Kai Lung, of the Labour Corps, calling out : "My hat, old top; Ah Song's wangled a Military Medal."'[117] In other words, less multilinguism than the ubiquity of English slang – in fact Lt J. B. Morton believed that the ubiquity of English slang and soldiers' songs was holding the alliance together.[118] But as early as January 1915 it was being realised that inadequate British teaching of languages was being shown up by the war: a correspondence in *The Daily Mirror* suggested that modern systems based on conversation rather than rote-learning of grammar would be seen as necessary.[119]

While multilinguism was to be expected from the nature of an international war that involved people being stationed in countries away from their residence, the mingling of groups within each national grouping involved the bringing together of languages. The French army embraced Occitan and Breton, as well as standard French, and the particular form of French called 'petit français' developed for officers to speak to *tirailleurs* from Senegal.[120] The British Army had speakers of French from Canada and Guernsey, Gaelic from Scotland, Irish and Welsh; there were Maori-speakers from New Zealand, and South African soldiers brought Afrikaans (also to be seen on the text of victory medals for South African soldiers); American indigenous languages were brought to Europe by Canadian and American forces; several languages were brought to Europe by Ghurkas and Indian troops from South Asia.

Skill in foreign languages was noted and often its contribution was recognised: at the Villa Trento hospital in Italy, staffed by English nurses

FIGURE 1.3 A German postcard sent to Manchester in September 1918 by a British soldier.

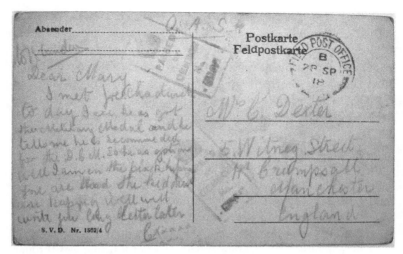

FIGURE 1.3 *Continued*

and VADs, 'the skill in the language acquired by many of our nurses', added to the value of the hospital's work.[121] Generally, where British soldiers knew other languages, this was limited to a little French or more rarely German, or some Hindi, but it is notable that an Indian soldier remarks that the Military Secretary to the India Office General H. V. Cox 'knows Hindi very well, and spoke to us in that language'.[122] Aubrey Herbert was an exception, having what he called 'a fairly fluent smattering of several eastern languages'.[123] Stephen Hewett recognised that 'it is a useful thing to have some facility with the language' (French in this case),[124] and though Lancelot Spicer wrote 'my French has improved greatly as a result of a month down here',[125] and a 9th Royal Scots private's diary noted 'a "would-be linguist" [saying] *où êtes-nous monsieur*',[126] more common were observations of failure to speak French: 'I'm tired of buying eggs and milk in execrable French',[127] or 'Trying to speak French. A splendid failure'.[128]

Language learning and teaching took various forms. Sgt John Ward, wounded and transferred to the management of a Chinese convalescent camp, taught himself some Chinese,[129] while a convalescent Portuguese officer tried to learn English from the VAD nurse tending him.[130] Language courses for British soldiers were advertised in trench journals and regimental and military magazines,[131] including in the *Navy and*

Army Magazine, Hugo's courses in 'French, Spanish or even German', and Belgian refugees in Reigate advertised their services to teach French and Flemish to British soldiers.[132] Evidence for more casual teaching includes M. MacDonald teaching English to French troops,[133] a stereograph photo titled 'Lessons in French', showing three American soldiers studying with a woman,[134] and parodies of language-teaching in trench journals – an advertisement for 'Specialists in Dead Languages' and 'Bad language by post', and a test on slang.[135]

Most language learning though was incidental, and involved picking up the most necessary terms. Within two weeks of his arrival in Egypt James Jones had picked up the term 'backsheesh',[136] and Belgian refugee children in Scotland were reported to have speedily picked up the local accent.[137] Some of this involved the traditional British embarrassment when faced with French: Adèle De L'Isle reporting that she is intending 'to learn to "parley-voo"'.[138] A more enticing way of learning was through contact with the opposite sex: Badshah Khan in a letter home noted that when British troops were away from the trenches 'it was "bonsoir madame"',[139] while RSM Harry Atkin 'spen[t] a pleasant evening with the girls trying to make something of the French language'.[140] Rather more cynical evidence comes in the American Expeditionary Force description of a French girl as a 'sleeping dictionary'.[141] A card from Berthe Brifort to Billy indicates that such relationships involved language acquisition in both directions.

FIGURE 1.4 Three American soldiers receiving lessons in French. Stereoview photograph, published by the Success Portrait Company, Chattanooga, Tennessee.

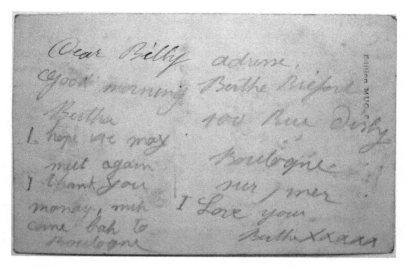

FIGURE 1.5 Card from Berthe Brifort to Billy, hoping to see him again. The image shows a studio photograph of a woman with a British soldier, and the legend 'Doux Souvenir'.

> *Many phrasebooks were available in 1914/15, but few in Flemish, a language with greater difficulties: for the average British soldier this was an unknown language. Phrasebook publishers did not recognise its importance at the Front; even if they had had pronunciation guides the dialect of West Flanders is distinct from other dialects.*

Lt Cecil Down's servant was presented with a copy of 'useful French phrases' when he left for France,[142] and while the BEF distributed a thousand French dictionaries at the Front in 1915, many Australian officers equipped themselves with such books before arriving in France.[143] Though the *Publishers' Circular* in September 1914[144] noted the limitations of phrasebooks, commenting on the pronunciation guide in *The Briton in France* (eight editions 1906–1918) that it was 'funny' – '"Kahrt der Frohngss" sounds more like German than Carte de France' – by January 1915 they were proposing that 'it would appear to be the duty of the State to supply [the soldier] with reliable language guides'.[145] A soldier's letter published in the *Daily Mail* in January 1915[146] stated that 'nearly everyone carries a book or pamphlet containing English and French sentences', though with only 'a vain hope of finding a sentence that will help him out'. *Home Chat* claimed that '[a]s a practical man, Tommy is no believer in the shilling phrase book, even with phonetic pronunciation. He prefers to hear the phrase with his own ears, and write it down in his own way'.[147] Many phrasebooks were available in 1914/15, but few in Flemish, a language with greater difficulties: for the average British soldier this was an unknown language. Phrasebook publishers did not recognise its importance at the Front; even if they had had pronunciation guides the dialect of West Flanders is distinct from other dialects. *War-Time Tips* suggested that the soldier 'buy an English–French dictionary and study it', but not an English–Flemish one.[148]

It emerged also that German publishing houses had prepared phrasebooks for German soldiers, which were clearly designed for campaigning abroad, such as *Deutsch-Französischer Soldaten-Sprachführer* (1914), also available as *Deutsch-Englischer Soldaten-Sprachführer*, by Siegfried Haasmann, which contained phrases such as 'Are you a deserter? Write down why!' British phrasebooks did not take such a peremptory approach, being firmly based on the tourist model, and retaining much of the tourist phrasebook's organisation and choice of statements for translation. The *Mayfield French Conversation Guide* (1914) was quickly adapted to take a small supplement with words such as 'mounted infantry' and 'gunner' and phrases such as 'I have a pass' and 'Have you seen the enemy?' (but not 'trench' or 'barbed wire') before moving on to the more familiar (for the time) tourist phrases 'Where does one procure tickets?' and 'At what time does the post office close?'[149] More dedicated phrasebooks such as *How to Say it in French* (1914) showed a British soldier greeting a French soldier on the front cover, and included terms for 'the battle field' such as 'give me something to drink please', and 'how many wounded?', but still included 'the smoking carriage' and 'could you repair my bicycle please'. As an indication of optimism, despite the horrific casualties and the pro-war feeling of 1914, it finishes with 'let us hope peace will soon be declared' and 'cheer up'. *What a British Soldier Wants to Say in French* (Wimereux, 1914) and *The British Soldiers' Anglo-French Pocket Dictionary* (1915) both, like *How to Say it in French*, carried pronunciation guides, but the *English–Flemish Military Guide* (Poperinghe, 1915) omitted this; all of these characteristically work from the principle of speaking rather than being spoken to. Carreras enterprisingly produced a series of four English–French dictionaries and phrasebooks to be included within Black Cat cigarette packets; the printers' pragmatic approach to French included using an inverted 5 in place of 'ç'. These phrasebooks tend to show an uncomfortable mix of tourism and military activity, requests for a footbath alongside 'have you heard firing lately?',[150] or 'I place you under arrest' with 'have you nothing cheaper?'[151] Henry Buller's *The Soldiers' English–German Conversation Book* ('for the man at the front') published in 1915 is far more practical, with inclusions such as 'cessation of firing' and 'I must search this house', and ends with a poignant section 'Tommy In Friendly Talk', which provides conversational material such as 'let us have a smoke' and 'how long were you in the trenches?', imagining a range of possible scenarios, from hospital to Christmas truce to prisoner of war camp or even armistice. It was revised and re-issued in 1939.

Multilingual phrasebooks offered publishers an attractive product, apparently useful, though probably less so in practice. Melik David-Bey's *Manuel de la Conversation Française, Anglaise, Turque & Russe* (Paris, 1916) mainly comprised non-military phrases, which could indeed have been ignored while the useful ones would still be useful; there would have been limited opportunities to use phrases such as 'To the opera, I am so fond of music', but it was always going to be helpful to be able to say 'the town – the little town – the houses' and '*Avez-vous du vin?*'.

Its inclusion of the four languages from the context of the closing Gallipoli campaign and the development of the Salonika campaign, involving French and British forces from October 1915, and Russian forces, along with Serbian and Italian units, from summer 1916, indicates less a practical book for interpreters or soldiers than an enterprising publisher catering for the perception during the war of the value of being able to communicate in other languages. Enterprising, opportunistic or just lazy, the 1918 (eighth) edition of the phrasebook *The Briton in France*, unchanged from the edition of 1906, still gave details of how to get to Brussels via Harwich and Antwerp via the night boat and the Belgian State Railway, as if the war had never happened.

Civilians in Britain probably had about as much contact with Flemish as did the British soldiers in Flanders, since the north-west of Belgium quickly became a militarised zone, with the local population making up no more than 15 per cent of those present in the 'unoccupied' zone. Very few Flemish-based terms entered soldiers' conversation, and those that did –

Bandagehem, Dosinghem, Mendinghem – significantly are parodies of place names. One soldier did note that when Flemish speakers spoke French it was easier to understand, because they spoke slower and with an accent closer to that of English-speakers.[152] Comfortingly perhaps, some German soldiers also found Flemish hard to understand,[153] while in Dundee in November 1914 there was some surprise that communication in French or Flemish with Belgian refugees was successful at all,[154] and in Glasgow Flemish classes for hosts of refugees were proposed.[155] But the soldiers had little successful contact with Flemish speakers: John Bullock, the protagonist of Henry Williamson's *The Patriot's Progress* has a dispiriting encounter with a prostitute who swears in Flemish,[156] R. H. Mottram notes that the 'Flemish–French dialect [is] not easily understood',[157] and the private's diary of the 9th Royal Scots, February–March 1915, remarks on 'comments made in guttural Vlaamsch, which no-one understood'.[158]

The most obvious obstacle faced by British soldiers in France was how to communicate with French people. The ability to speak a little French was not uncommon throughout the armies of men who enlisted from 1914, and contributed towards easier relations with locals – though looking back after the war the 'Miscellany' writer of the *Manchester Guardian* reckoned that 'only a few advanced linguists [in a shopping situation] went so far as "je prong"'.[159] Among the officer class holidays abroad and education made the ability to speak French more common,[160] and might, as in the case of 'other ranks' soldiers such as R. H. Mottram, lead to a safer posting as an interpreter. Most British soldiers picked up a few words, but many found that extended conversations were beyond them; any soldiers who could speak at all fluently, as could Manning's Bourne in *Her Privates We*, were pounced on as informal interpreters. And with commerce as an incentive, it was reckoned that by 1917 most of the inhabitants of the combat zone and its hinterland had a working knowledge of English. In extraordinary circumstances there was inevitable breakdown – Aubrey Smith failed entirely with his French and his billet-owner's little English to explain how to make a jam roly-poly pudding.[161]

For non-officers the record of documentation shows regular conversations partly in French, partly in English, frequently involving some Tommy French or Trench French – utterances such as 'no-bleedin'-bon' – and particularly occurring in estaminets, and including some swearing. Horace Stanley's diary includes a scene where rhyming slang is thrown into the mix too, concluding with a French woman saying, 'out bleeding bird and winder, bonne'.[162] This kind of code-switching was described as 'Arf an' Arf' language.[163] French and English side-by-side were also frequently found as captions on soldiers' postcards, sometimes incongruously, as in the tongue-twister song 'Sister Susie's sewing shirts for sailors', translated pointlessly as *Nini travaille aussi pour les soldats*.[164] Bilingual texts occurred in other war-related contexts – an advertisement in the *Navy and Army Magazine* 20 March 1915 for a civilian badge gives the motto as both 'lest we forget' and *n'oublions jamais*.

Another phenomenon was the casual dropping in of foreign, usually French, words and phrases into communication. Lancelot Spicer writes 'fresh milk – well, we never see it in the trenches – seulement le lait condensed'.[165] A postcard sent to 'Angleterre' hopes it will find the addressee 'in the pink as it leaves me in that awfull condition compree', and another sent to 'Ella' in Glasgow from France ends 'yours lovingly, Cheero, Salute'.[166] A soldier sent a postcard home to M. Wilson in Peterborough on 1 October 1914 with the words 'Au revoir mon cher maman, Bert',[167] his eagerness to use French not hampered by correct word-endings. John Masefield describes his voyage to France: 'everyone was sick but myself, spuage universal, so to speak . . '. This practice is to be found in diaries as well: Cpl R. D. Doughty writes in his diary for 11th October 1916, 'Gun Officer all day. Nothing much doing only trying to forget London. Tres Bon, I don't think. On duty tonight.'[168] Walter Shuttleworth wrote on 22 August 1917, 'Letter from Nellie Mason makes absurd statement that I write tales of woe. Trés [sic] fâché,'[169] and Bombardier Spires wrote, 'Haslers and I regularly visit the 'Au Nouveau' estaminet as the ale is not so bad and the oeufs were certainly good.'[170] *The Pow-Wow* 26 February 1915 has a pastiche of the Arabian Nights titled 'Un Petit More-So'; the war environment was renewing a practice of dropping French words and phrases into English that has been a regular practice for over a thousand years.

In this environment of French being the primary 'other language' it was natural that French should be used as a lingua franca. 2nd Lt Cyril Drummond reported that during the Christmas truce in 1914 the conversation between Irish and German soldiers was in French,[171] and Cpl A. E. Lee had a conversation with a wounded Bavarian sergeant in no man's land – 'we had a good old chat in schoolboy French'.[172] French was the standard lingua franca in communication with the Turkish army, but a French/English mix was more common for the British army's communications in France and Flanders – R. H. Mottram describes an elderly woman in Poperinghe saying 'Monsieur, est-ce bombarde soon finish?'[173] The process of French people speaking English to arriving

FIGURE 1.6 Postcard sent 'On Active Service' in 1917: 'Am getting on tray-bon now. Hope all are well. Love, Arthur.'

FIGURE 1.7 Postcard sent from Bert to his mother in October 1914, while 'On Active Service'. Note the use of 'Angleterre'.

troops began at the port towns. Donald McNair reported residents of Cherbourg picking up and shouting the appropriate response to 'Are we downhearted?',[174] and Lt Cecil Down reported 'the Franco-Belgian woman's war cry "Chocolat, good for English soldiers"'.[175] French and Belgian children were often noted as picking up English: Graves documented children pimping their older sisters at Cherbourg,[176] Douie heard children at Etaples selling 'three apples – une pennee',[177] and A. M. Burrage remembered a small boy near Bavincourt selling newspapers shouting 'Bloody good news for the Ingleese!'[178] Frequently, as here, the documentation shows transcribed accents, usually indicating that the accented English was understood: Henry Williamson describes French boys begging in English, saying 'biskeets and booly biff',[179] and a postcard in the series 'Sketches of Tommy's Life' by Fergus Mackain shows French children shouting 'Orangeez! Ah-pools! Shock-o-la!'[180] Adults' speech is transcribed too, and taboo terms were of especial interest: Bombardier Spires noted in his diary that as he had lost his cap and had to wear his helmet, the local estaminet proprietor insisted on calling him '"M le Pisspot".'[181] Harold Harvey describes a local Frenchman saying, 'Vat your vife say if she see you in ze water?'[182] British advertising copywriters naturally made use of this, regularly employing 'ze' for 'the', or extending the idea into applying recognisably French syntax to English, as in the Army Club cigarette advertisement, in which the 'Sous Lieutenant Aviateur' says 'But since I am arrive here . . . I essay the golden tobacco of the English':[183] its counterpart lies in a British nurse saying to a French soldier, 'Tasy vous toot sweet or je vous donnerai la colleek'.[184]

French use of English was naturally not always successful; editing would have benefitted the text in a few bilingual postcards, such as 'A Zeppelin thrown down in the Vardar marshes', 'Reims cathedral, fired from the Germans', or 'Rimains of splendie church after the bombardment'. French-speakers picking up inappropriate slang as well as incorrect English was of particular amusement: Gibson gives the example of a Flemish café owner telling her customers, 'Messieurs, when you 'ave finis, 'op it',[185] and Douie records a Belgian saying "Ello, my boy! Me speak Eengleesh',[186] the transcribed accent alerting the reader to the speaker's foreignness. And while the environment of foreign languages gave scope for teasing – Masefield records French wounded soldiers saying to anglophone nurses 'Seester, what is Will you kiss me mean?'[187] – Aubrey Smith records a sharp conversation between a British soldier arriving at Rouen and a French women selling oranges, which ends with her saying 'You damn fool'.[188]

A number of English words were taken into French as well: *L'Argot de la Guerre* by Albert Dauzat included:[189]

bizness, for work or business, a longstanding usage in Paris
souinger, to bomb, from 'swing', originally 'donner un swing', probably from boxing
uppercut, eau-de-vie, also from boxing
rider, pronounced 'ridèr' – chic, especially in the language of the cavalry (Dauzat states *le rider est le cavalier anglais, donc le cavalier chic* – a case of the French looking to the English for style)
ours, horse, maybe picked up from Londoners
go, meaning 'ça va'
come on, meaning just that
tanks, which Dauzat translates as *les auto-mitrailleuses ou les auto-camions blindés* (armoured) – *blindés* itself meant 'tanks'.

Eric Partridge adds to this list the following wartime adoptions:[190]

Sops, planes, from Sopwith, cf. 'taube' for German planes.
Finish, meaning 'there's no more', a mirror of the anglicisation 'finee'.
Strafer, taken from the British adoption of the German strafen, so a bounced-on adoption.
Coltar, wine (coal tar).
Afnaf, 'either not too well pleased', or 'satisfied', or else 'exhausted'; imitative of the cockney "'arf 'n 'arf".
Olrède, alright.
Lorry, with the plural *lorrys*.

From Déchelette can be added *saucissemen* ('Germans', the term seldom documented as being used by anglophones) and the ironic *billard* ('billiard-table', for no man's land, also to be found in Partridge).[191] A French trench journal, the *Télé-Mèl*, produced by a section of telegraphists, borrowed its title, with altered spelling, from the *Daily Mail*. And at least one word was bounced back: Fraser and Gibbons record 'chicot' meaning verminous, coming from the French *chicot*, itself an adoption from the American 'hitchy-koo'.

Some mixed English/French conversations were given the label 'pidgin': a Chairman Cigarettes advertisement runs:

When Tom and Jacques meet in a trench
They parlez-vous in 'pidgin' French.
Says Tommy 'prenez cigarette?'
And Jacques exclaims 'Oui, oui, you bet'
. . .
'Who ees zis Chairman zat I see?'
'He's top man at the feed, compris?'[192]

While not actually a pidgin (though some aspects of Tommy French would count as pidgin), this shows one of the labels given to this kind of speech at the time, another being seen in a review of a performed sketch called 'My Lonely Soldier', which used the term 'broken English' to describe a French woman's attempts to speak English.[193] Successful Franco-English communication in Europe seems to have depended on the management of key words – *compree, fini, chocolat, vin*; an ability to pick up vocabulary might be the essential factor to make communication work: Ian Hay[194] describes a Sgt Goffin managing to make a successful purchase with 'I want vinblank one, vinrooge two, bogeys six (*bougies* – candles), Dom one. Compree?', where 'Dom' refers to a bottle of Benedictine, the sergeant having the habit of naming wines after the largest word printed on the label.

Some German words were adopted into French, particularly by prisoners of war; Partridge lists several including *arbeit* (work), *kartoffel* (potato), *krank* (ill), but he notes that *pfennig* was pronounced also as *fennich* or *péniche* (barge), that *ersatz-girl* meant a temporary sweetheart, and that *verboten* was often pronounced *faire de beau temps*.[195] A former PoW administrating a Russian PoW camp in Germany after the war noted the word 'mould', describing the demoralisation produced by boredom, frustration and malnutrition.[196] Capt Gilbert Nobbs, in a prison hospital in Germany, noted that a French orderly used only one word of German, *nix*, 'which he used on every possible occasion to express his disgust of the Germans'.[197]

Many Central Powers soldiers were familiar with English – several Austrians picked it up while working in America and Canada,[198] and immigration from Germany into Britain had doubled between 1861 and 1911, at which time the figure was over 50,000 annually. Perhaps the effect of so many Germans living and working in Britain and widely picking up the language led British soldiers to assume that German soldiers would speak English, or failing that, what would have been to them the most obvious foreign language, French. Pte L. M. Baldwin made a lasting friendship with a wounded German soldier who spoke English and French, and though this soldier was well educated,[199] his facility with the language was not isolated. Adèle De L'Isle reported that many of the wounded Germans that came through her ward spoke English,[200] and the *Daily Express* reported on German prisoners saying 'Germany, thumbs up', and 'bad luck – two down', on hearing of the loss of two Zeppelins;[201] another newspaper article reported on a German prisoner being able to say his comrades were 'in the soup' when their field-kitchen was bombed – the paper described it as a 'ghastly pun';[202] if intentional it indicates considerable confidence with the language. Though British soldiers knew or picked up a few words of German, particularly those that most affected them, such as *strafe* or *Minenwerfer*, fluency was rare. V.A.D. Emma Duffin spoke German to wounded soldiers,[203] though she and her colleague found some of the dialect speech difficult, Aubrey Herbert

CODE-SWITCHING

For soldiers of all nations involved there was a commonality of experiences on the Western Front, which was both reinforced and reflected by the use of each other's slang. A *Punch* cartoon of 11 April 1917 (p. 247) shows a British soldier guarding a German prisoner. The German scowls as the British soldier says to his mates, 'You wouldn't think it to look at 'im, but when I says "'ands up," 'e answers back in puffick English, "Steady on with yer blinkin' toothpick," 'e sez, "an' I'll come quiet."'

A later cartoon (20 March 1918, p. 184) shows a British officer in an Italian shop; he asks for apples, but the woman serving says, 'Non, niente. English "napoo"'. According to the *Daily Record* (29 December 1915, p. 5) French soldiers had picked up and were using the pronunciation 'Wipers' from British soldiers. But code-switching or competence in a second language allowed more than just the adoption of foreign terms: according to Brophy and Partridge in *The Long Trail*, *dégommé*, the French for 'sacked' or 'demoted', was picked up by British soldiers as 'ungummed', and developed into 'unstuck' in the phrase 'to come unstuck'.

spoke German to a captive at Gallipoli,[204] and Walter Blumschein was asked by a British soldier only 15 metres away 'Haben Zie Zigarren?'[205]

The mixture of English, French and German in conversations was common, and a mark of the need to communicate in conditions of stress: Aubrey Smith notes it as 'the eternal remark' when the French say to British soldiers, 'Allemagne caput',[206] while Emma Duffin noted a dying German soldier say to her, 'Schwester fini'.[207] Graves noted a conversation between his own troops and Germans opposite which involved English, French and German, one German soldier being happy that the English had at last learned some German;[208] in another incident a wounded German soldier says 'Mercia, kamerade ... tres bon English soldier', in a muddle of languages.[209] A problem in this situation was highlighted when a German soldier surrendered to Sgt Bradlaugh Sanderson 'and said something like "merci"': Sanderson thinks at first he is saying thank you in French, but concludes he was asking for mercy in English.[210]

The more unfamiliar the context, rather than the language, the less likely it was that successful communication would develop; thus, Arabic in Egypt was more likely to be picked up than Greek, because of the British Empire's association with Egypt. By December 1916 in Salonika, according to The Times, British soldiers had managed only the phrase 'Hidy bros' (the equivalent of 'Buck up!'). This was 'reinforced by gesture and "Hi! Johnny See!"', while the Greeks had picked up only 'stop' and 'finish'.[211] Harold Lake in In Salonica with our Army wrote 'I have seen new drafts come out to Egypt, and I have heard them a fortnight later with all sorts of Arab slang at the tips of their tongues ... Our men bring back words in many dialects from India, and the South African war made some additions to our vocabulary. But there is another tale to tell in Macedonia. Why it should be I cannot imagine, but no one seems to pick up the language. At the end of my own time I only knew three words (for "eggs" "water", and "go away" or words to that effect)'.[212] 'Transport Officer' in Gallipoli reckoned that half of Anzac slang was 'Egyptian Arabic, picked up in Cairo', while he believed that 'Tommy's slang is largely derived from Hindustani'.[213] But no instances have come to light of Arabic being used as a lingua franca between Allied and Turkish troops, though pre-war British troops were accustomed to using non-European languages – a Hindi slang long used between British and Indian soldiers was recorded in Kut before the surrender, by a British soldier, P. W. Long.[214] In this regard the long-term linguistic familiarities produced by trade, conquest and colonialism probably had more effect than western literary culture, educational curricula, diplomacy and European travel. The naval equivalent of the army 'buckshee', 'cumshaw', was derived from pidgin communication with Chinese people; 'goody-la', from the Chinese Labour Corps term for 'good', was, according to Brophy and Partridge, taken over for facetious use and became a catchword.[215] But not everyone was going to become an ad hoc linguist: Emma Duffin reported in her diary on a Russian soldier who after serving with the Australians for a year 'could hardly speak English at all'.[216] British soldiers serving in Russia during the war and afterwards in support of the White Russian armies picked up a few terms, transcribed as 'spassiba' (thanks), 'xaroshie/ sharoshie' (good), 'bolos' (Bolshevik fighters), 'do svidanya' (goodbye),[217] and 'tavarish' (mate). On 2 October 1918 Pte W. Brock wrote home to London from the North Russian Expeditionary Force that 'my knowledge only extends to names of things such as Bread (Kleb) (Skolka) How much (Catorie Chassi) whats the time (Spazebow) thank you (Neet pominair) don't understand (Eggs) Ya, cet, sa Tea (chai) Gidea (where) . . .'; he then notes that 'if I had stopped down the line much longer I should have learnt a lot mixing with the people'.[218] Following the pattern of Western Front slang, 'carachou, nichyvoo' were the counterparts of 'napoo', 'dobra' (good) was extended to 'niet fucking dobra', and 'skolka' (how much) developed into 'skolkering' (black market trading).

Multilinguism during the war provided the potential for bonds between people, the opportunity to learn, and the environment for chaos. In the Austro-Hungarian armies twelve languages had official status; the equivalent of the Field Service Postcard was printed in eight languages. But the use of Czech, Italian and Serbian raised questions of disloyalty, even though these were languages of the Habsburg Empire, while the use at the front of English or Russian – enemy languages – did not. In August 1914 an artillery gunner was shot by a French sentry because he did not understand the challenge,[219] and George Barker remembered his disappointment at not being able to communicate with some Gurkhas he met – 'they might as well speak to the moon'.[220] One of the most distressing misunderstandings was over the supposed German 'Corpse Utilisation Company': according to a British soldier, who got it from a German prisoner, this unit was boiling corpses 'to make fat for ammunition making and to feed pigs and poultry, and God knows what else besides . . . Fritz calls his margarine "corpse fat", because they suspect that's what it comes from';[221] in the report on the incident in *The Times* the soldier says 'mind, I don't know that it's true, but he told me', which should have set some alarm bells ringing. The misunderstanding possibly arose from hard-nosed German slang, which renamed the commission that assessed recruits' fitness for active service as the *Kadaververwertungsgeseelschaft*, or 'carcase-grading factory'. Cartoonists in *Punch*[222] and trench journals mocked the idea, but probably some real distress was caused. Misunderstandings could also prove advantageous: Lt Cecil Down's Scottish servant was impressed when on asking for 'twa oofs' he was given three;[223] the story is told elsewhere, appearing in *Punch* on 21 April 1916 (p. 287), so may be apocryphal, or a common occurrence.

The quest for effective communication across language barriers went on to the end of the war and beyond. Cavanders introduced 'the "American Doughboy"' in their advertising campaign for Army Club cigarettes at the end of the war,[224] showing him reading a book entitled *French and English Phrase Book*, and saying 'Can't make nothing of this gol-darned French phrase book. All about the wooden leg of the gardener and the pens of my aunt, and that kind o' junk', referencing the phrases of school exercises. The American *Thirty Second News* for November 1918 has several documentations of disappointment, of soldiers not being able to speak French, of misunderstanding, and of attempts at lingua franca collapsing into American slang. An American cartoon book *When I was in Germany* dating from after the withdrawal of American troops in 1923 contains considerable code-switching into accurate German:

Lebe wohl Fräuleins – I'm through.
Each Mädschen I have met
I'll say good-bye to you – and all my chocolate
I'm through with all spazieren
And even being near 'em ...

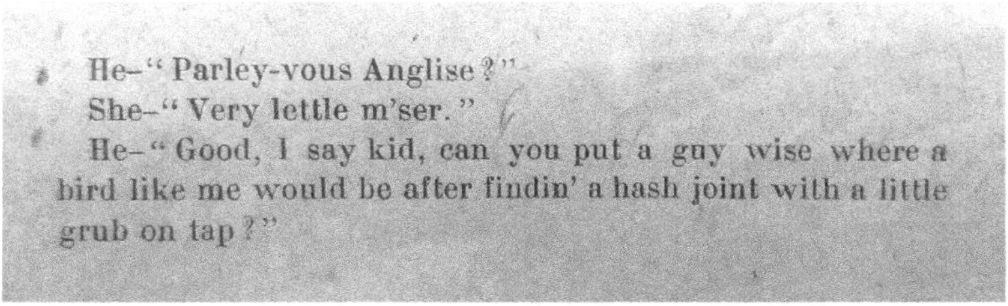

He–" Parley-vous Anglise ?"
She–" Very lettle m'ser. "
He–" Good, I say kid, can you put a guy wise where a bird like me would be after findin' a hash joint with a little grub on tap ?"

FIGURE 1.8 From the *Thirty Second News*, November 1918, the journal of the American 32nd Division, nicknamed *Les Terribles*.

2 LANGUAGE AT THE FRONT

Words: sources and trajectories

Words and phrases came from a variety of sources, old army slang, criminal slang, street slang, school slang, rhyming slang, topical events, common home experience, music-hall songs, other languages, close observation of the experience of the trench. There was interest in etymology, as well as the words themselves, during the war: Ward Muir, a lance corporal in the R.A.M.C., wrote in *Observations of an Orderly* 'Whether the derivations of army slang have been investigated I do not know. It appears to me a subject worth examination.'[1] Cadet N. R. wrote in *The White Band* a brief entry on the etymology of 'Uhlan',[2] while in 1917 the *Manchester Guardian* carried three paragraphs on some Hindustani (Hindi/Urdu) and gambling origins of slang, hoping that the subject would be studied in future[3] (an earlier column, written on 4 June that year, had suggested the slang was in too much of a flux for it to be done yet).

Claims for the origin of slang expressions also pitted Britain against other anglophone countries: 'some' as an intensifier was felt to be an Americanism, and there was some concern about the influence of American slang – 'The new Whitehall officialdom is far sunk in the more generally adopted colloquialisms of Canada and the United States.'[4] 'But I say, kid, *some* cigarette' was the way Cavanders characterised an American sailor. But 'a Bachelor of Science' writing to the *Birmingham Gazette* claimed the use of 'some' in this way 'at least thirty years ago' in Cornwall,[5] and the *Burnley News* quoted a correspondent claiming the term's use in Lancashire, rather than its originating in America.[6] And while the guardians of British English feared the influence of American slang, *The Times* correspondent in New York in 1918 observed that 'the Americans [were] showing a much greater facility in acquiring British slang than the

Tommies in learning American slang.[7] Certainly on reading Jonathan Lighter's *Slang of the AEF* it is noticeable how many of the terms just did not appear in the record of British soldiers' speech.

Eric Partridge's 1933 study of army slang described several words which predated the war, many of them having been in army use for many decades; criminal slang – 'make', 'nab', 'nail', 'scrounge', 'snaffle' and 'win' were pre-1830, while 'as to the slang that arose in India, nearly all of it dates from the period of the Indian Mutiny or from the subsequent . . . occupation of India by the British Army'.[8] A 'King's bad bargain' was centuries old by 1914, as were 'clink' and 'cage' for holding offending soldiers, while 'push', 'padre' and 'grouse' were nineteenth century terms. In the military environment terms came together from various sources: the 'padre' might be mockingly called the 'amen-wallah'; and 'binge', according to Partridge, was possibly a mixture of Lincolnshire 'binge', meaning 'to soak', and 'bingo' – spirits: it was pre-war Oxford University slang, taken to the Front and adopted by other ranks soldiers. 'Jipper', nautical slang for gravy, evolved into 'gippo', sitting alongside 'gypo', an Egyptian. The large number of words from Indian languages – khaki, cushy, bandook, gone phutt, dekko, rooty, kutcha, muckin, chokey, bolo the bat, pukka, chit, coggage, booka, bobbajee, dum-dum, doolally, wallah, and Blighty – many of which have stayed in spoken English, anchor the British military experience of the time in contact with Indian culture. Military contact with African languages had brought 'pozzy', and South African troops brought 'mainga', while army slang had acquired several words from Arabic from the involvement in north-east Africa – bint, burgoo, iggri, imshi, buckshee, mungaree. These words were passed on through the army during the war, rather than through direct new contact with Arabic-speakers or Indian soldiers; very few new adoptions of words from these languages occurred, though Fraser and Gibbons list 'cooker' from the Ghurka 'kukri', and Downing's *Digger Dialects* (1919) has the earliest documentation of 'iggoree', more often 'iggry', from the Arabic for 'quickly'.

Before the war itself became the almost exclusive topical news story,[9] one non-associated term shows how quickly words were both taken up, and recorded: in the fourth week of September, while the B.E.F. were settling in trenches facing the German lines along the route of the River Aisne, the press was reporting the story of Jack Johnson's brush with the law (Johnson was the black heavyweight boxing champion). Johnson's name had been reported in the British provincial press ten times during

August 1914, mostly to do with prospective matches, but not at all from 1 until 19 September. On 22 September the story broke that Johnson had been served with a summons on 17 September, following a parking infringement, the newspapers reporting the following day the full story of the incident, including Johnson's alleged aggressive reaction. Within two days the *Sheffield Evening Telegraph* (24 September 1914) was reporting that when a large shell landed 'our boys dub the pillar of smoke which it makes "Black Maria" or "Jack Johnson"'. 'Jack Johnson' became the standard term for a heavy German shell giving a large cloud of smoke, but was also applied to the guns that fired the shells; there were also 'JJ's,[10] 'black Johnsons',[11] and both 'Jacks' and 'Johnsons'.[12]

Words and phrases continued their development during the course of the war. 'Blighty', from the Urdu *biliayati*, meaning 'a foreigner', was adopted in India by British troops and colonials, and was immensely popular during the war, to the extent that frequently soldiers addressed their postcards and letters home to 'Blighty' rather than 'England' or 'Britain'. A coveted wound that did not do life-changing damage but

FIGURE 2.1 Soldiers' 'On Active Service' postcards, sent between February 1917 and October 1918, addressed to Blighty.

would take the soldier home, was called 'a blighty wound', or 'a blighty one', or simply 'a blighty'. Soldiers with a 'Blighty ticket' were called 'Blighties', 'a blighty touch' was a self-inflicted wound,[13] but 'the Blighty touch' was a mysterious ability projected onto one V.A.D. nurse by wounded soldiers, supposing she had the ability to decide which wounds merited treatment in Britain.[14]

Other developments were less celebrated. Ernest Weekley, in *Words Ancient and Modern* (1926), wrote of the word 'raider' that 'when air raids on London began to be really unpleasant, a large proportion of the alien population [sic] took to evacuating the capital, as soon as the evening shades prevailed, and camping in the villages of the home counties, where they were commonly known as "raiders". The inhabitants of one village, stricken with compassion at a first invasion, but unable, for many reasons, to offer house-room to the "raiders," provided them with all they could spare in the way of tents, rugs, and mattresses. When they arose in the morning, they found that their visitors had folded their tents like the Arabs and silently stolen away, transitively as well as intransitively'.[15]

The extent to which terms were used, in terms of time period, individuals, groups, locations, is hard to gauge. Wilfred Owen in his letters used the word 'tamboo' for a shelter (it derived from the Persian and Hindi *tambu*, so was presumably an Indian Army adoption), but few others used it. 'Bugwarm' for a tight dug-out in a trench is known but was seldom used. 'Our present billet is a big house only 600 yards from "sandbag street" or the firing line; everything has a nickname out here', wrote Pte P. Gilbert, Duke of Cornwall's Light Infantry,[16] but apart from here and in a poem in the *Sporting Times*[17] other documentation has proved elusive. There was a vogue for saying 'over the lid' in the summer of 1916, but it was recorded at other times also. Obviously the introduction of new weaponry or equipment, where it can be dated, gives a date 'after which' for the requisite terms: the introduction of corrugated metal huts in late 1916 gives 'elephants', recorded from 1917; the 'gaspirator' appeared in 1916.

Experience common to men from urban households on different sides of no man's land gave rise to common expressions: margarine was 'axle-grease' and *Wagonschmiere*, the German stick-hand-grenade was a 'potato-masher' and a *Kartoffelstomper*, a bomb giving off black smoke was a 'coalbox' and *Kohlenkasten*. Anglophone soldiers took the word *Trommelfeuer* and, finding it appropriate, used the idea as 'drumfire'. From the continuous experience of being told *il n'y a plus* – 'there's none left' – by

French bartenders and shopkeepers, anglophones developed 'napoo', while the Germans called a lager *naplü*, and a cognac *naplüchen*.

Enthusiasm for etymology gave the academic community an audience: the writer of 'Are the Germans really Huns?' in *The Pow-Wow* (9 December 1914) correctly showed that the Allemani, whose name developed into the French *Allemagne*, derived from forms cognate with the English 'all men', indicating their heterogeneity. But contested and multiple etymologies were an inevitable aspect of the study of new terms. 'Archie', the name given to anti-aircraft fire, is widely recognised as coming from the 1909 song 'Archibald Certainly Not', written by John L. St John and Alfred Glover, notably performed by George Robey. The term is documented from very early in the war,[18] is noted by Brophy and Partridge[19] as having 'pride of place' in Issue 2 of the *Wipers Times*, and gained wide acceptance, extending to its use as a verb, 'to Archie'. The song refers to a man being told by his wife not to expect intimate relations after their honeymoon night, which explains the definitions, or explanations in Cassell's *New English Dictionary* (1919):

[nickname from the popular song, 'Archibald, certainly not,' with allusion to the fewness of the hits made], n.pl. (Soldiers' slang) Anti-aircraft guns or shells; the anti-aircraft force.

and Collins' *Etymological Dictionary* (1922):

Archies n.pl. the anti-aircraft force; also, the guns and shells. The name is said to have been given, owing to the fewness of the hits, from the song, 'Archibald, certainly not.'

A different version is given by Ernest Weekley in his *An Etymological Dictionary of Modern English* (1921):

Archibald, Archie: 'It was at once noticed at Brooklands [where much aviation development and testing was carried out prior to 1914] that in the vicinity of, or over, water or damp ground, there were disturbances in the air causing bumps or drops to these early pioneers. Some of these "remous" were found to be permanent, one over the Wey river, and another at the corner of the aerodrome next to the sewage farm. Youth being fond of giving proper names to inanimate objects, the bump near the sewage farm was called by them Archibald.

As subsequently, when war broke out, the effect of having shell bursting near an aeroplane was to produce a "remous" reminding the Brookland trained pilots of their old friend Archibald, they called being shelled 'being Archied' for short. Any flying-man who trained at Brooklands before the war will confirm the above statement.'

COL. C H JOUBERT DE LA FERTÉ,
I M S [Indian Medical Service] ret.

Both of these are fully viable, and not necessarily mutually exclusive; a more likely interpretation is that complementary sources cemented the use of the term. The multiple sources and experiences of language made multiple etymologies and reinforcements inevitable – Fraser and Gibbons reported that 'cushy' was 'popularly said to be derived from Cushion', while noting that it had a history dating back to the Hindi word for 'pleasant'; Partridge agreed that 'it is not absolutely certain that it does not represent a shortening of *cushiony*',[20] which was the view of John Nettleinghame.[21]

But enthusiasm for the etymology of war language led some into conjectures that were more optimistic than wise. 'Gone west' excited many suggestions, but had a wider range of sources than at first thought of: the 'Miscellany' writer for the *Manchester Guardian* 25 September 1917, p. 3, wrote that he had discovered the Chinese phrase *hui-hsi*, meaning 'returned west', or 'gone to heaven', Buddhist heaven being 'in the west'. Dubious etymology, folk etymology, and missed usages were part of the business of the public and academic interest in slang. Brophy and Partridge omitted the interpretation 'breaking wind on parade' for 'dumb insolence', which Fraser and Gibbons had given in 1925, and did not include it in the 1969 edition of *Songs and Slang of the British Soldier 1914–1918*, though Partridge included it in his *Dictionary of Slang and Unconventional English*, dating the usage to 1916. Some attempts at etymology might have been better left unsaid: 'H.V.W.' wrote to *The Observer* suggesting that 'wangle' derived from 'angle', because it involved getting something by '"fishing" in the slang sense';[22] and Ernest Weekley's entry in *An Etymological Dictionary of Modern English* (1921) for 'Botulism' betrays a lasting resentment against Germany:

Botulism
Ger. Botulismus, discovered and named (1896) by Ermengem. From L botulus, sausage, being caused, in Germany, by eating same. See newspapers Apr 24, 1918.

The names given to the prototype tank 'Little Willie', and its successor, 'Big Willie', are widely supposed to be poking fun at the Kaiser and his son, particularly following the relentless cartoon pastiching of them in comics and magazines.[23] Alternatively the term 'the Wilson machine', from the name of one of the designers, has a good claim for being the source, becoming 'Big Willie' and 'Little Willie' after the development of the second, larger machine. In several cases what may be happening is a reinforcing through parallel sources or associations, which might strengthen the name. Multiple sources might lead back to an ultimate commonality: in *Her Privates We* (1929/30) 'Bourne, thinking with a rapidity only outstripped by her precipitate action, decided that the Hindustani "cushy" and the French "coucher" must have been derived from the same root in Sanskrit'.[24] 'J.R.H.' in *Notes and Queries* proposed that 'fed up' had been acquired by British troops from Australian soldiers during the Boer War (1899–1902),[25] while 'A.R.McL' recorded 'I am full of him' from 1877; he felt its link with the French 'j'en ai soupé', which the writer refers to, was no more than common feelings giving rise to common metaphors.[26] And the slang of the period did not exist in chronological isolation: 'scarper' was established slang in the late Victorian period, from the Italian *scappare* (to escape), and was reinforced by rhyming slang from 'Scapa Flow' (go).

Arguments persisted long after the war, in some cases up to the present. Was it myth or actuality that *Schweinhund*, beloved of Second World War film scriptwriters, was in use in the earlier conflict? Were Scottish soldiers really described as 'ladies from hell'? Both of these terms appear, *Schweinhund* in a signal intercepted off Gallipoli,[27] and in Adèle De L'Isle's diary – 'After Jerry had sampled the sort of fight we could put up if properly roused, he christened us "The Ladies from Hell".'[28] Argument continues over the origin of 'basket case', though the *Oxford English Dictionary* and Lighter's *Slang of the AEF* both carry the same clear citation referring to the war. 'Plonk' is possibly the most familiar contentious word, with a wide assumption that this term for wine emerged from the soldiers' shortening of 'vin blanc'. Though 'plink-plonk' and 'plinketty-plonk' were recorded by Brophy and Partridge, 'plonk' alone was a very common word for mud, as used in 'over the plonk', with 'to plonk' meaning to shell. Among New Zealand soldiers 'plonk' was also used for the transcription of the sound of a gun firing and a rifle firing;[29] it appeared in the expression 'Comment allez plonk?', while 'vim blong', 'vim blank', 'point blank',[30] 'vin blank' and 'von blink'[31] were used in place of *vin blanc*;[32] but never 'plonk' alone, which was first recorded meaning 'wine' in 1927.[33]

Arguments over the etymology of this or that phrase characterised the post-war correspondence in *The Athenaeum*: Nettleinghame dismissed Sparke's suggestion that 'to put the tin hat on it' came from trying to catch rats with a helmet, but quite reasonably and generously made the point that 'it is as impossible to find origins or first usages of such expressions as it is to differentiate between "taking the cake", "the bun", or "the biscuit"'.[34] J. Howard Randerson claimed to have initiated the use of 'no man's land' in August 1914, not for the space between the front lines, but for the effect of the German armies' advance through Belgium and France.[35] Not only lexis but phonology was disputed. 'J.R.H.' again in *Notes and Queries* judged the pronunciation of the first word of 'route-march' as rhyming with south-east English 'about' as a 'mispronunciation'; the editor of *The Pow-Wow* (2 December 1914) was 'emphatically of the opinion that "rout" [i.e. rhyming with "about"] is the correct pronunciation'. Siding with the second view, regardless of accent or questions of social class or J.R.H's view that it was a case of 'evil communications corrupting good manners', would seem to privilege the voice of the soldier over that of the observer.

Arguments over etymology continue to the present: in 2015 there were debates over whether 'putsch' had come from the wartime sense of 'push', whether a 'weather-front' had derived from 'Front', and whether the term 'chitty-chitty-bang-bang' originated in a wartime song involving a chit that allowed the bearer access to a brothel.[36]

Collecting words

Within weeks of the outbreak of war 'a glossary of terms for the man in the street' appeared under the headline 'War Terms' in the *Sheffield Independent*.[37] By November newspaper readers had become familiar with presentations of soldiers' language, either as single words, such as 'Boche', or short glossaries.[38] Glossaries were needed also for those managing and accommodating Belgian refugees,[39] soldiers wishing to speak French or Flemish, and women going to France and Flanders for nursing posts. Consequently by the end of 1914 the glossary had become a fundamental tool for understanding the war, for both civilians and the military.

Given the unfamiliarity of the language to British nurses, glossaries of Flemish were of immediate need for those dealing with wounded Belgian soldiers. In 'How to Converse with the Wounded Belgians' *The Sphere*[40] offered a list of questions and answers in English, French and Flemish. For those working with Belgian refugees, the *Yorkshire Post* provided lists of Flemish phrases and words, with pronunciation tips.[41] Glossaries of forces slang in newspapers catered for the fascination with slang that had developed during the second half of the nineteenth century; anything worked that allowed civilians to identify with the soldiers, sailors and airmen, and was clearly patriotic – slang generally being portrayed in the press as a sign that British forces would make light of their situation and thereby appear to be on top of it.

The format of these glossaries included comparisons between English and French slang;[42] incidental mention of a few terms;[43] groups of terms to do with one subject – money,[44] food,[45] money and food;[46] others were offered in letters[47] or as formal lists of slang and army terms.[48] The subject was of sufficient interest to warrant newspapers reporting on other publications' reporting of slang, the *Reading Mercury* reporting on the *War Budget*'s full page article on 'Trench Slang'.[49] *The Times* curiously did not publish a formal glossary of English slang during the war, but did print an article on French slang in March 1915, stating that words published in letters in the press were 'joyfully adopted' by newspaper readers.[50] Press reporting of slang, as glossaries or otherwise, helped redress the balance as regards army, navy and air force language; articles on navy slang appeared in the *Abergavenny Chronicle* (4 August 1916, p. 2), the *Daily Mail* (5 May 1917, p. 2) and the *Diss Express* (21 June 1918, p. 3), notably not papers local to naval bases, and the *Birmingham Gazette* printed an article on RAF slang on 20 August 1918 (p. 2).

While trench journals functioned as incidental glossaries of trench slang, formal and deliberate glossaries functioned both as celebrations, educative material for new recruits, and a space for satirical comments on army life. These might appear as a single expression, such as 'Pommes de terre frits – Bombardier Fritz' in *The Gasper*,[51] or as formally laid out lists. Murray Johnston's 'Aussie Dictionary' in Issue 1 of *Aussie* (January 1918) was a one-and-a-half-page spread comprising forty-one entries, including 'finnee', 'hopover', 'mud' and 'wind up', and significantly carries the note 'for the use of those at home'. Primarily though the glossary offered the soldier-writer an opportunity for satire: '*The Gasper* Guide to the War'[52] with 'Wrist-Watch – a good excuse for appearing late on parade'; 'Army

Terms and their Derivation'[53] with 'Trench – so called from the trenchant remarks from those inhabiting them'; and in the French trench journal *Poilu*, 'Définitions'[54] with 'Repos – temps consacré aux manoeuvres, revues, marches de nuit, etc.'[55] By the end of the war trench journal editors had developed the glossary/dictionary model into a range of ideas: the

IN FRANCE.

French : Pommes de terre frits.

English : Bombardier Fritz.

FIGURE 2.2 A single entry glossary in *The Gasper*, 8 January 1916.

Fifth Gloucester Gazette had 'A Guide to the Language' (Italian) with 'Take away the Stilton – Alley tootsweeto il stiltonoh', and 'A Short Dictionary of Military Diseases', including '*inflatio capitis, or swelling of the head*' in its July 1918 issue, and in its next issue (January 1919), 'Army Talk', which comprised 'a few hints on grammar and familiar words'.

The more the people at home were familiar with the idea of slang, the more connection could be made by sharing it, especially where this raised a smile. Postcards printed for soldiers to send home catered for this, in both English and French, with cards showing brief slang glossaries or lists. An English card includes 'Napoo', 'over the top', 'ticket for Blighty', while a French one shows a French soldier with a list of what he will bring home on leave, including '*saucisses*', a '*marmite*' and twenty-five '*cloches à melons*', all slang terms for items encountered at the Front.

Glossaries also appeared as inclusions in memoirs, such as *A Yankee in the Trenches* (1918) by R. Derby Holmes, with a six-page glossary, Arthur Empey's extensive 'Tommy's Dictionary of the Trenches' in *Over The Top* (1917), and Thomas O'Toole's curiously titled 'Tommy's Private Language' in *The Way They Have in the Army*[56] – the view that this is a 'private language' is given both before and after the glossary. Maximilian Mügge gives seven two-column pages of 'war words' at the end of *The War Diary of a Square Peg* (1920), using the word 'slanguage' to describe the talk of the men he served with in the infantry, and showing specific interest in expressions such as 'by gum', 'p—off', and 'put a sock in it', but also some curiosities, such as 'at the toute', 'sprado' (butter), 'compray', 'couty', 'deadomer', 'jipper', 'filbert' (head), 'gobby', and 'iky'.[57] Ward Muir in *Observations of an Orderly* collected several expressions in a military hospital bathroom, from which he made some assessments of the language (that rhyming slang would unfortunately catch on, and that the 'facetious irony' of war slang was its strong point), but it is his prognosis that is most interesting: 'Some day these etymological mysteries must be probed. Perhaps the German professors, after the war, can usefully wreak themselves on this complex and obscure research. Meanwhile the above notes are offered not as a serious contribution to a subject so immense, but rather as a warning. The infectiousness of slang is incredible; and this gigantic inter-association of classes and clans has brought about a hitherto unheard-of levelling-down of the common speech. Accent may or may not be influenced: the vocabulary certainly is. Nearly every home in the land is soon going to be invaded by many forms of army slang: the process in fact has already begun. If we were a sprightlier nation the effect

FIGURE 2.3 Two cartoon slang glossary postcards. The French card was sent in July 1917. The card in English was sent from the Front; the writer asks if 'Mamma [has] been on the booze lately', and says 'I shall probably be in the line again by the time you receive this'.

FIGURE 2.3 *Continued*

might not be all to the bad. But most of our slang-mongers are not wits. "He was balmy a treat," I heard a soldier say of another soldier who had shammed insane. That is what we are coming to: it is the tongue we shall use and likewise (I fear) the condition in which some of us will find ourselves as a result'.[58]

It is notable too that these glossaries were reported on in the press, the *Yorkshire Evening Post* reporting on O'Toole on 20 March 1916 (p. 4) and quoting Ward Muir extensively on 17 August 1917 (p. 4). This interest in war-lexicography continued after the war as newspapers reported on dictionary inclusions of wartime slang: 'War Slang – Additions To the Dictionary' reported the *Daily Mail* 17 December 1919 (p. 4), on the inclusion of 'fed up', 'eye-wash', and 'napoo' and others in Cassell's *New English Dictionary*, while the *Illustrated London News* reported on the inclusion of 'napoo', 'get the wind up', 'brass hats' and 'over the top' in the new edition of *Brewer's Dictionary of Phrase and Fable*.[59]

Two key glossaries in English appeared near the end of the war, W. H. Downing's *Digger Dialects* (1919), and Lorenzo Smith's *Lingo of No Man's Land* (1918), which was published largely in support of the recruiting mission to induce British subjects living in the United States to enlist. Very distinct in tone, Smith's was realist and at times carried a cynicism that was not ideally suited to his task, with the inclusion of 'suicide club', 'Mad Fourth' and 'Irish Die-Hards', both describing soldiers who had made a suicidal charge. Downing was responsible for some first documentations, such as ''alf-a-mo' for a moustache, and 'Aussie' for a wound, corresponding to 'a Blighty', and was notably diligent in collecting words to do with sex, such as 'knocking-shop' and 'short-arm'; his collection also embraced words that Australian soldiers encountered from other languages, such as 'ferangi' and 'capisco'. Downing's book helped fix war slang in the culture of Australia, cementing the culture of the war in the country's identity.

Towards the end of the war there was an awareness that unless some methodical collecting was put in place there was a possibility that the wealth of war terminology and slang would be lost. E. B. Osborn's article in the *Illustrated London News* 25 September 1918, 'War and the Word-maker' proposed that some words would remain in the language as a memorial to the conflict – which, given how quickly the most typical ones disappeared, was clearly not the case. In November 1918 Archibald Sparke started a correspondence on war slang in *Notes and Queries*, which went on until March 1919, and started again in 1922; Ernest Baker initiated a correspondence in *The Athenaeum* in May 1919 which went on until December, and A. Forbes Sieveking put together a list of terms from former soldiers working for *The Times*, which was published in *Notes and Queries* in October 1921, and laid emphasis on the need for 'collection and classification of the slang produced by the war, and its historical and philological relations to that of previous periods'.[60] December 1921 saw an article in the *National Review* by Edgar Preston, commenting on Sieveking's project and noting that both French and Italian lexicographers were making collections of war slang.[61] In the autumn of 1921 the Imperial War Museum put out a call 'to old Army men for lists of slang phrases which were used in the trenches';[62] in this the museum was seen to be reacting to collections of French and German war terms, which had been published before the end of the war, such as Albert Dauzat's *L'Argot de la Guerre* (1918) and Karl Bergmann's *Wie Der Feldgraue Spricht* (1916). Edward Fraser and John Gibbons, authors of *Soldier and Sailor Words and Phrases* (1925), were catholic in their collecting, incorporating several pre-war expressions which had been 'either adopted as they stood ... or altered and adapted to suit existing circumstances'; they also acknowledged that their collection was not definitive, and invited further contributions, in itself an acceptance that the language of the war was still, in 1925, fresh in the minds and mouths of their readers. John Brophy included in his anthology, *The Soldier's War* (1929), a glossary on the grounds that 1914–18 was already beginning to take on 'a "period" flavour', and before long 'the book may be unintelligible without this glossary'.[63] The following year he collaborated with Eric Partridge in *Songs and Slang of the British Soldier* (1930). *Songs and Slang of the British Soldier* went through three editions between 1930 and 1967, picking up an addition to the title – *The Long Trail – Soldiers' Songs and Slang 1914–18*; each new edition built on the previous with contributions from readers 'whose wartime memories were then comparatively fresh and unconfused'.[64] After the first edition Eric Partridge went on to present several collections of soldier slang in *The Quarterly Review* (1931), in *A Martial Medley* (1931), and *Word! Words! Words!* (1933), and in E. B. Swinton's *Twenty Years After* (1936–38).

In September 1939 another British Expeditionary Force was in France, and an article in the *Derby Daily Telegraph* 25 September (p. 6) reported that 'it is just as if the clock had stopped for 21 years and had now been restarted. As then, so now: "pain", "oeufs", "coffee-or-lay", "no bon", "tray bon", and "encore" still make up the average soldier's vocabulary'.[65] Not just a repeat of the vocabulary, but also of the reporting of it.

Fighting over words

Language functioned both as a weapon, as a field of conflict and as a trophy. The appropriation of any German expressions, particularly those like 'hate' and 'the day' which were effectively propaganda terms, showed the British making fun of German earnestness. 'Hate', deriving from Lissauer's *Hymn of Hate* (see p. 207) was adopted to mean the dawn and dusk artillery or infantry shooting; 'Germany's place in the sun' featured in Von Bülow's speech in 1898 in regard to Germany's intention to be part of the colonial process – 'In short, we do not want to put anyone in our shadow, but we also demand our place in the sun' – and was regularly mocked, as in 'Australia's place in the sun'[66] and 'French take German Congo. Another Place in the Sun Lost'.[67] 'Der Tag' (the day) symbolised the day when Germany would successfully challenge the world; it was the subject of a pastiche poem in *The Gasper*,[68] as well as of a patriotic play by J. M. Barrie, and was mocked by an officer recorded in Malins' *How I Filmed the War* (1920) – 'My word, we haven't heard a blessed thing for days. Have you really come to photograph "The Day"?'[69] 'Kamerad', the surrendering soldier's plea, was taken over to mean 'to surrender', 'a surrendering soldier' and later as a verb meaning 'to kill prisoners',[70] 'strafe' was taken over so successfully that the *New English Dictionary* (1919) gave a citation of a mother saying to her child 'Wait till I git 'old of yer, I'll strarfe yer, I will!' The recorded words of an Austro-Hungarian officer taken prisoner on the Italian Front show that 'strafe' had made the return journey, as he 'exclaimed in surprise: "Engleese! Bang! Bang! Some Strafe!"'[71] 'Ersatz' changed from its meaning as 'replacement' (*Ersatzbataillon*) to 'cheap substitute' or 'poor' as in the *Daily Express* headline 'Ersatz Oratory' on 26 September 1918, or the post-war 'German "ersatz" system' of clothing, which the *Manchester Guardian* reported as involving 'paper shirts and collars'.[72]

Fraser and Gibbons imply that to a certain extent there was also a process of appropriation by the military of terms used by the press – 'frightfulness' certainly, and 'steam-roller', which the press invented as a term to describe the size and power of the Russian army, but which Fraser and Gibbons claim was 'taken by the Services and used in a derogatory sense'. Despite the moral condemnation inherent in Churchill's use of the term 'baby-killers' to describe the German fleet's bombardment of towns on the east coast of England, H. M. Denham felt able to describe the action of his ship in firing at a farm in the Dardanelles as 'real "baby-killing"'.[73]

In studying the record of language during the conflict it is noticeable that considerably less attention was paid to language in the Navy and the Air Force. Fewer words moved from the naval experience to the Home Front and to the Army, though naval glossaries were printed in the press. Possible reasons are the lower numbers of personnel involved, their having less contact with the civilian population, and the traditional way that naval staff tended to live in or near port towns. Much naval terminology or slang, some of it very old,[74] stayed within the Navy, e.g. 'bracketing' for range-finding by firing; 'bloke' for captain; 'neaters' for rum; 'ord' for Ordinary Seaman'; 'snottie' for midshipman; or indicated exclusion of the non-naval world, e.g. 'soldier' for an incompetent sailor – a 'soldier's wind' was, according to Fraser and Gibbons, an easy wind that anyone could sail in. In a sample from Fraser and Gibbons comprising 25 per cent of the whole (pp. 90–170, 'ever since Adam was an oakum boy' to 'Ally Sloper's Cavalry') there are 696 entries, of which seventy-one are specified as naval and twenty-two as air force terms. Few naval terms have survived to the present in general speech: among them are 'sweet Fanny Adams', 'a flap', 'a gadget', 'show a leg', and 'do you want jam on it?', of which only 'a flap' originated during the war, as one of three stages of getting ready quickly – a buzz, a flap, and a panic[75] – and most of them are seldom documented (for example 'gashions', meaning 'an excess of anything', 'Jimmy the One', denoting 'the First Lieutenant on board ship' and 'Monkey's Island', meaning 'the upper bridge of a warship'). In contrast to army slang, a few terms from naval slang entered common civilian speech without being recognised as such – 'pongo' for soldier, 'pond' for sea – while others were taken up by soldiers and after 1918 were more thought of as soldiers' terms: 'bully-beef', 'gadget', 'jam on it', 'flag-wagging'.[76] 'Erk', originally a below decks term for a navy rating, was taken up by the air force as slang for a mechanic, and was retained into the Second World War. Given the horrific nature of actual sea-warfare it is strange that fewer imaginative or cynical terms were documented: 'survivor's leave' was the term used by a sailor to describe his time ashore after being torpedoed.[77] In four wartime newspaper articles on Naval slang[78] only the last gives terms which were specific to the experience of the war – 'hostilities' for men who signed up for the duration, and 'distasters' for Royal Naval Divisions. Boyd Cable, a soldier-writer, used

STRAFE

'Strafe' was acquired from the widely used German motto *Gott strafe England* (God punish England). England (Britain), and later Italy, were to be punished for entering the war against Germany and Austro-Hungary as an act of will rather than self-defence, Britain specifically having made it a 'world war' through bringing in its colonies. The German expression was used within the territory of the Central Powers as graffiti, as a franking motto on correspondence, as a legend on badges, and on a wide range of inventively designed charity stamps. The adoption of 'strafe' by anglophone troops and later civilians downgraded its force, as it came to be associated with annoyance rather than fear; the change of meaning in the process of adoption was an act of conquest in itself.

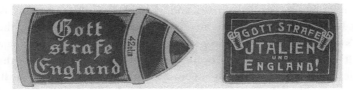

FIGURE 2.4 Two German 'poster' stamps; a German postcard sent in November 1917; a British postcard indicating the downgrading of the word 'strafe'.

"STRAFE" THE BARBED WIRE

FIGURE 2.4 Continued

the term 'jaunties' to describe the Royal Naval Brigade, as recorded by Eric Partridge in *A Dictionary of Slang and Unconventional English*, but he stated that he had not seen it anywhere other than in Cable's *The Old Contemptibles* (1919). While much slang was shared between the army and the air force – 'sausages', 'archie', 'wind up' (and Boyd Cable, an infantryman, was probably the first to use in print the term 'dog-fight' for what had previously been an 'air fight' or 'air duel')[79] – airmen quickly developed their own slang: 'the British airman is an adept at inventing slang terms', wrote the *Birmingham Gazette*, 20 August 1918 (p. 2). Partridge noted in his *Dictionary of R.A.F. Slang* (1945) that the Second World War RAF was still using a few words from the period 1914 to 1918, but 'only or mainly by the men over forty or in new senses'; but in comparing the slangs of the three forces he noted that 'the richest of all is that of the Army ... the Navy's slang, not quite so extensive as that of the Army ... [and] the Air Force had a small body of slang'.[80] A lot of RFC and RAF slang and particularly American air force slang was imaginative, cynical and long-lasting, though less disseminated to the civilian press at the time. Ernest Baker, initiating the correspondence on slang in *The Athenaeum*,[81] mentioned a few terms of 'what may be called "air-lingo"' – 'bank' (to shell), 'zoom', 'huff' (kill), and 'hickboo' (air-raid), with the pre-war 'bus' for plane; elsewhere in the correspondence only Eric Verney[82] mentioned 'interesting Air-Force slang', specifically 'quirk' and 'spike-bozzle' ('quirk' was an inexperienced airman, and 'spike-bozzle' meant to destroy completely), as well as 'bus', 'drome' and 'joy-stick'. Fraser and Gibbons dedicated considerable space to air force slang, with terms such as 'conked out', 'comic business', 'tabloid' (a Sopwith plane with many good points, so concentrated goodness), 'parasol' (a monoplane, with wings above the pilot), many of which were taken up by Brophy and Partridge; but in his *Slang To-day and Yesterday* Partridge dedicated less than half a page to RAF slang.[83]

The sinking of the *Lusitania* in 1915 sparked riots in several British cities, in which shops with German owners' signs were targeted. German philology was around the same time directed at English, with an article by a Professor Neumann on the decline of English: on 1 May 1915 the *Daily Chronicle*[84] reported 'Language of Britons Decaying – Dutch [sic] View of English Working Classes'. The article, based on a report in the *Frankfurter Zeitung*, comments on Professor Neumann's view 'that the language, despite its increasing use in all parts of the Far East', is showing 'marked indications, not only of phonetic decay, but of decay in the capacity of the language to express ideas'. Professor Neumann's ideas seemed to be largely based on the observation of migrant communities in America retaining their first languages, but also on observation that in India and China 'the language has become drugged with exotic terms', with 'thousands of forms in use which are not English, and which are pressing on pure English with disastrous results.' Examples of 'insidious interlopers' given are 'Pagoda, monsoon, verandah, shawl'. Some of this may have been influenced by the mood of lexical purism proposed by the populist German Language Union (*Allgemeine Deutscher Sprachverein*, ADSV), founded in 1885, which campaigned against adoptions of French and Greco-Latin-based vocabulary and words from English. Professor Neumann was naturally patronised in the *Daily Chronicle* article – 'like so many of his kind he is most amusing when most serious' – but German philology was itself later obliquely mocked in an article in the *Globe* (24 May 1918): 'With your admirable command of foreign idioms you very possibly know our cant London phrase: "Where Maggie wore the beads." Well, Fritz dear, that is where you are going to get it.' This quote was pointedly used by Ernest Weekley in his 1921 *An Etymological Dictionary of Modern English*, despite Weekley's being Professor of Modern Languages at Nottingham University at the time. But there were voices that complained about the use of foreign terms in English; 'hamburgers' might be relabelled as 'Salisbury steaks', and Horatio Bottomley proposed that the Prince of Wales should drop his motto *Ich dien* on the grounds that it was 'in the hateful language of the Hun'.[85] But under the headline – Wanted: Reduced Language Rations, the *Yorkshire Evening Post* ran a brief article on 5 February 1917:

> Criticising the language of Lord Devonport's appeal for voluntary rationing, 'The Londoner' in the 'Evening News' observes: All that he says is in an official jargon of Latin English: none of it is in the language that we simple folk talk and understand. Listen to this. The Controller wants to say that poor people eat more bread than fresh meat. What he says is that 'With many in such circumstances meat is only intermittently comprised in the scale of dietary.' What a jargon! I should like to hear how a Controller would describe a lost brown leather purse.[86]

The complaint is explicitly against Latin English, but seeks to maintain this position without explicitly favouring Germanic English. On 1 September 1917 the same newspaper ran the following:

> Is the English Language Vulgarised?
>
> Mr George Moore's Strong Views
>
> Mr George Moore, the author, holds that the English language is becoming hopelessly vulgarised and barbarised.
>
> 'People won't take the trouble to speak or write ordinary, decent English,' he told Mr. Arthur Machen [of the 'Angels of Mons' fame], of the London 'Evening News'. 'Why do people write "terrain", "badinage", "point d'appui"? Then we had a very good phrase, curtain fire. That has become "barrage". We used to speak of a smoke curtain, which is excellent; now we speak of a "smoke barrage", which is nonsense. We are getting away from the idioms of our own language. The other day I saw "esprit de factory" in an evening newspaper. And why do the people one meets at lunch talk about "gaffe" and "raffine"? It isn't that they speak French; no, but they seem unable to speak English.'

'You see English has lost so much already. It has lost "thee" and "thou". It has lost such words as "hither", "whither", "thither", "whence", "yonder". People don't say "Whither are you going?" but "Where are you going?" Instead of "yonder" they use "over there" '[87]

The argument was getting hopelessly muddled as nationalism pushed rational thinking aside. As the *Athenaeum* correspondence came to an end in December 1919 it was followed by a letter from Andrew de Ternant reminding readers that a short time previously there had been 'agitation against the use and for the removal of Hun (or rather German) names of places in England'.[88] Fortunately this had come to nothing, but there had been attempts to downgrade the status of 'enemy languages' in various ways. As early as October 1914 a journalist in *The Cheltenham Looker-On* was proposing that the study of German in schools should be dropped in favour of Spanish or Italian, as 'the German is characteristic of the German race, and we feel we do not want to be reminded of the existence of that race',[89] and James Crichton-Browne, a pioneer in the field of mental illness who had supplied research material to Darwin, believed that a proposal in 1917 to establish a chair of German language and Literature at the University of Edinburgh was 'inopportune, unpatriotic and discreditable'.[90] Meanwhile, a report in the *Liverpool Daily Post* stated that the *Frankfurter Zeitung* was calling on German citizens to 'root out the language of our enemies from public signs and notices',[91] and the Austrian authorities in Trent, Trieste and Zara banned the use of Italian in public notices, street signs and newspapers.[92] A proposal by the 'German Clerks' Association' printed in the *Hamburger Fremdenblatt* observed that the pursuance of foreign trade in English had 'helped the English to extend their position in the world'. By demanding that German foreign trade be carried on in German 'we can damage the English enormously, because the greater part of their usurped importance in the world would collapse'.[93]

This aspect of the conflict extended over all the theatres of war. Pidgin was in use in the Allied takeover of German possessions in the South Pacific in 1914,[94] and was parodied in the expression for a young officer – 'makee learn'. In 1916 it emerged that linguists in Berlin had attempted to create a dialect to oust English-pidgin for use in territories controlled by Germany; this attempt was unsuccessful, and no doubt galling to the German officers who 'had to communicate with the natives, and even give orders to their own troops, in pidgin-English'.[95]

Control and censorship

'We have been warned to be more careful than ever of what we say'[96]

On 23 February 1916 Amy Shield wrote from No. 12 General Hospital Rouen a letter in a green envelope saying, 'Sorry this way but my letters from here are censored!'[97] Evidence of censorship was clearly visible on every letter and postcard sent from the Front, the censors' stamps in red ink changing design every year. Censorship was part of communication, as Shield knew, her use of the 'green envelope' requiring her signature to the statement 'I certify on my honour that the contents of this envelope refer to nothing but private and family matters'; such a letter would not be 'censored Regimentally', but 'the contents are liable to examination at the Base'. Officers were allowed a few green envelopes a month, but other ranks saw them more rarely, though an order of November 1916 stated that troops were to be given one per week; they were bartered between troops – in 1916 the price seems to have been 50 centimes and, with luck, three cigarettes.[98] The green envelope generated its own slang: 'green letter is at a standstill',[99] 'a green one',[100] 'sticky jack',[101] 'Am writing green, hope to post tomorrow'.[102]

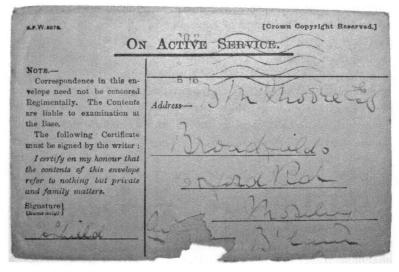

FIGURE 2.5 The green envelope enclosing Amy Shield's letter, 23 February 1916.

The official view of censorship was that it served three purposes: checking that no information of use to the enemy was accessible, monitoring the morale of the troops, and that potential attacks on troop morale did not get through to the troops. Censorship of mail from soldiers was far more evidenced than civilian mail censorship, but by 1918 the War Office was employing around 5,000 people to censor mail to soldiers, and more diligently, mail to neutral countries. The statistics for mail show an enormous amount of correspondence to be checked – there were 12.5 million items of mail leaving the postal depot at Regents Park every week for the Front alone, which computes to 2,500 items of correspondence per censor per week. But censors were empowered to notify police, who in some cases searched offices and confiscated offending material.[103] Information on the process of censorship of correspondence to soldiers remained sketchy, perhaps deliberately so since maintaining high levels of post would boost morale; a four-page article in *The Illustrated War News* of 24 October 1917 (pp. 30–3) on 'The Campaign of the Postal Censor' states that the unit 'distributed mail . . . taken in from the Post Office . . . to various sections of the Censorship', before passing it back to the Post Office, but concentrated on the censoring of mail to British and German PoWs, the detection of sensitive information and contraband, the unit's translation section, and the staff canteen. A photograph showed a warehouse full of confiscated mail 'stacked away until the end of the war, when, perhaps, they may be forwarded to their destination.'

Mail from soldiers was censored by junior officers, while the 'Home Fleet General Order No 43' (2 August 1914) required that on every ship 'one officer should be detailed to carry out the duties of censor', with more than one officer on larger ships. Censorship was a matter of personal initiative, likely to be rigid where it came to place names, and no doubt caused friction from time to time. The censor's discretion and advice probably helped smooth over occasional family difficulties, but Capt McDonald's revelation of the 'take a good look at the floor' story (see p. 107) indicates that good stories did not always stay inside the envelope. The evidence of censorship on the millions of soldiers' postcards and letters was not just the stamp and the censor's signature but the scratching out of place names, largely pointless but dutiful, which, along with the ubiquitous 'somewhere in France', added to the mythologising of place at the Front. Thanks to repeated mentions in soldiers' memoirs, the presence in the material culture of the war of so many soldiers' postcards and letters, and the more recent digitisation of these, studies of wartime correspondence censorship have concentrated almost exclusively on mail from soldiers, itself an indication of the lasting dominance in both popular and academic culture of the soldiers', rather than the civilians' verbal mediation of the war.

The censorship office based at Boulogne had the task of reading letters sent to and from India, including from wounded Indian soldiers in Britain, requiring close reading in any of seven languages. The particular role here was to detect signs of dissatisfaction, with a weekly report to be prepared, showing sample letters in translation; this task, undertaken by a team of up to five men, former interpreters with Indian cavalry regiments, involved reading and translating where necessary over 30,000 letters per week.[104] As soldiers were aware that information about the survival of comrades might be deemed sensitive, writers' codes for this and other matters developed; these involved mechanical coding, by means of adding signs, symbols or numbers, according to an agreed code, or the use of parables and puns.[105] This might range from a code as simple as a wounded Sikh soldier advising his brother not to enlist by writing, 'Think over what I say and you will understand what I mean when I say "stay in the village",'[106] to references to black pepper, common code for Indian troops: 'what is the condition of the market for black pepper? That which I brought with me has all been finished . . .' (Tell me how recruiting is going in India. All the original Indian contingent are dead or wounded . . .).[107] Similar codes were used by Welsh soldiers writing home in Welsh, for whom there seemed to be some confusion as to whether writing in Welsh was permitted,[108] but so many letters in Welsh have survived that it appears that censors' discretion and trust allowed free passage to correspondence in the language. This itself allowed the passage of information which would not otherwise have got through, not by virtue of being in Welsh, but through the obfuscating wordplay that was not immediately seen through by the censor. Ifor ap Glyn notes one letter where the writer puts in Welsh that he could not say where they were, but noted 'that they eat apples here'; in English the censor would have instantly spotted the reference to Etaples.[109] Pte W. Brock, writing home from Russia in 1918 states 'where I am now . . . is about 70 miles south of an important town with a heavenly name no doubt you can guess it'.[110] Coding operated in a wide range of fields within the forces, perhaps the most successful instance being the use of the word 'tank' to conceal the nature of the armoured vehicle.

COLOUR-CODING

'Khaki' was adopted into English from an Urdu word during the early 1860s, and by the 1880s the colour was used for operational units working with the (British) Indian Army. The word soon appeared in army slang and by the turn of the century it was used in non-military slang in the UK, as in the term 'khaki election' – an election where military issues were of major importance. The term 'in khaki' was used after the adoption of the colour for army uniforms, to mean 'in uniform', changing from implying a visual description to an occupational description – effectively a soldier was 'in khaki' even when not wearing khaki. The first uniforms available for men enlisting in 1914 were blue, known as 'Kitchener's blue', the earliest ones supposed to be unwanted transport and postal uniforms; even the quickly-developed version was not consistently available, and new recruits trained in anything from red tunics to canvas fatigues and their own clothes. The sponsors of the first Pals Battalions made it a point of honour to clothe their recruits in actual khaki. Blue uniforms with white details later became the uniform of convalescing soldiers; a *Punch* cartoon of 11 September 1918 (p. 165) refers to convalescing soldiers out on the town as 'blue boys'.

By early 1915 'in khaki' was being used in recruitment posters. One poster asked 'the Young Women of London' 'Is your "Best Boy" wearing khaki?', while another commissioned by the Parliamentary Recruiting Committee asked, with much more punch, 'Why aren't you in khaki?' Australian (Australian English being often more direct than British English) posters urged men to 'Get into khaki'. Despite the term's association with the army, 'khaki' could have less than positive connotations: *Home Chat* in January 1916 warned its readers that the attraction of a uniform, a quick romance and a wedding might be followed by disillusion and solitude – the perils of 'khaki-love'. Languages other than English colour-coded their servicemen;

FIGURE 2.6 German postcard, sent in October 1915: 'We trust in grey and blue, in the fleet and the army, we build up Germany's victory on land and at sea.'

Germany had 'Grau' and 'Blau' (soldier, in *feldgraue* – field gray – and sailor in blue), while the French 'bleus' and 'bleusailles' were new recruits.

Censorship passed into general culture, from the use of references in fictionalised memoirs celebrating the feats of regiments such as the 'Blankshires',[111] long after the war, to comic picture postcards showing messages pre-blacked out, the question 'Who wrote "We have left the place I mentioned to you in my last letter home"?' in the *Fifth Gloucester Gazette*, and the poem on 'The Censaur' in *The Gasper* (1915):

The Censaur is half-beast, half-man:
Which seems a reasonable plan:
Since if there's blame for what is done'
Each puts it on the other one.

Information about where a soldier was stationed could fairly easily be given without troubling the censor: Vivian Stevens, writing home on 3 April 1916, says 'Yes, I am 2 miles east of where Father says',[112] while 2nd Lt J. Macleod conveyed his whereabouts via the initial letter of each line of a letter.[113] These tricks in correspondence should be seen in the context of a culture that enjoyed codes such as 'the language of flowers' and 'the language of stamps', in which the angle of the stamp conveyed one of a set of meanings.

But a wider sense of coding seen throughout the linguistic mediating of the war shows a complex relationship between language, speaker and experience. Soldiers needed to express a range of reactions to their situation without increasing the stress on their readers, while, as can be seen from responses in the lines of soldiers' correspondence, civilians' letters convey hopes and reassurances, with occasional desires to know 'what it is like'. From soldiers' words, protection is a key theme. Cpl W. Hartley writing to his parents (there may be a double layer of editing here, as the letter was published in the press), gives a description of being attacked with liquid fire ('horrifying in its beauty'), shrapnel, lyddite, whizz-bangs and Jack Johnsons, 'coupled with heavy rifle and machine-gun fire'; 'the place was strewn with wounded and dying'. Yet Cpl Hartley prefaces this with 'all of us thought we were in for a certain do this time'.[114] In this case the event is framed by a phrase which belittles it before we meet the description. Belittling was a common rhetorical device, addressed both to another, and to the soldier himself: Lancelot Spicer, writing home in October 1915, wrote that the 'shell fire was not altogether pleasant. I ... wished to heaven that they would stop annoying us with their beastly shells',[115] while another soldier, in his diary in 1917, wrote, 'the shells began to pepper along close to us', conveying both unpleasantness (heat) and triviality.[116] Some of this was survivors' bravado – Pte G. Broadhead wrote in his diary, 'Usual carry on. Bit of a strafe in the afternoon'[117] – the text belittles the threat, allowing the writer to feel he is more likely to survive this kind of bombardment.

Postcard messages are a particularly rich field for coded and controlled messages; not necessarily to do with giving accurate coded descriptions, phrases such as 'We are at present busy and unsettled'[118] convey an idea of the writer trying but being unable to say what is going on. Suggestions of what the writer might be going through, in a letter sent to his son, presumably another soldier on leave – 'I caught it hot, I am glad you are at home, as you can give some idea of what it is like here from the papers but not all',[119] this draws the reader in to a complicit understanding of a multi-layered relationship with information. The formulaic repetition of comments – about the weather, the writer's health, whether the soldier has received news from home, or a parcel, thanks for cigarettes – show minimal differences from the Field Service Postcard; their sequences of clichés, 'in the pink', 'keep smiling', 'always merry and bright', display a rhetoric of banal emptiness, but equally a statement of the fundamental, that the soldier was able to send such a message, to say anything at all; the appeal of the picture postcard was that it could look full, while having little content. Letters were often more problematic, being very much expected from soldiers, but often finding the writer had little to say. Some, like that one from Rifleman William Taffs to his 'best girl', ended up being about a rat-hunt in a barn;[120] another, sent from Charlie to Bessie in October 1917, thanks Bessie for her letter, apologises for not writing, says the writer is busy, discusses the weather, notes that someone is well, hopes the war will end, notes other people are well, sends regards and notes that someone else will write soon.[121] A popular song at home in 1916 urged people to send only good news when writing to soldiers:

> Send him a cheerful letter
> Say that it's all ok.
> Tell him you've ne'er felt better
> Though it's all the other way.[122]

Codes often merge into clichés, as soldiers describe themselves as 'merry and bright' or 'in the pink'; the continuous use of the familiar countered the unfamiliar, the constantly present unpredictability of life

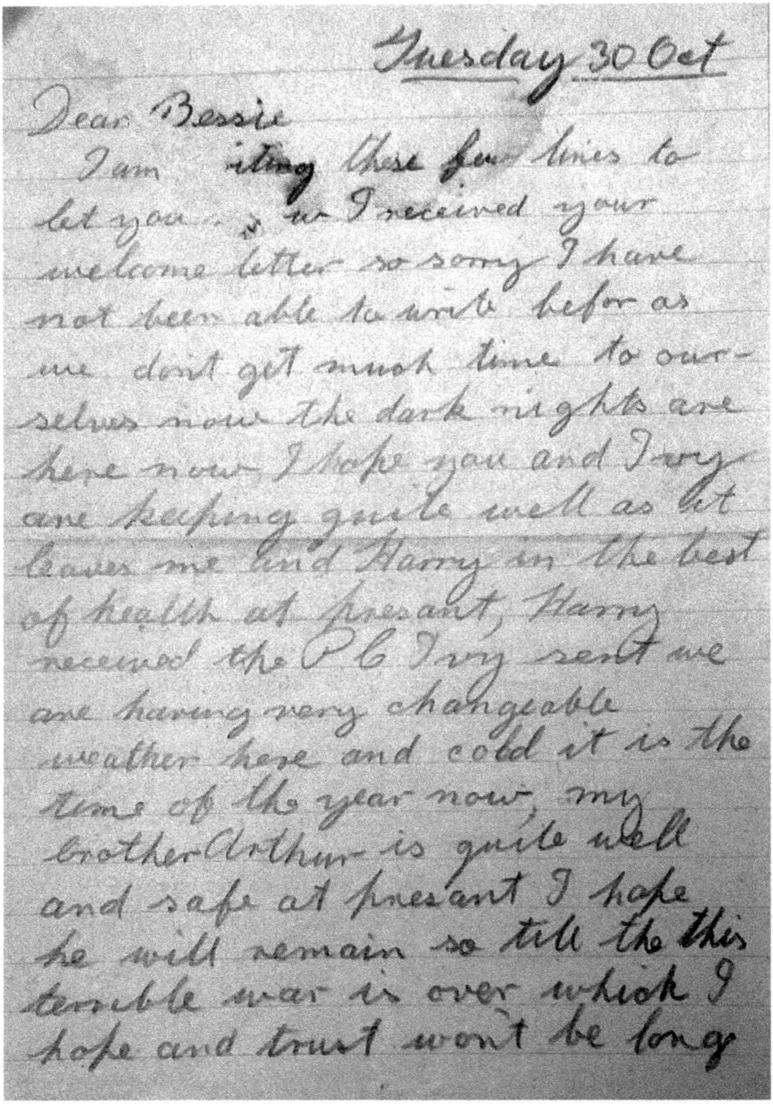

Tuesday 30 Oct
Dear Bessie
I am writing these few lines to
let you [illegible] I received your
welcome letter so sorry I have
not been able to write befor as
we dont get much time to ourselves now the dark nights are
here now I hope you and Ivy
are keeping quite well as it
leaves me and Harry in the best
of health at presant, Harry
received the P C Ivy sent we
are having very changeable
weather here and cold it is the
time of the year now, my
brother Arthur is quite well
and safe at presant I hope
he will remain so till the this
terrible war is over which I
hope and trust won't be long

FIGURE 2.7 Letter from Charlie to Bessie, 30 October 1917.

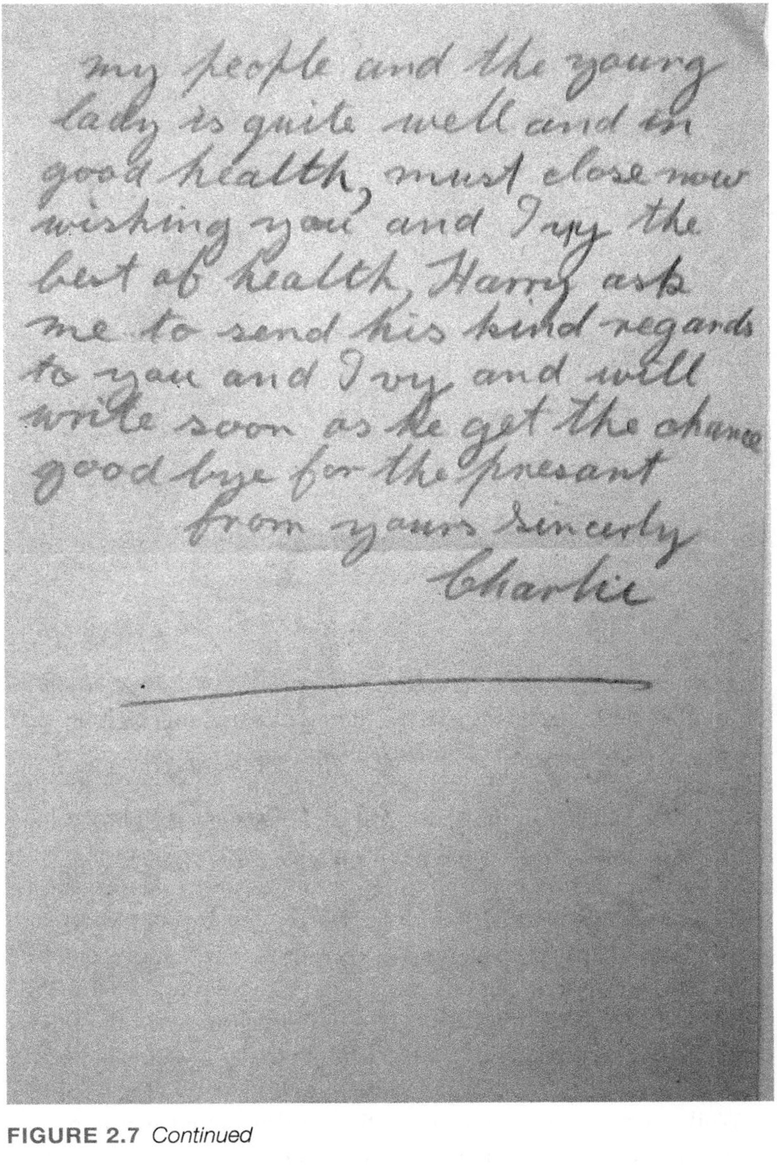

my people and the young
lady is quite well and in
good health, must close now
wishing you and Ivy the
best of health, Harry ask
me to send his kind regards
to you and Ivy and will
write soon as he get the chance
good bye for the present
from yours sincerly
Charlie

FIGURE 2.7 *Continued*

FIGURE 2.7 *Continued*

or death, creating a stasis that could counter the fear of death. Certainly a tradition of understatement and the hiding of emotion, especially fear, was expressed in a pattern of understatement and phlegmatic comments that undoubtedly helped people 'carry on'. 'Getting peppered pretty hot, aren't you?' asks a heavily under-fire 2nd Lt of Capt Gilbert Nobbs; 'Rather lively', he replies.[123] The excited glorification of combat, as in the *Vivid War Weekly*, a penny magazine mixing combat and romance stories, could balance its gung-ho drawings and its repeated use of 'glorious' with the euphemistic 'he must have done heavy execution with his six hundred bullets a minute',[124] echoing 'our men … did some execution among the Germans' (see p. 133), the language of the formal memoir and official report; officialese used in this context tells the reader, 'you do not need to know the details'.

While rage seems to have been the burden of much war poetry, soldiers in the combat zone needed some way of surviving – a way of protecting themselves which involved protecting others at home, codes again being employed to fix levels of information the writer was prepared to allow the reader access to. Harold wrote a card to Miss J. Morris at Bedford Place, London (a well-off address, though she may have been in service there), on 26 March 1916 stating 'we are all at a new part of the line now and expect some real dirty work here'.[125] In a letter home to Sydney, Pte Ernie Hough pulled himself up when he felt he was conveying too graphic an account of men dying: 'I am afraid I am making this note a little strong for you'.[126] It was rare for a soldier to imply involvement in fighting; instead the word 'busy' is used to let the reader know that the writer is actively doing what war involves, but that no details are to be expected. An environment of censorship helped here, taking the responsibility away from the writer. A writer says he is 'more busy than I have ever been in my life, but it will only last a day or two longer I hope. I haven't had any clothes off or my boots even for two nights'.[127] 'Lively' and 'unsettled' were used to indicate that the writer had been involved in shelling or fighting; 'Am perfectly well. Letter following. Had some hard work last night, hard but healthy', wrote Cyril on a postcard, 4 March 1916. Essentially whatever was written in any code was less important than 'Am perfectly well'.

Formulaic writing, as on a picture postcard of the destroyed village of Foncquevillers (Funky Villas) with the message 'Hoping it finds you in the best of health as it leaves me at present',[128] may have been learned in correspondence offices before enlistment. In a letter home – 'Dear Mother' – Will writes 'Just a few lines to let you know that I am still well and in good health hope you are the same and have got rid of the flu we are having grand weather here now hot enough for anything during the day', takes up a quarter of the text and could be a letter from holiday or boarding school.[129] Certainly clichés and formulaic writing allowed the filling up of letter space without the writer having to provide frightening information, but equally this was the contemporary language of correspondence. The multiple-choice format of the Field Service Postcard was so reductionist that it became almost pointless to tick in the boxes – 'I am very busy just now so will not be able to write letters for some days, no need to worry, will send a field card at times', wrote Walter to 'My dear Rose' on 8 August 1917. The multiple-choice approach to information became so much part of this abroad-to-home correspondence discourse that it was re-used for holiday postcards for decades afterwards.

While selectivity or parcelling reality to protect those at home was commonplace, downright mendacity was also part of Front-to-home communication. There was a variety of incentives – the context of the heroic 'our boys' trope, the potential to strengthen the nerves, the chances of getting away with it; Sgt Bernard Brookes admitted in his diary that he had got away with telling tall stories to newly arrived soldiers, noting that 'the biggest liar always gets the largest audience'.[130] Masefield reported catching out two young Australian recruits, and met a gunner who, in censoring his battery's post, had read the words 'The enemy are shelling terribly as I write & I may be blown to pieces at any moment, but I would not be anywhere else. I am proud to be out here, doing my bit for England' – the man had in fact 'never been under fire, & was writing in a base, & "his bit", that he was so proud of, was cleaning latrines, he being useless at anything else'.[131] Information spread like this easily got out of control: in July 1918 Andrew Clark was told by a tramp of a 'glorious victory', which had no substance at all, and for a while in September 1914 it seemed that few people in Britain did not believe that a Russian army had been brought by train from Scotland to the south coast. This story, according to the *Hull Daily Mail*, emanated from a 'Berlin telegram' in Rome; '"the Press Bureau did not object to the publication" of the statement'; supposedly the War Office was keeping the press quiet about it, but 'on reliable authority, we learned of the landing of Russian troops at Hull from Arcangel, and of the passage of thousands of Russian troops, with horse, guns and full equipment, from Hull, Newcastle and Scotland, . . . to the South'.[132] Six days later the Press Bureau stated there was no truth in the story, and that it should be 'discredited'.[133]

If rumours were an example of information getting out of control, they were in contrast to the concept of 'cheerfulness' pushed at people continuously. Troops were incessantly praised for their cheerfulness, their singing on the way to the Front, their joking under pressure; *The Somme Times* responded to it in their 31 July 1916 issue in the form of an advertisement offering to cure the reader of optimism; the first question to identify the condition was 'Do you suffer from cheerfulness?' This was in the face of such assaults on the mind as a YMCA service in the field with the motto 'Keep your head down and your heart up!',[134] and Sunlight Soap's advertisements proposing 'Cheerfulness opposed to Frightfulness. Cheerfulness is uplifting. Frightfulness is a millstone round the neck. Cheerfulness will overcome Frightfulness. *Cheerfulness at Sea – Cheerfulness on Land – Cheerfulness in Trenches – Cheerfulness in Factory – Cheerfulness at War – Cheerfulness at WORK. Sunlight users are always cheerful*'.[135] The injunction continued after the war, as the *Daily Mail* reckoned that the strikes of 1919 would be overcome 'by smiling'.[136] The concept of cheerfulness was to be found in the most unlikely situations: Sir Douglas Haig praised the work of the Gas Services, particularly the 'very heavy work and great courage and devotion on the part of the personnel employed; ... all demands have been met with unfailing cheerfulness and carried out with the greatest efficiency'.[137]

This should all be contextualised within a verbal culture of phlegm, understatement and self-control (see p. 284 – stiff upper lip). Capt E. H. Wyndham described as 'a very trying day' one in which his trench had been shelled for 16 hours continuously, a position had been lost, retaken and given up, with the loss of several men;[138] Ian Hay described the German artillery as 'distributing coal',[139] while Pte Broadhead described this as 'Fritz sent a few shells as a reminder'.[140] Mottram described a heavily shelled area as 'unhealthy',[141] and Kate Luard said of a wounded officer that 'Like so many he was chiefly concerned about "giving so much trouble"'.[142] The words highlight the contrast between self-control and the massive loss of control in the speaker's environment; the control of speech as a manifestation of the need to maintain control.

Avoidance

It is a familiar experience in language use that we make things a little less real by not naming them; this is seen most in our avoidance of saying the name of a disease, our use of euphemisms or abbreviations. For the sociologist Alfredo Niceforo writing in 1912 it was manifested in the survival of a primitive avoidance of naming death: 'to pronounce the name of death, to speak of a dead person, is to provoke ... a material contagion between death and the man who has spoken'.[143] Eric Partridge, who was at Gallipoli and later in France, noted the irony in military slang, quoting Brophy's idea that with irony 'some of the terror disappeared, together with the pomp, from war and military glory'.[144] Partridge proposed the flattening out as a mixture of dysphemism and euphemism, taking down the exalted, and lifting the debased: euphemism is 'indulgent where the other is pitiless; kindly where the other is mocking; discreet where the other is brutally frank'. Added to these was the Greco-Roman tradition of meiosis, palliative or placatory devices, which took many forms during the war, pulling the frightening closer to create a less frightening reality, pushing the reality away into foreign or impersonal terms or generalisations, or refusing to name it at all. The mix of languages and new fields of language all helped in this process, allowing people to protect themselves and each other from the reality of their situations, often at the same time that they were exaggeratedly acknowledging the horror of what was happening to and around them.

For a basic range of how avoidance was used we can compare a postcard, a literary memoir, and a report. On 23 October 1915 'W.C.A.' wrote to his mother in London that 'I have come out of the Ts. well & we are resting for a while', avoiding using the word 'trenches'; in *In Parenthesis* Jones writes 'the more solicitous disposed themselves in groups and . . . rather tended to speak in undertones as though not to hasten or not disturb, to not activate too soon the immense potential empoweredness – and talk about impending dooms – it fair gets you in the guts';[145] and Fussell describing Alexander Aitken's realisation that 'the use of euphemistic adjectives, such as "sharp", "brisk"' in descriptions of fighting carried specific meanings in terms of the number of casualties.[146] In the first of these we see the writer protecting his mother, and allowing her to move over the fact that her son had been in the trenches; in the second David Jones describes a kind of superstition by which we lower our voices so as not to 'call on' what we are talking about; and Fussell and Aitken describe the use of code to avoid saying '50 per cent of our men were killed'. While the first example appears to quickly gloss over the reality, it equally draws attention to itself, like an exaggerated voiceless speech act that adults use when children might be listening. David Jones touches on a trope in use since Greek culture gave palliative names to the Fates – the Kindly Ones – in an attempt to meliorate danger. The third example packages reality in an impersonal way, a defining methodology of 'the report'.

In *The Attack*, a sound dramatisation made in the 1920s, an officer gives instructions: 'Look here Corporal, don't forget when you get into the Boche trench you must work your way up to the right, and then clean up that big Boche dug-out as you go past'. 'Clean up' here is clearly a euphemism for killing or capturing men; conversely in *War Letters* Lt W. B. Spencer writes of his own potential death as the familiar 'if anything did happen' or 'should anything happen'.[147] But with many codes terms can vary between users, and at different times: thus it is difficult to know exactly what is being described when encountering the terms 'knocked up', 'knocked down', 'knocked out' or 'knocked over', all of which are used frequently to described the experience of being shelled in trenches.

While there is ample documentation of slang words for the enemy, the use of any term carried the power to make the enemy real. There is documentation of avoidance of giving the enemy a name at all, though, while refusing to grant the enemy the power of a name, using 'he' or 'they' makes the enemy appear more familiar, closer even. As early as January 1915 this was noted:

> When talking to French people the British soldier does not usually say 'Boches'; he prefers to be more correct, and so makes a sound which must be spelt Ollermon. And, to be perfectly accurate, most British soldiers do not find it necessary to use anything more descriptive than 'They' or 'Them'.[148]

This quite powerful acknowledgement of the enemy as the counterpart of the self was picked up by writers: David Jones writes 'they were at breakfast and were as cold as he, they too made their dole' and 'Mr Rhys and the new sergeant were left on his wire; you could see them plainly . . .; but on the second night after, Mr Jenkins's patrol watched his bearers lift them beyond their parapets',[149] 'they', 'his' and 'their' referring to the Germans. Sassoon also used 'They' as the title of a poem about 'the other', but here it is the wounded and altered British soldiers who are a challenge. A variation appears in Sydney de Loghe's *The Straits Impregnable* where the Turkish soldiers at Gallipoli are described as 'the other blokes'.[150] The form 'they' is seen in other languages, for example in Jean Rogissart's autobiographical novel *Les Retranchés* (1955), in which Gavin Bowd notes that '*ILS*', used to describe the German occupying forces in the Ardennes, is the only fully capitalised word in the book.[151]

Similar to 'they', 'it' referenced what people preferred not to utter. The widespread use of 'it' to describe the experience of the war, or the war itself, worked as avoidance and as creating a relationship of both knowledge and distance. Many soldiers write of 'being in it'; though 'it' cannot be said to represent anything in phrases such as 'in the thick of it', often there is a sense that 'it' does mean 'the fighting', 'the war', 'the area of danger'. David Jones's closely observed *In Parenthesis* has soldiers in a bar, one of them saying 'We shall be in it alright';[152] Sgt B. W. Carmichael wrote of 'housing fit for NCOs who had been through it' and Rifleman F. White wrote 'you'd be lying in bed with your wife and you'd see it all before you'.[153] Or there was the frequently used phrase 'to get it'; like 'going under'[154] it combined the quickest passing over of the actuality of death with an awful simplicity of the essence of war. Its fellow phrase 'to cop it' was clearly more final than 'to cop a packet'. 'I've got "*It*" badly' says a soldier talking about flu;[155] something very clear is being referred to, and the utterance of it avoided, in '1914 closes with the hope that we shall soon be "in it".[156] 'It' was the unspeakable and the too well known – David Jones has his soldier observe 'not much use hearing It coming', where 'It' may be poison gas, an unheard shell, or death in any form.[157] 'It' acknowledged the existence of the war as an entity, a business so inconceivable and yet so known that it defied expression on both counts. 'It' was the great thing that hung over the world from 1914 to 1918 and beyond.

Officialese, avoiding the personal, was well equipped to manage avoidance language. As 'quarter-bloke's English'[158] (such as 'rifles, soldiers, for the use of') removed the narrative linear structure from the language in place of a reductive taxonomy, officialese reduced 'men' to 'rifles' and 'soldiers' to 'rank and file'. The *1st Life Guards War Diary* for 12 October 1914 reads:

BRAINE – French 1st Corps on our right. Lost 600 men in ten minutes in an attack early this morning. Ran into a wall of machine guns. Lovely day.

Here a clipped and flat tone reduces all observation to the same level. There were various style choices which removed the personal; Fussell noted how official euphemism blossomed during the war, especially the use of the passive voice to push personal responsibility into the background.[159] Ian Hay catches the way in which staff officers pushed away their failure to get supplies to the front line: 'How many men are deficient of an emergency ration?'[160] If officialese played with language for its own purposes, then it created an environment whereby others could extend the game for theirs, usually mocking authority. But direct communication of horror might be incidentally hindered further. If gunners accidentally fired on their own troops, Capt E. R. Hepper could describe this as getting 'some premature in the neck'.[161] In a diary the writer knows what it means, but also knows that it is an insider term, excluding but also protecting the uninitiated.

As so often, wordplay, irony, sarcasm, and cynicism provided other ways of looking at the banality of death, pain and loss. The simplest form of this, personalising and familiarising the enemy, gave the Germans names that were almost comforting – 'Mister Boche',[162] 'Old Man Fritz';[163] 'Cousin Fritz'[164] or 'Hiney'.[165] The same was evident in the widespread naming of guns and projectiles, and the personalising into individual names of both enemy and ally. More threatening material, especially

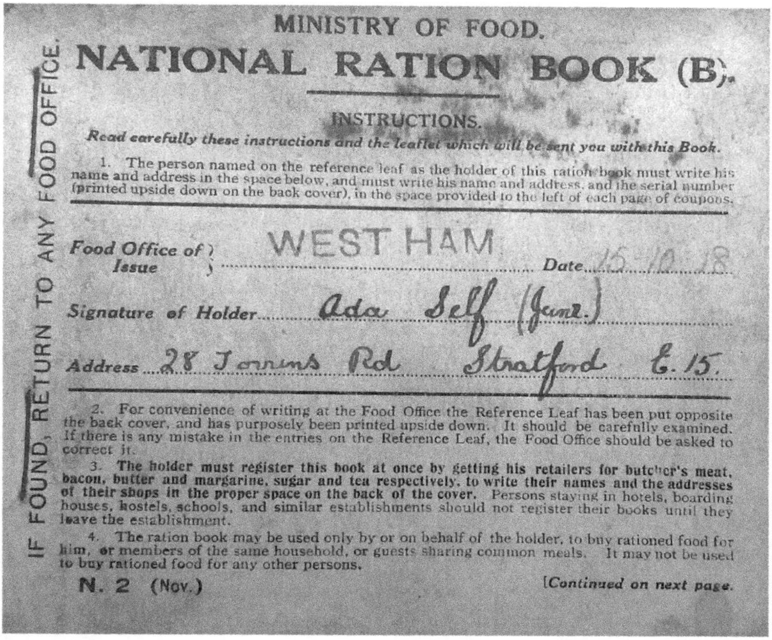

IF FOUND, RETURN TO ANY FOOD OFFICE.

MINISTRY OF FOOD.

NATIONAL RATION BOOK (B).

INSTRUCTIONS.

Read carefully these instructions and the leaflet which will be sent you with this Book.

1. The person named on the reference leaf as the holder of this ration book must write his name and address in the space below, and must write his name and address, and the serial number (printed upside down on the back cover), in the space provided to the left of each page of coupons.

Food Office of Issue WEST HAM *Date* 15 10 18

Signature of Holder Ada Self (Junr.)

Address 28 Tonnins Rd Stratford E. 15.

2. For convenience of writing at the Food Office the Reference Leaf has been put opposite the back cover, and has purposely been printed upside down. It should be carefully examined. If there is any mistake in the entries on the Reference Leaf, the Food Office should be asked to correct it.

3. **The holder must register this book at once by getting his retailers for butcher's meat, bacon, butter and margarine, sugar and tea respectively, to write their names and the addresses of their shops in the proper space on the back of the cover.** Persons staying in hotels, boarding houses, hostels, schools, and similar establishments should not register their books until they leave the establishment.

4. The ration book may be used only by or on behalf of the holder, to buy rationed food for him, or members of the same household, or guests sharing common meals. It may not be used to buy rationed food for any other persons.

N. 2 (Nov.)

[Continued on next page.

FIGURE 2.8 Ada Self's ration book, issued in November 1918. The instructions note that 'For convenience of writing at the Food Office the Reference Leaf . . . has purposely been printed upside down', presumably allowing the document to be read simultaneously by two people facing each other; civilians as well as soldiers were exposed to an increased level of officialese.

shells, could be 'un-named' as 'a few "big stuff" went over us'[166] or 'heavy stuff sent over', which rendered certain locations as 'unhealthy'.[167] Belittling language like this was allied to the romanticising 'gone west', 'pushing up daisies', and 'being a landowner in France', all of which pushed reality away and provided a filter for violent death. Trivialising campaigns or raids as a 'show' or a 'stunt' of course fooled nobody involved in them as to their seriousness, but gave some superiority to the speaker in comparison. Light irony, borrowing terms such as 'liveliness'[168] to describe fighting, or calling the operating theatre 'the pictures'[169] raised the status of the speaker over his environment; heavier irony, such as calling the Spanish Flu 'the plague',[170] challenged it. Downright cynicism faced the horror directly like medieval representations of Hell, and stared it down: speaking of some wounded Germans helping wounded British soldiers, their guard says 'They have to be [good]. If they weren't, I'd let the daylight into them';[171]

'Anzac soup' was the term used to describe a watery shell crater holding the corpse of an Australian or New Zealand soldier;[172] RFC and RAF pilots in training were in the habit of destroying planes to such an extent that they were called 'Huns'.[173] Some of these shock still; in a general sensibility so stunned by the cheapness of life reality did not matter.

Another way to avoid reality was to express it in a different language. This is often seen in situations of accidental death, or reprisals, the incidents of war that disturb, but which one can do nothing about, except shrug them off. 'I am more sorry than I can say about this [the death of a comrade], mais c'est la guerre, I suppose', and later '[retaliation to a raid is strong] mais c'est la guerre'.[174] The term became so debased that it was applied to any disappointment caused by the war, thus trivialising the war (Masefield used it to describe his annoyance at mail getting held up[175]). The rarity of instances of 'such is war'[176] indicate the normality of the French version. A curious incident of the use of a foreign language in a case of reprisal is related by Walter Brindle who describes how anti-personnel bombs are dropped on a camp of the CLC (Chinese Labour Corps) wounding several; they go to a nearby infantry camp, acquire some Mills bombs and deliberately throw them into a PoW camp, 'and with them fired the following question: "You like um, plomb? Eh you like um plomb?"' Brindle describes the event as 'very comical at the time'.[177] While we have no mention of Chinese being used as well, what we do have is the description of an atrocity being carried out in a foreign language.

Mediating one's own 'unacceptable' was done with linguistic resources. It was perhaps the nature of the articulate 'citizen war' that it could be so. There can be little doubt that the killing of prisoners and the wounded took place during the war, and sworn accounts are sworn accounts. Graves gives two reports 'two first-hand accounts' that he heard, which prove that these stories were told, not that they took place; tellingly he describes atrocities against prisoners 'a boast, not a confession'.[178] For George Coppard the shooting of surrendering men was 'the extreme treatment',[179] while A. M. Burrage wrote that 'men are threatened with a shortage of rations if they take too many prisoners', a roundabout direction to shoot surrendering men.[180]

On 26 February 1916 the editorial writer in the trench journal *The Gasper* wrote about the need for weapons that would 'go one further than poison gas and the flammenwerfer, and take a little of the burden off his [the infantryman's] shoulders'. By this time the British had been using gas, unsuccessfully at first, for five months. But it was not at first officially called 'gas'; the outrage launched at the Germans for introducing clouds of poison gas to the battlefield would have been hollow unless it could be demonstrated that they alone were responsible for it, though soldiers on both sides felt it was an unacceptable weapon. Sir John French noted in 1915 that 'I much regret that during the period under report the fighting has been characterised on the enemy's side by a cynical and barbarous disregard of the well-known usages of civilised war and a flagrant defiance of the Hague Convention.'[181] Yet within three months the British were using 'the accessory'; other nicknames developed – 'bottles', 'rogers', 'rats', 'mice' and 'jackets' – but the cold officialness of 'accessory' is still disturbing. A few weeks after its introduction Robert Graves's unit was told that an attack was to be preceded by 'forty minutes' discharge of the accessory'; a footnote states that 'severe penalties [would be imposed] on anyone who used any word but "accessory" in speaking of the gas'.[182] But a few weeks after that, on 6 October 1915 Lancelot Spicer wrote 'It does not seem to have been mentioned in the papers that we used gas, although I can't see that there can be any harm in saying it as the Germans must know, many of them having died from it'.[183] Spicer's assessment that the information was being kept secret was partially right, but he missed the point that avoidance of the word was to protect the British troops not so much materially as morally. Of course, the soldiers had their own caustic take on this: 'gassed at Mons', the response to enquiries regarding an absent man, mocked authority and the inaccuracies of the Home Front, and commented fatalistically on their own situation.[184] When one discharged soldier unwisely tried using 'gassed at Mons' as an excuse for slow work, he was fined £3.[185] In the period of the publishing of memoirs, ten years after the Armistice, there seemed to be fewer qualms about naming the weapon; 'the gas projectors . . . went off . . ., hurling opened cylinders of gas on to the enemy position'.[186]

Not knowing protected both soldiers and civilians in many ways; the majority of deaths in the combat zone of the Western Front were caused by artillery,[187] from guns like the French *soixante-quinze* that could fire a projectile over five miles, to the German *Pariser Kanone* with a range of eighty miles; and the editorial writer of *The Gasper* 8 January 1916 wrote that for the infantry much shooting was speculative: 'we don't even know how many Bosches we have butchered . . . one may have fallen; six may have fallen'. For the heavy artillery the question was practically meaningless: 'How many do you reckon we killed?' is the first line of Apollinaire's poem *Peu de Chose*, dated 13 October 1915:

Odd how it does not affect you at all . . .
Each time you say Fire! the word becomes steel that explodes far off[188]

The gunners never had to know the reality of the explosions they were responsible for. Linguistically too, distance, to the point of removal, moved people away from the reality of war.

Wordplay

Wordplay served several roles, the avoidance of failure, the fun of invention, a sense of creativity amid destruction, parody and downgrading, and alteration of the unfamiliar towards the familiar. All of these overlap.

Many will be familiar with the sense of embarrassment at school at being required to speak French with a French accent, or German with a German accent; for many of us the response is to avoid speaking at all. This, combined with the inability to create anything like a French accent, with no useful models, makes reasonable a lot of the supposedly failed attempts of British soldiers to speak standard French, such as that by a soldier known to John Crofts as 'Scrounger', who pronounced *briquet* as 'bricker'.[189] It is easy to think of this, and 'parley-voo', 'buckoo', 'toot sweet' and the rest as mocking the French pronunciation, of belittling it by removing part of its identity; if so, we need to ask whether this was deliberate or an attempt to replicate the sounds of the language as transcribed in phrasebooks. Examination of a sample of phrasebooks from the first year of the war show that the given pronunciations are not so far from what is usually recognised as 'Tommy French':

> *What a British Soldier Wants to Say in French* (1914): seel voo play, bon-joor, vang, ler pong (the bridge), kaffay, bokkoo, tray bong
> *How to Say it in French* (1914): ray-ponday, boh-coo, du pang, jombong (ham), du buff (beef), du lay (milk), maircy, we/nong, un frong, parlay voo
> *The British Soldier's Anglo-French Pocket Dictionary* (1915): frongsay, savay
> *French Conversation* (1914): pong (bridge)

Large numbers of cheap phrasebooks were printed, opportunistically perhaps – Carreras produced a series of four, to be given away in packets of

Black Cat cigarettes; the *Anglo-French Pocket Dictionary* got to at least nine editions, over 57,000 copies; *What a British Soldier Wants to Say in French* was printed in Pas-de-Calais with its British price printed on the cover; *How to Say it in French* attracted buyers by stating that profits from sales would go to the War Relief Fund, while *French Conversation* was a standard tourist phrase book with an added section on 'Military and Hospital Phrases'. The transcriptions given above are not exclusive to wartime – *The Briton in France* (1906) gives 'oo-ee' and 'nohng', *The French Phrasebook* (1913) gives 'pah bokoo', 'tray beeang', and 'toot ah koo'. The 1904 Board of Education Regulations for Secondary Schools established that a modern foreign language should be part of the four-year course, so, for many soldiers going to France, French would have been familiar, if forgotten. Considering how much time British soldiers spent in Flanders, and how little Flemish permeated through to soldiers' speech, schooling and phrasebooks as well as contact with locals have to be considered as sources for 'Tommy French'.

But 'napoo', from *il n'y a plus*, and 'sanfairyann' from *ça ne fait rien*, or 'just a minute' from *estaminet* are more than creditable attempts to speak French, as they become new English words with distinct meanings. There are a number of possible interpretations for what is happening here, blending into each other: an acknowledgement of being in France, and mixing with French-speakers; a bit of showing off; a very long tradition of wordplay; a colonialist approach to the local, of pulling it into an English framework, making minimal concessions to the local; even a recognition of the longstanding link between English and French. Jimmy's 'I said, "Tray Bong"',[190] 2nd Lt Keay's 'it is a bon job',[191] Brophy and Partridge's 'japan' (*du pain*) and 'umpty-poo' (*un petit peu*), 'sink faranks' (*cinq francs*)[192] and 'cat soo' (*quatre sous*)[193] all convey a sense of enjoyment of the potential of language. Exactly the same kind of wordplay could be done with more familiar language, 'Georgius Rex' on the cap badge being turned into 'Gorgeous Wrecks', and Montreuil being renamed 'Geddesburg' after Sir Eric Geddes, Director General of Transportation, established his headquarters there in 1916. The process could be extended: 'toot sweet' could give 'to do something on the toot', i.e. on the double, 'sanfairyann' became 'snaffer', and 'somewhere in France' slipped into 'summers in France'.[194] Faux childishness made a periscope into a 'look stick', and mock-trivialising made a senior officer's visit to the trenches into a 'Cook's tour' and staff memoranda into 'Comic Cuts'. The home press and the civilian world echoed this mood with wordplay such as 'assasinaucracy'[195] and 'Austrich'.[196] Evidently the same thing was happening across no man's

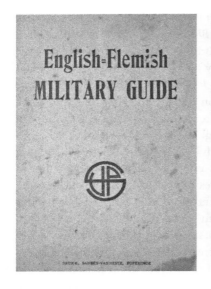

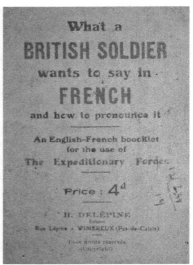

FIGURE 2.9 Some of the dictionaries and phrasebooks available to British soldiers in France and Flanders, from 1914.

land, where the typical name for a pilot, Franz, gave rise to the verb *sich verfranzen*, to get lost.[197] Even Arabic could be played with: the Egyptian Labour Corps were known as 'the Calm Laylas' from their song '*Kam Layla, Kam Yom?*' ('How many nights, how many days?')

While there were no doubt frequent instances of British soldiers teasing the French by teaching them obscenities and bizarre rhyming slang (see p. 36 Horace Stanley), there were also honourable attempts, and typically British glorious failures, to communicate in French: Brophy and Partridge tell the story of the soldier who knew the French for 'milk' warning the owner of his farm billet that the cow had got loose with the words 'Madame! Madame! Dulay promenade'.[198] Brophy and Partridge label this story as 'immortal' in appreciation; at the time soldiers enjoyed the hit-and-miss adventures of language: Rifleman William Taffs wrote, 'I was a scream yesterday in the shops. My French is the absolute limit. I go in the shop with a carefully prepared sentence, they never understand but only laugh at. I beat about the bush an awful lot until the place is a mass of broad grins. . . . The other chaps with me laugh too, but I notice they get me to get the things for them'.[199] Essentially empirical, this approach to language was usually going to work through its positivity and its humour, unlike the heavy-handed satire of Horace Wyatt's *Malice in Kulturland* (1917) with its clumsy allegorising of Humpty-Dumpty as Army-Barmy, and:

'Twas dertag, and the slithy Huns
Did sturm and sturgel through the sludge;
All bulgous were the blunderguns,
And the bosch bombs outbludge.

Inventiveness with language at this time spread across several media – newspapers, letters, diaries, postcards, trench journals. Playing with words and sounds created 'tres beans' from *très bien*, and extended it into 'fray bentos',[200] 'having the wind up' became 'windy', which became 'breezy',[201] and a Scottish soldier was called 'Tammas McAtkins'.[202] 'Mesopolonica' was a particularly fortuitous conjunction of Mesopotamia and Salonika that highlighted the soldiers' attitude to unknown foreign parts, while there is a razor-sharp wit in the Australian terms for those who enlisted in successive years of the war: the 'tourists' of the first year, out for adventure, followed by the 'dinkums', genuinely fighting for Australia, the late-coming 'deep thinkers', and the 'Noah's doves' for those who arrived too late, with 'methusiliers' for those who should have been too old to fight. Some of the expressions, such as the American 'swiss cheese air', for turbulent air pockets, require understanding of the environment, while 'tinned cow' for condensed milk is instantly recognisable.

No doubt some of the apparent wordplay came from a longstanding phenomenon whereby simplifications or apparent mistakes become standardised – the poetic 'Morpheus' became 'murphyised'. 'Landslip' for 'landship' (tank) shows that the idea of the mistake could be played with. Other forms of wordplay appear rarely, showing that what often is seen as general usage through the period and across the whole area was more likely used for a period, among a set of people, or even an individual: to 'hop over the parapet' occurs occasionally, but 'sandbag street' (the front line) is very rare,[203] and given its source, may be a regional term. Similar instances of regionality are 'Gribbles', used by Northampton soldiers of Kitchener's Army for comforts sent out from a fund established by a Mr Gribble of Northampton, recorded by Fraser and Gibbons, and the Kitchener's Army Battalion called the Hull T'Others.

Wordplay raises the question of authenticity, in terms of breadth of use and the privileging of the Front. Individual or nonce expressions are hard to label as 'soldiers' slang'. 'Tobo' for tobacco,[204] in postcards sent to Fownhope in Herefordshire may be a local or family expression, unrecorded elsewhere; Dawson's soldier saying of German prisoners 'If they weren't [well-behaved], I'd let the daylight into them'[205] is very creative, but it may be Dawson's or the soldier's one-off creativity. When Brophy and Partridge say of 'cannon-fodder' 'a journalistic expression, only used with the implication of quotation, by soldiers', or when Fraser and Gibbons say of 'mad minute' 'newspaper coined expression', there is an implicit evaluation – 'not soldier slang' – which debases as 'journalese' such inventions as 'limpet' (someone with a government desk job), 'cuthbert' and 'ladies from Hell'. And journalistic interpretation, made at the time and with no benefit of research over extended location or time, inevitably made claims based on quick impressions: a *Yorkshire Evening Post* correspondent's assessment of 'Nosey Parker' as 'one name [for a tank] being used more than any other at the front' is really not borne out by other documentation.[206]

Inventiveness also extended words into different parts of speech: Weekley noted the use of 'to rhondda' (from Lord Rhondda, government food controller from 1917), meaning 'to appropriate', and *Cassell's New English Dictionary* (1919) recorded the verb 'to Lusitania', meaning 'to

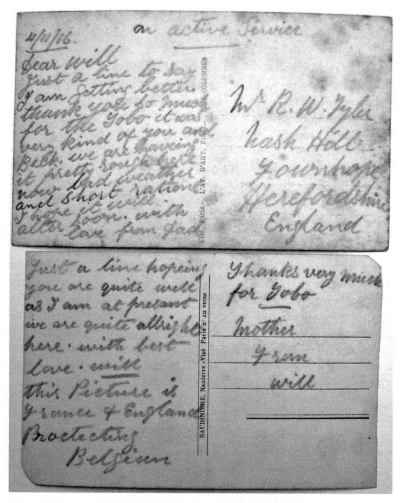

FIGURE 2.10 Two cards from members of the same family, both saying thank you for a gift of 'Tobo'.

torpedo passenger ships'. Slang terms made the transmission easily: the sound-description 'crump' became the verb 'to crump'; 'napoo's sense of 'dead' was transferred into a verb, meaning 'to kill'; and Williamson shows the movement from one part of speech to another – 'You know what to do with the kamerards – kamerard them with three inches in the throat'.[207] Similarly Eric Verney in *The Athenaeum* recorded 'to shanks it' meaning to walk (from 'Shanks's pony'),[208] and a battery firing too early and hitting their own troops was 'prematuring' – 'the Battery denied that they were prematuring into us'.[209]

Partridge believed that soldier slang had an association with the criminal underworld and cockney verbal culture, which may have had some influence on the growth of rhyming slang at the Front. The same *Yorkshire Evening Post* article records the use of 'a drop o' pigs' ('pig's ear', beer), 'a laugh and a titter' (bitter), and 'I'm so frisky' (whisky),[210] while Ward Muir records 'plates of meat' (feet)[211] being used by an Australian soldier, though not necessarily picked up in France. The *Notes and Queries* correspondence (1919–22) recorded a lot of rhyming slang: 'grasshopper' (copper), 'china' (mate), 'bushel and peck' (neck), 'Cain and Abel' (table), 'cough and sneeze' (cheese), though all of these were around long before the war.

Belittling one's own side, presumably in a good-natured way, produced 'snake-charmers' and 'flag-waggers' (buglers and signallers), 'cherry-nobs' for the military police, and 'canaries' for the army instructors and sanitary orderlies, who wore yellow brassards. The roll-call of nicknames for regiments dated back to long before the war: the 'Mutton-chops' for the Royal West Surreys, whose emblem was the lamb and flag; the 'Virgin Mary's Bodyguard' for the 7th Dragoon Guards, with a large proportion of Catholic soldiers; the 'Lavatory Lancers' for the Westmoreland and Cumberland Regiment. Fraser and Gibbons listed thirty-nine pages of them, including the rather more bitter wartime 'Rob All My Comrades' (Royal Army Medical Corps) and 'All Very Cushy' (Army Veterinary Corps).

The same kind of wordplay was going on in German, with its long tradition of military language, and in French: Partridge's chapter on *Slang of Three Nations*,[212] including pre-war language, is a journey through the world of metaphor: *Abfrühstücken* ('to breakfast away', to be wounded), *dépoter son géranium* ('unpot your geranium', to die), *être etalé* ('to be laid out for display', killed), *avoir un petit jardin sur le ventre* (not unlike 'pushing up daisies'), *Kilometerschwein* ('kilometre-pig', foot soldier), *auf Gemüsetour gehen* ('tour the vegetables', look for something to scrounge). Unsurprisingly similar terms appeared on both sides of no man's land, for example 'she bumps' ('we're being shelled') and *es pumpert*.

French wordplay included the names of trench journals (*L'Echo de Tranchéesville, Le Tacatacteufteuf, Journal Embuscophobe*), but the most enthusiastic extensions were to the word 'boche': Sieveking in *Notes and Queries*[213] notes *Bochonnie* ('Germany'), and from French trench journals

Le bochophage ('boche-eater') and the nonsense word *Rigolboche*, while Fraser and Gibbons add *Bocheser* ('to germanise'), *Bochonnerie* ('German foul play'), *Bocherie* ('German cruelty'), *Bochiser* ('to spy'), *Bochisme* ('German "Kultur"'); Olivier Leroy, in *A Glossary of French Slang* (1922), adds *bochie* ('Germany'), *bochisant* ('Germanophile') and *bochisme* ('*Kultur*').

Puns were common and apparently enjoyed; they are found in trench journals, letters, newspaper advertisements, songs, picture postcards: an advertisement for Beecham's Pills shows a soldier with a machine-gun under the banner 'A Good Maxim To Remember'.[214] Simple puns like this required little invention, but the increasing awareness of other languages gave scope for more intricate intra-lingual puns, beyond the *trois*/twa and the inevitable *oui*/wee beers jokes. *The Fuze* carried a joke in French based on the sound similarities between *femme* and *faim*.[215] Or mixing visual and verbal communication: the 9.45 inch trench mortar was known as the 'quarter to ten'.[216]

PUNS

Puns as a form of rhetoric were widespread during the conflict. 'Dug-outs' were both shelters in trenches and retired officers recalled to the colours to help train the new armies. The involvement of French allowed multi-layering: the *Sunday Mirror*, 25 February 1917, p. 7 carried a cartoon of an ex-soldier delivering coal asking his customer whether she wants 'coal a la carte' or 'coal de sac'. Trench journals are liberally decorated with puns and semi-homonyms between English and French: 'Who asked for "weak nerves" when all he wanted was "huit oeufs"?' (*Fifth Gloucester Gazette*, 12 March 1916), as well as the more straightforward 'Rumour hath it that an Intelligence Department is not necessarily an intelligent Department' (*The Gasper*, 28 February 1916).

But puns could also convey popular propaganda and pathos: 'Boche' was always useful for downsizing the enemy by sounding the same as 'bosh', while Passchendaele morphed into 'Passion Dale', its association with heavy losses of Canadian

---

troops giving this an official name status after the war, a remembrance which makes the some/Somme pun all the more difficult to later observers.

FIGURE 2.11 Photograph of seven cavalry troopers, with the chalked board locating them 'Somme where in France'.

Avoidance, a theme that comes up repeatedly in this study, was a strong contributor to the language developed in various branches of the army. The voices of the army became easily recognisable in terms such as 'wastage', or 'the accessory', where the avoidance of direct description – here, the acceptable number of troops killed in an operation, or 'poison gas' – were seen to be either removing moral problems, and thus making an officer's job easier, or avoiding recognition of the unacceptable and painting a propagandist picture of combat. Though the term 'officialese' had been around for 30 years by 1914, it was the First World War that familiarised millions of people with its manipulation of direct language. In its extreme form it allowed a voice that is impersonal, neither active nor passive, allowing a dehumanising of soldiers, as when Ian Hamilton writes 'At the end, I told them I had asked for 95,000 fresh rifles' rather than so many 'men'.[217] Similar usages are 'order to off-saddle received',[218] and the repeated uses of 'entrain', 'embus', and even 'disentrain'.[219] The dehumanising power of this is seen in Graves's narration of a soldier charged for 'committing excreta'.[220] When in Bairnsfather's cartoon Colonel Fitz-Shrapnel receives a message from GHQ asking him 'Please let us know, as soon as possible, the number of tins of raspberry jam issued to you last Friday', this reflected the exasperation junior officers felt at the endless requests for information from quartermasters and staff officers; Lancelot Spicer gave another example – 'the number of men who have not cut their toenails for the last fortnight (giving reasons)'.[221] Given that shelling was directed as much at the supply lines as at the firing trenches, continual reporting of such information was necessary, if tiresome. The supplies process was responsible for another linguistic form, known as 'quarter-bloke's English'; Brophy and Partridge characterised it as *Gum Boots and Thigh Boots* were in Quarterese described as *Boots, gum and Boots, Thigh, Soldiers, for the use of*'.[222] What happens here is a word order that places ideas in order of importance rather than the usual syntactic form, a kind of ranking; the same concept appears in Sidney de Loghe's transcription of the instructions for the firing of a battery: 'Guns in action! Aiming point right-hand edge of Battleship Hill! Line of fire five degrees five minutes right! Corrector one-five-ough – three-three hundred! Angle of sight three degrees three-five minutes elevation! One round battery fire!'[223] While operational orders and records had to be given in abbreviated form – 'Heavy gunning about 7 pm, so saddled up 1st squadron. Quiet again, 9 pm. Went up to Headquarters. Likely to move tomorrow. Orders to move came, 6 pm'[224] – these occasionally failed to sit comfortably with standard English syntax, as in 'I in command of rearguard of ourselves'.[225] New vocabulary too came from officialese, though as H. M. Denham said of 'mine-bumpers',[226] not everyone understood it. Nor did everyone in authority like it – General Allenby disliked the term 'camelry' which had emerged as a counterpart to 'cavalry'. Clearly some of it did not lodge in the mind – *War-Time Tips* had to remind prospective soldiers that the question was not 'Who goes there?' but 'Who comes there?',[227] but ANZAC, claimed by some to be the first English acronym, and invented by desk clerks in Egypt in 1915, has to be one of the most felicitous terms to come from the period.[228]

The anglicisation of place names in France and Belgium is a well-known aspect of British soldiers' linguistic problems and solutions. The process raises the question of how these came about; the still successful humour of the result should lead us to look for the process of word-creation. There is no evidence for the origin for calling Ypres 'Wipers', so we are thrown back on internal or circumstantial pointers. Wipers is the most well-known anglicisation, but the place was also called 'Eeep' and 'Eeprees'; the first example comes from John Buchan writing in 1919, who said that '"Wipers" [was] not a name given by the British private soldier. He called it "Eeep." "Wipers" was an officer's name, gladly seized on by journalists and by civilians at home',[229] though the *Sunderland Daily Echo* quoted a *Manchester Guardian* correspondent who felt that 'Wipers' was a 'horrible word ... a relic of our first expeditionary force, the personnel of which were better fighters than scholars', and one which was dying out, thankfully, due to there being by 1917 'more educated men in the ranks'.[230] Veteran RFA gunner (i.e. non-officer) Percy Bryant interviewed in 1975 pronounced it 'Eeprees'.[231] Herbert McBride wrote that '"Eéps" was the word that went up and down the line, that being the Flemish pronunciation of Ypres',[232] presumably the pronunciation coming from a local guide.

Given that there was little contact there between British soldiers and Flemish speakers, the greater likelihood is that exposure to the name was through its French pronunciation, which would have come into English as 'Eepra', or reading the French or Flemish spelling (Ypres/Ieper), which would have given 'Eepres' or 'Yeper'; the local Flemish pronunciation is more like 'Eeper'. Both officers and men would have heard it pronounced 'Eeper' or more likely 'Eepra', the second (French) pronunciation from interpreters, liaison officers and estaminet-keepers – the last of these recorded as speaking French more often than Flemish.

'Wipers' seems to be a deliberate joke based on the first letter of the French spelling. The standard English pronunciation, with a bit of knowledge as to how French pronunciation works, would have given Buchan's proposed 'other ranks' version, 'Eep', or 'Eepr'; with a bit less knowledge of French, but making a good attempt, this would easily come out as 'Eeprees'. It is worth remembering here that there is plenty of evidence for British soldiers being prepared to have a go at French, and in many cases to set themselves to try to learn a bit: in a recorded dramatisation *In the Trenches* directed by Major A. E. Rees in 1917, which has both authenticating and absurdly unrealistic aspects, cockney private Reginald 'Tippy' Winter is spotted reading a French manual, though his chum Ginger claims he is doing it only to be able to speak to French girls. Brophy and Partridge[233] claim that though 'Wipers' was the soldiers' pronunciation in 1914 and early 1915 'the majority of the troops seemed to harbour a suspicion that French was not properly pronounced by the same rules as English . . . The commonest methods of tackling Ypres were "Eepray" and "Eeps"'. Brophy and Partridge also give the form 'Ips' as used. But the amount of documentation of the soldiers' imaginative use of 'Wipers' is difficult to ignore, from the limerick which has 'Ypres' rhyming with 'two snypres' and 'the Argyll and Sutherland pypres',[234] to the mournful ballad with its chorus of 'Wipers in the wet' printed in the *Yorkshire Evening Post* (2 November 1918). H. S. Clapham in *Mud and Khaki* written from diary notes (4 February 1915) states that he wandered into a church at Ypres and noted the use on local tombstones of 'Wyper' 'from which it would appear that Tommy is, after all, justified in his speech',[235] indicating awareness of some discussion of the subject at the time.

There are two other factors: the medieval Ypres Tower at Winchelsea which, Fraser and Gibbons point out, was always called the 'Wipers Tower'; and we should not underestimate the post-war influence on this question of the *Wipers Times*. Altogether the evidence would indicate that the joke version of Ypres came from officer-level wordplay based on the written/printed word, while the 'have a go' version came from spoken language among the other ranks; Partridge states that the 'Wipers' pronunciation 'was encouraged by the powers at the very beginning of the war',[236] suggesting the possibility that other pronunciations may have been a reaction against authority. There is also evidence of regional variation from a poem written by Pte Robin of the Argyll and Sutherland Highlanders, printed in the *Stirling Observer* 18 September 1915, which has Ypres rhyming with 'keepers'.

The Portsmouth Evening News, *in an article discussing the pronunciation of Ypres, Ghent, Compiegne and Aisne, stated 'Fortunately we have Przemysl already, and have agreed to call it Primrose Hill.'*

But there was an influence on soldiers' pronunciation before many of them got to Flanders. 'Wipers' was quoted widely in the regional press,[237] quickly spreading into general consciousness. As the city's name became fixed in public consciousness newspapers were continually asked how to pronounce it: generally the answer was 'Eepr'.[238] The *Nottingham Evening Post* pointed out that the question had been 'answered several times recently',[239] though its 15 October 1914 issue had given the pronunciation as 'Yeeper'.[240] Other variations were 'Ee-pre' in the *Newcastle Journal*[241] and 'Eep-rh' in the *Berwickshire News*,[242] while the *Yorkshire Evening Post* suggested 'we should not rule out "Eepray" as inadmissable'.[243] The same paper had previously given the local pronunciation as 'ee-per'.[244] Other place names caused worry for newspapers: the *Sheffield Evening Telegraph* offered the pronunciation of Yser as 'probably "Eessaire" 'but we do not guarantee this',[245] while the more confident *Liverpool Echo* gave it as 'eeser (slightly stressing "er")'.[246] The *Aberdeen Journal* gave the pronunciation of Thiepval as 'Tee-ay-val',[247] but Przemysl confounded many: the *Birmingham Daily Post* noted that there was a 'general agreement here to call the place either "Jemizzle" or "Shemozzle", the latter being the more favoured in the East End because it is an old piece of Yiddish slang.'[248] The *Motherwell Times* was more respectful if no more helpful, offering the pronunciation 'przhem-isl – pronounce as if all one syllable';[249] the *Portsmouth Evening News*, in an article discussing the pronunciation of Ypres, Ghent, Compiegne and Aisne, stated 'Fortunately we have Przemysl already, and have agreed to call it Primrose Hill'.[250]

It is clear that some pronunciations developed from reading and others from hearing: Jonathan Lighter lists 'bokoo frankies' (*beaucoup francs*) which would have come from hearing, and 'three beans' (*très bien*) more likely to have come from reading; 'silver plate' (*s'il vous plaît*) could have come from either. Clear patterns of etymology can be seen in other place name anglicisations. In the case of the wonderfully dismissive change from Albert to 'Bert', the French pronunciation of the town is nothing like the anglicisation, lending weight to the proposal that this case derived from the written or printed word. Moo-cow Farm/ Mucky Farm (Mouquet Ferme), About Turn (Hébuterne), Armentears/ Armentiers (Armentières), Inky Bill (Ingouville) and Ocean Villas (Auchonvillers) clearly are examples of anglicisation from sound, as are, from the Flemish, White Sheet (Wytschaete) and Dickybush (Dickebusch). But the anglicisation of Bois Grenier as Boys Grenyer depends on spelling, as do Dogs Knees/Doing it (Doignes), Aches-and-Pains (Aix-les-Bains) and Business (Busnes), the French pronunciation not resembling the anglicised version. Gertie Wears Velvet (Godewaersvelde) is less clear, but the Flemish spoken version would have been fairly difficult for the untutored British soldier to unravel, so the anglicisation here possibly comes via both paths. In any case the anglicised versions travelled along spoken paths with speed, and settled quickly to what sat comfortably in the various accents of the British Army as Hoop Lane (Houplines), Plugstreet (Ploegsteert) and the delightfully pragmatic Pop (Poperinghe). Sally on the Loose (Sailly sur la Lys) indicates a nod in the direction of knowing some French, while Ruin (Rouen) pretends nothing, and Extra Cushy (Estree Cauchy) called out for anglicisation. There is not extensive documentation of Armentières as Arm in Tears, and the compromise 'Armentears/Armentiers' seemed to cause so little trouble that R. H. Mottram felt 'it may be said to have entered the language'.[251] The curious renaming as 'Coxgrove' of Coxyde (Koksijde) may indicate a personal reference, or perhaps a decorous version of an obscene nickname for a letter of condolence.[252] In passing, it is comforting to know that the German soldiers also played with place names, turning Neufchatel into Neuschrapnell and Pérenchis into Bärenschiss ('bearshit').[253]

FIGURE 2.12 In October 1918 Rifleman Fred Walker was stationed near Houplines, written in his diary entry for 5 October as 'Hoop Lane'.

The invention of names is a clear instance of the individual and the group trying to regain some control over a bewildering situation: the names and nicknames developed through wordplay show people expressing their will and their determination to not shut down. Naming a gun 'scene-shifter'[254] or 'Christians Arise'[255] are reactions to situations, cynical and dismissive in the extreme, and simultaneously noting the effects of and belittling the guns. The opportunities afforded for naming tanks, largely at the discretion of their commanders, provided a range of names that show creative thinking, beneath the range of sentiments from patriotism to sentimentality to irony to revenge: Iron Duke, Lady Wingate, War Baby, Hyacinth, Oh My Word, We're All In It Together, Lusitania, Destroyer.

Humour

How is it that so much humour has survived? Or is it maybe that what people wanted to record was the humour, to compensate for the unending dreariness punctuated by moments of extreme horror? Humour no doubt helped both soldiers and civilians get through, and is an essential part of the record of language; does it still raise a smile, and does it help us understand the experience any further? The range of humour recorded is an indicator of people finding, and significantly wanting to record, an experience away from the casualty lists, the squalor and degradation of the Front, the fear, the anger and the hopelessness. The range is also an indicator of the amount: in presenting a range of different kinds of humour, this section goes some way to presenting the extent to which humour was part of everyday language use.

Humour among the horrors of trench life included jokes, puns, satire, wordplay, gallows humour, and those curious incidents of the bizarre – the unburied arm used as a hook for a pack or as a geographical marker, or the laughter of relief, as at the look on a man's face when he gets his foot caught while trying to escape from a grenade.[256] Laughter at the bizarreness of the situation, or at the relief of survival, or of something happening to someone else, was a continual occurrence at the Front: 'somebody slipped in a shell hole and the laughter was positively hyenish'.[257]

Alternatively, being cheerful ('cheery and bright' and 'merry and bright' are the phrases met with most often) was 'the only way to keep going out here',[258] 'to mix jollity with other matters is all one can do out here. There's so hanged little joy or laughter floatin' about that you have to jolly well create it, or languish in gloom'.[259] There were claims of spontaneous humour under fire – 'Many of the wounded who have been invalided home were asked whether this humour in the trenches is the real thing, or only an affected drollery to conceal the emotions the men feel in the face of death; but they all declare that it is quite spontaneous'.[260] For one young officer it was necessary to 'hang on to one's humour like grim death, otherwise I think you are bound to crack'.[261] But the general feeling is that, certainly after 1914, soldiers' humour was ironic, hard, reactive to the situation and frequently very creative. 2nd Lt Arthur Clarke described it as 'sometimes rather twisted but most always to the front'.[262] What the trenches produced was a 'war humour' that was reactive and referential, a verbal and situational humour that was bound to be more successful than performative or pictorial humour, by virtue of the circumstances; and by being reactive and referential it depended on and created an inner circle of those who understood, a 'free-floating circuit of logic independent of the outside world, uniting initiated soldiers by their fluency in the real knowledge of the war'.[263] As a way of reacting creatively to circumstances its influence was longstanding: for example, Paul Fussell believed that 'with the war, irony became the dominant mode in English literature'.[264]

The ironic, the cynical, and the satirical produced a range of verbal humour reacting to various aspects of the nature of the war. The writers and editors of trench journals saw these publications as a way of applying the culture of social satire to the situation of being in the trenches, the prosecution of the war, both politically and by staff officers, and the hiatus between the soldier and the civilian. Deeply territorial to individual regiments, columns such as 'Things we would like to know', 'Things overheard on the March', or 'We know, but we shan't tell' reinforced the insider identity with overt or thinly disguised references to known people, events or situations. In a sense the trench journal produced a closely parallel view of the world, a play version which showed the deadly effects of the real thing in a disorienting way. These allowed a blurring of the border between reality and fantasy, offering a possibility that this was all a joke that nobody could really understand: an advertisement in the *Grey Brigade* for 'The Handy Pronouncer – Every name of importance correctly pronounced. No more blunders. Turn up the index and there you are. Thus Yser, Ypres, and other places need cause no alarm. Also: the automatic saluter, our boomerang bullet'.[265] While most trench journals satirised the war, the parallel view of the *Wipers Times* and its later manifestations created its own version of the industrial-scale destruction in satirising practically anything within reach – page 4 of *The Somme Times* (31 July 1916) has a limerick about a young girl being blown up and an anti-love poem to a trench mortar. As *The Kemmel Times*[266] its advertisement page offered insurance for dug-outs, house ventilation, even the notice of a 'film play' called 'Gas'; while enjoying praise from the home press – the *Dublin Daily Express* described it in 1917 as 'probably the most remarkable newspaper ever published'[267] – the *Wipers Times* took merciless shots at the journalism of Hillaire Belloc and William Beach Thomas, renamed as Belary Helloc and Teech Bomas. *Fall In* offered a narration of a day in 1956 with the war still going on,[268] and *The Ghain Tuffieha Gazette* carried an article about the investigation of the theft of a bun and the subsequent trial.[269] A model in many trench journals is the mock–glossary satirising the home press's interest in soldiers' slang; *The Gasper* produced one that includes 'Officer: a private in the UPS [University and Public School] Battalions. Wrist watch: a good excuse for appearing late on parades'.[270] The 'parallel world' nature of the Front is seen also in the application of British place names to trenches, creating a parody of both places; senior officers visiting the trenches were doing a 'Cooks Tour'.

Paralleling the authorised destruction going on, soldiers applied satire to the language that was dealt to them. Officers called daily memoranda from staff HQ 'Comic Cuts', or soldiers, in the reverse process, used 'officialese' on non-official subject matter – thus, taking the model of a person acting as a substitute for someone of a higher rank being called 'acting ...', bully beef with biscuit was called 'acting rabbit pie'. 'Mesopolonica' mixing Mesopotamia and Salonika, mocked the remoteness and apparent irrelevance of both places, while soldiers mocked the terminology of enlisting by wishing 'roll on duration'.[271] Taking a swipe at the traditions of the army, the aristocracy, and the bizarre nature of the war as family argument between the royal houses of Europe, the term 'The Kaiser's Own' was applied to the King's Royal Rifle Corps (whose badge, a Maltese Cross, resembled an Iron Cross), to the 2nd City of London Fusiliers, and to a company of the Manchester Special Constables Brigade and a labour battalion of the Middlesex Regiment (both due to the number of naturalised Germans serving).[272] If irony carried a sense of challenge through humour then wartime irony was seen after the war in German resentment, the black-bordered stamps pastiching stamps of former colonies, the stamps urging Germans '*nicht vergissen unser Kolonien'* (don't forget our colonies), and strong irony was evident in the attempt by a Hamburg shipping company in 1922 to name their vessels provocatively as 'Hun', 'Boche', 'Pirate', and other names used against Germans. The company was persuaded to drop the idea.[273] A discourse of resentment was manifested in the sense of outrage at the material destruction of north-eastern France and western Flanders: an extensive series of postcards published in France showed villages and towns shattered to matchwood, with captions saying *'après le passage des barbares'* or 'Combles, what's left of it'.

> The tiredness, the inexplicability and the absurdity of it all was summed up in the expression noted by Archibald Sparke: 'when everything seems to be going wrong . . . the soldier turns to sarcasm, and says, "Well, we're winning"'.

The sense that the soldier should 'be allowed his grouse' respected the creativity of much grumbling, the nature of humour as a safety-valve, and realisation by both soldier and authority that there was a line that could

CAMPAGNE DE 1914-1916

COMBLES (Somme). — Ce qu'il en reste! — What it is left of it.   ND. Phot.

FIGURE 2.13 A 'resentment' caption, the card sent in January 1917; the censoring officer has made an attempt to erase the place name.

be stretched, but not broken. Bruce Bairnsfather's cartoons, using the typical cockney soldier who has seen it all, Ole' Bill, provided a model for grousing, so successful that the caption 'Well, if you knows of a better 'ole, go to it' became widely applied: '... every gun we have in this section is going to fairly give Bosche jumps; in fact he will have to find a "better 'ole." This remark caused considerable laughter'.[274] The expression provided the title for a 1917 film and another in 1926 starring Charlie Chaplin, and was cemented as a name for a character-type, seen in the report of the 1928 British Legion pilgrimage – '"Look at them blarsted trees", said an "Old Bill" of the party'.[275] Irony could be fairly harmless – soldiers who complained about the quality or paucity of food had long been reprimanded for 'wanting jam on it', and 'wanting jam on it' became a term for hoping for a betterment of anything. But irony could be hurtful: American Expeditionary Force slang included the term 'toyshop' for the factory in France that produced camouflage materiel, and the interpretation of their own initials as 'After England Fails'. Beyond this lies gallows humour, the wit of the territory where care is no longer an issue; James Kilpatrick describes troops in 1914 going into their first action shouting 'Early doors, this way! Early doors, ninepence!',[276] but a more plausible comment when going over the top is 'Do you want to live for ever?'[277] Civilians were not fully protected from this – a postcard shows a boy waiting to hit a fly that has landed on his father's bald head, with the caption 'if that fly don't move soon it'll be figurin' in the casualty list'; Coningsby Dawson related how, after nights of Zeppelin raids in London, a paper-seller said to him, 'They forgot us.' 'Who forgot us?' I asked. 'The bloomin 'Uns. I was expecting them last night.'[278]

By the end of the war gallows humour had become the norm. The tiredness, the inexplicability and the absurdity of it all was summed up in the expression noted by Archibald Sparke: 'when everything seems to be going wrong ... the soldier turns to sarcasm, and says, "Well, we're winning"'.[279]

The AEF glossary, compiled by Jonathan Lighter, shows some extremely hard expressions – 'permanent rest camp' for cemetery, 'meat-grinder' for battle-front[280], 'second children's crusade' for Boy Scouts – but Anzac slang was sharp too, and possibly a little wittier: 'Fanny Durack' was 'The hanging Virgin of Albert Basilica (i.e., the champion lady diver)' – the statue at the top of the spire had been hit by a shell and for years leaned over below the horizontal.[281] The humour in this depended on very sharp understanding that the appropriateness of the words would just outweigh any distaste. A less harsh quick-wittedness, deriving from the largely oral urban culture of music-hall comedians having to work with unforgiving audiences, produced examples of verbal wit that would have graced later radio-comedy scripts – indeed perhaps here is the beginning of that link between the army and radio comedy that flowered after the Second World War and through National Service in the 1940s and 50s. The quick verbal wit that characterised dense urban societies was easily transferred to the trenches: Aubrey Smith recorded one soldier asking a French woman, '"how many oranges for a penny?" "Two for seexpence," replied Mademoiselle. "Phew! Chuck us 'arf a one then."'[282]

Pte Robert Sturges described being on a night patrol in no man's land when a star shell would light up the area – 'At such times we flattened our noses into the mud, kept perfectly still and made a noise like a corpse'.[283] Capt R. McDonald censoring his men's letters read one which said 'Dear Jeannie, I am expecting leave soon. Take a good look at the floor. You'll see nothing but the ceiling when I get home'.[284]

The fund of shared verbal knowledge in songs and catchphrases provided scope for variation. John Brophy pointed out that when considering the origin of First World War song lyrics the style of material to be considered should include 'Christmas card verses or parish magazine poetry' as well as 'personal abuse'[285] – again that mix of polarities that embraced both the Sunday School and the all-male workplace. Brophy also points out the songs' lack of universality – the essential situational references that exclude the outsider – and the fact that so many were parodies, often sung by one inventor against existing song lyrics, reacting to the soldiers' circumstances and deliberately and, in the case of hymns, defiantly rejecting expectations of both the lyrics and the level of respect for authority. Many of the songs survived decades – even into 1960s school playgrounds – with 'Mademoiselle from Armentieres', 'The Bells of Hell go Ting-a-ling-a-ling', 'Far Far from Wipers I Long to Be' and 'Old Soldiers Never Die' passing into folklore as recognised if not fully remembered. Humorously obscene lyrics, encouraged by the all-male environment, flourished, and many, protected by their nature as verse, and therefore having a structural link to the classification of 'literature', have survived much more widely than passing comments using the same terminology. Matching content to the natural rhythms of English speech probably contributed to the longevity of the song, hence the survival of

nonsense lyrics like 'inky-pinky-parley-voo'. Shoeing Smith C. Williams'
song (though he felt some of it was too strong to record) was performed
in an all-male environment, was known and frequently repeated but
admired as an individual performance, had lyrics which were obscene
and a non-sequitur, and it stays in the mind:

> I once knew a fellow
> His name was Ben
> He had nine of a family
> (nearly ten!)
> … Now all you gents
> If you want any more,
> I've an apple up me arse
> And you can have the core![286]

Catchphrases in the same way took the known and changed it to
a new known, owned by the soldiers, affirming their existence by
adapting a well-known phrase, sometimes one specifically directed
or donated to them by the authorities or the press; Brophy and Partridge
point out that music-hall catchphrases were common for the first
months of the war, but the soldier's 'first disillusionment' led to the
alteration or ironic use of 'the fine phrases which had stirred his heart
into the patriotic desire to enlist'.[287] 'That's the stuff to give them' became
'that's the give to stuff them',[288] and 'Are we downhearted? No!' became
'Are we downhearted? No! Then you bloody well soon will be!'
Occasionally documented is the facetious use of unchanged catchphrases,
such as Colonel Nicholson's comment on the possibility of a truce in
1916 that could have ended the war – 'and what would mother have
said then?'[289]

The enemy or enemy actions as an object of derisive humour were
more often seen in the civilian world. This kind of humour quickly grew
from reactions to the news coming from the German invasion of Belgium,
and was generally quite aggressive. Wry comments about the war tended
to be the province of the servicemen and women, and civilian phrases
like 'Business as Usual, during European alterations' seldom outlived the
first months of the conflict.[290] More in keeping with the national mood
was a staged photograph of a German falling from an aeroplane,
illustrating how he had captured the plane and its French aviator on the
ground, forced him to take off, but was thrown out when the pilot looped
the loop; this was presented as 'Resourcefulness sometimes introduces an

element of humour into the most perilous situation.[291] The presentation of death or mutilation as humour is not typical of soldiers at the Front; the record of Tommy humour against Germans is much more verbal than visual. Under the headline 'The Green Howards' Joke':

> A racy account of the 2nd Yorkshires at the front appears in the ' Green Howards' Gazette.' The bomb throwers (says the writer) are a great adjunct to the brigade. The bombs are made out of old jam tins: and it is related how, when one Pure Plum and Apple, bearing the maker's name, had succeeded in reaching it's destination, the following plaintive remark was heard from the German trenches: 'Mein Gott, these English, these shopkeepers, how dey vos advertise!'[292]

And an 'official joke' from what is described as 'the official newsheet' of the Royal Engineers: 'Owing to the frequent adulteration of flour with sawdust in Germany, a child was born in Berlin with a wooden leg.'[293] The 2nd Division Christmas Card for 1917 shows a German soldier mistaking the Christmas star for star shells. German humour was naturally castigated as heavy-handed: under the headline 'German Humour': 'The following witticism of Jugend apparently appeals to the German, for it is widely reproduced in the Press: "The musicians at a London concert refused to play the Siegfried Idyll, by Richard Wagner. If the musicians were English they need not have hesitated to play the piece, for the audience would not have recognised it"'.[294]

A challenge to current sensibilities is the popularity of puns in the early twentieth century. From their widespread use over a range of situations it appears that puns were generally accepted – they appear frequently in trench journals, in soldiers' postcards (see 'Somme/some'), even the booklet title *Huns Ancient and Modern* is a semi-pun on *Hymns Ancient and Modern*. Some of these seem ponderous now, especially in advertising: the advertisement for Sanitas disinfecting fluid with the caption 'Did anyone say there was a GERMany anywhere?',[295] or the advertisement for Sunlight Soap with the caption 'It's the SAVON that you SAVE ON – Tommy, dear',[296] or the editorial for a trench journal that hopes 'it will be a HOOGE success',[297] Some of those in the military are a little more subtle, such as the divisional sign of a polar bear, referring to its commander's name, 'Snow', or the apocryphal pun across languages: 'A popular joke that spread like wildfire told of the cockney [NB] soldier who was about to enter a dugout in a newly captured German trench. With a Mills bomb in his hand he shouted down the dugout steps, "Anybody there?" Back came the answer, "Nein." "Nine, eh? Well bloody well share that amongst yer," and he hurled the bomb down the steps'.[298]

If puns were a knowing humour there are many documentations of incidental and accidental verbal humour; the fact of their documentation shows people putting importance on recording this as part of daily life. Adèle De L'Isle relates the story of an invalided soldier who was told to cough into a jar so that the doctor could test his sputum – he accordingly coughed into the jar, leaving nothing but air inside;[299] a soldier newly arrived in Gallipoli is asked if he knows where Oxford Circus is, and '"Rather!" I told him, proud to throw light on his ignorance, and I began to tell him, till he cut me short by snapping that he wasn't talking about London, but the trenches'.[300] Communication between people with different sociolects could always lead to confusion: Pte Davies finds himself on a charge – 'It was all along of the missus bein' took bad—'er wot I lives wiv, Sir—an' me 'oppin' it, and arsking for no leave. Of course I cops out and Colonel, 'e says, speaking very quick, "I suppose, my man," ses 'e, "I suppose you realise the gravity of wot you was doing?" Thinking as 'ow he wants to know if I sees *now* wot I done I ses, "Yessir," meaning as 'ow I sees now as I ought to 'ave put in for leave and 'opped it if leave didn't come orf. "O, you did realise it, did you?" says the ole man. "Yessir," ses I. "That makes it ten times worse," ses 'e, "twenty-eight days detention!" Corporal on p'lice tells me as 'ow I ought to 'ave sed "No, Sir!" me not realisin' nothin' at the time. But 'ow was I to know wot 'e meant?'[301]

Post-war investigations into wartime language produced their own incidental humour: *Notes and Queries'* first collection of 'English Army Slang' was made from 'contributions kindly sent in by the following members of *The Times'* staff', giving the names of 'Mr Beaumont, Mr Benest, Mr Cohen, and so on, a total of 17 names, all presented as 'Mr ...' An early entry in the glossary is 'Erb. Substitute used when a man's Christian name is unknown'.[302] A fantastic idealisation of Anzac slang appears in a glossary in the *Cairns Post* in March 1918: 'Heinie – A pen-name for the German soldier. Possibly suggested by the name of the well-known poet';[303] there was some confusion here though – 'the Canadians call their enemy Heine and not Fritz' was a comment in the *Yorkshire Evening Post*.[304] Unintentional humour in phrasebooks was inevitable given their stumbling transition from aids for tourists to well-meaning but one-directional guides for soldiers. *The Huns' Handbook*, published in 1915, as a representation with cartoons of a captured copy of *Tornister Wörterbuch Englisch* (A Knapsack English Dictionary), exploited this mercilessly with drawings of short-sighted Germans slowly reading out 'The mayor will certainly be shot', or in a shop holding up the book and asking the indignant assistant, 'Have you got socks?'[305] Seriously intentioned phrasebooks could create curious sequences of phrases presumably not recognised by the author:

I am an airman
I have an aeroplane
There goes an airship
It is ascending
It is descending
I wish to make a flight
My aeroplane is damaged
Is the engine damaged?
No, a wing is broken[306]

Phrasebooks were hampered by unfamiliarity with the reality of military procedures, by an apparent desire to use English of such formality (to avoid misunderstandings) that it looked more like English spoken by a foreigner than by a first-language speaker, and by providing little in the way of potential answers to the statements given.

Humour during wartime challenges the observer to reconcile, if such a thing is possible, the extremes of being under bombardment and the naïve silliness of some popular culture. How did men in the trenches or in rest camps react to *Comic Cuts* ('the paper that tickles our Tommies') with its spelling 'sosige', if they had seen observation balloons fall from the sky in flames? Or were such events safely distant? The name of a *Comic Cuts* 'Germ-hun' commander, Captain Stuffleheimpotsteinheinitz, is not so far from 'Karl Schnitzel-Wurzel' in the *Fifth Gloucester Gazette*,[307] or 'General von Sauerkraut and Hauptmann von Götzer' in *The B.E.F Times*,[308] but all of them contrast strongly with the actuality of 'Fritz'. Through the record of trench journals, letters, memoirs, there are continual riddles, simple jokes, comic alphabets, pastiches of the 'And then there was one' poem model, all of which display a worrying simplicity, at times almost childlike. *Made in the Trenches* gives a full page cartoon of the Chinese whisper 'Troops advance, send reinforcements'

"Whoever makes an attempt on one of my soldiers will be condemned to death."

[*Page* 10

FIGURE 2.14 One of Charles Graves's cartoons for *The Huns' Handbook* (1915).

becoming 'Going to a dance, send three and four-pence';[309] *The Fifth Gloucester Gazette* has:

Q. What is the difference between a 5th Gloucester and the Kaiser?
A. One makes Will ill, the other ill will.[310]

The Gasper[311] gives 'Over the Top':

> Sergeant Sauerkraut: You should emulate the Prussian Guard. They
>   think nothing of going over.
> Fritz: Nor do the Saxons!
> Sergeant S.: What! The Saxons go over?
> Fritz: Yes, to the enemy!
>   (Ten days No.1)

If this looks like schoolboy humour, many of those reading it in the trenches were little more than schoolboys.

Swearing and the documentation of extreme speech

When examining language phenomena during the war it is necessary to look at a huge number of terms emerging from conversation, wordplay, and dialogue with 'others', whether speaking the same language or in meetings between languages, dialects, and accents. Terms are used in situations of extreme stress and immediacy, where it is conventional to use terms which are spoken but not written.

The model of language development is generally perceived as progressing from the combat zones and the rest and administrative areas to the home areas. In this model a certain kind of language is seen as being created in the front line, seen variously as 'the most authentic', 'the real', 'the soldiers' slang', or even 'Trench Talk'. Looking at the progression of this model in terms of movement in the other direction, there is an implication that the 'most real' language would have been that used under bombardment, during combat, or, at its most extreme, at the point of killing or dying. For these we have very little documentation, too little to give any sense of what was typical, normal, or what might give any model for the people in these situations. We have indications here and there – Turkish soldiers saying 'Allah' as they died (Aubrey Herbert), dying French soldiers calling 'Maman' (Masefield), a soldier using the bayonet and shouting out training ground instructions (Graves). But we do not know what most people shouted, cried, whispered under bombardment, or while choking from gas.

In documentation, often a widely used expression might exist only as an omission – blanks or documentation that people swore. And given that our evidence largely comes from documentation that required the observation of social conventions, these words could not be written down. A letter sent to *The Athenaeum* in 1919 as part of an extensive correspondence on soldiers' slang, makes the point:

> You realise that after four years the early slang got hopelessly *démodé* towards the end of the conflict. But, as you know probably, the one word that won the war was the well-known obscenity containing four letters. From generals downwards everyone used it, and everyone was comforted by saying it. No dialogue pretending to represent military conversation ever rings quite true because this essential word is omitted. Of course, in public writings it can't be very well referred to, but only those who have soldiered out here realized what a companion in adversity that little word has been.
>
> **CLAUDE H. SISLEY**, 2nd Lt.[312]

Sisley points out that slang changed a lot during the war, and that early slang would be seen as way out of date by 1918, and that the use of 'fuck' was not limited to one class of men (and he does not specifically say that women did not use it). After the main point about the ubiquity and apparent absence in documentation of the word, Sisley observes that the expletive was also a palliative. For Brophy[313] 'most men who served in the army were coarsened in thought and speech', giving three words (fuck, cunt and bugger) which were 'uttered in every other sentence when soldiers spoke among themselves'; 'fuck' or 'fucking', like 'bloody', functioned, almost like the sound of a shell, as 'a warning that a noun was coming'. 'It became so common that an effective way to express emotion was to omit this word'; thus for greater urgency a sergeant would say 'pick up your rifles' rather than 'pick up your fucking rifles'.

So, we know that the word was used (see *Digger Dialects'* entry 'Fookers' and 'Carksuccers'), but there is little documentation to show how or when it was used, other than from rare documentations, use in fiction (implicitly corroborated by Sisley's comment), and individual observations from Brophy and Sisley etc. of frequent and widespread use at all times and across the entire military social scale. In his preface to *In Parenthesis* David Jones writes 'I have been hampered by the convention of not using impious and impolite words, because the whole shape of our discourse was conditioned by the use of such words'.[314] Away from the Front, in hospital in Bournemouth, Senior Assistant Surgeon Godbole noted that you did not hear people say 'bloody' or 'damn',[315] implying that 'bloody' and 'damn' were generally expected.

More common than records of words used are casual or obfuscated documentations of swearing happening: Charles Kendall observed of troops in London in October 1916 that 'their language may be coarse ... a finer looking lot of men I never saw';[316] Gunner Frank Spencer noted that getting the telephone wires at the Front to work required 'lavish use of the new revised and enlarged edition of the English Language';[317] 'we left behind us a trail of dust and of profane French and English'.[318] Particularly there are records that the words cannot be written down: Harry Atkin wrote in his diary on 10 September 1915 'We frequently shout to Fritz across the way but the language is not fit to record';[319] obscenity in songs was widespread – 'I couldn't in all decency repeat what came in the middle [of a song]'.[320] Being away from 'the mellowing influence of home-life and the concomitant feminine graces of womankind'[321] was one cause of the prevalence of swearing, a view supported by another observer who attributed the supposed increase in swearing at the Front to the large numbers of men together 'without the refining influence of women';[322] for this writer, though 'the soldier was always noted for his lurid language' there were 'large numbers of men [who] cannot say a dozen sentences without swear words' – a notably smaller proportion than that given by Sisley. Swearing in the trenches seemed entirely natural to a correspondent for the *Birmingham Daily Post*: 'profanity seems natural here, for the bullets are profane little things, and swear at you as they pass'.[323] Cursing under shellfire was common, and Cpl Mitchell noted: 'Some men crouched in the crowded boat ... while others cursed with ferocious delight'.[324]

Swearing was of course not unnatural to a vast number of men in the new armies: their home and work background was transferred to the Front – *The Times* reported a discharged soldier who in court stated that 'he had heard some swearing in the army, but his wife's language "took the biscuit"'.[325] Capt A. Lloyd of the Church Army noted that the pre-war army swore less than the men of the new armies, bringing their language habits with them; he had heard 'far worse language in the Lancashire mills than I ever heard in the barrack-room'. For him, the language of swearing was changing: 'if you want to hear some really hard selected swearing, full of new oaths, you should go to the University cadet battalions'.[326] He also noted that swearing in the Navy was 'quite as terrible' but 'not so interesting' as swearing in the army. One of the profoundest changes in language during the war was in the prevalence of swearing among those who had previously avoided it, as learning to swear, for those who did not, was seen as necessary both for social acceptance, and pragmatically as a means of coping: 'The majority . . . acquired the habit of using obscene and blasphemous expletives . . '.[327] One battalion padre recognised his charges by their language – 'I couldn't see you but I knew where you were from the language that was coming up. I knew it was the Church Lads Brigade and I've never heard anything like it in all my life'.[328]

Indeed for many swearing was seen as essential to army life – 'if a man doesn't swear when he's in the Service there must be something the matter with him',[329] and the standard simile for swearing, 'to swear like a trooper', had been in use for a century. A short story in *Made in the Trenches* has an officer 'burst into a torrent of swearing'; when his companion complains he says 'Time was when I was a nice-mannered person in a quite respectable business house. I suppose that must have been about a hundred and fifty years ago. Since then I have learned the art of vocal expression as constructed for military usage. Everybody does it'.[330] One of Graves's 'very Welsh Welshmen, who had an imperfect command of English' nevertheless had managed to pick up the expression 'bloody bastard'.[331] Coningsby Dawson in *Living Bayonets* tells the story of a soldier's progress from a weak link to hero involving learning to swear,[332] and in this sense swearing was part of being a soldier, or rather, because of its ubiquity, part of the uniformity of being a soldier; Tim Cook notes one Canadian soldier's comment on how slang was 'pass[ed] along from unit to unit',[333] an act of uniformity, and that opting out meant removing oneself from the soldiery. Similarly young Canadian soldiers taught themselves to swear excessively to prove their identity as soldiers.[334]

Yet there were many for whom this was a problem, either because they had come from homes where swearing was not the norm, or where religious observance condemned swearing, or because swearing exacerbated class awareness and discomfort; in many cases these were combined. Tim Cook quotes a Canadian mule-driver who was 'amazed at the cursing' when his own language seldom exceeded 'damn' or 'darn'.[335] Any problems attendant on men of different social classes mixing, problems which in the British Army the setting up of the Pals Battalions had to some extent bypassed, were revived by swearing, which strongly declared class difference. Just as 'bloody' had become a class marker,[336] swearing of any kind carried connotations of class, and of place. Charles Douie remarks on 'two very old soldiers, whose home address was well east of Aldgate Pump, addressing the German army in familiar, if deplorable language.[337] Coningsby Dawson by August 1918, having previously shown an interest in the language of his fellow-soldiers, was describing them as 'coarse men, foul-mouthed men'.[338] Plymouth Brethren member Donald McNair's letters home referred to a 'most respectable looking young man' whose 'torrent of pure and unadulterated swearing, punctuated with incessant blasphemies, was unique'; later he had to share living space with four men who were 'utterly low-class and foul-mouthed louts – I certainly have nothing in common with them, and find it difficult to put up with their wantonly pointless, witless and filthy conversation'.[339]

As soon as men re-entered the company of women adjustments were made; Emma Duffin reported that one of her charges 'used the 'Pygmalion' word to me' (bloody), but she made him apologise.[340] One young woman had to learn three words in Chinese to send away men from the CLC who were prohibited from making purchases in the YMCA canteen where she served in France; though told that the words were 'the most frightful swearing', she never found out their meaning, but continued to use them to effect.[341]

Though some officers used foul language, swearing was seen as the attribute of the men – William James Newton remembered swearing at an officer during a football match at the Front in 1915, and feeling that it was essential to apologise afterwards.[342] Officers turned a blind eye, or indulged in mild or occasional swearing: 'a few lusty curses delivered when things looked bad would often have a steadying effect'.[343] Some chaplains attempted to clean up soldiers' language at the Front, and they were not alone. Douglas Haig was very disapproving of obscene language, and on one occasion reprimanded a colonel who had not only let his men on the march sing a very bawdy song, but had joined in himself.[344] At the other end of the scale a number of people were shocked at the supposed profanity of some of the songs performed at a camp concert in Essex in September 1916; a Mrs Sargent was 'of the opinion that soldiers' ears should not be wounded by such expressions', the term in question being 'bloke'.[345] These extremes aside, there are even in trench journals expressions of disapproval of swearing, some tongue in cheek, such as in the trench journal *Carry On: The Trotters' Journal*, where one of the things that are specified as needing a 'pull-through' (with a piece of cleaning rag) is 'Company Sergt.-Major Flannery's language'.[346] But these are nevertheless indicative of something people would recognise:

C.O. 'You say the Sergeant used foul language to you?'
Recruit 'Yes, sir (with a blush), he called me a-er *ruddy* fool.'
C.O. (reflectively) 'A *ruddy* fool, eh! – and you didn't like it?'
Recruit 'No, sir, I certainly did not.'[347]

For some the reaction was strong: 'to think that young striplings of sergeants and corporals should use the foulest of language to men in the execution of duty was utterly appalling to me';[348] while for others it was just tiresome: 'one got so very wearied of hearing everything being described as f-cking this and f-cking that, the very word, with its original indecent meaning, being at length a mere stupid and meaningless vulgarity.'[349] Some of those who had become accustomed to swearing tired of it: Robert Graves, dealing with discipline infringements by soldiers in camp, noted that the 'obscene language, always quoted verbatim, continued drearily the same.'[350] Or swearing failed to do the job it was supposed to do: 'I fell into the frozen shell-holes three or four times, and soon exhausted all the swear words I ever heard, and was reduced to vulgar blasphemy';[351] Charles Douie describes a 'nightmare march' at the end of which the men are 'almost too tired to swear', and in speaking to their guide he uses 'language which was excusable only in the circumstances'; but the guide has 'developed an absolute indifference to popular opinion.'[352]

'Fuck' and 'fucking' made the most impact on those who observed soldiers' language, probably because of the disparity between their extensive use at the Front and the limited exposure to them of many people away from the Front; John Brophy, writing 'After Fifty Years' as an introduction to the 1969 edition of *The Long Trail – Soldiers' Songs and Slang 1914–18*, felt he could restore many other words to the texts of soldiers' songs – arse, balls, ballocks (sic), piss and shit, and also bugger, but not yet 'fuck' and 'cunt' which he 'jibbed at';[353] Robert Graves notes the early gas helmet's name 'goggle-eyed booger with the tit',[354] the 100th Brigade were known as 'the black-buttoned bastards',[355] and David Jones in *In Parenthesis* has 'that shit major Lillywhite', and 'bastards' applied to shell-splinters.[356]

The majority of swearing was mild and might even then have passed as little more than a marker of class. 'Blooming', 'blinking', 'ruddy', 'bloody well', 'gorblimey', even occasionally 'bugger' appear in letters, postcards, memoirs and recorded dramatisations.[357] Pte S. Fraser used the expression 'silly buggers',[358] and Lt C. Greaves described the first day of the German advance in March 1918 as 'a bugger',[359] but these may be post-war interviews or texts; it is noticeable that Graves spelled it 'booger', 'bugger' still being of doubtful legality. 'Lumme' and 'blimey' become standard indicators of soldier speech, emphasising the prevalence of cockney, and, as an indicator of how war changed the language, there was discussion as to whether 'damn' and 'bloody' were swearwords at all. Holmes in *A Yankee in the Trenches* gives a glossary which includes 'bloody', which 'is vaguely supposed to be highly obscene, though just why nobody seems to know';[360] The *Daily Mirror* gossip writer in November 1917 remarked that 'Brigadier-General Elles' picturesque use of "damn", in his signal to his tank commanders, has made the word popular. Yesterday we had Lord Rhondda saying about the Huns that "we would give them a damned good lesson before the finish". The word is, I believe, banned on most music-hall stages, but with such fresh examples of its forcefulness the ban may be lifted'.[361] Comparison between the popular and provincial press of 1911 and that of 1919 shows a more than doubling of the use of 'blimey'.[362]

Casual swearing is documented in a range of ways, none of which show swearing to be anything other than natural: in 'With the Bombardiers' in *Made in the Trenches*, if water drips down a man's neck he 'will immediately swear, straighten his back, bump his head, swear again',[363] 'Blimy' is the caption for a drawing of a soldier ducking to avoid a hand grenade;[364] 'you find yourself in a shell hole, knee deep in mud and water, sprawling about against the slimy sides. Several swear words follow'.[365] Graves reports a conversation between a stretcher bearer and a Welsh soldier in his regiment: '"Who's the poor bastard, Dai?" … "Sergeant Gallagher … silly booger aims too low … it breaks his silly f-ing jaw …"'; the soldier also swears in Welsh, using 'Deoul' ('the Devil'), a comparatively mild term.[366]

Apart from the obvious use of dashes, e.g. E. H. J. in a letter to *The Athenaeum*[367] – 'There is a very queer phrase denoting "nothing" – "- all!" No record of war slang is complete without it' – the printed dash records awareness that swearwords cannot be printed, and that swearwords were used, and, depending on the audience, that the reader knows the likely word being alluded to. Thus *The White Band* gives 'Australia's War Song',[368] with a very good cartoon of a grinning soldier; the first two lines set the rhythm – 'Fellers of Australia, Blokes an' coves an' coots', which set up the chorus:

> Get a ---- move on.
> Have some ---- sense;
> Learn the ---- art of
> Self-de ---- fence.

Apart from dashes, there were several ways of avoiding swearing while making it clear that it was only the form of swearing that was being avoided. Graves records the use of obscene language by a soldier called Boy Jones, in 1917; the offended bandmaster, described as 'squeamish' reported it as: 'Sir, he called me a double effing c–'.[369] David Jones writes 'you use the efficacious word, to ease frustration'[370] – and the first part of 'efficacious' shows clearly what he is referring to; Brophy and Partridge list 'blurry' as a common euphemism for 'bloody';[371] a cigarette advertisement in *Punch* uses p-d-q,[372] while H. M. Denham at the Dardanelles refers to a coxswain as 'a young b.f.';[373] the still current 'effing and blinding' is used by Lance-Sergeant J. L. Bouch, probably in a post-war interview;[374] and *In the Hands of the Huns* substitutes *verfluchter* for 'damned'.[375]

It was not all a dreary procession of 'fucking bloody bastard' (Coppard stated that 'the enemy were always "bloody bastards"'[376]), though this clearly served a useful role in giving form to the expression of despair in the trenches. There was humour and invention, such as the postcard showing a man in court saying to the judge 'he called me German and used other filthy language', reputedly an actual event. Coppard noted that 'after a particularly foul and original sentence [a pent-up bloke's] face would beam at the cheers which acclaimed his efforts'.[377] And some of the local place names supplied combinations of syllables that called out to be used: Fraser and Gibbons noted particularly that Krakenhohe, a German town passed by after the Armistice, was 'adopted' as a convenient swearword. There is evidence for soldiers from Canada feeling that their swearing was superior to British swearing: 'the Canadian swears more. His language is richer and more original . . . [English swearing] . . . is hackneyed and lacking in ideas. He swears with a sort of apology in his voice, whereas the Canadian is conscious that he is inventing phrases which are his own, so he has a pride in his own language. . . . This originality tends to make him a more dangerous opponent'.[378]

Soldiers' casual swearing or swearing at the situation or the enemy was deemed more or less acceptable by the end of the war – 'the cussed Huns have got my gramophone' was fine in May 1918 for an advertisement in *Punch*.[379] At the unveiling of the war memorial at Stainforth Capt Tyas told the audience that 'a man who could swear and let out his feelings was a much better soldier than a sulky man', and that he 'did not care whether a man died swearing or not'.[380] The extent, nature and impact of

FIGURE 2.15 Postcard sent in February 1916.

swearing might be judged by the traces it left on the local population, for which we have little long-term evidence. Inevitably there were cases of men teaching the locals swearwords they did not understand the import of, and delighting in hearing them with foreign accents: 'I think the French girls who repeated and threw back at the men all the bad language they heard had little notion what it all meant.'[381] Van Welleghem thought that British soldiers were saying 'Fake Belgium',[382] but one French woman picked up nothing more harmful than 'you damn fool';[383] if this was indicative of how soldiers swore at civilians, they appear to have been as capable of controlling their speech as they were of censoring their postcards home. R. H. Mottram gives a picture of British troops behaving in a way that appears the polar opposite of the effing and blinding Tommy: 'How often have I not seen twenty or thirty of them packed into some little Flemish kitchen, treating the peasant women with elaborate Sunday-school politeness, ... tittering slightly at anything not quite nice, and singing, not so often the vulgar music-hall numbers, as the more sentimental "Christmas successes" from the pantomimes'.[384] Soldiers, as we all do, were able to temper their language and behaviour to the circumstances. On these grounds we should consider that self-censoring of swearing applied to memoirs was an authentic aspect of the language of the war.

Transcribing the sound of war

The cliché of the sound of the guns at the Somme being heard from Blackheath, in south-east London, masks the reality that artillery fire at the Western Front could be heard from the south-east coast of England for most of the war, and, with the right meteorological conditions, from much further away. Andrew Clark noted in his diary on 17 July 1918 that bombs in Flanders could be heard at Brooklands, ten miles from the coast, near Chelmsford in Essex, when the tide was at its lowest.[385] The closer to France, the louder and clearer the noise could be heard: Graves writes of Sassoon, 'Down in Kent he could hear the guns thudding ceaselessly across the Channel, on and on . . .'.[386] Florence Billington noted that from England you could not only 'hear the guns firing, . . . if you were out in the dark you could see the flashes over in France, of the actual war going on',[387] and in France away from the Front 'the reports from all the guns mingled in a curious oppressive rumble'.[388] Reports in 1915 stated that guns could be heard from the Yser Front in Amsterdam, across the entire breadth of Belgium.[389]

For some soldiers the noise at the Front was constant: in a 1971 interview for *The Listener* Robert Graves stated that 'noise never stopped for one moment – ever'. Lancelot Spicer wrote in a letter: 'For the past 10 days or so we have been living in a small cottage less than a mile from the Boche front line. And yet at times it has been so quiet that one could almost believe one was back in England, say in Sussex. At other times the guns make such a row you can barely hear yourself speak. At night sometimes it is absolutely quiet, at other times you can hear nothing but the pop-pop-pop-pop of the machine guns'.[390] Vivian Stevens wrote to his parents on 3 April 1916 of 'pure country air & surroundings & it is so peaceful & quiet with the farmers ploughing spoilt by the noise of guns in the nights'.[391] In contrast Charles Douie described how on the first day of the Battle of the Somme 'the thunder of our barrage was such that orders could not be heard',[392] while Neil Tytler wrote that 'Every order to the guns has to be written on slips of paper, it being absolutely impossible to make anyone hear the spoken word'.[393] Amongst this mayhem and the 'roar of falling buildings'[394] and while 'being continually shelled by the enemy'[395] soldiers noticed birdsong, and the noise of insects.[396]

The loudest noise was that of the heavy artillery, sometimes miles behind the the front line, description of this including similes and imitative words. Thunder features heavily, 'the ceaseless thunder of the guns',[397] 'the guns thundered',[398] 'our own guns thundered overhead';[399] Graves records one of his comrades saying 'where the gunder ended and the thunder began was hard to say'.[400] Guns also roared – 'the roar of guns audible for hours',[401] and sometimes these similes overlapped with imitative descriptions: 'the sudden whoop and roar of battery fire'.[402] Imitative words include 'an occasional loud boom',[403] guns 'banged away like mad',[404] Masefield's 'bong of a big gun',[405] or the 'continual banging' Harold Watts wanted to get away from, in a letter dated June 1916. The continuous noise of artillery is often referred to: 'the boom, boom, boom of the guns continually carry on'.[406] For some commentators the sound was beyond description: 'many veterans said that no one could capture the sound of a massive bombardment'.[407] The continuity of the environment of noise is seen in the use of the same words to describe the sound of the gun and the sound of the explosion, both sent and received. Masefield gives 'the roar of a shell bursting far off',[408] while Lt W. Carr described a German bombardment as 'the loudest clap of thunder you have ever heard'.[409]

From mid-1916 massive bombardments were employed to destroy morale as much as flesh, a strategy maintained through the rest of the war. As the shells exploded in the air or on or below ground they caused 'shakings and concussions',[410] a 'noise, incessant and almost musical, so intense that it seemed as if a hundred devils were hammering in my brain';[411] 2nd Lt A. Lamb wrote 'the din is terrific',[412] which could at that time mean 'great', 'very good', or 'terrifying', or all three. The soundscape of the Front seems so extreme and disconcerting that it is a wonder men were able to function, let alone manage the perception of noise, but George Coppard wrote that 'several times I noted the similarity of sound when bullets found their mark in the head'.[413] Men in the trenches, while being subjected to some of the loudest noise, were supposed to make as little noise as possible, in order both not to give evidence of a gathering of troops and to hear the tiniest noise that would signal a raid or the release of gas – Graves describes 'sorting out all the different explosions' and picking out 'at once the faint plop! of the mortar that sends off a sausage'.[414] David Jones notes the banning of cowsons (ear-muffs) because it was so essential to be able to hear,[415] but high-velocity shells gave no warning and were called 'stocking footers'.[416] Fears were exemplified by the rumour reported in the *Manchester Evening News* 1 December 1914 that the Germans were developing a 'silent gun', working on pneumatic, electric or silencer principles; and Canadian soldiers at the Somme faced a shell which they named 'Silent Percy'.[417] Even at a distance from the front line soldiers were reminded of what they had faced or would face: 'the hoomp! of distant shrapnel bursts'.[418] Distant sounds like the 'distant drone of the Gnome engine'[419] and the 'hum of aeroplanes'[420] might signal assault from the air, while at any moment there might be the sound of a new weapon, the hiss of a gas-grenade or the 'chunk, chunk, chunk, chunk' of a tank.[421]

Most people got through it: 'The noise is terrific, but one gets used to it' wrote Lt B. Willmott, 2nd Essex Regt.[422] Graves eventually managed to sleep through it,[423] and others seemed to find it an annoyance more than anything else – George Williams' diary for 6 April 1916 has 'Heavy Bombardment by our Artillery 9–10pm awful row'.[424] Others did not; temporary or permanent deafness was a standard symptom of manning a gun, or even passing by one being fired: 'the main impact of an 18-pounder gun firing is the compression of the shell leaving the muzzle as it goes forward. When you were in front of the guns, you got into that compression'.[425] Aubrey Smith records that he was deaf for two hours after being near a gun firing,[426] an officer reported 'a continuous din that was deafening',[427] Pte Stanley Woodhouse during a period of a night strafe reported that 'the noise was simply deafening',[428] while *The Army and Navy Magazine* 15 May 1915 reported on 'naval "gun-deafness"'. The same magazine a week earlier stated that the noise from guns was 'nerve-shattering', while 'Wagger' in *Battery Flashes* wrote of a soldier going 'dotty with noise'.[429] Though it depends on the need for a rhyme, there is a strong truth in the soldiers' song:

We are the boys who fear no noise
When the thundering cannons roar[430]

It was essential for people to be able to read noise. Noise was information, especially the noise of the shell in flight; instantaneous recognition allowed a decision to be taken on the direction to throw oneself, or whether not to bother. 'We know by the singing of a shell when it is going to drop near us, when it is politic to duck and when one may treat the sound with contempt'.[431] Graves's sergeant advises his men 'Listen by the noise they make where they're going to burst'.[432] Edmonds indicates how essential this was: 'another shell came, giving the least of warnings. It burst before us after so short a roar of coming that the brain had no time to appreciate it'.[433]

Discussion of the transcription of projectile sounds involves looking at descriptive, onomatopoeic and metaphorical terms. Some descriptions of sounds verbalise the chaos of shelling – Henry Williamson's use of 'Flash-flash-WOMP-WOMP' and later 'Whizz, Wang, Zip. Crack. Jagged splinters' and 'Zzzzzzuzz-CRASH'[434] create a soundscape of the combat zone highlighted by clearly intelligible details. The soundscape is made up of the 'pop-pop of rifle fire' and the 'swish and moan of the shells',[435] the crump of explosions and 'continual "plonks"'.[436] The gap between the simplistic nature of the noise-words and the actuality of topographic, materiel and human destruction can be challenging, but apparently simple names can be informative. The simple-sounding 'whizz-bang' for example tells us a basic fact about the nature of the shell's speed: 'Whizz-bangs were a torment to us. They travelled faster than sound. If you happened to be near the receiving end, you first heard the thing burst, then the whizz of its approach and lastly the boom of the gun that fired it'.[437] But this scientific observation was not universal: 'Its name derives from the fact that the noise it makes is a whiz, followed at once by the report of the burst',[438] or 'Whizz-bangs are small shells, that don't give you time to say Jack Robinson. All you hear is a whizz and a bang' wrote Pte J. Bowles.[439] The name was not universal, one report using the term 'fiz-bang'.[440] The description of 'The Johnsons' in the *Wipers Times* for 12 February 1916 – 'A Shout. A Scream. A Roar' – tells us equally that the sound of the shell in flight would be heard after it landed.

Soldiers regularly give evidence of their awareness of the distinct noises made by different projectiles: relating the story of an attack, a soldier writes 'amidst it all the rifles and the machine guns made their peculiar noise'.[441] The sound of bullets always fascinated, the marker of 'one to one' combat: bullets 'whine',[442] they 'piped and moaned',[443] 'some whine plaintively, some shriek overhead, and some have an almost vicious hiss',[444] but the soldier is warned that 'only the bullet that goes by makes any noise': 'the pellet with your name and number inscribed on it is not giving any warning of its approach';[445] as bullets travelled faster than the speed of sound over the short distances of no man's land a soldier heard only the displacement of air caused by the passing of the bullet, not the one coming towards him, hence the interest in transcribing the sound that effectively meant a temporary reprieve from injury or death – 'occasionally machine-gun bullets whizzed over us'.[446] LCpl E. Edwards, sceptical of the 'bullet with your name on it' legend this produced, contributed to the *Yorkshire Evening Post* an article in which he details three different kinds of bullets and the noises they make: 'the ordinary commonplace bullet … is quite a decent noise, more like a swift-flying bee', the 'reversed bullet … makes a rich hum like a whistling rocket', and the 'explosive bullet makes an ear-tingling crack as it whizzes by, which makes one deaf for the time'.[447] Bullets otherwise are described as 'pinging and hissing',[448] 'phitting'[449] or making the sound 'zip'.[450] They ricochet with the sound transcribed as 'ping',[451] or land as 'patter'[452] or, for the bullet which hit him, 'pf-ung';[453] sometimes the sound is described as 'plonk',[454] or 'the plink-plonk of a bullet'.[455] A report in the *Marlborough Express* described the noise as the 'Zip-zip, hissing and cracking of bullets' followed by 'plonk – only a Hun bullet which has buried itself'.[456] Pte Leslie Sanders described bullets as going '"crack-plud!" as they bury themselves in a parapet'.[457]

Rifle fire was characterised as the established 'rattle of musketry',[458] the 'rattle of rifles',[459] 'the incessant rattle and crack of rapid, heavy fire'.[460] Rifle fire and machine-gun fire may be described together as a 'rattle' or 'crackle'[461] – 'rattle' was also the sound of the Lewis gun,[462] as well as 'poppity-pop-pop-pop'.[463] Individual rifle firing is often the innocuous-sounding '"poop" of a rifle'[464] or 'popping of rifles',[465] which extends into the 'pop-pop-pop-pop' noted by Spicer.[466] A wider range of terms were used for machine-guns, 'tap-tap-tap-tap-tap',[467] 'Tap! Tap-tap!',[468] 'phut-phut-phut',[469] 'the chattering of our machine-guns nearby',[470] 'pitter-patter' from a distance ('the sound was unmistakable'),[471] 'far-away racketing'.[472] Identification by sound was possible: 'A machine-gun was firing. Sergeant Jackson said, "It's all right it's one of ours", but I had my doubts. A Maxim sounds *ta-ta-ta-ta*, but a Nordonfeldt sounds *tut-tut-tut-tut*'.[473] Given the imitative nature of these sounds it is no surprise that French and German transcriptions of machine-guns are similar: Apollinaire transcribes machine-guns as 'ca ta clac' 6 October 1915,[474] Masefield gives the sound of the mitrailleuse as 'tick, tick, tick',[475] and Grimm gives 'taktaktaktak'.[476] In a mix of visual and aural description the traversing action of the machine-gun is recorded in 'the occasional "Swish! Swish! Shish!" of the bullets as it swung round in our direction'[477] and 'that sissing noise'.[478]

Shells in flight needed to be identified quickly, the different shapes and velocities giving different sounds. Oil-drums, packed with explosives and scrap-metal 'hummed',[479] bursting shells 'throbbed',[480] or 'whizzed'.[481] The terms used often give a strong picture of the level of threat: Charles Edmonds was near one that fell with 'a low sibilant roar',[482] while there was less danger from 'a few shells whistling over our heads' wrote Henry in a postcard home from Gallipoli.[483] Distance and danger may explain the wide range between shells 'sighing',[484] or 'like the wind through telegraph wires'[485] and 'screaming'[486] or 'screeching'.[487] 'Pussy cats' was the name given to empty shell cases falling,[488] less aggressive but still capable of doing great harm. Sometimes shells were described as landing with a 'plonk': 'All of a sudden I heard a sissing noise over my head . . . it was a shell about to drop. Plonk! It lands just beyond'.[489] The sound of the close explosion of a shell was usually transcribed as 'bang': 'The scream and bang of an occasional shrapnel' is described in a report from Gallipoli,[490] while LCpl Edwards reports 'bang' as the noise of a shell in a trench. Midshipman N. K. Calder describes in his diary the explosion that sank HMS Vanguard as 'a hell of a bang' (9 July 1917).[491] 'A wounded soldier' reported his experience of battle as 'a terrific bang – and then a nurse asked me to "sit up and drink this"'.[492]

Charles Edmonds' description of the noise of gas shells, even a dozen years on, is indicative of the heightened awareness necessary for survival: 'Flutter, Flutter, Crump! Came the shells. Whirra, Whirra, Phut!' compared to a high-velocity shell 'Whoo-Whoo-Whoo-WHOO-CRASH!'[493] The distinction was important in terms of the instantaneous protection needed. The liquid in gas shells made them easy to recognise by sound, 'hooting' or 'twittering',[494] but their landing was often barely audible. Larger shells usually gave some warning of their approach and their descriptions show a passage of time. The 'coal-box' 'whines through the air like a drowsy fly' followed by 'an ear-splitting roar',[495] or comes 'screaming and tearing up the field';[496] a similar description, 'shells ploughed up the field with a great roar', comes from Pte Thomas Lyon in 1915.[497] One of the most frequently used descriptions was 'crump', a clear description of the explosion slightly muffled by soil. A glossary published in the *Derry Journal* defines the 'crump' as 'a German five-point-zero shell',[498] but the term was used to describe both shell, sound and explosion: 'a heavy crump burst on a knoll close by',[499] 'a resonant "crump" louder and more obvious, transmitted by the air',[500] and probably other shells: 'a big crump has burst within 6ft of me, blinded me with the flash of its explosion, and scorched my flesh with the hot gases emitted',[501] and a 'heavier crash, as some large "crump" was imported'.[502] The description of splinters and fragments of hot metal convey a sense of violence as well as sound: they 'hiss'[503] or 'shriek'.[504] Aubrey Smith at the Second Battle of Ypres described a 'crashing shrapnel barrage over our heads',[505] while Charles Foxcroft in the poem 'Travail' gives 'swish' as the sound of shrapnel.[506]

Smaller shells were given rather dismissive names – though 'pipsqueak' described the report and flight of the shell;[507] Wainwright Merrill gives the sound of a pipsqueak as 'plunk-whiz-boom' – the sound of firing, flight and landing,[508] while the Australians, dismissive of most things, described a Stokes shell as a 'mouth-organ' because of the noise made by air passing through the holes in the base of the shell.[509] Very lights 'whished'[510] and lighter shells 'whispered'.[511] Trench mortars seem to have made variable noises: LCpl Edwards describes an 'almost silent hum', they 'give no warning but just go zip-bang!',[512] they 'whinney'[513] or give a 'raucous screech',[514] or, for at least one German, a soft sound – '*das leise Schsch*'.[515] 'Duds', and more rarely 'blinds' (given as 'the technical adjective for a "dud" shell')[516] had been around for a long time, but it was still proposed by A.H.B. in correspondence in *The Athenaeum* (1 August 1919) that 'no one who has once heard a "dud" fall can have any doubt of the onomatopoeic origin of the word'. Though evidence shows an earlier origin, it may be that onomatopoeia in the period 1914 to 1918 strengthened the word's popularity. It is not hard to see how onomatopoeia would carry the sounds of war across into metaphor and literary expression. Often description of combat drifts into expected metaphors – 'a battery of guns on the right sang out',[517] or 'death whining and screaming'[518] but there are surprises such as George Barker's 'I try to run but my limbs are like lead. Plonk za! A near shave that time' from *Agony's Anguish* self-published in 1931, which, like Henry Williamson's descriptions, seems more futurist or Dada than war memoir. Continuous artillery fire was described as *Trommelfeuer* in German, translated and used in English as 'drumfire', and carrying an impression of the hearer being inside the drum. While the 'heavies' roared, other weapons were likened to animals, especially dogs: a VAD notes 'the barking of the "Ack Ack"',[519] Aubrey Smith notes the 'bark of our 18-pounder',[520] and a caption to *The Battle of the Somme* (1916) has 'The vicious bark of the Canadian 60 pounders'. A more dismissive approach is shown by Neil Tytler: 'the disgusting noise of the Archies yapping like a pack of toy Sipperkes'.[521] In this animal simile scenario Edmonds describes the flight of a gas shell as like a hit partridge[522] and the machine-gun inevitably becomes a woodpecker.[523] German writers favoured animal similes: Hans Grimm's eponymous Schlump (1929) sees a shell explode – the fragments 'hissed through the air like a thousand cats, some wailing and howling like cursed souls'.[524] The poet August Stramm likened the 'howling of the heavy shells' to the sounds of wild beasts. Somehow in this industrialised war that destroyed land and trees, nature not only appeared to assert itself but even to mock the proceedings. 'T.H.H.' wrote to *The Times* quoting a letter from his son 'somewhere in France'; the sound of shells falling close by was heard, but with no explosion, which was disconcerting. It turned out that the noise was coming from chickens who had begun to imitate the sounds of the Front.[525]

In the bewildering world of the Front soldiers grasped for sounds they knew; just as the metaphor of the machine-gun as office machine tells us about the environment of the citizen-soldier, so descriptions of shells passing tell us about the world back home.

Often machine-guns were likened to typewriters,[526] a sound image which transferred back to the offices of Britain in an extraordinary advertisement for Burroughs Adding machines showing a woman firing a machine-gun from an office desk.[527] This was extended to other office equipment, such as Kalamazoo Loose leaf Account Books, who advertised with the line 'What the Machine Gun is to an Army the Kalamazoo is to an office – it holds the line with fewer men'.[528] In the bewildering world of the Front soldiers grasped for sounds they knew; just as the metaphor of the machine-gun as office machine tells us about the environment of the citizen-soldier, so descriptions of shells passing tell us about the world back home. Specifically high-passing or fast shells were frequently likened to trains and trams. Brophy and Partridge document the name 'tube train' for 'a heavy shell passing well above with a rumble',[529] a rather contradictory metaphor, while less benign shells were compared to express trains: a shell from a long-range gun 'shrieked past like an express train',[530] the 'Ypres Express'[531] or, a local reference for the Leinster Regiment, the Roscrea Express.[532] Americans preferred the terms 'street-car' and 'trolley-car'[533] for non-threatening shells passing high overhead, and 'freight cars' or 'freight trains' for the shells that concerned them more.[534] In flight the largest shells sounded like 'huge traction engines running through the air',[535] or 'a tramcar turning round a corner'.[536]

Given the extent, complexity and range of noise caused by the combat one word sufficed for absence of killing: quiet.

Killing, dying, and the destruction of the body

The core experience of the war, fighting, was couched in terms that both communicate and obfuscate. 'We are fairly amongst the fighting now' wrote a soldier in the Mediterranean Expeditionary Force to his family in Manchester,[537] and 'have had a cut at them this time' wrote Guardsman Boorer in October 1914.[538] At times combat could not be hidden or sanitised, and was described in terms of fury, rage, a total loss of control; 'Seeing the wounded getting cut at by the German officers, the Scots Greys went mad'.[539] Such behaviour was seen in the same terms as 'atrocities', which were, in the press, usually couched in terms of the animal or the loss of civilisation, the German perpetrators being described as 'uncaged beasts', 'pitiless brutes' acting with 'unbridled savagery' and 'disgusting brutality'.[540] Killing prisoners, by either side, though not described as an atrocity, carried the same associations: following the news of the German naval bombardment of British east coast towns 2nd Lt Arthur Stanley-Clarke wrote 'we mean to take it out of the Germans the first opportunity we get and I am afraid the toll of prisoners will be small as the men are a bit savage';[541] Robert MacLeod wrote 'Gas shell attack 5 to 6 a.m. Made me wild. Don't want to take prisoners after this'.[542] Or a terrifying pragmatism might take over: Coningsby Dawson describes a 'chap here who's typical of this spirit of treating war as an immensely sporting event . . . a short while ago he . . . captured three Germans; on the return journey across No Man's Land something happened, and he lined up his prisoners and shot them'.[543] Though Lancelot Spicer wrote that 'they always say the further away from the front line that you get the more warlike you become',[544] retaliation changed men's minds. There were many processes at work which facilitated the business of killing: the great range of many of the guns, the impersonalised killing nature of gas and mines, the depersonalising of men by blind discipline, or by uniform naming as 'Fritz' or 'Tommy',[545] or by describing men as 'rifles' or 'bayonets'. The death of comrades sparked a desire for revenge, though this conflicted with notions of sportsmanship; revenge was seen as 'a state of mind very dear to the Teuton',[546] and thus un-English. However, the record shows frequent instances of revenge as an expressed motive; considering the Zeppelin raids on Britain, *The Gasper* editorial for 28 February 1916 realised that retaliation in kind would 'give to the Germans the very victory that we mean to win', but equally felt that too much scrupulousness in not using weapons considered as unacceptable put British soldiers under greater pressure. The writer felt that 'we, who have to pay the price of this pusillanimous scrupulousness, are not quite so particular as to how we do it'. John Masefield, seeing at first hand the effect of gas and flame-throwers, wished for an escalation of weapons: 'let her [America] invent the damnable & bloody machines that she alone can invent, & then let her make them by the hundred thousand, & let them be deadlier than hell . . .'.[547] Charles Douie's 'anger and bitterness . . . against those who had wrought this destruction' were so great that even 11 years on his anger 'could find no expression in words'.[548] Capt Charlie May's diary records his reaction to the loss of a comrade: 'We all feel wild to get at the beast and hope we may string him up on the wire . . . one day we'll get at him with the bayonet. We'll take our price then for Gresty and all the other hundred thousand Grestys slain as they were standing at their posts'.[549] Though in the early part of the war gas had been seen as 'such a filthy form of fighting',[550] pragmatism led to its adoption, though a comparable pragmatism allowed the retention of moral superiority by referring to it as 'the accessory', 'bottles', 'rogers', 'rats', 'mice', and 'jackets'. Lancelot Spicer acknowledged that 'retaliation is strong', and shrugged it off with 'mais c'est la guerre'.[551]

On the other hand, there are plenty of references to a fellow feeling with someone who was doing the same job, but for a different commander. Arthur West wrote 'for the Hun I feel nothing but a spirit of amiable fraternity that the poor man has to sit just like us and do all the horrible and useless things that we do',[552] and typical of a 'quiet sector' was that described by Edward Shears: 'We discovered, to-day, what strangely friendly relations prevailed in our part of the line. Neither side was very securely entrenched, and the infantry on both had adopted the principle of "Live, and let live."'[553] Compassion was by no means rare: 'I know of several instances wherein our wounded have been treated kindly by the Turks' – Pte Hough described this in sporting terms as 'they have done nothing offside';[554] in January 1919 a Royal Army Medical Corps officer recalled a German observation balloon officer directing British stretcher-bearers in no man's land, offering the comment 'there are one or two decent Huns'.[555]

Generally conversation in the trenches under a bombardment was pointless, as nothing could be heard; Brophy claimed that the troops sang little or not at all in the line or on the way there.[556] A. M. Burrage remembered that under shelling he crouched, moaning 'Oh, Christ, make it stop! Oh, Jesus, make it stop! It *must* stop because I can't bear it any more! I can't bear it!'[557] Metaphorically artillery might talk, but this was very much journalese.[558] The result of shelling was one of the most difficult experiences to suffer and to express: for Arthur West 'seven men killed by a shell as soon as we got in the trench: beastly sight!'[559]

Between periods of watching, waiting and being shelled were raids and hand-to-hand fighting; Aubrey Smith described fighting as a 'chimozzle' or a 'scrap',[560] though a 'shemozzle' was also an attempted raid that turned into a mess.[561] Being wounded in a fight meant the possibility of being carried back to safety, and even to Blighty if the wound was 'a Blighty' or 'a Blighty one':[562] 'really one gets almost to hope for a gentle wound', wrote Lancelot Spicer.[563] But also there was the chance of lying for days in no man's land: Pte H. Baverstock was hit above the knee and lay waiting to die, but two stretcher-bearers reached him, giving him the opportunity to observe his wound, remembered as 'a gaping hole with a terrific bulge on the opposite side';[564] the details of a wound might be easier to observe in others than oneself: Flora Sandes, hit alongside her comrades by a 'shower of bombs', wrote that one of the men 'had his face split from nose to chin', but for herself the experience was 'a feeling as though a house had fallen bodily on the top of me'.[565] VAD Emma Duffin could not put into words a description of a wound, only her reaction to it: 'I don't think in my life I have seen a more horrible sight'.[566] Other nurses were more able to put experiences and sights into words, though still more metaphorical than those of the soldier's own words: one man 'got an explosive bullet through his arm, smashing it up to rags above the elbow. He told me he got a man "to tie the torn muscles up"'.[567] The way that the metaphor ameliorates the business can be seen in the range of soldiers' terms for wounds and being wounded. In Eric Partridge's fictionalised account soldiers are 'badly "smashed-up"', or have 'got it in the neck' – not necessarily meaning being wounded in the neck (Partridge puts both expressions in inverted commas);[568] New Zealand soldiers 'got smacked';[569] 'I only got a tap in the back' wrote Sgt Benjamin Cope[570] – being 'tapped' and 'pipped' were recorded by Fraser and Gibbons, Brophy and Partridge, and Philip Gibbs.[571] Wounds ranged from being fatal – for Eric Partridge this was a 'daisy-pusher'[572] – to Rifleman William Taffs' reaction: 'I felt pretty dicky at the time – I must have got a little gas in my lungs'.[573] Wordplay allowed a wounded man to deal with his condition by belittling it; being operated on was 'going to the pictures',[574] the state of being ill from a wound or war-related injury was 'being knocked up',[575] or, in 'The

New Army Slang', 'washed out'.[576] After the war a wounded soldier described himself to James Beck as 'a crock'.[577] There was too an avoidance of saying 'flu' – Dora M. Walker dealt with a colonel who asked to be directed to a hospital, saying 'I've got "*It*" badly'.[578]

In four years of incessant killing it was almost obligatory to find different ways of saying 'he was hit', 'he died' or 'he was killed': a soldier was 'napooed',[579] or, for Bulgarian soldiers, 'he has gone to Sofia';[580] in American slang men were 'bounced off', 'bumped off', 'huffed', 'knocked off';[581] they were 'knocked',[582] 'popped off',[583] they 'copped a packet',[584] they 'went under',[585] 'konked out' or were 'knocked out',[586] were 'off it',[587] or, used everywhere, they had 'gone west'; the dead were 'pushing up daisies', were 'over the hill',[588] or 'somewhere in France'.[589] Commonplace expressions gave nobility – 'so many old friends were taken from us',[590] and 'The Manchester's pet fell with his master',[591] but more cynically a French term was 'to get your jaw smashed'.[592]

The frequency and range of terms that mask killing using metaphors, jokes, simplifications, nonsense words, and officialese, are such that the simplicity of 'Hun killing'[593] can be all the more shocking. The directness Remarque uses in *All Quiet on the Western Front*, whether it be the description of stabbing a man – 'I strike madly home, and feel only how the body suddenly convulses, then becomes limp, and collapses'[594] – or the description of revenge/atrocity killings,[595] show how language protects by communicating circumspectly. Examples of the range of ways that killing could be parcelled are: 'men got sploshed', 'had a splosh at', 'put two of them over', 'scotched',[596] 'I 'anded 'im a plum',[597] 'let the daylight into them',[598] '"get home" with the bayonet',[599] 'they've done him in',[600] 'our men did some execution among the Germans',[601] a bullet 'found its billet'.[602] Matthew Wright evaluates some of the most short and simple notes on comrades' deaths as 'by laconic New Zealand standards – amount[ing] to deep emotion', just as 'news back to families was couched so as to cushion the blow'.[603] Of all the wartime situations where destructiveness was balanced with creativity, pain with care, this must be one of the most stark.

To counter the interference of thought or emotion bayonet training was scripted. Men were taught to shout 'in, out, on guard' while charging and stabbing dummies,[604] and Graves reported a young soldier 'automatically' shouting this while bayoneting a German soldier.[605] It would be a mistake though to believe that killing was only ordered and mechanical, driven by revenge, hatred or need. Coningsby Dawson in the preface to *With Lancashire Lads* makes no apology for the idea of 'slay and spare not', adding that he was thankful that the war came at a time when he was 'young and fit [and] thoroughly able to take part in it'. Sidney de Loghe describes the destruction of a Turkish gun team as, 'There were no horses; there were no men. And many souls were speeding up to Allah';[606] for George Mitchell wanting to bayonet a Turk there is the disappointment of 'I have not been lucky enough to catch one yet';[607] John Easton's 'Broadchalk' in *Three Personal Records of the War*[608] has men shooting 'with yells of laughter and cheers', describing them as firing 'as one shoots at a fair', reminiscent of the battle cries of 1914 (see p. 106). As the war dragged on, it became a business of relentless numbers of people killed and killing – 'killing squareheads is all we think about',[609] and 'we are killing a lot of Germans – considerably more than they are killing of us'.[610]

Semi-scripted battle cries attempted to excite soldiers to kill, but did not always work: 'Our platoon officer 2/Lt. E.M.Gould led us yelling, "Remember Belgium, Remember the Lusitania." We yelled back, "**** Belgium and **** the Lusitania!"'[611] In Gallipoli different mentalities and attitudes showed in the opposing battle cries: Aubrey Herbert noted that while the Turks cried 'Allah!', New Zealand soldiers cried 'Eggs is cooked!', a phrase picked up from barracks in Egypt.[612] One sergeant at Gallipoli used old army slang, 'Imshi!', the Arabic for 'Go!', to encourage his men over the parapet.[613] Cynical or improbable, these words of killing can be contrasted with the words of dying. Aubrey Herbert again noted the word 'Allah' used by dying Turkish soldiers, while on the Western Front men, and boys, called on, maybe for, their mothers. Masefield wrote of a French man he met who had wandered over the Marne battlefield where 'perhaps for miles there was a sort of moan of Maman, Maman, from hundreds and thousands of dying men'.[614] Lynn MacDonald's interviewees for *They Called it Passchendaele* (1978) records several soldiers, British and German, whose last words were 'mutti', 'mum', or 'mother';[615] Holmes records similar instances.[616] As death was seldom painless, the 'shrieking and groaning' of dying men was common in no man's land,[617] often articulated in the common language of the Front – 'men go to their deaths with curses on their lips'.[618] Capt Bell died with the words 'Oh – damn',[619] Charles Douie recorded a hit man shouting 'Christ, my God!',[620] and Masefield watched a wounded French soldier look at his wife, 'and said "Maigre", which means excrement, and died'.[621] Most human perhaps are Graves's observation 'I've been hit',[622] Emma Duffin's ward Courage, who says 'Oh sister, dear, I am dying',[623] and Pte Nixon's 'I heard Tommy Winkler go "Ah!" he was my mate – and he was gone – just like that'.[624] Masefield met a French soldier who had seen two instances of men singing as they died, one after being shot in the head.[625]

The fatalism that grew through the course of the war (soldiers stopped going to church parade as 'we were becoming fatalists')[626] was expressed in terms of a system that would determine life or death – a bullet would have 'your bloody number on it',[627] your 'number was up',[628] or you would 'lose your number'.[629] If the randomness was brutal and could not be fought against, the *Portsmouth Evening News* recognised the way soldiers' language faced down this brutality with their own as 'the dauntless spirit with which our soldiers face death', in the phrases 'to be put in a bag' and 'to be scuppered'.[630]

Many of the men of the new armies from urban centres (30 per cent of all industrial workers had enlisted by January 1916,[631] before conscription) would have seen industrial accidents; the rapid escalation of weaponry in the war of attrition from autumn 1914 quickly taught men the effects of industrial warfare on the body. Shock at what shrapnel and shelling did shows in the descriptions by young officers, not normally exposed to this kind of thing; the possibility of carrying on perhaps depended on bland description, people managing to accept what they saw without the cushioning assistance of metaphors. Cyril Helm wrote of the effects of a shrapnel shell on a young gunner subaltern in October 1914: 'The poor fellow was brought in to me absolutely riddled. He lay in my arms until he died, shrieking in agony'; Ernest Shephard wrote after a heavy bombardment in July 1915, 'One man, Pte Woods, was found in 8 pieces, while others were ghastly sights, stomachs blown open, some headless, limbs off, etc.'[632] Kate Luard, working as a nurse, wrote in her diary for 15 December 1914, that she had spoken to a stretcher bearer who had carried a man who 'had his face blown off by an explosive bullet', and a month later was able to write herself of treating 'One man with part of his stomach blown away and his right thigh smashed'. The introduction of poison gas brought the need to find ways of describing its effects: 'the noise of the poor devils trying to breathe was sufficient to direct us ... The effect of gas is to fill the lungs with a watery frothy matter which gradually increases and rises till it fills the whole lungs and comes to the mouth; then they die'.[633] The spatial nature of the trench led to a high proportion of head-wounds: 'Sangster had half his head blown away and died an hour later;'[634] but the whole body was vulnerable: 'Gresty – a lad who was a sergeant of mine – was the worst, his body full of gaping holes'.[635] Some nurses managed to deal with this with professional enthusiasm: the writer of *A War Nurse's Diary* wrote of 'an officer . . . with huge wounds in his abdomen, while his intestines were absolutely riddled with shot. The surgeons cut out twelve feet of entrails, and he made an excellent recovery!'[636] For Angela Smith nurse Eleanora Pemberton's dispassionate description of the absence of parts of the body, with the substitution of a number for the soldier's name, 'provides her with the power to express the horror with authenticity'.[637] Supposedly restrained accounts from commanding officers to bereaved families show, if not the reality, at least the expectation of a population becoming by 1917 inured to the nature of death at the Front, its degrees of mercy, even desirability: 'your brother was shot through the head with a bullet . . . his death appears to have been instantaneous'.[638]

More of a challenge was finding the language for the regular occurrence of the body being blown to pieces. For many soldiers this disintegration was a deep fear, despite the fact that death would be instantaneous; Sgt Paul Dubrulle in the French army wrote 'To die from a bullet seems to be nothing; parts of our being remain intact; but to be dismembered, torn to pieces, reduced to pulp, this is a fear that flesh cannot support and which is fundamentally the great suffering of bombardment'.[639] The terms used often employ 'blow', the explosive reference also conveying the lightness, the slightness, of the human form: 'blown to pieces',[640] 'blew the man and horse to pieces',[641] 'blown to atoms',[642] 'blown to buggery';[643] or 'men and horses were splintered to ribbons'.[644] More brutally, men might become 'raw meat',[645] 'human wreckage',[646] 'a mess of human wreckage',[647] they might 'be demolished',[648] or just 'splashed'.[649]

What, apart from the need to bear witness, was seen as the purpose of graphic description? Referring to the use of this kind of writing in Henri Barbusse's widely read *Le Feu*, translated as *Under Fire* when it was published in Britain in 1917, Sassoon was urged to 'do a Barbusse' for pacifist purposes,[650] but there is little evidence of people being shocked by descriptions of the destruction of the body to an extent that urged them to agitate for an end to the war. The post-war story became more complex, particularly during the boom in war memoirs 1928–32; for Dan Todman, the success of *All Quiet on the Western Front* provoked both a rush to 'capitalise on Remarque's success', particularly his use of horrific description, but also a reaction by those who felt that it was painting an unbalanced picture of the experience of the war.[651] Bearing in mind the factual portrayal of death in the 1916 film *The Battle of the Somme*, still the British film most watched in cinemas, there is an uncomfortable possibility that in words as well as in film, presentations of realistic death fascinated; for Lawrence Napper[652] 'it is clear that the depiction of death was an attraction' in the film; why should it not be in words? While the desire to read it was distinct from the need for the writing of it, both served therapeutic purposes.

Death and the destruction of the body led to another trope, the need to find ways of describing the destroyed body and the reaction to it. Familiar images are related, the dead man's hand or leg sticking out of the trench: 'they would shake its hand: "Alright mate?"',[653] or 'the men using [a dead German soldier]'s feet to hang their water bottles on'.[654] But in this language people became things; Charles Edmonds describes the contents of a shell crater as 'two curious things. They were muddy grey in colour – clothes and boots and faces'.[655] What survives of men's bodies mingles with the uniforms that will survive them, as 'chips of bone and rags of clothing. The rest is putrid grey matter'.[656] Reaction to this assault on the senses focuses on smell. The smell of corpses envelops the environment: 'This was the battlefield of stenches, of caked blood, of dirty bandages, lice, rats, eternal mud, and the smell of rotting corpses'.[657] 'We wear our respirators because of the awfull smell of the dead', wrote T. Harold Watts in a letter home, posted on 18 June 1915. Masefield wrote of French soldiers describing as 'camemberty' corpses that had become unfrozen in a spring thaw.[658] For one supply officer 'the whole atmosphere [of Vailly] was tainted with the odour of burning and the disgusting smell of putrefying flesh'.[659] Notable is the change post-war, in which these same remnants of flesh that had previously been 'a shocking compost of clay, bodies and rags',[660] become 'the very substance of man's sacrifice' (see p. 275), and soldiers' remains are generally referred to as 'bodies', whatever their condition, or the amount that survived.

Despite the fall in attendance of church parades there was a strong cultural model for the environment of the Front, which appears regularly. 'A Veritable Hell' was the headline used for an article about the Italian front in October 1916;[661] after his first stint in the front line in December 1914 Wilbert Spencer wrote home 'I wonder how many people realise what hell the trenches can be';[662] the Front was 'a perfect inferno of guns',[663] 'hell with the lid off',[664] 'hell let loose',[665] 'Hell on earth',[666] 'hell in the clouds',[667] 'damned hellish misery',[668] 'a hell of machine-gun fire',[669] 'nerve-wracking hell'.[670] It was extended to 'a raging inferno',[671] 'an inferno, real damnation' and 'the slaughterhouse',[672] where the enemy were 'fiends incarnate', 'a lot of mad devils' and 'satanic'.[673] A wounded Indian soldier wrote home that 'this is not war. It is the ending of the world',[674] a common Hindu metaphor for the war; a gentlemen's outfitters' advertisement claimed it would not be profiteering 'during Armageddon'.[675] And within the great hell there were micro-hells, an area of no man's land so emptied of anything that it was known as 'Sahara';[676] and not one but several 'Hell-fire Corners'.[677]

Failure

The mythology of the experience of soldiering proposes that soldiers should be allowed to grumble. A. J. Dawson proposed that it was a 'very English' trait: 'So long as there's a little intermittent grousing going on you can be quite sure of two things—that there's nothing wrong and that the men are in good spirits and content. If there's no grousing, it means one of two things—either that the men are angered about something, in which case they will be unusually silent, or that we are up against real difficulties and hardships involving real suffering, in which case there will be a lot of chaffing and joke-cracking and apparent merriment'.[678] Stephen Graham felt that grousing was 'damp anger and will never ignite to action, never flame out in mutiny'.[679] Grousing was an army tradition, one which had been engrained in army language since the 1880s, and which Partridge believed dated back earlier to the Crimea and the Indian Uprising. 'Grousing' was thus seen in a positive light 'only excusable in a soldier, for it's his privilege, and though he grouses he never shirks'.[680] Grousing was a self-administered control, a prophylactic against being a soldier, not against doing what a soldier had to do. When *The Gasper* had 'a grouse to air' it was not against lack of supplies or discipline, or anything to do with the pursuance of the war, but against letters from home asking how many Germans the recipient had killed.[681]

Though grousing was seen as a safety-valve against a breakdown in discipline, major difficulties did arise, and required a renegotiation of language. 'Mutiny' was what happened in Russia, Germany or Austria; it did not happen to allies on whom you were totally dependent, even the French. 'Riots' and 'disturbances' happened, but were explainable, if not excusable, on the grounds that they were about the living conditions of 'our boys' (and the Etaples incidents were ultimately blamed on the MPs and the 'canaries'); during the war 'mutiny' existed only as a potential, for example in the form of words used to prosecute and fine Sylvia Pankhurst in November 1918, for 'attempting to cause mutiny, sedition or dissatisfaction'.[682] The actions at Etaples and Boulogne in September 1917 and at Le Havre in December 1918 were conspicuously under-reported, though major disturbances which took place on home territory could not be ignored. In March 1919 Canadian soldiers at Kinmel Camp, near Rhyl, awaiting demobilisation rioted, resulting in the deaths of five men, with injuries to a further twenty-one[683] – newspaper reports gave varying figures for the casualties. The activities here were reported as 'disturbances',[684] 'Camp Riot',[685] and 'Rioting'.[686] The *Lancashire Daily Post* reported that, according to the camp commandant Col M. A. Colquhun, one man had 'raised the red flag in an attempt to introduce Bolshevism', while the *Western Times* reported that 'a cry, "Come on Bolsheviks" was raised by Canadian soldiers, said to be Russian'. Yet the headlines for the *Western Times* article include the innocuous sounding 'Canadian Troops Get Out of Hand'.

The *Derby Daily Telegraph* reported that when the offenders were brought to court martial 'the charges were mutiny and failure to suppress mutiny'.[687] It appears that 'mutiny' could be used when suppressing and punishing this kind of action, but there was an effort not to raise the importance of protest while it was happening by giving it the title of 'mutiny'. But at the same time such a loaded term could be treated light-heartedly: in November 1918 the *Yorkshire Evening Post* reported the story of a Canadian battalion mascot that had been sold for beer-money, provoking a strike by some of the men. The article reports: 'It caused the only mutiny in the story of the battalion'.[688] Mild though this might be, this incident did involve an action taken against authority; in 'Another Camp Riot', an article in the *Sunderland Daily Echo* reported on fighting between black soldiers and white soldiers awaiting travel to America and the Caribbean, following an outbreak of insults and retaliation, which had been largely controlled by fellow-soldiers.[689] The newspaper reported that 'nothing very serious happened', though the word 'riot' was used, just at it had been for the incident at Kinmel Camp.

Over the past hundred years some debate has taken place, not explicitly, as to whether the incidents at Etaples in September 1917 should be called 'mutinies', 'riots' or 'disturbances'; in this case protests about an arrest in the training camp led to a fight with military police, an accidental death, a large-scale breakout from the camp, drunkenness, fighting, a court martial and one execution. In 1930 the *Manchester Guardian* carried an article about 'The Mutiny at Etaples',[690] while in 1982 Lt Col C. E. Carrington had no hesitation in referring to 'the Etaples mutiny'.[691] For Jay Winter the incident 'that has been described as a mutiny was nothing of the sort', and it is 'stretching the term considerably to call this set of events a mutiny at all';[692] for Dan Todman in his discussion of the 1986 BBC production of *The Monocled Mutineer*, based on the events, the word 'mutiny' appears both within quotation marks and with none.[693]

While strikers during the war were seen as working against the war effort, and were deeply resented by soldiers, terms of mutiny were not applied to them, nor to striking workers after the war. For these situations metaphors of conflict were applied: one union compared an employers' federation pamphlet to 'the most dangerous of the poison gases used in the late war',[694] while Lloyd George's secretary Philip Kerr called for 'a manifestation of the trench spirit' in requiring trades unions to accept lower pay.[695] 'Mutiny' seems to have been a taboo word, something that could not exist within the British forces: its seriousness was debased in the Navy, where the word was used as a slang term for rum or grog.

Descriptions of fear used terms that parcelled it as the contrary to bravado – 'funk', a term originally used for smoke, being extended to 'funk-hole', either a crater to shelter in, or a safe desk job, away from the fighting; or 'getting the wind up', with its range of extensions; or simply 'nerves'. The popular view was that 'out of a hundred men, five are generally cowards, ninety-five are ordinary individuals, and one is rashly brave',[696] rather than the potential for cowardice and bravery being present in almost all; A. M. Burrage's view was that 'most of us were cowards . . . but there are as many shades of cowardice as there are shades of a primary colour'.[697] Soldiers' comments indicated that group mentality and reaction to quickly-changing circumstances could change men instantly – despite the famous 'ladies from hell' epithet, Graves's anti-Scottish adjutant reckoned that 'the Jocks ... charge like hell – both ways'.[698] Combat naturally provoked extreme fear, inexpressible fear – Richard Holmes describes the men in retreat as 'broken'; the gunner who saw these men 'throwing away their rifles as they ran ... wholly demoralised' described them as 'calling out to us as they passed that Jerry was through and it was all over'.[699] For one soldier admitting to having to give up a position could be wrapped up with the picturesque term 'flitting',[700] which avoided the admission of defeat. Richard Tobin, interviewed in the 1960s described the feeling of going over the top as 'fear has left you – it's terror',[701] while 'Tippy' in the sound dramatisation *In the Trenches* describes the feeling after his act of heroism as 'I'm all of a tremble – it's a rotten cowardly feeling'.[702] Anticipation surely terrified many, in waves, from being conscripted to waiting to go over: one soldier sending a postcard home from Folkestone wrote 'Feel very much upset at leaving you all but will try to cheer up for all your sakes'.[703]

And in truth not all soldiers were reliable, competent, or capable of controlling their fear. Moran, usually sympathetic to the soldier's position, described the Trench Mortar Company or the Machine Gun Corps as where a battalion would 'send its rubbish',[704] Cpl George Ashurst described men selected for a working party as 'duds',[705] Capt Slack described how 'it was getting on in the war [1916] when we were getting very poor material out',[706] and Ian Hay has Capt Blaikie 'weeding out . . . shysters'.[707] The age-old link between armies and criminals showed in a commonality of slang: the army terms for a lock-up, 'clink', 'chokey', 'jug', all originated as criminal slang, and there was a widely held view that the criminal world had provided the army with much of its slang.

The ultimate military crime, desertion, was 'going over the hill', or 'going over the hump',[708] perversions of 'going over the top'. The punishment for desertion was 'to suffer death by being shot', for 'misbehaving before the enemy in such a manner as to show cowardice'.[709] MacDonald's interviewee, Capt C. S. Slack, charged with carrying out such an order, wanted to know nothing about the execution, and wrote to the soldier's mother that he had been 'killed in action'.[710] Graves claimed that 'executions were frequent in France'; in May 1915 he found evidence for around twenty executions, but noted that a few days later these were denied in Parliament.[711] Fraser and Gibbons record the phrases 'on the pegs' and 'up for the long jump' for 'awaiting court martial'; 'up for the long jump' sounds more ominous in the circumstances.

While many memoir writers mention fear in code words – 'windy', 'funk', 'nerves' – few refer to fear as openly as Charles Edmonds, writing in 1929: 'Now the cold fear clutched at the bowels of men', 'a tremendous sense of realisation came over me – I hardly know if it were fear or excitement', 'I thought the human spirit could endure no longer postponement of the terror'.[712] Lord Moran notes both the exhilaration of achievement and survival – '"A" company had an officer and thirty-eight men, but their tails were up, the effect of going over the top was apparent, they were well pleased with themselves', but probably is reserving judgement in 'Quite a number of our men appear to consider it necessary to accompany them [three prisoners] across no man's land . . .'.[713] No doubt a sense of pragmatism tempered actions in no man's land, and this was after a successful trench raid. A general attitude in favour of keeping or getting away from the Front is seen in the hope of getting a Blighty, and the opportunist advice to a friend in hospital – 'Don't forget to swing the lead and stop there'.[714] While 'swinging the lead', 'scrimshanking' and 'working your ticket', all terms for avoiding dangerous or onerous activity, were presumably widespread, the difference between sensible self-preservation and cowardice might be simply a question of 'getting away with it', a term Fraser and Gibbons include in their glossary of *Soldier and Sailor Words and Phrases*.

One of the greatest areas of failure related to language was the sense that language itself was simply not up to the job of describing the experience of the war. This can be approached in a number of ways. Language clearly did not fail, since there are several frighteningly graphic descriptions of fighting and its aftermath, but there are probably as many expressions of these being indescribable:

I cannot describe the sights I saw[715]
The whole thing is too ghastly to write about[716]
It is unspeakable[717]
Great God, what do you expect one to say? Great God, what am I to say?[718]
It is an impossibility for me to describe all that happened[719]
No one can imagine what it is like, only those who have been through it[720]
Bodies were lying on bodies like stones in heaps (which no words can be found to describe or relate)[721]

The penultimate of these propose that no words ever could create the image of the scene for those who had never been present, but the final quote creates an image, and goes on to deny the possibility of creating an image. It is as though the whole concept of the function of language is disrupted, but perhaps not destroyed. John Masefield, in a letter to his wife on 9 March 1915, wrote:

I don't think that people in England can realise what this is; I know they do not. Words cannot describe it, except as crime and infamy, and a stinking filth . . .

Clearly language could work – and there were ways round the problem. In a letter sent to the *Daily Mail* and published on 26 November 1914, Pte W. Kirk, of the 1st Bedford Regiment, wrote that:

> I cannot describe what it is like out there, but you can guess by these figures. Our 1st Battalion has been in seven engagements, and reinforced three times with over 100 men each time. It started with 1,200, and has now got 400 and 3 officers left. The 2nd Battalion started with 1,200 and has 300 men and 3 officers left. Other regiments are worse off than us.

This trope of describing the experience as something that cannot be described, and then offering a way to understand it, appears fairly early in the war. Though Kirk invites the reader to guess, his is a mathematical description, one of numbers of killed men, ultimately the purpose of the fighting.

Examining terms such as 'the indescribable' in a verbal context reveals that many things were expressed as 'inexpressible' at this time. Death and grief are frequently 'inexpressibly sad',[722] but also the index of a report is 'inexpressibly tedious',[723] the 'gentleness of heart' of Christ is 'inexpressible',[724] the silhouette of the latest Royal Worcester corsets is 'inexpressibly smart',[725] Charlie Chaplin looks 'inexpressible!',[726] and the 'repulsiveness' of the living conditions of men at the Front is 'inexpressible'.[727] War always has 'inexpressible miseries and horrors'[728] but the comfort of knowing oneself safe in the combat zone is also 'inexpressible'.[729] 'Inexpressible' clearly means something, the expression that one is not able to express something – it is less the failure of the language than the failure of the speaker.

There emerges a distinction between indescribability in writing and describability in speech; possibly the presence of the living witness provided a reassurance that such appalling events could be survived.

Arthur Marwick in *The Deluge* proposes that after the Battle of the Somme people at home were unable to know the 'foul horror' of trench warfare – 'they saw the glory, but not the sordid filth of trench life';[730] he quotes 'one young soldier' as writing, 'There are some things better left undescribed'.[731] There emerges a distinction between indescribability in writing and describability in speech; possibly the presence of the living witness provided a reassurance that such appalling events could be survived. It is probable that among those soldiers who had left school at fourteen there existed a sense of how the written language should operate, and they were unequipped to match this to their experiences. But they were more comfortable with spoken English, even in such a subject. In a letter to 'Arthur' sent on 18 June 1916 T. Harold Watts writes:

> We wear our respirators because of the awfull smell of the dead. I'll never get the sight out of my eyes, and it will be an everlasting nightmare. If I am spared to come home, I'll be able to tell you all about it, but I cannot possibly write as words fail me. I can't describe things.

It is likely that there was a gender divide here; Marwick quotes another soldier as writing 'Everyone out here considers it only fair to one's womenkind to hush up the worst side of the war',[732] while Mabel Lethbridge in *The Great War Interviews* (recorded 1964) remarks on 'soldiers' strange lack of ability to communicate with us, to tell us what it was really like'.[733] (see p. 257).

In many cases memoir-writers state that an experience or a thing is indescribable, and then go on to describe it clearly, often with the proviso that this can be done only dispassionately. A. M. Burrage gives a good example of this in *War is War*:

> Stretcher-bearers were coming for the man who still lived: our job was to clear up the mess. We picked up unspeakable things with our hands, putting them into sandbags. . . . The only way to live out there was to turn one's face against sentiment and regard human flesh merely as flesh.[734]

This, however, is after the conflict, and the great outpouring of graphic memoirs were published long after 1918. But the atrocity reports of 1914 had set out an acceptable language of horror, and from its publication in December 1916 Barbusse's *Under Fire* provided to millions of readers of French and German the graphic language for understanding and describing the Western Front, accessible in English translation from June 1917 (an advertisement in the *Manchester Guardian* described it as 'the book which all France and Germany have read, and all Britain is now reading'[735]) the potential of its language to provoke revulsion is seen in the pacifists' comment to Sassoon to 'do a Barbusse'.[736] But this was an exception. The trope of inexpressibility and the failure of words surrounds the war, not just combat and being shelled or living in a trench dug-out, but all the facets of the war. Masefield wrote in *The Old Front Line*, 'The tumult of these days and nights cannot be described or imagined';[737] elsewhere 'Words fail me to express the admiration I feel ...';[738] and VAD nurse Emma Duffin's realisation that her words to the mother of a dying soldier were only 'the futile words that one says because one must say something'.[739]

> *it was not a failure of language, but a view that, for the individual, language, particularly written words, and the enormity of the experience were not matched.*

Fussell proposes that what was really happening here was not an inability but a choice, the choice not to describe, and that 'unspeakable' actually is a code for 'nasty',[740] though a stronger word might be more appropriate. It is another instance of how putting experiences into words makes them real a second time, which was both generally avoided and was carefully used in the treatment of shellshock. Writing (and not saying) that war experiences were inexpressible was a deliberate description, a statement that the experiences could be understood only as being of such extremity that they stood beyond written words; it was not a failure of language, but a view that, for the individual, language, particularly written words, and the enormity of the experience were not matched.

3 US AND THEM

Race

Nineteenth-century Europe saw the establishment of states from what had previously been smaller principalities, kingdoms, duchies, autonomous regions and city-states. The aftermath of the Napoleonic Wars saw the emergence of the Kingdom of the Netherlands in 1814, the Kingdom of Belgium in 1830, and the Grand Duchy of Luxembourg in 1839. The establishment of the Austro-Hungarian dual monarchy to include the kingdom of Croatia–Slavonia was completed in 1868, the German state was established in 1871, and the final setting of Rome as the capital of the Kingdom of Italy took place in the same year. During the second half of the century anthropology and palaeontology were operating within an imperial and colonial framework to establish some kind of scientific rationale for how human beings saw each other as 'us' and 'them'. Photography and anthropometrics allowed processes of data-gathering and measuring to be used to bolster arguments that the European states' control of the world's resources was both natural and inevitable. Race was established as a rational way of understanding and managing the world, and became an essential part of understanding the concepts of 'us' and 'them' in the war in Europe.

The determination of nation by ethnicity and language, as opposed to religion, became dominant in the late-nineteenth century[1] and afforded opportunities for the creation of identities based on perceptions of anthropometrics closer to home and on ethnocentric views of historical migration. For France, the German invasion sparked off a re-affirmation of 'a form of "national spirit" in the national language', while for the German-speaking countries the 'purification of the language' was an aspect of the struggle for dominance.[2] In this context words such as 'Slav' and 'Hun' were easily enlisted for the purposes of propaganda at all levels.

Unravelling how these terms were used and understood, and how they were etymologised in terms of race history, gives a view of how the war was both rationalised racially and given a deeper emotional meaning. The area is complex, frequently contradictory, and its language operated with several distinct intentions and embodied several interconnected perceptions. Involved are stories of identity, imperialism, pseudo-science, and the politics of survival.

King George V's speech after the Armistice embraced 'the English-speaking race, dwelling upon the shores of all the oceans.'

Language, as shown above, operated as a major determinant in the making of national identities, but several of the states involved in the Great War had many languages; France, with a strong national identity, had Occitan, Gallo and Breton speakers as well as standard French speakers, and the Belgian army had Flemish and French speakers; German *Flamenpolitik* attempted to create an ethno-linguistic connection between German and Flemish culture in Belgium; the Austro-Hungarian military had to manage twelve languages. Frequent references during the period to 'language' and 'race' together show how the perception of interdependence determined one idea of 'race'. The preface to Olivier Leroy's *A Glossary of French Slang* proposes that the study of slang might 'throw an interesting light on the psychology of the French and English-speaking races'.[3] L. B. Swift, quoted in the 'Correspondence Course in Patriotism',[4] states 'This record [of various "Anglo-Saxon" rights] is the peculiar and crowning glory of the English speaking race', and King George V's speech after the Armistice embraced 'the English-speaking race, dwelling upon the shores of all the oceans'.[5] In an article titled 'The Empire', in *The War Illustrated Album De Luxe*, 1915, Sir Gilbert Parker, MP wrote, 'There is only one race throughout the British Empire', indicating how the muddle of physiology, culture and language was ultimately at the service of political pragmatism.[6]

But one nation might have two races, as the War Gossip writer in the *Yorkshire Evening Post* explained '. . . Belgium was divided into two races, the Flemish and the Walloons, different in language, in faith, in manner of

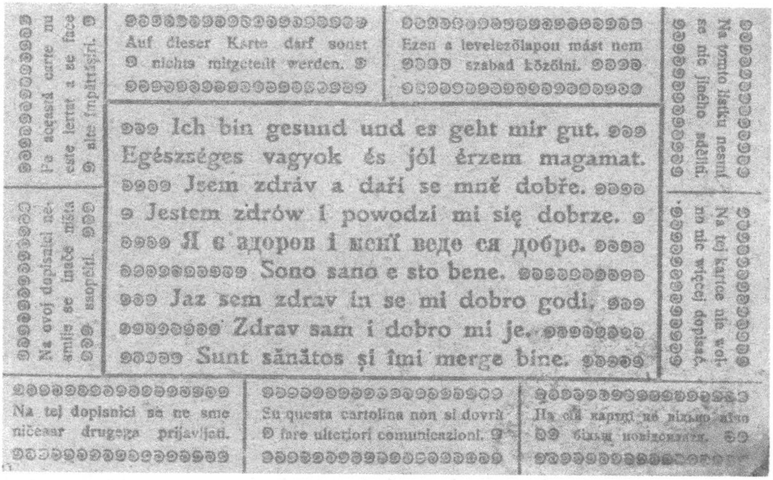

FIGURE 3.1 Multilingual postcard used by the Austro-Hungarian army, allowing the sender to say only 'I am well and everything is fine'; the nine outer boxes warn, probably with no irony intended, that no other message can be sent.

life, and I knew that they hated each other heartily'.[7] Czechs, within the Austro-Hungarian army, were suspected of disloyalty,[8] and their language became a marker for suspicion, as seen in an interview with some Czech-speaking PoWs in Russia: 'we are brothers [with the Russians], and speak the same tongue; we are one people'.[9] Equally, racial difference is marked by the inability to speak a language. Richard Fogarty shows how a particular kind of French was used to create a demarcation of Senegalese soldiers in the French army in Europe,[10] while a VAD nurse at the Front noted of Senegalese soldiers that they 'could not even speak French';[11] significantly pilgrims in France in 1928 noted that an Algerian trader bargained 'in perfect French'[12]. For black or Indian soldiers racial difference might be highlighted by parodies of accent, such as a Sikh soldier's 'gib him plent ob dat'.[13] VAD nurse Adèle De L'Isle, strongly aware of accents and languages, notes of a Senegalese soldier in her care that he not only speaks French, but 'he speaks fluent French'.[14] In this context it is noticeable that the slang of the black troops in the American Expeditionary Force, where it differed from that of the white soldiers, was not collected, and as Jonathan Lighter points out, what was represented was governed by conventions of the pastiche black accents of the minstrel show, with the occasional 'man' thrown in.[15] For the United States the position of black soldiers continued to be an issue without resolution: while in captivity behind German lines some white American soldiers were brought before a camera and 'in order to humiliate [them] still further they were photographed standing between six negroes',[16] the black PoWs' views not being recorded. The Canadian authorities also had reservations about 'accepting negroes for military service'.[17] Graves, in a few sentences, shows the attitude of white Europeans to the non-white troops in France: a French woman describes them as '*animaux*', for the British they are 'semi-civilised', and for the Germans their presence at the Front is 'one of the chief Allied atrocities'.[18]

For America the problem of a vast number of citizens from German family backgrounds led to the invention of 'hyphenated Germans': 'fourteen million hyphenated German-Americans hoped all things and believed all things good about the statesmen of their fatherland'[19]. Early on the term was shortened: Wilhelm II had 'German hyphenated hirelings' in America',[20] and 'hyphenated', 'hyphenates', and even 'hyphens' alone carried the accusation of disloyalty: 'Hyphenated German views',[21] 'Dooley on the hyphenates' and 'German hyphenated fellow-citizens',[22] 'hyphenated agents of German propaganda',[23] the various forms spread outwards to further objects of political condemnation: Theodore Roosevelt's views of Sinn Fein made a link with 'pro-Germanism' in America – he 'denounced the hyphenated',[24] but, commenting on the German names in the American army in 1918, *New York World* stated 'Hyphens may be found here and there in this country, but in France the American Army is American'.[25]

Anglophile Jews in America were indignant about any view of the German–Jewish press being linked to the Anglo-Jewish press, *The Times*' correspondent stating that 'the small band of German Jews who seem to have intimate relations with the German Embassy is clearly unable to keep their race in line'.[26] The relation between support for the Allies and family or community history was a continuing tension, expressed in the British press in terms of race: 'Italians, Germans, "squareheads", and all the rest of them find each his own little racial community'.[27] Across the border in Canada there was another issue, that of the French–Canadian community, 'the French–Canadians as a people, or "race" (as they term themselves)', though Armstrong was clear in stating that she was following French–Canadian use of the term, and not proposing any anthropological significance for it.[28] Many of the French–Canadians were not interested in supporting a 'British' war; long after the war Armstrong's analysis of the situation in 1915 retained the French–Canadian use of 'race': 'in times of racial conflict the animosity displayed towards English-speaking Canada is extended to Britain as well'.[29]

The term 'martial races' reputedly developed from the assessment of the Indian uprising in 1857, but by 1914 it was being used in the press and political speeches considerably more widely; it was shorthand for the recruitment of unemployed young men from economically depressed areas of Britain – Scottish Highlanders were a martial race[30] and Lloyd George's recruiting speeches pointed out that the Welsh were 'one of the most martial little races of Great Britain';[31] for Irish MP John Redmond 'the Irish are now, as always, a martial race'.[32] The Jews were probably not a martial race,[33] though ready to fight for their adopted country,[34] nor, during the South African war could the Boers be allowed to be thought of as a martial race, though to explain the lack of British military progress they were 'a brave and an indomitable race, if not a martial race, a foe in every way worthy to confront British troops'.[35] The Hunan were a martial race,[36] and the Japanese and Chinese were martial races.[37] In the summer of the outbreak of war Britain's allies the Servians (still 'Servians' rather than 'Serbians' at that date, though the change happened quickly) were a martial race,[38] and the French were 'the most martial race in Europe'.[39] The Germans were naturally a martial race.[40] But the British, though ready to rise to the occasion, needed to be seen as non-belligerent; so, while Earl Beaconsfield believed 'ours is a martial race',[41] Lloyd George believed that the English 'have ceased in the ordinary sense of the term to be a very martial race'.[42] It is not easy to make sense of this: the general idea is that some 'races' appear to be quicker to take up arms, a potential which can be realised by a 'non-martial race', i.e. England, whose defence against any criticism of being non-martial lies in her history of warfare. By the Armistice victory was seen as partly due to 'the martial races of India':[43] 'her soldiers sustained in many theatres of war, and under conditions the most diverse and exacting, the martial traditions of their race'.[44] A letter from Senior Assistant Surgeon J. N. Godbole to a friend in Poona indicates that in his experience at least Indian soldiers in England experienced a different kind of language from that which they had heard at home: 'The people ... are pleased to see us ... We do not hear the words 'damn' and 'bloody' at all frequently, as in India. But this only applies to those who have not seen India'.[45] Though measures had been taken to ensure that morale among Indian soldiers was not affected by overt racism ('the King has given a strict order that no trouble be given to any black man in hospital'[46]), and frequent temporary close relationships born of adversity sprang up between for example Anzacs and Indian soldiers,[47] long-term linguistic markers and patterns remained: Dhunjibhoy Chinoy used the English word 'natives' to describe Indians in a letter written in Parsi,[48] and an article in the *Ypres Times* recalls a Pathan officer named Mir Dast, being called 'Mere Dust' and then 'Sheer Mud' 'by his British friends'.[49]

> *For Herbert Johnson writing in the sensationalist* Vivid War Weekly *the contest was thus between 'a nation of sneaks' and 'white men.'*

Alongside all this was a sense that the 'white race' depended on solidarity, a concept that was used by German politicians to condemn Britain's use of non-European troops. Thus Prince Bülow, as reported in *The Times*, accused Britain of 'high treason against the white race'.[50] 'The white man', with connotations of fair play, duty, missionary zeal, muscular Christianity and the bringing of civilisation was a slightly different concept, possibly based on obligation rather than fear, though nevertheless justifying imperialism; applied to the conflict this bolstered accusations of 'unfair' weapons such as poison gas, tactics such as fake surrenders, and the bombing of civilians. For Herbert Johnson writing in the sensationalist *Vivid War Weekly* the contest was thus between 'a nation of sneaks' and 'white men'.[51]

There were during the war rumblings of how the resentment against the memory of Afro-Caribbean slavery, Muslim resentment at Russo/Franco/British domination of Western Asia, and the whole balance, or imbalance, of power worldwide, might be manipulated. The diary of German sailor Richard Stumpf mentions the idea that 'the Mohammedan population of [Egypt] will also take the opportunity to overthrow the English despotism',[52] and there was a persistent rumour that Germany might, via Mexico, exploit white suppression of black people in the Southern States of the USA: 'A plot to procure a negro rising in the Southern States and to establish a negro Republic in Texas is spoken of' (among 'new and sensational disclosures regarding Germany's intrigues').[53]

If there was some awareness that the concept of the 'white race' had rendered itself meaningless by the war, but that race was a determinant, then a conflicted Europe would have to be understood in terms of race. Heather Jones states that 'for many Europeans between 1914 and 1918, "race" meant multiple things – not only biological "race" but also ethnicity or nationality – and understanding of the term also changed during the war. Within the wartime world-view, not only the non-European or imperial world was defined in terms of racial hierarchies; under the influence of social Darwinism, the different nationalities and ethnicities of Europe itself were also seen as distinct "races"'.[54] The emergence of this sense of race in the European context can be seen in a number of cultural developments in the nineteenth century: the use of mythologies in music, particularly German and Scandinavian, pageantry in England and the rejection of the 'Norman' in favour of the 'Anglo-Saxon', including lexical rejection of Latin-based words,[55] and even what might be termed 'nationalist paleoanthropology'. Following the discovery of 'Neanderthal Man' in 1856 and 'Cro-Magnon Man' in 1868, the focus of the hunt for human origins in Europe had moved back to Germany with 'Heidelberg Man' in 1907, at the time of worsening relations between Germany and France, and the establishment of the *entente cordiale* between Britain and France. In 1912 the fragment of human skull which came to be known as 'Piltdown Man' was first sent to Arthur Woodward, Keeper of Geology at the British Museum (Natural History) by Charles Dawson, with a letter that described it as a 'portion of a human skull which will rival H. Heidelbergensis in solidarity'.[56] Competitive racial divisions in Europe were being pushed back to prehistory. On the outbreak of war European racial competition was already potent, and ready to be used for propaganda purposes: 'the German intellectual classes' had misled the German people 'as to the position of the German race in the world', wrote Wynnard Hooper, City Editor of *The Times*.[57]

British verbal culture, in keeping with the promotion of the Anglo-Saxon during the second half of the nineteenth century, repeatedly referred to the 'Anglo-saxon race'. The Anglo-Saxon race 'irrespective of flag'[58] included all English-speaking nations, though how this involved 'hyphenated people' (see p. 150) is only clear if they were different races within a nation, speaking different languages, as seen in Belgium, and presumably parts of Britain. But as well as Anglo-Saxon they were also 'the British race'.[59] Usually when the subject refers to combat, it is the 'British race' involved rather than the Anglo-Saxon race: Haig's letter to

Robertson, Chief of the Imperial General Staff, after the beginning of the Somme offensive praised the 'fighting power of the British race',[60] echoing a longstanding view of the British soldier: 'the reputation of the race for courage and coolness'.[61] There were specific characteristics, naturally different depending on where the opinion was coming from: 'I saw, too, how in physique the people of that island race of ours stand out above the other races',[62] balances an Australian view of the Brits as 'a race of mild curates',[63] the American James Beck's view that 'if this were an ordinary war I could well understand that Great Britain would come out of it with the simple remark, "Well, let's have a cup of tea. What's the next event?"',[64] and a post-war view of the British army in France as 'a race of egoists'.[65] Other characteristics were vaguer: 'the best is never got out of the Anglo-Saxon race until it is in a tight place'.[66] But these might be more recognised than defined: Masefield saw it in a combination of casualness and proficiency – 'we are a queer race'.[67] Cpl John Streets' poem 'An English Soldier' begins 'He died for love of race', which looks to be sentimentalising a complex set of reasons why and how people enlisted and survived or died, but at the time resonated with a view of wartime Europe as a conflict between cultures and languages as much as nations;[68] one writer in the book celebrating the 1928 British Legion Pilgrimage felt that the story of the raid on Zeebrugge 'filled our minds with "pride of race"'.[69]

The main British concentration as regards race during the war was on the 'German race', also described as the 'Germanic race' or the 'Teutonic race'. A strong view of what this constituted, to the British observer, was given in a letter in *The Times* from Stanley Roberts, which was summarised as 'the Teutons are a chosen race', who should strive for predominance. The 'Teutonic race' was generally typified in France and Britain as barbaric, naturally militaristic, and highly self-organising; there was a begrudging respect for organisation and efficiency, though this could be accounted for as a result of authoritarianism and 'the mechanical drill system of the Teutonic race'.[70] British journalists' reports of barbarism attached to the race were condemned by the pro-German Swedish writer Sven Hedin: 'During the first phase of the war the British press accused the Germans of barbaric cruelty to their prisoners and to wounded opponents. Not for one moment did I believe these reports but for the sake of the Teutonic race I wanted to uproot this calumny and to bring to light the truth'.[71] But in the British press the term 'Teutonic race' served as a simple, convenient and frequent marker for why the Allies needed to fight rather than negotiate: 'any wrong committed by the Teutonic race against its neighbours was approved by Heaven because the world-domination of Germany through war was part of the Divine scheme',[72] and 'the machinations and barbarianism of the Teutonic race'.[73] 'Teutonic' remained a marker of condemnation after the end of the war with 'Teutonic arrogance',[74] 'Teutonic mendacity',[75] and 'Teutonic cunning'.[76]

After so many decades of colonial dominance and consequent racial privilege, outside Europe, the emergence of a power making European racial claims of rights to power was a challenge to Stanley Roberts, who observed that Britons were a mix of Latin and Anglo-Saxon: Germany's claim that 'If you are born a Celt or a Slav there is no hope for you'[77] was part of the German ruling classes' bombast. But the fear of German European, and subsequently world, domination was expressed in terms of race elsewhere: 'The Germans aim at nothing less than the domination of Europe and of the world by the German race'.[78]

'Pan-Germanism' had changed from the idea of the unification of German-speaking peoples in Europe to the fear of German political expansionism. Yet within Germany there were distinct divisions: Richard Stumpf felt that the Prussians despised the 'quiet, patient Bavarians';[79] 2nd Lt Cyril Drummond reported that during an unofficial truce, when a Dublin Fusilier was killed, 'the Saxons immediately sent over and apologised, saying it hadn't been anything to do with them, but from those so-and-so Prussians on their left';[80] and the Saxons were claimed in one instance to be getting on so well with the British troops facing them that the authorities had had to stop mutual visits across no man's land.[81] In some sections the antipathy between Saxons and Prussians was exploited: 'opposite one section of our centre the Germans for some time waved flags and took considerable pains to inform out troops that they were Saxons. It is possible that the different light in which we regard Saxons and Prussians is realised'.[82] Cross-no-man's-land communication even created the potential for a change in the disposition of the armies: 'While our guns were giving the Prussians opposite us hell, the Saxons opposite the Middlesex applauded the hits. Later they shouted across, "We are being relieved by Bavarians tonight. Give us time to get out and then shoot the ---s"'.[83] The *Illustrated London News* couched this in what would have been seen at the time as a racial connection – 'Saxons and Anglo-Saxons fraternising'.[84]

The racial characteristics of other peoples facing the British soldier were less distinct. It was easy to lump together the various peoples of the Austro-Hungarian Empire as numerous peoples with vaguely exotic names: 'hordes of Croats, Magyars, Slovaks, Swabians, Rumanes, and other races of the Austro-Hungarian Monarchy',[85] 'hordes' indicating a fear of uncontrolled invasion. Turks were frequently described as 'dirty' or as 'the unspeakable Turk',[86] 'a stubborn fighter', 'as tough as the Germans', but 'no one can tell how a Turk will behave under any given conditions; the Turks themselves do not know how they will behave'.[87] Har Dayal (1884–1939), an Indian Nationalist revolutionary, certainly had no good word for the Turks: 'the Turks, as a nation, are utterly unfit to assume the leadership of the Muslim world. They have been, and are, only a predatory tribe, without culture and political capacity . . . The Turks have no brains; that is the plain truth. They can fight well, but they cannot administer or organise. They have been in possession of a vast empire for several centuries; but they have no great or noble national literature . . . The Turks could not sing or speculate, as they are really very low in the scale of mental evolution'.[88] The result of the Gallipoli campaign would seem to argue against this. K. A. Murdoch's letter to the Australian Prime Minister claimed that 'the British physique is very much below that of the Turks',[89] but this view was naturally condemned by Ian Hamilton.

Just as 'the Balkan Wars' covered a complex series of conflicts, the term 'the Balkan races', even though they had 'varying aims and aspirations',[90] swept into a convenient group a mass of connected and conflicting cultures. For those without knowledge of the complexities, the term 'race' did not help: R. W. Seton-Watson, the influential academic who was involved in the creation of Jugoslavia and Czechoslovakia, in a letter to *The Times* 16 September 1914 talked about 'common Southern Slav patriotism', 'the Serbo-Croat race' and the 'Serb, Croat and Slovene race'.[91] Political expediency and the stereotypes from popular culture filled in the gaps. Before they entered the conflict, the Bulgarian nation were described by the Kaiser as 'the most vigorous of all the Balkan races',[92] while it was reported that Bulgarians were believed by Russians to be unnecessarily thrifty.[93] 'The people of Montenegro . . . are extremely bellicose . . . of a peculiarly proud and warlike temperament',[94] while 'the native of Macedonia . . . possesses in full the laziness of the true Oriental and the fascinating tricks of a nation of beggars'.[95] Another soldier's view was that the Greeks were 'a lazy, dirty lot, and such thieves'.[96] The idea of 'dirt' was a strong determinant – the defeated Balkan army in 1918 was described as 'arrayed in Serbian loot, with here and there a filthy uniform':[97] among Britain's allies, the Serbs, having moved on from 'Servia' to 'Serbia' in the autumn of 1914, 'are not dirty people', Mr Hogarth was at pains to assure his audience at a lecture in Oxford in 1915.[98]

British soldiers were also exposed to the difficult relationship between the majority of France and those French citizens living close to the border with Flanders, for many of whom Flemish was their first language. The expression '*les Boches du Nord*' was levelled at these people, echoing the attempts by the German occupiers of Belgium to develop an ethnic relationship based on language. R. H. Mottram, acting as an interpreter and working with a Flemish and a French colleague, relates in *A Personal Record* how the French interpreter ('he disliked his Flemish-speaking compatriots') looks at the names Nordpeene, Bolleseele, Merkeghem on a map and says 'Can we be in France?' His Belgian colleague claims Charlemagne as his military ancestor, whereupon the French interpreter states, '*Charlemagne, c'était tout simplement un boche!*'[99]

The French interpretation of racial grouping that included Flemings under the term 'Boche' refers to the Franco-German assessment of the war in racial terms as a conflict between 'Boche' and 'Welsch', a German term cognate with 'Welsh', meaning 'foreigner'.[100] In effect these are balancing insults: the German *Welsch* at that time carried meanings of 'Roman, Italian, French',[101] and links to the use of 'L'Union Latine', primarily an idea of a connection between France and Italy. An article in the *Manchester Guardian* about fighting in Galicia states that this is where 'the Slavs first became a distinctive race. . . . the two opposite ends of the same Alpine race; the Frenchman and the Russian, are cousins, with an alien northern Teutonic race coming between them to disturb the family unity. Of course, Europe is a hotchpotch of races, and none of us are very pure in our stock, but there is much more than idle fancy in believing that the religious peasant of Brittany is of blood kin with the devout villager of Russia.'[102]

The Kaiser and his advisers were clear that the approach to war was along lines of race: in May 1913 Wilhelm II wrote on a report that 'The struggle between Slavs and Germans can no longer be avoided and will surely come'.[103] The same views were held by the German Chief of the General Staff, Moltke[104] but the Chief of the Austro-Hungarian General Staff, Baron Franz Conrad, felt that for Austro-Hungary a 'racial conflict' would be problematic as it would involve nearly 50 per cent of the empire fighting 'against their racial comrades'.[105] Seaman Richard Stumpf believed that 'at the outbreak of war, our enemies, especially the Russians, expected that the races living along the Danube and the Theiss would come over to their side'.[106]

During the course of the war German propaganda castigated the French and the British for using non-white troops, as a threat to the supremacy of the 'white race'; this had its foundation in centuries of racism, manifested pre-war in the atrocities in German Southwest Africa (1904–7), which were seen in terms of 'racial struggle'.[107] German wartime propaganda against African, Caribbean and Asian troops mirrored the language of the German High Command pre-war – not just 'disgusting Japs', 'filthy Cossacks' and the Kaiser's 1900 comment about Chinese people 'dar[ing] to look cross-eyed at a German', but 'detestable Austrians', 'ghastly Walloons' and 'dirty Americans'.[108]

Awareness of physique is a constant trope in British soldiers' perception of their enemies; it had been so in the early months of the war as it became apparent that the men of Kitchener's Army were typically unfit, undernourished and unable to manage the rigours of military life – and many reported feeling very well after a few months' training. But the enemy they faced were typically presented as short, fat, undernourished, short-sighted, crop-headed, and square-headed. The recent history of anthropometrics in determining a criminal physique opened the potential for an entire race, however the term might be applied, to be condemned as criminal. An anthropometric link between the criminal and the bestial had been proposed and widely taken up in the late-nineteenth century;[109] M. MacDonald's group of 'an undesirable class known as "suspects"', which included spies, people who had robbed dead or dying soldiers, or collaborators, are described as having 'crime and bestiality stamped on their faces'.[110] Fraser and Gibbons applied this thinking to their entry for 'squarehead':

A German. In its origin an old seafarer's term, suggested probably by the somewhat square shape of the typical Teutonic skull. The close-cropped hair of the German soldier on active service, noticed among prisoners, accentuated the idea of squareness, and gave the term currency at the Front in the War. The Squarehead or Nordic type of skull (*brachy-cephalic*) is a recognised form in anthropology, in contradistinction to the Longhead (*dolicho-cephalic*) type. Says a British authority on the subject: 'A very big proportion of the German people are Squareheads. The Saxons are nearly always Nordic, and a quite large proportion of the Prussian aristocracy also. These distinctions as they bear on the habits of the racial types have a bearing also on the callings they choose and the effects of those callings on physique and long life. The great majority of the police are of the Nordic type: so are soldiers and sailors. The Squarehead is almost extinct in these islands. Perhaps, very roughly, one person in 10,000 is an English Squarehead. But it is a very interesting fact that our murderers, in the majority of cases, are square-headed; and in the United States the proportion of murderers of the square-headed type is extraordinarily high.'[111]

Fraser and Gibbons's authority here may have been M. Descamps whose assessment of the Anglo-Saxon head as dolichocephalous and the German 'accurately termed a "squarehead"' was printed in the *Yorkshire Post* in May 1917[112] – and note here the apportioning of scientific and non-scientific terms. An article in the *Chester Chronicle* on 'The Human Body' by the famous anthropometrist Sir Arthur Keith proposes that if you compare a man from Strasbourg with a man from Nottingham there would be little to choose between them, but for the probability that 'the Englishman's face is the longer and narrower'.[113] The demarcation by head shape between Britain, France and Germany was given three days after the declaration of war between Britain and Germany in an article titled 'Nationality in Heads' in the *Sevenoaks Chronicle*, which posed the idea that heads became rounder nearer the equator: 'a Frenchman's head is much rounder than an Englishman's, while "squarehead" is a term often applied to Germans, the latter being very rounded, with the exception of the back, which is decidedly square'.[114] Austrians, though 'very good imitations of the closely-shorn, square-headed, heel-clicking Prussians',[115] were not referred to as 'squareheads', though the description by French–Canadians of the British as *têtes-carrés* implies that the term carried a sense of German-style militarism that could be carried across national boundaries.[116] The effects of anthropometrics were seen in the physical 'grading' of soldiers – A1 down to C3 – which became part of everyday language: 'I am A1 and hope you are too' is a frequent phrase in soldiers' postcards home from the Front.

One incident indicates how terms like 'squarehead' and 'Boches du Nord' mattered: in 1917 a young German officer stationed in Alsace (under German control since 1871, much to the resentment of its French-speaking inhabitants and France itself) 'while instructing his men, insulted the French flag, and called Alsatian regiments "Wackes," a nickname meaning "square-heads," and frequently used by the people of Alsace–Lorraine in a jocular way, but hotly resented by them if used toward them by others'.[117] The taking over of an insult name and its application as a group identity name, only for the use of insiders, is a familiar trope in slang; its use in this circumstance shows the power and sensitivity of slang.

The casual positive and negative characterising of nations, cultures, skin colours, language groups, and so on was easily applied in wartime. The British were 'a race of clean fighters and honest manhood',[118] German troops were told that Maori soldiers cooked their prisoners,[119] VAD Emma Duffin 'might work like a black all night',[120] 'the Arab is not a cleanly creature',[121] '"Chinks" going home',[122] 'the two men [German prisoners] are obviously of the bestial type',[123] 'a Slavonic-featured, black-bearded, sneaking-eyed face',[124] 'it's a pretty tall order for the French to put black Senegalese cannibals into Red Cross uniform',[125] it goes on and on. An internee from Leeds in the Ruhleben camp in Germany wrote home saying 'we have formed an amateur dramatic society ... A few days ago a variety entertainment was given here ... New cinder paths are being made in camp by a gang of negroes, who are paid out of the relief funds'.[126] But from within the camp there was documentation of the language of established racial segregation: 'Mr Cohn's remarks concerning our coloured compatriots appear to have caused a little resentment. It is only natural, however, that the children of Israel should not find favour with the descendants of Ham'.[127] Early-war attempts to show racism being pragmatically laid aside in the Belgian army include a very staged photo for the British war press: 'There is no time now for the "colour-bar," and black and white fraternize freely in the titanic struggle against the German invader',[128] runs the caption. The War Office limited the involvement of the British West Indies Regiment primarily to support and labour duties in France, though their involvement in the fighting in Palestine produced two awards of the Military Medal, and the government's reluctance to bring black soldiers from Africa to the Western Front was questioned in Parliament on 11 October 1916 with the words, 'Why we should not employ more coloured troops I cannot understand. It is simply prejudice'.[129] Robert Houston MP went on to read out a postcard claiming to be from an Englishman living in Switzerland: 'The writing is in German character. I cannot read the communication as the language is so filthy that it is impossible for decent ears to hear it. But I will try to give you the contents without the adjectives, as I do not wish to shock the sensibilities of any hon. Members. "Sir, you suggest in the 'Daily Mail' of 25th September[130] to bring millions of negro soldiers to overrun Europe and to slaughter decent white people. You are nothing but a so-and-so and a so-and-so to make such a vile proposal. What is wanted now is a call to the mob in London to rush the blooming House of Commons and to cut the blooming throats of all you so-and-so s of politicians who made the war and profit by it."' Houston's letter to the *Daily Mail* asked what would be the *'moral'* and *'physical'* effect [Houston's italics] on Germany of putting 'three millions of coloured troops . . . into the field'. Despite the successes of black troops in Africa in the first two years of the war, readers of the popular and provincial press in Britain in 1916 would be more likely to see the word 'negro' associated with news of lynchings in the United Sates, court reports in Britain, minstrel shows, the boxer Jack Johnson, and the raising of labour battalions overseas;[131] the British West Indies Regiment was excluded in 1918 from a general pay rise on the grounds of their classification as 'natives'.

There were voices of reason in this world of racial claim and counter-claim. In 1915 the biologist Peter Chalmers Mitchell's book *Evolution and the War* showed that the German claim for dominance through strength being 'a natural process' had nothing to do with Darwinian evolution, and that 'racially the Germans are a mixture of three primal stocks, like every other nation in Europe'.[132] Sadly, this, like the *Manchester Guardian* observation that 'Europe is a hotchpotch of races, and none of us are very pure in our stock', was unlikely to find favour with the average British citizen assailed with headlines like 'Brute callousness of the Teuton Race'.[133] Fears of racial domination might be no more than a bogey,[134] but it was a widely used bogey. After the Armistice, and particularly its interpretation as the defeat of Germany's attempt at world domination, the war was analysed again in terms of evolution and the 'struggle for survival' in Robert Munro's booklet *From Darwinism to Kaiserism* (1919), which proposed that the German *Weltpolitik* was a misinterpretation of Darwinian natural selection in that 'the absence of morality in the operations of the organic world was accepted by the German military authorities as a justification of their guilty conscience'.[135] Munro gives an idea of historical war as 'survival of the fittest',[136] whose outcomes might not produce 'the progress of humanity', while he implies that the recent war, a 'carnival of bloodshed and misery', was actually to do with 'the British people and their Allies . . . fighting, not only in self-defence, but for the freedom of all nations, as well as the preservation of the landmarks of human civilisation'.[137] But the rhetoric of race is constant throughout the text, and depressingly points forward to that of the 1930s.[138]

The end of the war, and the demise of one episode of 'racial domination', brought a revival of the hopes for racial harmony that had been proposed in Roberts' September 1914 letter: 'This war at least ought to teach us, if not them, one lesson – namely, that civilisation is not the property of any one race or nation, but something after which all nations and races must strive';[139] 'The English and the French must get rid of race-prejudice and pride. The Orientals must lay aside distrust and rancour'.[140] But Japanese attempts to use the concept of racial equality to secure its status, to resolve migration problems between Japan, Britain and British Dominions, and the United States, and to assist in the securing of Japanese support for the League of Nations, failed on a number of grounds, primarily Britain and America's rejection of the idea of universal racial equality.[141]

For British people language and pseudo-science were conflicting bases for ideas of race; outside the bombast of propaganda, language made more sense than anthropometrics as a basis for racial division within Europe. When a group of prisoners from Bohemia and Moravia were questioned as to their feelings about their Russian captors 'they replied, in a quite matter-of-course way: "We are brothers, and speak the same tongue; we are one people"'.[142] Though the unification of Flanders with the Netherlands, desired by many who had seen the Flemish language promoted by the German army of occupation,[143] was not to happen after 1918, linguistic boundaries formed the basis for many of the new countries of Europe.

Naming the enemy

Cartoon characteristics gave soldiers and civilians a clear image of the enemy, which lasted for most of the war. Germans believed the British to be greedy, both personally and geopolitically, while the British believed the Germans, specifically the Prussians, to be militaristic and despotic. French cartoons frequently portrayed Germans as pigs, while the reverse view portrayed the French as peasants. Although the German visual cartoon view of the British soldier in 1914 was less Kipling's Tommy Atkins and more an emaciated Flashman with lank hair and pillbox hat, the German High Command expressed reluctance early on to use pejorative terms against the British in the prosecution of the war, guided by article 22 of the Hague Convention of 1907 respecting the Wars and Customs of War on Land.[144] No such thoughts inhibited the epithets Britons used of Germans.

The various terms used of Germans in general and German soldiers in particular carried different implications, were used by different people, and at different times. The model proposed by Partridge – that 'Boche' was 'used mainly by officers and journalists; fire-eating colonels preferred *Hun*;

the Tommy said *Fritz* in 1914–15, *Jerry* (from *Gerry* – German) in 1916–18'[145] – is too simple, and has been extended by researchers such as Doyle and Schäfer,[146] looking rather at the intentions behind the use of 'Hun', 'Boche/Bosche', 'Alleyman', 'Fritz' and 'Gerry', as well as their respective time periods. Partridge proposed that both 'Hun' and 'Bosche' were uncommon after 1915,[147] while Brophy and Partridge claim that after 1915 Fritz became 'less frequent among private soldiers than "Jerry"'.[148]

Effectively all were used from 1914 onwards, and though individuals and journals had preferences (*Punch* for example liked 'Teutons' for older Germans in positions of power), the implications and inferences of the terms are clearer to see than generalisations on who used what, though it must be said that the Partridge model has created a powerful folk etymology of the terms. Fraser and Gibbons state that 'Hun' was expressive of anger against the Germans, that it 'first came in as a generic name for a German through the newspapers, as an epithet of disgust', but that it was not taken up by the services, other than the Air Force.

Fraser and Gibbons give 'Alleyman' along with 'Fritz' as 'the usual army names for the enemy in the earlier days of the War', giving way to 'Jerry'; 'Fritz', though it certainly continued in use through to 1918, was after the first year gradually superseded by 'Jerry', according to Brophy and Partridge. Though 'Fritz', like 'Jerry', seems to be an attempt to personalise the enemy, it was no more to do with the individual than were the stereotyped names given to the male of any nation – Taffy, Jock, Ivan or Paddy; the glossary of war terms, 'English Army Slang as used in the Great War', in *Notes and Queries* in October 1921, included 'Fritz' as both 'A German' and 'A German aeroplane, shell, or anything aggressive'. Bearing in mind that this glossary is of 'army slang', 'Fritz', 'Jerry' and 'squarehead' are given equal weight as 'A German' ('Heinie' is defined as 'German (American word)', implying potential use as an adjective as well as noun).

'Boche' and 'Bosche' excited those interested in language during and after the war, both in terms of origin and use. Fraser and Gibbons state that it was 'taken up in England by the public in general and the Press' – no mention there of the army – and go on to propose its development from Parisian slang about 1860 to general French use after the Franco-Prussian War of 1870–1; but it was not sufficiently widely used to feature in *L'Éclipse*'s *Dictionnaire de L'Argot Parisien* (1873). The word's etymology was discussed endlessly. Brophy and Partridge's view, derived from Dauzat, is that it emerged from the phrase *tête de boche*, in which *boche* was short for *caboche*, the whole phrase meaning an obstinate person. The Germans having a reputation in France for stubbornness, *allemands*, the standard French word for Germans, became *allboches*, shortened about 1900 to *boches*; propagandist posters revived the memory of *allboches* by employing the term *Sale Boche* (dirty boche). They note that fascination with the word can be gauged from the publication of R. Lestrange's *Petite Monographic du mot Boche* (1918). A. Forbes Sieveking quotes from Albert Dauzat, writer of *L'Argot de la Guerre* (1918), to indicate the sense that 'boche' was essentially a racial term.[149] An article in the *Manchester Guardian* notes also that in the Marseilles dialect the word 'boche' meant a ball.[150] The *allboches/sales boches* pun features in English writing – the *Manchester Guardian* brought the phrase up again in February 1923, and John Masefield, enraged within the environment of the French frontline hospital, writes of 'these sales Bosches who have done this devilry' and 'the sales Bosches have learned they cannot win'.[151] Which raises the question of the spelling. Dauzat uses 'boche',[152] as does Déchelette.[153] Bosch (often spelled as 'Bosche') magnetos,[154] familiar to motorcycle mechanics and riders, may have had an influence, for some soldiers' diaries and letters show both forms in use by the same person: in his 1916 diary Pte G. W. Broadhead uses 'boche' on 26 September and 'Bosche' from 11 November; in *A Scholar's Letters from the Front* (1918) Stephen Hewett uses 'Bosches' on p. 46 and 'boches' on p. 107; and Capt E. Raymond's *Great War Diary* (2011) has 'Bosche' on 9 March 1916 and 'Boche' on 18 October 1917. *Illustrated London News* writers on 29 November 1915 (John Buchan) and 20 January 1917 use 'Bosche', while Lancelot Spicer uses 'Boche', and Lt-General Aylmer Hunter-Weston uses 'Boches';[155] but 'Bosches' was also used[156], as well as 'Boshe' and 'Boshes',[157] and *What's the Dope*, a post-1944 glossary of war terms, has 'Bosche' surviving into the Second World War. There seems to be no pattern to be deduced from this either in spelling or use of capitalisation,[158] but it does fairly counter Brophy and Partridge's claim that it was 'practically never used by the "other ranks" who preferred Jerry'. Seeing that the term was in use by all ranks it is no surprise to see it used by well-known writers – John Buchan and Arnold Bennett used it in writing for the *Illustrated London News*,[159] as 'Boche', though Robert Graves's poem 'A Dead Boche' (1918) was clearly meant to challenge. Journalists, as many commentators note, used the term enthusiastically, though as early as July 1915 *The Daily Mirror* told its readers that the word was out of use, along with 'Tommy';[160] *John Bull* was still using it in 1919 and a boys' adventure story book published in 1936, *Adventures at Greystones*, used it to recall the environment of hate in the war. Not all papers used 'Boche' – the *Daily Citizen*, an ILP

(Independent Labour Party) paper, avoided it, while using 'Germhuns' (13 February 1915) – and though the *Manchester Guardian* was still using it enthusiastically to the end of 1918 it does not appear in the paper after 1922. One example of how the use of the term spread socially is a report in the *Sheffield Evening Telegraph* in which boys who raid birds' nests are described as 'young Huns' and 'the budding Bosch'.[161]

As with many colloquial terms during the war, 'Boche' was pushed into several kinds of use. The standard plural, as in 'we are only ten yards from the Boches'[162] and 'a dozen of the Bosches'[163] implies a standard singular, but 'a Boche' is seldom used. More common is the plural form without 's', as in 'the Boche have been good',[164] 'murderous fire from the Boche',[165] 'Pilken Ridge, recently in the hands of the Boche',[166] or 'the Boche started "crumping" on our left'.[167] This partly merges into an abstract usage: 'The hatred of the Boche is much more pronounced'[168] or 'War is cruel and the Boche is bloodthirsty'.[169] Equally the term is used as an adjective, as in 'a Boche dugout'[170] or 'a Boche aeroplane'.[171] Some bombs were also called 'boches',[172] while rarely the term was used as an abstract name, like Fritz: 'Boche is "hating" us this afternoon'.[173] An extension of the word into a verb exists as 'the Bosching of Austria', a cartoon in *Punch* 10 July 1918, in the sense of exerting threatening pressure.

GUERRE 1914-1916. — Bataille de la Marne. — Chatillon-sur-Morin à 4 kil. d'Esternay, entièrement détruit par les Boches. — Chatillon-sur-Morin destroyed by the Boches — LL.

FIGURE 3.2 French civilian propaganda: a huge number of postcards published in France, with captions in French and English, showed photos of destruction on French territory, often explicitly blamed on 'the Boches'.

Certainly the French, with more history both of the term and of an antagonistic relationship with Germany, had no qualms about using the word, and it must have been easily recognised by any English-speaking soldier on arrival in France. A 1914 article in *The Times* states that the term is 'on the lips of every man, woman and child in the country'.[174] French postcards used the term frequently (*'jeunes "boches" prisonniers'* for example). It was naturally used in French-speaking Belgium, a British soldier being warned by a Belgian woman in Sevry on 10 November 1918 with the single word 'Boche',[175] and was the standard term used in Tommy French conversations with local people in Flanders and Northern France, the Armistice being marked with widespread exchanges of 'Guerre finie – Boche napoo!'[176] Some American soldiers had trouble with 'Boche': 'They may be "Boches" to the French and the British, but the Huns . . . will never be anything but "Bushes" to Uncle Sam's doughboys. It was too hard to get the proper pronunciation of "Boches".'[177]

German attitudes to the word were extremely negative; as a footnote to the curious story of the nail-filled wooden statue of Hindenburg, the *Manchester Guardian* writer states that while Germans did not mind being called Huns, 'all through the war the German rank and file became furious when they were called Boches'.[178] Germans seem to have been sensitive to the terms used to describe them: an early German–English soldiers' phrasebook equipped soldiers to say 'We are no barbarians, as people often say in France and in Belgium'.[179]

> An early German–English soldiers' phrasebook equipped soldiers to say 'We are no barbarians, as people often say in France and in Belgium'.

During the post-war occupation of Germany continued use of 'boche' fuelled resentment; the *Manchester Guardian* noted that the French use of the word in official documents would create 'a bitterness of feeling that will not easily be effaced'.[180] Divisions between French citizens from the occupied and free zones were exacerbated by the use of the word to describe those who had lived under German rule, with a French man being fined and required to pay damages for calling a French–Alsatian 'Boche', 'even if not preceded by the wartime "dirty"'.[181] In Paris itself there was a civil prosecution on 1 April 1919 when Mlle Dorziat was awarded £880 in damages against Mlle Blanche Toutain, who had called her a 'Boche', the defendant having to pay for the judgement to be publicised in ten French and British newspapers. The power of the word post-war is seen in the report that the French Academy were proposing to include it in the Academy Dictionary of the French Language, while omitting 'poilu'.[182] In post-war Britain the term caused fewer problems. *The Times* referred to how the occupied Belgians had managed to carry out 'Boche-baiting',[183] and a murder committed with a '"Boche" knife' was reported in July 1921;[184] *The Ypres Times*, a veterans' newspaper, had no problems about publishing the word,[185] and Rudyard Kipling felt able to say 'the Boche learned nothing from the last war', in 1933.[186]

The difference in tone between 'Boche' and 'Hun' is easier to recognise than to define; 'boche' perhaps had some resonance with 'bosh', a derogatory term for margarine common from the late-nineteenth century (from its place of manufacture, Hertogenbosch in Holland), and 'bosh' meaning rubbish, but both terms were used to ridicule Germans. The fact that Germans hated 'Boche' but did not mind 'Hun' highlights the source of the words – 'Boche' as an external insult, and 'Hun' as a term that originated from within the German military experience.[187] 'Boche' was temporary, while 'Hun' referenced a past, selective or inventive perhaps; thus from an Allied point of view 'the Boche' was redeemable, while 'the Hun' was not. 'Hun' implied a racial viewpoint, examined above, with its own discourse of physical and temperamental characteristics.

Kaiser Wilhelm II in an address to German troops at Bremerhaven on 27 July 1900 declared: 'Just as a thousand years ago the Huns under their King Attila made a name for themselves, one that even today makes them seem mighty in history and legend, may the name German be affirmed by you in such a way in China that no Chinese will ever again dare to look cross-eyed at a German'. *The Iodine Chronicle* December 1917[188] extended this into 'The Kaiser has said that he is a reincarnation of Attila the Hun': the word was a gift to Allied propaganda. Any ethnological claim to descent[189] was argued in articles such as 'Are the Germans really Huns?' in *The Pow-Wow*[190] and the pamphlet *Huns Ancient and Modern* (1918). The term seemed ideal for use in August 1914 as German troops overran Belgium, but it took a few weeks to catch on in Britain. The earliest references in *The Daily Mirror* in September 1914 were to the 'ancient Huns' (1 and 3 September, p. 5), then to 'German Huns' and 'modern Huns' (4 and 5 September, pp. 12 and 1), and only from 11 September as

'Huns' alone (11 September, p. 1). Illustrating the wide enjoyment of puns[191] the term 'Germhuns' was popular in 1914, and remained in use throughout the conflict. *Comic Cuts* (advertising itself as 'The paper that tickles our Tommies' and 'The Soldiers' Comic' in 1917) first used 'Germ-Huns' in its 31 October 1914 issue, retaining the phrase beyond the introduction of 'Huns' in the 12 December issue. The tub-thumping *John Bull*, which advertised itself as 'The Soldiers' Friend', had 'Germhuns', 'Germhun papers' and 'that Germhun Bartholomew',[192] and 'I hear that Germhunny is short of wool',[193] but also published a letter mentioning 'a German Hun';[194] the paper was still using 'Germhuns' in September 1917: 'he thinks like a Germhun'.[195] *John Bull* used 'Hun' and 'German' throughout, but not 'Boche'. 'Germhuns' was a populist journalists' term, ignored by Fraser and Gibbons and by Brophy and Partridge, 'not originally an army term' according to the Miscellany writer in the *Manchester Guardian* in early 1915.[196] The same article also claimed that the terms 'Germ-Huns' and 'Germs' were already out of date, noting also the use of 'Gerboys' by an officer in a comment on the youth of many German soldiers, and 'canaries', deriving from some soldiers' experience of German soldiers primarily as prisoners in the barbed wire holding stations. 'Germs' was a soldiers' term, widely used in Sgt Bernard Brookes' diary, presumably both an abbreviation and a reference to disease:[197] 'This show had been occupied by the Germs and then by the French from whom we took over. The filth and stench was too awful for words, one of our batteries striking rather unlucky in coming across Germs buried just under the surface when they started digging their guns in'.[198]

'Hun' was used in the singular and plural, as an adjective, and as an impersonal or abstract – 'I have not seen a complete Hun, but I have seen him in sections',[199] 'Ready for the Huns',[200] 'got all the Hun wire cut',[201] 'the Hun lines',[202] 'shells from the Hun',[203] 'all the Hun killing we were enabled to do',[204] 'the war against "the Hun" is over'.[205] And like 'Boche', 'Hun' could be extended: 'We wandered for a long time over Hunland',[206] 'Hunnish barbarities',[207] the 'Hun-bird',[208] and inevitably a pun, in 'Hunny Moon', a moonlit night for Zeppelins.[209]

The given characteristics of 'the Hun' can show how this epithet differed from others. *Huns Ancient and Modern*, while a heavy caricature, gives an idea of how some on the Home Front justified their distaste for Germany through historical views; as 'cherish[ing] war not as an instrument of noble purposes, but for its own sake', as 'drown[ing] men at sea' and believing 'Frightfulness' to be 'a pleasant conception'.[210] The Huns were 'a set of inhuman monsters'[211] and 'a nation of sneaks',[212] 'brutal',[213] ruled over by an emperor who was known by his subjects as 'the All-Highest'.[214] The sense of the term at the Front was formed less by outrage than by a sense of a military figure: there was an objectification – 'a large fat Hun'[215] – but 'the Hun' was not so much an individual person as an abstract figure, the enemy. On the Home Front any failure to work towards the war effort might merit being called a Hun: 'The manufacturer [of overpriced matches] may be British, but he is a Hun' claimed a writer for the *Manchester Guardian*.[216] 'I wish you to keep your eyes glued on the Huns at home';[217] 'they had to fight against German Huns, British Huns, and Taunton Huns . . . these so-called Christian employers were so mean, so Hun-like . . .'[218]

The use of 'Hun' was widespread across all sections of society during the war,[219] both among British officers and men, nurses,[220] Canadian soldiers,[221] civilians,[222] civilian internees in Germany,[223] and advertising copywriters.[224] However, Fraser and Gibbons state that 'the services did not adopt the name to any extent; except the Air Force, with whom it was the usual name for the enemy'. And the *Manchester Guardian*'s Miscellany writer for 13 January 1915 wrote '"Huns" may look very pretty as a column heading; it does not belong to the slang of the trenches'. The word was very popular in the press in 1914, and remained more popular than 'Boche', 'Fritz' or 'Jerry', with no sense of a decrease in usage as the conflict went on. It was still in use in the *Manchester Guardian* in early 1919, along with the middle-brow tabloid magazine *The Bystander*, which had published Bruce Bairnsfather's Ole' Bill cartoons, and in *John Bull*, which referred in January 1919 to 'the transport of Huns back to their own country'. Metaphorical use continued with the reactionary White Guards who took control in the German capital in January 1919 being described as 'raging like Huns in Berlin',[225] and references as late as December 1919 to 'Hun (or rather German) names of places in England' in *The Athenaeum*.[226]

Popular in 1914, and clearly picked up from French people, was 'Alleyman', with its variants 'Ollerman' and 'Allerman'. Fraser and Gibbons state that this, and Fritz, gave way to 'Jerry', and Brophy and Partridge give 'not much used after 1916'. In Charles Edmonds' *A Subaltern's War* the officer uses 'Boche', while the private uses 'Alleyman',[227] with 'Allemans' being used to describe a group of prisoners.[228] A soldier writing in thanks for a parcel (under a scheme whereby citizens with no immediate contact in the forces could support a serviceman), reads 'Thanks very much for the parcel, it is very good of you Im sure . . . This place has not been visited by the Allemands. . .'. The soldier is writing in a polite style ('Im sure'), and may be carefully avoiding slang, or may be indicating that even by July 1914 British soldiers were prepared to use French correctly when they wanted to. A variant of 'Ten Brown Bottles' published in *The Comet* (a troopship magazine) has 'nine anxious Allemands', the song also featuring 'seven boss-eyed Bosches', 'six horrid Hunlets', and 'three "K"-owardly Komarads'.[229]

Documentation of soldiers' use of 'Fritz' is seen from the autumn of 1914 – German type-characters tended to be called Hans or Carl before the war. Again there are abstract usages, though the plural form, usually as 'Fritzies', is less common. Usually the usage was in the form of 'Fritz sending his minenwerfer',[230] 'Fritz's efforts',[231] and 'Fritz quiet'.[232] Popular among junior officers and men, the name was used for Germans[233] also by the French, though 'Boche' was much more common. 'Fritzie' as a noun was popular with Canadian and American troops, less so with British soldiers: '5 or ten tons of Fritzie's bombs'.[234] The word did not make a comfortable adjective – Frank Hawkings' 'the water has all gone into Fritz trenches'[235] – or a plural: Ian Hay uses 'Fritzes'[236] but the usual plural was the impersonal 'Fritz'. 'A Fritz' was a naval term for a German submarine, seen in an article by John Margerison for the *Illustrated London News* featuring 'the Hun', 'the Fritz' and 'Fritz';[237] at Gallipoli it was the term for an aeroplane: '. . . as they passed over the Turkish lines they were attacked by a Fritz (Turkish or German aero-plane)'.[238] 'Fritz' tended to be less vicious, more tiresome, 'paying attention to our district again',[239] who 'has made a mess of everywhere round here';[240] the lessening of the threat in the name is seen in its extension into 'old Fritz',[241] 'old man Fritz',[242] 'cousin Fritz',[243] 'Unser Fritz',[244] and even, for a Tyneside Irish soldier, 'brother Fritz';[245] 'Brother Boche' was an occasional usage.[246]

Fraser and Gibbons mention an extremely dubious etymology for 'Jerry', namely that 'Fritz' became 'Fitz', which suggested 'Fitzgerald', and so 'Gerald', 'Gerry' and thus 'Jerry'. What was observed is that the 'Irish Rifles, Dublins and Munsters' used the term Jerry 'in their slang',[247] and that in the book *The Irish on the Somme* by Michael MacDonagh (1917) 'a Gerry', 'the Gerrys', 'a Gerry machine-gun', and 'Gerry' as a form of address to Germans, are used repeatedly. Elsewhere the spelling 'Gerry' appears rarely.[248] The general consensus is that 'Jerry' developed as a diminutive of 'German', fairly early on (Doyle and Schäfer give an example from September 1914, but in inverted commas – 'if the "Jerries" could shoot').[249] It had the advantage of easy usage as name, singular, plural, adjective and abstract, though 'the jerry' is rare – 'defend it in case the jerry attacks again'.[250] The abstract usage is common – 'Jerry began searching the wood with "heavies"'.[251] It also worked well with familiar usage – 'I thought Old Jerry's here',[252] 'our friend Jerry',[253] indeed Brophy and Partridge describe the term as being 'almost of affection'. They also give a 'more fanciful, if improbable' source in the supposed similarity between German helmets and chamberpots ('jerry' being a slang term for a chamberpot), but the term was in use long before the steel helmet was issued.

Any demarcation of meaning or connotation between these terms is made more difficult by the way sources frequently use two or more of them apparently indiscriminately. 'German' was a more neutral and sometimes respectful term, but was often used alongside 'Hun'. Emma Duffin had two German soldiers in her ward, known as 'the old Bosch' and 'the little Hun';[254] *Comic Cuts* has in the same story 'Germans', 'Germ-Huns' and 'Deutschers';[255] G. B. Manwaring in *An Officer's Letters* (1918) uses 'Hun', along with 'German', 'Fritz', and 'the Bosche'; Major M. Macleod uses 'the Huns' along with 'the Germans';[256] Pte G. W. Broadhead uses 'German', 'Hun' and 'Fritz';[257] *The Listening Post* uses 'Huns', 'German' and 'Fritzie';[258] and the *Sunday Post* (30 June 1918, p. 8) has 'the Jerry squareheads'. The inclusiveness with regard to names continued after the war, with 'A Blow For Fritz . . . the tenderest part of Jerry's anatomy'[259] or 'a Jerry steel helmet . . . removed by him from an offending Boche'.[260]

There were other terms – 'kraut', 'squarehead', 'Dutch', 'Prussian', 'Teuton', 'kamerad' – which show how the soldiers' language reflected what was of the most significance to them. Like the archetypal range of Inuit words for 'snow', words for the enemy reflected where the speaker came from, fashion and the value of using the current terms, the changing environment, the emotion of the moment. 'Kraut', more expected from the Second World War, was an American contribution, as in '. . . we just bet that Kraut was scared to death',[261] and 'You can't smash us, you sauer-krauters.'[262] Lighter's *Slang of the AEF* gives a range of spellings, 'kraut', 'krout', and 'crout', with the extensions 'kraut-eater', 'krauthead' and 'sauerkraut'.

'Squarehead' was a generic term for Scandinavian and German sailors before it was applied to German soldiers; in America it had been for decades applied disparagingly to Swedish migrants. A story reported in the *Liverpool Echo* refers to a longstanding animosity between British and German sailors, the latter referred to as 'square-heads',[263] while a brief article in the *Portsmouth Evening News* opens the category still wider: 'At sea the term "Squarehead" is indiscriminately applied to Scandinavian mariners, Swedes, Norwegians and Finns. A German, when he does occur, which is not often, is "Dutchy". Cf "Deutscher".[264] It seems to have come to the fore in 1915: "'Boche', as a name for the German soldier, is out of date now with "Tommy", I am told. His description is apt: the Huns he now always refers to as "squareheads". You know those German haircuts'.[265] The usage was as a noun: 'The "squareheads" have been very busy';[266] 'Give the "squareheads" a few good English volleys';[267] and occasionally as an adjective too: 'Some "squareheads" submarines had gone to intercept us'.[268] It is a puzzling term, capable of expressing a range of feelings depending on the context: contempt in '. . . the business of putting lead in square-heads'[269] and 'squareheads (Tommies' nickname for the Germans in the lagers [prisons])';[270] or humour, when a soldier captures two Germans with the words 'Come along you big square-headed gents, or you'll be late for the theatre'.[271] The anthropometric aspect of these, removing all but the physical characteristics, allows distancing and brutally racist perception. It is rare to find the term in memoirs other than as a racial description, but the press seemed to like its contempt and simplistic viewpoint. The *Newcastle Evening Chronicle* used the headline 'The Durhams' Scrap with the "Square-heads"' even though the letter from the soldier quoted does not use the word.[272] 'Dutchy', above, would be an anglicisation of 'Deutscher'; Partridge in *A Dictionary of Slang and Unconventional English* gives 'Dutchman: a German; "any North European seaman except a Finn": nautical colloquial . . '. The *32nd News* American trench journal uses 'Dutch' to mean 'German'.[273]

'Prussian' was a more serious term, including within Germany. The rise of the military in the Prussian state, and later the entire German state as it became dominated by Prussia, led to the idea internationally of Prussians as militaristic automatons, subservient to their ruler. This was underlined by reports of the supposedly more decent soldiers from Saxony or Bavaria disliking Prussians, a distinction that spread through the British army and served as a low-level moral boost;[274] for British propaganda writers any historical evidence of animosity on the part of other Germans towards Prussians, such as Goethe's 'The Prussian is cruel by birth; civilisation will make him ferocious'[275] was a godsend. The press enjoyed using 'Prussian', which both expressed their views of the ruling circle's bombast and the Kaiser's manners during earlier visits to Britain, and conveniently allowed the geographical locating of the enemy far away from the British royal family's German antecedents. Probably the first negative epithets to be applied to the Germans, early on there were 'The Prussians', 'The Prussian wolf' and 'Prussia's Iron Hell'.[276] The use of the word in the press increased tenfold on the outbreak of war, and extended into 'Prussianism',[277] 'Prussianisation',[278] and the wonderful 'People don't shove quite so selfishly, don't scowl at each other so Prussianly'.[279] For the troops, awareness of the level of training and resilience among the Prussian Guard meant that the word had fewer connotations of humour, though Boyd Cable's story 'The Blighty Squad' has a cheerful wounded soldier say to a sentry 'We're the blinkin' Prussian Guards'.[280]

'Teuton' and 'Teutonic' carried ideas of medieval knightly thoroughness and brutality, and was popular in the press; old German men in clubs were Teutons,[281] as were the archetypal British-hating internment camp doctors ('the hatred of the English had sunk deep into the heart of the Teuton'),[282] and obsessively efficient wiring parties in no man's land 'patrol with Teutonic thoroughness'[283] – 'Teutonic efficiency' and 'Teutonic thoroughness' are frequently found in memoirs. The 'Teuton' was primarily a soldier: 'in spite of all we say about the Teuton, he is taking his punishment well, and we've got a big job on our hands'.[284] The term also symbolised the, to the British, German lack of any sense of humour: 'the celebrated "Hymn of Hate" and various other popular Teutonic melodies'; or if there was a sense of humour, it was essentially medieval: 'A few have endeavoured to be humorous, after the ponderous manner of the Teuton, which nearly always suggests the jester's bladder suspended by a string from the end of a stick'.[285] However, parallel to this was a capacity for indicating knightly nobility: Crofts describes a wounded German soldier, sixteen years old, who had been lying in no man's land; as he meets 'the curious gaze of his enemies . . . his face was the ageless face of a Teutonic hero'.[286]

There is very little documentation of 'Kamerads', developed from the word German soldiers used when surrendering, being used to describe German soldiers, but it worked as a lingua franca term, seen in an observation by Major H. Bidder in 1916, who heard a soldier explaining to a French woman that the enemy had been nearly wiped out in fighting, with the words 'Kamerad napoo!'[287] There was a clear model of using words from a foreign language to describe speakers of that language: the French use of 'ya-yas' for Germans,[288] British and American soldiers using 'parleyvoos' for French people (which had been around for 100 years at least), and the German use of 'tuhlömong' and 'ohlala' for French soldiers.[289] Occasional uses of 'Hans' for the abstract German soldier were most likely individual usages.[290]

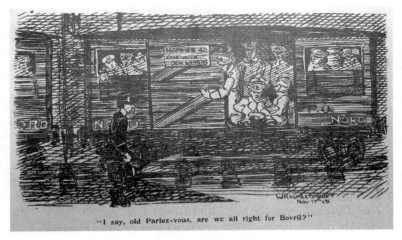

"I say, old Parlez-vous, are we all right for Bovril?"

FIGURE 3.3 *The Gasper*, edited by UPS Battalion soldiers, uses 'parlez-vous' rather than the more frequent soldiers' 'parley-voo'. 8 January 1916.

'Boche' and 'Hun' were not much revived in 1939, but 'Jerry', 'squarehead' and 'kraut' were; 'Fritz' was less common. Perhaps the first two had been too strongly linked to those who commanded and commented rather than those who fought and died. In post-war interviews, especially those made after 1945, it is very difficult to know whether the use of 'Jerry' is coloured by the more recent conflict. While there are dozens of markers of authenticity in these texts, there is also markedly less use of 'Fritz', and a notable absence of 'Alleyman', 'Hun' or 'Boche'.[291] This is not in any way to impute a lack of accuracy, but rather to highlight the way that the language of the conflict continued to develop and be influenced both by the Second World War and by a developing sense that 'Boche', 'Hun', 'Fritz', 'Jerry', and 'Alleyman' carried distinct connotations which emerged in memoir-writing, memory recall and story-telling. Neil Tytler's apparent callousness is both conveyed and allowed by his almost exclusive use of 'Hun', particularly the abstract 'the Hun', while in the words of the veterans quoted in MacDonald's *They Called it Passchendaele* there is a distancing from anger against the enemy in the widespread use of 'Jerry'. It was a feeling that could be seen soon after the Armistice: 'We no longer referred to them as Huns now that we were in Germany. Innate goodness of feeling prevented the use of that name, though indeed the German was never Bosche nor Hun to the rank and file, but always "Jacky" or "Jerry" or "Fritz." We soon learned that the Germans greatly disliked the appellation of "Bosche," which apparently was not absolutely meaningless but meant "ill-begotten" or something of the sort'.[292]

Austrian soldiers, if encountered, were called 'Fritz', or occasionally 'Hans Wurst', while Turkish soldiers were occasionally 'Abdul',[293] but usually 'Johnny' or 'Johnny Turk', or 'Jacko'.[294] In a 1964 interview Anzac veteran Frank Brent used the term 'Old Joe', rhyming slang from 'Joe Burke' (Turk),[295] while Aubrey Herbert recorded a New Zealand soldier receiving Turkish prisoners at Gallipoli with the words 'Come in here, Turkey';[296] Turks called Allied soldiers 'Johnny Kikrik'.[297] 'Johnny Turk' was around before and after the war, and was the name of a racehorse up to 1954. Brophy and Partridge record the use of 'burglars' for Bulgars, and the King of Bulgaria was 'Ferdy',[298] but a postcard with the caption 'When you meet the Bulgars knock the "L" out of them' serves as a clear indication of what they were usually called.

'Tommy' was the term most widely used by Germans soldiers to describe and address their British counterparts, though Fraser and Gibbons state that 'the khakis' was 'the usual enemy name for the British troops, used colloquially among the Germans on the Western Front, in particular during the earlier months of the war'. The German trench slang dictionary *1000 Worte Front-Deutsch* (1925) states that after 'Tommy' the main German epithet for British soldiers was *Fussballindianer*. The British were certainly obsessed with football – one of the army's main problems arising between them and local farmers was access to land for playing football; Lancelot Spicer reported that 'they object thoroughly to our playing on their grasslands. One old fellow told me that all the countryside around complained of the English Army, and that they would really rather have the Germans here than us'.[299] For the French, the Germans were Boches, and for as long as they used the *pickelhaube* they were 'Pointus',[300] and German artillerymen were referred to as Ernst, Otto and Michel; Partridge also notes Esnault recording 'ya-yas' as a French name for Germans. The Germans used *der Ohlala* and *Tuhlömong* for the French, a mix of humour and fear.[301]

How others speak

While it is fairly easy to imagine British soldiers having trouble speaking and understanding French when they arrived, it is more difficult to imagine the shock of those soldiers who did not realise that there would be people who could not understand English: 'Oh love a duck, can't the Froggies understand blinking English?' was the response of an exasperated Kitchener's Army man to 'I not understand'.[302] There was however, for many, an expectation of how foreign languages sounded, and during the war English pastiches of German, and to a lesser extent French, were widely disseminated. The main pathways for this were satirical postcards, magazines, cartoons and comics, for German, and Tommy French for French.

Three terms stand out in the frequent descriptions of the foreign languages anglophone servicemen and women encountered, 'jabber', 'babble' and 'chatter'; even when nurse Madge Sneyd-Kynnersley spoke French to wounded Belgian soldiers she wrote 'I jabbered French to them'.[303] VAD Emma Duffin's Egyptian servant 'chattered Arabic to me',[304] George Barker notes 'the excited babble from the Gurkhas',[305] German soldiers 'jabber'[306] ('I could hear them jabbering away'[307]), and 'a Rochdale officer' wakes up to hear a French woman 'chattering away like a jackdaw'.[308] All these imply fast speech which the listener cannot understand, but 'jabber' and 'babble' also imply foolishness and lack of control: significantly the shell-shocked soldiers in Sassoon's 'Repression of War Experience' 'jabber among the trees'.

Written pastiche German used a number of catchwords, changes to consonants, and specific words, particularly 'hoch', 'vos', and 'mein Gott', the use of 'v' for 'w' and 'd' for 'th' to imitate German speech sounds, the substitution of 'k' for 'c', and the reduction of tail-questions into 'isn't it'. Also there were cross-language puns, imitations of German syntax, and wordplay based on German names, often used with visual caricatures of Germans, to make fun of the German language, particularly its pronunciation of English. The popular press was a great user of pastiche German: in the *Sheffield Evening Telegraph* a brief article gives what became an archetype of supposed German deception, using British uniforms to ambush British troops, in which the Germans apparently shout 'Nein, nein, leedle mistake; ve vos not Shermans; ve vos der Vilts' [Wiltshires]; 'The British then charged with the bayonet, and the Germans "Vilted"'.[309] A satirical poem 'A German on Jutland' begins: Ven we set out ter meet der foe, / Von Tirpitz – none are wiser – / He say you pring soom Pritish shell / As keepsake for der Kaiser'.[310] Elsewhere an advertisement for Chairman Cigarettes has German soldiers surrendering, saying 'Ve vos your brisoners, Kamerad, you give us Chairmans, isn'd it?'[311] And at the end of the war the American trench journal *Thirty Second News*, November 1918, has a woman saying 'Tings iss on der pum aind id?' The advertisement for the Press Art School 'Nein!

Nein! I vill the Press Art School not join!'[312] incorporates German syntax too. There is occasional use of this demonstration of how German works and how it is different from English, in trench journals[313] and dramatisations,[314] continuing the propaganda need to maintain the view that Germans were ridiculous – 'I believe that if the Germans beat us and invaded England they would still be laughed at as ridiculous foreigners'.[315] This was all part of a general tendency to patronise foreigners and foreign languages: in November 1914 *Home Chat's* apparently pragmatic advice on the pronunciation of Przemysl, 'most people think out a pronunciation for themselves and say "Prizzymizzle – or whatever you call it"', masked a deep-seated combination of insularity and arrogance.[316]

Key words signifying pastiche German were 'hoch', recognisable from the soldier's song 'We are Fred Karno's/King George's army', with the line 'Hoch, hoch, mein Gott';[317] 'Himmel', used as a standard expression of surprise;[318] and 'vos'. 'Vos', or occasionally 'vas', was from the German *was*, the pronunciation of 'w' as a 'v' being familiar to thousands of anglophones from the large number of Germans working as waiters in Britain before the war. A cartoon in *The Bystander* has a Prussian Polish soldier talking to a Russian Polish soldier: 'You gif me your flag und I gif you mine, and ven ve get back ve vos both decorated, ain't it?',[319] where 'vos' is used for the verb 'to be', and incidentally the German has picked up some colloquial English. The syntax joke could be extended too so that it signified German speech without the need for 'vos' and so on: 'Brother Bosche's motto appears to be: "It is a fine morning. There is nothing in the trenches doing. We abundant ammunition have. Let us a little frightfulness into the town pump"',[320] providing a speech-model for a century's worth of caricature German military officers.

Some of the wordplay with German was typical of puns crossing languages – General von Kluck was regularly 'old one o'clock'; 'Kamarade, gib mit vater; ze Englisch vos not bullies!' 'What's he on about Bill?' 'Oh, chuck him a can of "bully"'.[321] Much of this depended on a knowledge of German. The manipulation of German, and of German rendering of English, while being noticeable, was not by any means universal or necessarily satirical. Gilbert Nobbs writing of his time as a PoW transcribes German, in a passage carrying no signs of humour, thus: 'Ze English zey have been firing ze long-range guns here, big guns. Zay carry twenty-seven miles. Ve moved dis hospital two times – yah'.[322] Readers of magazines like *Punch* had been exposed to this kind of transcription before the war: in 1912 *Punch* carried two cartoons with

German-speakers, a German visitor saying 'Vaitor, I speak der English not moch. Vill you der nodis exblain', and a 'Teutonic bandsman' saying 'Ja, dis time I blay faster und finish first'.[323]

One area where this mattered was in the detection of spies. Spy-panic was at its height at the beginning of the war and gradually died away, but there are instances of language anomalies, almost shibboleths, being used to catch spies. Fraser and Gibbons tell the story of two Australian officers at Gallipoli, who are suspicious of a major who joins them and advises them on a direction of firing. They ask him 'are you fair Dinkum?', and the reply 'Yes, I'm Major Fair Dinkum' gives him away as a spy.[324] A. M. Burrage is told by his sergeant to 'shoot anyone who can't properly pronounce the consonant "W"',[325] while At the Crossroads ends with the spy revealing himself by his German word order – 'the King's messenger a lie tells'.[326]

French transcriptions of German overlap with English transcriptions. The 'Hoch, hoch' is there ('Hoch … Hoch … c'est un morceau de roi'),[327] 'kamerad' is usually 'kamarat',[328] 'mein Gott' becomes 'Mein goot!' while 'nicht gut' remains as is (Le Mouchoir 25 October 1916, p. 4), and 'kaput' becomes, in an English translation of a French report, 'capout'.[329]

While German in both French and English was rendered to create comic effect, there was some care taken to avoid this happening in the transcription of French in English, by avoiding excessive transcription. A poem in the Northern Mudguard uses 'z' in place of 'th', and this, with the occasional 'Engleesh' and 't'ink' (for 'think') suffices to portray a French person speaking English.[330] A rhyme for Chairman Cigarettes has the French character say 'who ees zis Chairman zat I see. He takes ze cake, And I vill one more Chairman take.'[331] This is described as being in 'pidgin' French, yet he says 'Oui, oui, you bet', speaking not 'pidgin' French, but standard French and colloquial English, with minimal French markers, apart from the 'v' in 'vill'. More typical is the February 1918 quoting of a French liaison officer, which is in standard English – 'Are we all here? Yes, and we shall stay here'.[332] Markers of French accents in the transcription of words spoken by poilus were noticeably absent in British newspapers during wartime, and the only identifiable French accent in cartoons in Punch for the first six months of 1917 is that of a civilian.

Given the environment of transcribing the sounds of other languages it is not surprising that the written corpus should transcribe the multiple accents of English, as 'Stratford-atte-Bowe mingles west tribe modulated high and low';[333] Aubrey Smith waiting for his troopship at Southampton found soldiers from all parts of the British Isles creating 'a regular babel of heathen tongues ... the variety of dialects was most disconcerting'.[334] Kipling and Wells had brought this into mainstream literature, and works by Kipling had cemented its role in transcribing the speech of soldiers. While it is rare to find colonial accents transcribed, memoirs and diaries contain a wealth of transcribed accents from within the British Isles. Scottish and cockney accents feature most frequently, though the London accent ranged over much of the urban and rural south. Transcription of Scottish accents as well as written dialect ranged from the simple 'wee scrap of paper' in a postcard featuring a Scottish soldier, to Ian Hay's 'There's no Chumney-stalks in Gairmany' 'Maybe no; but there's wundmulls. See the wundmull there – on yon wee knowe!' 'That's a pit-heid!'[335] Adèle De L'Isle, working as a VAD, transcribed 'Jock's speech as 'I'm ta dry the noo, but I'll clane 'em if she'll come an' do the "spitten" part'.[336] Scottish newspapers naturally were happy to publish Scots dialect texts, especially if they highlighted the Scottish soldier's experience in France: 'I reeze the sowans an' seerup, the kebbuk an' the scones, / An' Bawbie hearkens, blushin' at ma "mercis" an' "tray-bons"';[337] but this is altogether distinct from the accent transcribed in 'oh, we did'na expec' them back at all; they went hame the Seterday with their deescharrge – medically unfeet. Dinna ken what they'll do either, as they did'na luk as if they'd a bawbee atwixt them'.[338]

The Scottish accent had a reputation for impenetrability, never mind that there were several Scottish accents. Aubrey Smith tells of a policeman who 'shouted out a lot of nonsense in broad Scotch ...: honestly I could not understand a word ...'.[339] Charles Douie tells of being stuck in a shell hole with his company commander: 'Suddenly two Highlanders fell on top of us, and proceeded to engage each other in conversation, apparently of a humorous character, but virtually unintelligible.'[340] For at least one French estaminet-keeper the same problem arose: 'a private in France' wrote that 'I walked into an estaminet the other day and found the proprietor struggling to understand some Gordons. I stepped into the breach and straightened out the tangle. Afterwards he said, "Je comprends bien les Anglais, et je comprends les soldats d'Irlande" (here he threw up both hands), "mais je ne comprends pas les Ecossais." I told him that it was difficult for me to make them out at times and he was delighted.'[341] The troopship magazine *The Comet* carried the usual 'Things we want to know' column including 'If a few lessons in Scotch would not be acceptable to enable the Englishman on board to understand some of their friends from north 'o the Tweed. And ... failing this, an interpreter may be appointed.'[342] Pronunciation difficulties led to renaming of trenches: Peter Chassaud reports that in the

La Biselle sector the 51st Highland Division marked their taking over of trenches from the French by renaming them, and when English troops took over from Scots they also renamed them; in both instances the reason given was that the earlier names were hard to pronounce.[343] Douie recalls teasing a Highland major by mispronouncing Sauchiehall Street as 'Saucy Hall Street', the major subsequently requiring alcoholic support.[344]

Variations of cockney and the London and south England urban accent dominate transcriptions of British soldier slang, as they dominate advertisements featuring soldiers, recorded dramatisations, post-war films and the wider personifications of 'Tommy' saying 'Gorblimey', 'Arf a mo, Kaiser', or ' 'eave 'arf a brick at 'im'. In a cartoon postcard a child with a paper hat and wooden sword is called home with 'Hi, Kitchener! Yer muvver wants yer!'; or from *Scoops* by Harry Greenwall: 'It was like this 'ere. Yer see we came along together, neither 'im nor me knowing where we was going. Nobbler, as perky as you please, asks an orficer. . .'.[345] Adèle De L'Isle describes a wounded cockney soldier called Snowball: 'His coster language was often difficult to understand. His ideal was his "Muvver." "She's a brick, she is. Many a fick ear she's give me when she's caught me aplying shove-'a'ny, an' she ain't no bigger'n you, leastwys, not in 'ight, but roun', oo lor! She'd mike four o' yer"'.[346] 'Ullo! Wot's wrong now Tom? Wot's run up agin yer this time? . . . Cawn't you hear me a callin' yer? . . .' appears in *Fall In*.[347] Greenwall describes the cockney accent as having a 'twang', and it is the accent which tends to be most energetically transcribed.

Less frequently occurring are transcriptions of Irish accents and speech patterns, such as Malins' 'Shure, sor, and it's gas shells the dirty swine are sending over',[348] Emma Duffin's 'his mother was after dyin' and 'Sure you have till humour him, the cratur',[349] or 'he had a stick uv dynamite in his pocket whin wan uv thim ran over him'.[350] Kipling, continuing his enthusiasm for the pre-war soldier's accent, transcribes accents of soldiers in his *The Irish Guards in the Great War*: ' 'Twas like a football scrum. Every one was somebody, ye'll understand',[351] is most likely a middle-class voice given the reference to rugby, to be compared with the words of a soldier whose false teeth had been broken in an attack: 'I've been to him [the doctor], Sorr, and it's little sympathy I got. He just gave me a pill and chased me away, Sorr'.[352] An exchange reported in *The Bystander* includes some Tommy French: 'Do you mean to tell me that you . . . have lost your rifle?' 'Mais wee, sorr, napoo.'[353]

Welsh accents are transcribed very rarely – Graves gives an example of some officers, 'strictly brought-up Welsh boys of the professional classes', one of whom, 'very Welsh', says 'I did was my fa-ace and ha-ands', the transcription catching the drawn-out vowels, and a 'very Welsh Welshman from the hills, who had an imperfect command of English . . .: 'Sergeant tole me was I for guard; I axed him no . . .'.[354] More common are transcriptions of Northern English accents: John Crofts has a 'stolid Yorkshire miner' saying 'A'reet, a'reet',[355] Aubrey Smith transcribes a Northumberland sergeant as saying 'brought soom [bombs] along' and 'all you've got to do is take the pin oot and buzz it',[356] and Ian Hay has a soldier from Manchester saying ''alf clemmed'.[357] Cpl Harry Ogle carefully transcribes a North Country accent: 'I don't say you know nowt about it, but acts as if you don't, bein' in a 'urry, an' I'm goin' to schoo'master you'.[358] Capt Billy Congreve wrote in his diary the words of a Durham man: 'I come to a trench and in I tumbles, roight on top of two other blokes, One of 'em was dead, t'other aloive.'[359] These cases show middle-class officers noting and in text imitating the sound of regional accents used by men of what was a different social class. Some transcriptions are recognisable as North Country, without any details of the speaker's origin: Emma Duffin gives 'wot a fooss',[360] and W. H. Downing's *Digger Dialects* in a rare use of something other than cockney for a typical British soldier accent, gives 'fooker' as the catch-all Australian slang for a Tommy. West Midlands accents are occasionally noted – 'Some hail from a place, which is known to the natives as Berminghum' and 'Yo' see it's like this 'ere. Ah uster be the champion lead swinger of this little lot . . .';[361] and 'when they knew that I came from Birmingham, I got the accent thick and fine "Gor blimey, 'ow are ye, then, ole townie?" came the rich, Black Country accent'.[362] Mottram in *Journey to the Western Front* remembers a Norfolk accent, given as 'Them Jarmins! Feverish beggars I calls 'em. 'Ont let y' sleep'.[363]

What became clear during the war was the predominance of the London accent, and identification with London, in the army's 'other ranks', and specifically of the army in the trenches. The first British place names used as trench names were London street names, and these remained a strong source for trench names, with Sassoon and Blunden noting how the West End cropped up along the line.[364] An advertisement for War Bonds not only links the front line to London, but draws a direct line making London the portal through which the whole empire experiences the war: 'There, on the bloody fields of France, the Londoner reaches the true "outer defences" of his own great city – of the island homes of Britain – of the British Empire!'[365] This may all have been a fiction – a complaint was published in the *Birmingham Mail* that not all London soldiers were '"h"-less Cockneys',[366] and E. B. Osborn in his introduction to *The Muse in Arms* complained about the 'strange literary convention whereby the rank and file of our fighting men ... are made to speak a kind of cockneyese of which no real Cockney is capable';[367] for many Kipling was at the root of this misconception. But if it was a fiction, it was a fiction that preceded the war: a brief article from 28 July 1914 proposed a direct linguistic connection between London and the army, claiming that 'London slang is daily adding to its extensive vocabulary. "Look at 'im 'aving a dekker at you," I heard a woman with a baby on her knee say to a friend. ... It must have been introduced into London slang by soldiers home from India.' This was from the *Manchester Guardian*, and published in the *Yorkshire Evening Post*.[368] And a close relationship between army slang and cockney seems to have been a given in discussions of slang during the war: Julie Coleman quotes a review of *Kitchener's Mob* (1916), which highlights the author, J. N. Hall's fascination with cockney.[369] The overwhelming majority of accents in post-war sound dramatisations of the Front use cockney accents, with local markers, such as 'Lumme', adding to the representation of the war in the 1920s as an identifiably cockney experience.[370]

> *What became clear during the war was the predominance of the London accent, and identification with London, in the army's 'other ranks', and specifically of the army in the trenches.*

Cartoons in *Punch* that involved the services show the development of this. Throughout 1912 there were eight cartoons, which show 11 standard voices, 10 cockney voices, 2 Irish voices, and 3 Scottish voices, cockney voices making up 38 per cent. For January to July 1917 there are 35 with identifiable cockney or urban south-east England accents, 39 with no accent shown, 1 Geordie, 3 Irish and 8 Scottish accents; cockney voices here make up 45 per cent, an increase of 18 per cent.

Publications such as *500 of the Best Cockney War Stories* (1930), the mention of Piccadilly and Leicester Square in what became the identity-marking 'Tipperary', and the continuation of Bruce Bairnsfather's 'Ole Bill in *Fragments from France* after the war cemented the relationship between London and the Great War. T. S. Eliot in the introduction to *In Parenthesis* in 1937 writes that 'as Latin is to the Church, so is Cockney to the Army, no matter what name the regiment bears'.[371] Partridge felt equally that Parisian slang transformed was one of the three main components of poilu slang,[372] and the author Herbert Vivian wrote an article for the *Daily Express* in which he 'translated' Parisian slang into cockney, using the iconic 'muvver'[373] (Greenwall's Driver Smith goes into a shop in France and asks 'Got any Woodbines, muvver?'[374]).

What also became noticeable was how one accent was seen as a cuckoo in the nest of other accents. On 20 March 1915 the *Birmingham Daily Mail* carried an article titled 'The War and Slang', which included: 'What shall we say when to the full diction of the Birmingham street arab there is added the colour of Oriental words picked up from the lips of returned warriors? As thus: "'Ere, Bill, maro the silly ooloo. Strike me pink yer burra guddha watcher mean? Ye've pukeraoed by [my?] bhiddees. 'Ere, where's the Khubber-ka-khergaz? Let's have a dekko. What's won? Well, if this ain't a nice bloomin' Komofick. Nor 'arf." Yes, it sounds promising.' A development noted by some was that the cockney accent was influencing Scottish accents: 'In the army you will hear a Scotchman doing what he never did before – dropping his aitches. He has caught it from his English comrades. You will hear him say "Not 'arf" – an inane tag which, despite its popularity in London, failed to find any foothold north of the Tweed before the war. "Not 'arf'" was mouthed by Sassenach comedians on the music-hall stages of Edinburgh and Glasgow, and was grinned at for what it was worth: the streets did not adopt it. Now the streets will hear it and will use it: it is one of Jock's souvenirs from his campaign.'[375] John Crofts notices a Scottish soldier 'using a purely Sassenach idiom ['a baastard, ain't it'] which he has picked up somehow'.[376] Philologists such as John Nicholson had already noted that railways, the telegraph and school boards were killing local dialects,[377] as urban accents spread out into hinterlands, the urban south-east accent most of all; working-class urban accents permeated the army – before conscription nearly a third of Britain's industrial workers had enlisted in the forces.[378]

Occasionally non-European accents were transcribed, South Asian, or Chinese, such as a Lascar saying 'tea-veree-hot' in a private's diary of the 9th Royal Scots, February–March 1915, but American documentation of African American speech is widely seen, usually in contexts disadvantageous to the speaker, such as misunderstandings, anecdotes or cartoons. That names from within the Indian army community caused problems can be inferred from the comment on the back of a weekly washing chit from February 1916: 'How would you like to pronounce these names every day?'

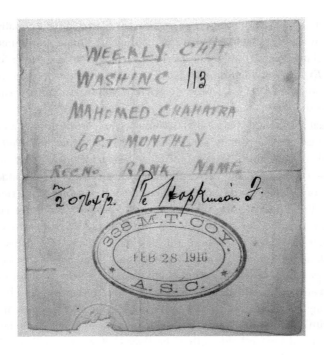

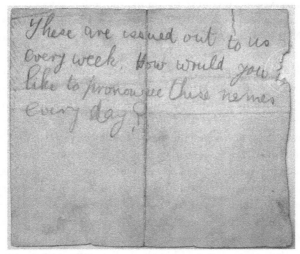

FIGURE 3.4 Pte F. Hopkinson conveys his concerns about the pronunciation of Indian names on a chit, the word 'chit' coming from Hindi.

Other languages in use within the BEF, South African, Anzac and Canadian forces included French, Maori, Afrikaans (seen on bilingual victory medals), and Asian languages including the Nepali of the Gurkhas, Marathi, Urdu, Gurmukhi, Hindi, Pashtu and Gujerati.[379] The experience of the regular army staff of decades of using Indian languages[380] meant that there was a strong awareness of the need to use a wide range of languages for efficiency. As well as linguists being involved in censoring letters home from soldiers using Indian languages, Indian recruiting posters and Field Postcards were printed in Urdu, and trench names were written in Indian characters.[381]

In addition to this there were languages other than English used within the British Isles which were used and managed in various ways. Recruiting posters were printed in Welsh, with few if any using Irish or Gaelic text, but there is evidence for Scottish and Irish Gaelic speakers in the forces. An entry in the Berliner Lautarchiv, a dialect and accent study among British prisoners of war made from 1915, shows a recording was taken of Duncan Gunn, a soldier whose first language was Gaelic. There had been Irish Gaelic speakers in the British Army for centuries and references to the speaking of Irish Gaelic appear frequently: an article in *The War Illustrated* about the use of clubs as trench-weapons by both sides is headed 'Erin-go-Bragh' (success go with you)[382] – the phrase was also used by Irish visitors to the battlefields in 1928;[383] Brophy and Partridge note the word 'skite' as coming from the Irish 'blatherumskite' (it more likely came from the Scots 'blatherskite'); and there was uproar in Ireland when a court martial president was reported as making disparaging remarks about the Irish language, an article in the *Derry Journal* quoting a question asked in the House of Commons by Alfie Byrne MP noting the 'Irish speaking soldiers of the Connaught Rangers and the Munster Fusiliers and other Gaelic-speaking soldiers at the front'.[384] Many of the Royal Guernsey Militia who volunteered for the 6th Royal Irish were French-speaking,[385] and there were even, as seen in *A Book of Manx Songs, compiled for the use of Manxmen and Manxwomen serving in His Majesty's Forces* (1915), fragments of Manx being circulated among troops.

Some situations arose with the management of these languages, particularly Welsh. The different worlds of the army and home are shown in the lack of clarity as to whether Welsh could be used in writing letters home,[386] and one diary shows a soldier using Welsh until he arrives at barracks, when he promptly switches over to English. Lloyd George (whose first language was Welsh) in September 1914 stated that he

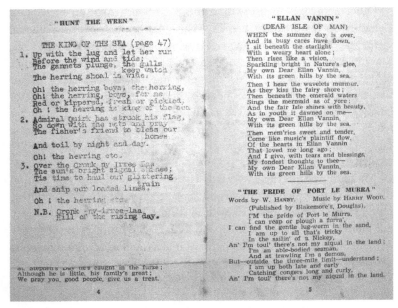

FIGURE 3.5 From *A Book of Manx Songs*, published in 1915 'for the use of Manxmen and Manxwomen serving in His Majesty's Forces, and the Manx Societies throughout the World'.

wanted to see 'a Welsh army in the field',[387] but the Welsh Corps was a source of disagreement between Lloyd George and Kitchener, who ordered that Welsh should not be spoken on the parade ground or in billets.[388] However, possibly as a result of Lloyd George's initiative, a large amount of recruiting literature was produced in Welsh, and soldiers not only wrote home in Welsh throughout the war, but were, after a ban in 1916, quickly repealed, permitted to speak the language while training in Britain.[389]

There is no evidence to suggest that the use of languages other than English proved problematic in the BEF at the Front, in the way that was experienced by other multilingual country's armies. The Austro-Hungarian armies had to manage up to a dozen languages on an equal footing, sometimes with results reminiscent of Jaroslav Hasek's *The Good Soldier Schweik*; longstanding tensions regarding Breton soldiers resurfaced in the years 1914 to 1918 as Breton monolinguism was strongly linked to Breton separatism. M. MacDonald describes a 'foreign legion' in which he served in the French army, with Russian, Italian, Rumanian,

Spanish, and other languages spoken; within this corps were Alsatian soldiers fighting for the liberation of Alsace from Germany, who spoke their first language, German, much to the anger of their colleagues; the group was eventually ordered to use French.[390]

Naming our side

'Tommy' as a generic name in France for the British soldier took the place of 'un godam' according to John Masefield;[391] not having been involved in a European war for several generations, for the British and for a few Europeans 'Tommy' was associated with service in India, Africa and the colonies. The term had come originally from a generic name for soldiers serving in the Napoleonic wars, and was popularised by Kipling. It was specifically a name for 'other ranks', not officers, was seldom applied to NCOs, and never, according to Partridge, to colonial troops like himself – though Grace Pulvertaft mentions meeting 'an Australian Tommy' in her diary entry for 11 November 1918.[392] However, far from being a universally accepted and cherished term, 'Tommy' was widely disliked. 'An Ensign of 1848' wrote to *The Times* 23 October 1914:

> May I ... suggest that the time has now come ... to put a period to the use of the nickname 'Tommies'? ... To hear these British soldiers referred to in deprecatory patronage as 'Tommies' by those who stay at home ... is unseemly and exasperating.

It was not an isolated sentiment. In the *Liverpool Daily Post* there was a report on the Manx Legislative Council and the House of Keys:

> Yesterday, in connection with the provision for relieving soldiers' estates from duty, the Attorney-General strongly protested against soldiers being popularly called 'Tommies'. The term, he said, was ridiculous and offensive, and would not be allowed in any other country.[393]

'Tommy' was at the bottom of the status-ladder in the army, which may have been a difficult association for the enlisted soldiers of Kitchener's Mob, many of them carefully aware of their class status. As an article in the *Birmingham Mail* put it 'Those who are well educated, and have given up excellent situations and comfortable homes for the sake of their country, naturally resent being patronised as "Tommies" who cannot speak the King's English, and whose place of origin is assumed to be Houndsditch or the New Cut'.[394] Or maybe Kipling's 1892 poem 'Tommy' had for long established in the public mind that the private soldier was both socially and militarily expendable. There is a possibility too that the term was associated in older people's minds at that time with older meanings of 'tommy', such as those given in J. C. Hotten's *Dictionary of Vulgar Words, Street Phrases and "Fast Expressions"*, (1865), in which the meanings given are 'bread, generally a penny roll', and 'a truck, barter, the exchange of labour for goods, not money'. Any surviving association of the enlisted and conscripted soldiers with a trade or a consumer perishable could not have helped – 'Tommy' as the basic material of a war in which a raid was carried out by 'a couple of officers, some NCOs and the rest were ordinary Tommies who went over'.[395]

There was also an English identification to the word – Welsh soldiers were 'Taff', Scottish soldiers 'Jock' individually, and 'the Jocks' as a group ('Scotties' if they were London Scottish), while Partridge records 'The Micks' for the Irish Guards. The naval equivalent was 'Jack', and the emergence of a separate identity for the RFC and RAF brought 'George' for an airman, recorded by Brophy and Partridge. 'Kilties' as a term for Scottish soldiers was not common, even among the writings of soldiers in Scottish regiments: Stephen Graham, author of *A Private in the Guards* (1919), and Cpl O. H. Blaze, 1st Battalion Scots Guards, author of 'A prisoner of war in Germany' in *In the Line of Battle* (1916), both use the term once (pp. 321 and 18 respectively), Graham preferring 'Jocks' and Blaze using the names of regiments. Brophy and Partridge claim that it was 'taken from popular journalism and used only mockingly, sometimes for the purpose of starting a row'. Michael McDonagh used 'kilts' for Scottish troops in *The Irish on the Somme*,[396] but this metonymic image is rare, though the principle – 'rifles' and 'bayonets' for 'men' – was long established in military language.

'Tommies' was used for the infantryman in other armies, underlining its class and rank status:

... a letter written soon after his arrival in France in the spring of 1915 by Captain Lionel William Crouch described his amusement at 'watching a group of our chaps surrounding a French Tommy who was endeavouring to teach them French'.[397]

Other non-British Tommies appear in *The Rochdale Observer*, which has 'a fat French Tommy',[398] while the *Daily Gazette for Middlesbrough* has 'the Italian "Tommy"'.[399] To stretch the mind further, six months after the Armistice, the *Daily Mirror* described the political instability in Germany with some antipathy towards 'Prussian officers' lording it over 'German Tommies'. Weekley even has a 'Roman tommy'.[400] 'Tommy' also functioned as an adjective, in 'Tommy-cooker'.

The name became a plaything for the press, a widely-used sign of familiarity with the troops, another supposed authenticator. The *War Budget* March 1916 played with the name using the headline: 'Tammas McAtkins's water ration'. Did soldiers bridle at this? Brophy and Partridge noted 'Tommy' as being used by English troops only derisively, or 'when imitating the style of a newspaper or a charitable old lady'.[401] Enid Bagnold recorded a much earthier, and certainly less literary alternative: 'I wonder when people will stop calling them "Tommy" and call them "Bill". I never heard the word "Tommy" in a soldier's mouth: he was a red-coated man. "But every mate's called 'Bill', ain't he Bill?"'[402] Bagnold's text carries two notable points, first the association of 'Tommy' with the red-coated Victorian soldier of Kipling's poem, and secondly the importance of Bruce Bairnsfather's observations of life at the Front, 'Old Bill' both reflecting and reinforcing the troops' language.

The documented dislike of Tommy opens up a Pandora's box of myths. *Poilu*, the widely-used equivalent of Tommy in the French army, was 'liked as little as British soldiers liked "Tommy"';[403] *bluets*, a press invention, was not liked either.[404] The French preferred to call themselves 'les hommes' or 'les bonhommes',[405] though M. MacDonald, who enlisted with the French army in August 1914, refers constantly to 'Jean Pitou' as the preferred name.[406] Olivier Leroy refers to *bleu* and *bleusaille* for a young soldier, but not *bluet*;[407] more common terms were *pioupiou* and *pitou*. To rub it in there is evidence that the Russians disliked the term 'steamroller',[408] and Australian soldiers became 'sick of the word' Anzac.[409] Worst of all, 'Tipperary' was not sung incessantly. Fraser and Gibbons state that in deference to the Old Contemptibles, the first British army in Flanders and France, many of the New Army units did not sing it; and for the same reason it was not played at the St Barnabas pilgrimage to the Menin Gate in Ypres in 1925 – 'if anyone had struck up the Old Contemptibles life-and-death song, many in that gathering would have looked away'.[410] Major Bruce Taylor wrote in 1916 that 'We practically never hear *Tipperary*';[411] there were plenty of parodies though, not all of them obscene. Even the society magazine *The Lady* responded to the composer Ethel Smyth's statement that she wished that she had written it, with the comment that 'it is not gay, it is not solemn, it is not inspiring, it is not ennobling'.[412]

There were other general terms used by soldiers, which referred to the amount they had to carry: PBI (poor bloody infantry) is recorded by Brophy and Partridge, and Fraser and Gibbons give 'trays', 'Christmas tree', and 'something to hang things on'. Fraser and Gibbons give 'Kitch' as the nickname for someone enlisting in one of the new armies. Partridge records the occasional use of 'swaddy', not connected to 'squaddie', and 'Camel Corps'.[413] 'Bing boys', a widely used term after 1916, referred to a show in London,[414] and merged with the Canadians who called themselves the 'Byng Boys' after their respected commander General Julian Byng. There were in use a few imaginative references to marching – and to those soldiers destined to march. 'Foot-slogger' – 'Foot slogging over Belgian ways' was noted in the article *The Route March*, in the *Fifth Gloucester Gazette*[415] – was originally 'foot-wabler' or foot-wobbler' in Grose's *The Vulgar Tongue* (1785), a term of contempt for the infantryman much used by the cavalry. Related names were 'gravel-grinder', and 'mud-crusher'. There were similar terms in French and German, German terms being particularly graphic – *Dreckfresser* (mud-glutton), *Kilometerfresser* (kilometre-glutton), *Fusslatscher* (foot-shuffler), *Lakenpatscher* (mud-crusher). According to Partridge only the Germans were resigned to the term *Kanonenfutter*, 'cannon-fodder', but there are signs of it creeping across into English: George Barker writes 'but after all we are only "cannon-fodder"',[416] and Jonathan Lighter records the expression 'fokker-fodder'.[417]

As regards the question of when and by whom the terms 'men', 'boys' and 'lads' were used, there were no hard and fast rules. 'Boys' was chummy between soldiers, 'men' was common to officers when giving instructions, 'lads' used by civilians was patriotic and grateful; 'boys' was used by civilians when worried or protective, 'men' was for soldiers when attacking, 'lads' was for decent admirable young men. There were regional variations, and variations dependent on the field of text – journalism, official reports, letters from home, memorials – variations so vast that categorisation is probably worthless; but the following observations and inferences may be suggested.

'Boys' and 'lads' tend to invoke togetherness, association, and equality. In Wilfred Owen's words 'Gas! Gas! Quick, boys!' in *Dulce et Decorum Est*, the use of 'boys' matches many other texts – Ian Hay in *All In It, K (1) Carries On* (1917) uses 'boys' throughout when one soldier is talking to other soldiers. In a De Reszke Cigarettes advertisement a lance corporal is quoted as saying 'I shall recommend them to the boys'.[418] 'Our boys are splendid' writes Harold McGill, noting a German prisoner holding a piece of bread 'one of our boys had given him'.[419]

In describing comradeship Charles Edmonds writes 'all things were bearable if one bore them "with the lads"'.[420] 'Lads' had a regional association – George Barker, writing about soldiers from the Manchester area,[421] uses 'lads' and 'laddies', while Neil Tytler's *With Lancashire Lads and Field Guns in France* (1922) was published in Manchester. 'Our boys' is common for describing group actions – 'as I fell I heard our boys cheering',[422] 'our boys had had a time getting across the canal',[423] 'it was in the last stage of the battle that our boys cut in'.[424] When an attack is being described 'our men' or 'the men' is more often used, giving more gravitas: 'our men unflinchingly advanced across the open ground',[425] 'Prompt to the second, our men go over the top in a grand assault';[426] but an 'Armour-plated Hun 'plane ... used to mow down our lads',[427] and 'our lads was mown down'[428] convey a sense of ownership and protection; the Realistic Travels company who published stereoview photographs throughout the war used 'lads' when describing dead British soldiers – 'The lads who fell at Hooge', 'brave lads fallen in morning raid'. Cpl Shaw's later words, that they were 'losing men all the time' and 'the men were falling back in the trenches', convey less sense of pity. The use of 'lads' for associative purposes – 'Xmas hamper for khaki lads'[429] – though looking blunt now, probably had some commercial success at the time.

> *The choice of words at times seems at odds with the situation, men who had killed other men being called 'boys', boys of sixteen being expected to be 'men'. Enid Bagnold, continually questioning the words she heard and used, wrote 'I can't think of them like the others do, as "the boys"; they seem to me full-grown men'.*

The sense of care and protection is evident in the use of 'boys' throughout in *A Red Triangle Girl in France* (she worked in YMCA establishments for US soldiers), and the vulnerability of the soldiers is expressed usually in the use of 'boys': for VADs Emma Duffin and Dora Walker all wounded soldiers were 'boys'.[430] This is carried on into post-war writing about visits to France and Flanders, where 'boys' embraces 'men', 'husbands' and 'sons': 'we had our "iron rations", as our boys had had,'[431] 'how the boys hated that!'[432] 'Boys' conveyed loss more than did 'men' or 'lads': 'the gloom came down again because the boys had gone that day'.[433] The choice of words at times seems at odds with the situation, men who had killed other men being called 'boys', boys of sixteen being expected to be 'men'. Enid Bagnold, continually questioning the words she heard and used, wrote 'I can't think of them like the others do, as "the boys"; they seem to me full-grown men'.[434]

'Bhoys', as transcribed from Irish accents,[435] and from nineteenth-century American slang, was popular among soldiers; from postcards there seems to have been an association with performance rather than Irish culture, as the word appears in descriptions of groups of soldiers.

As regards names between the Allies, these were variously predictable or imaginative. Partridge and Leroy note that the French called the

FIGURE 3.6 Photograph of a group of soldiers in camp; the barrel is labelled 'Quinine No. 11 B'Hoys'.

English/British 'Angliche',[436] but Partridge records they also had the word *'anglaiser'*, meaning 'to steal'. In turn anglophones referred to their French allies as 'parleyvoos', 'dee-donks', 'ohlalas'[437] and of course 'froggies'; Portuguese were 'Tony' and 'pork and beans', Italians 'eyeties'. Partridge lists for French slang: for the Italians, 'macaronis' and 'Taliens'; for Serbians 'Serbos' or 'Dobros' (from the Serbian for 'good'); for Belgian soldiers 'piotes'; for Greeks 'Grecos'; for Russians 'Ruskis' and 'Rousses' (the English version 'Ivan' seems fairly tame); for Bulgarians 'Bulbuls' or 'Bougres'. Olivier Leroy's *Glossary of French Slang* (1924) includes 'rosbif' still for English, and 'choucroutemane' for German; 'choucroute' is sauerkraut, and 'mane' may be a French transcription of the English 'men'. *Piou-piou* was a longstanding name used by French soldiers for themselves.

Germans also had names for the individual parts of their services, not exactly corresponding to Tommy, Jack and George: Ernst for an artilleryman, Fritz for an infantryman, and Franz for an airman.[438]

Sex and gender

Gender culture around the period of the First World War idealised the position of the bachelor. Married men were popularly presented in music-hall songs and picture postcards as henpecked or disappointed, overloaded with the sudden arrival of babies, and seeing their free-roaming activities curtailed. An underlying misogyny framed women as potentially predatory, to be punished for impersonating WRENs, showing 'swank' and wanting to 'get off with officers';[439] a postcard shows a soldier struggling with four women, with the caption 'The Territorial: receiving the attack!' The correspondence on war slang carried on in *The Athenaeum* post-war included the note that observation balloons had been called 'maiden's prayer' or 'maiden's delight'.[440]

Actual sexual activity at the Front involved extremely limited access to brothels, more access to French soft-porn postcards, innuendo in trench journals, and imaginably more macho talk than has been documented. Attempts to initiate sexual relations with local women ranged from variations on 'Vous jig-a-jig avec me', usually associated with men on the march passing women,[441] to the more one-to-one 'Vouli-vous promenade avec moi?'[442] Sometimes soldiers struck lucky, but the constant movement of troops meant that most relationships were short and hurried. R. H.

FIGURE 3.7 Postcard sent in July 1918.

Mottram claimed that 'the great ambition of most of the girls of the place [Bailleul] was to marry a "sergeant Nouvelle-Zélandais"; I do not know how many succeeded;'[443] probably not as many as those who kept 'a souvenir', i.e. a soldier's baby.[444]

Brothels provided a quicker resolution, but often the weariness and age of the sex-workers combined with the disappointment of the environment to put many young men off;[445] Makepeace quotes Frank Richards being in a group of three who walked out of a brothel and 48 hours later 'each one of us had picked up with a respectable bit of goods'.[446] The fear of venereal disease, and the punishment for acquiring, and more specifically hiding it, helped to confuse many young men; Winnie McClare wrote home to Canada that 'the worst of London is the girls that run around the streets there . . . it is an awfull temtation when they act like that. An awfull lot of fellow that go to London come back in bad shape and are sent to the V.D. hospitals'.[447] The brutalising of sex, like the brutalising effect of swearing, gave a blunted view of sex, occasionally prudish ('short arm' for penis), but more often expressed in terms such as 'jig-a-jig' or 'a bit of dick'.[448]

A different view is that proposed by the idea that brothels were tolerated as fulfilling a necessary function for married men,[449] sexual activity seen as no more than physical: Graves reported censoring a lance corporal's letter in which the man wrote to his wife that the 'French girls were nice to sleep with, so she mustn't worry on his account, but that he far preferred sleeping with her'.[450] The view that sex was an undesirable necessity is reflected in the name given to brothels – *maisons tolérées* – not least its being in French, continuing the anglophone tradition of using French to avoid speaking directly about sex. There were, according to Ellen La Motte,[451] several women who stayed in unoccupied Flanders as sex-workers; Williamson's description of prostitutes as 'proper little pushers' refers to women pushing prams.[452] Behind the teasing of Pte Tippy in *In The Trenches* for learning French 'to speak to the French girls', which makes him a 'bad lad', there is a complex and competitive attitude to sex.[453]

Semi-erotic French postcards depended on the visual, while English ones depended more on verbal titillation, of the familiar seaside postcard type. French postcards, hand-tinted and studio photographs in enhanced colours, showing French soldiers improbably in full uniform engaging with women in complicated underwear, were available to British soldiers, and were occasionally sent home. 'How does this suit you my dear?' was

The unhinging of the demarcation between the terms 'boys' and 'men' can be read as part of a broader loosening of parameters, beyond the familiar images of men in drag in soldiers' concert parties. Shellshock, creating hysteria (this period being the first time that 'hysteria' was applied to men), was seen as 'unmanning' men, blasting them into female territory; hysteria itself was, according to Karl Bonhoeffer, as presented in *Shellshock and Other Neuropsychiatric Problems* 'a female affair antebellum',[454] indicating the effect of the war in breaking down the barrier between men and women. As the war drained countries of working-age men, and women took their places in the visible service industries, the assumption by women of male dress and activities was widely expressed as 'women becoming men'. The sexually provocative magazine *Fun* carried a brief letter on Christmas Day 1915, headlined, 'The Changing of Sexes': 'It is a notable thing of late that girls are becoming more masculine and fellows more feminine'. The article goes on to imply that changes of costume, as women took jobs such as drivers or window-cleaners, were linked to physical changes in gender dominance within relationships.[455]

A verbal regendering of the male appeared as a compliment given by Germans to kilted Allied soldiers, from Scotland, Canada or England – 'Ladies from Hell' appears repeatedly in memoirs, as the title of R. Douglas Pinkerton's 1918 memoir of his time with the London Scottish, in A. Corcoran's *The Daredevil of the Army* (1918, p. 139), in *Over There and Back*, by Joseph S. Smith (1918, p. 192), and in *Private Peat*, by H. Peat (1917, p. 175). Soldiers repeatedly reported its use to the press, enjoying their reputation for engendering terror, but significantly there is no documentation in German of its use. 'A lady working among the troops', as reported in the *Western Mail* (13 March 1915, p. 7), offered the actual German word *Höllenweiber*, but added 'I suppose; it was told me in English'. The responsibility for the term was thus projected onto the enemy. The first part of 'ladies from hell' faces the question of gender raised by the kilt, but the second half of the phrase stares down challenges to the soldiers' masculine power. It is noticeable that the term was enthusiastically taken up again in the Second World War.

In the opposite direction a cartoon in *The Bystander* (3 April 1918) shows a female bus conductor giving a female window-cleaner a light, cigarette to cigarette, their figures androgynously attractive, before a fainting elderly woman. 'Oh, my grandmother', runs the caption, 'In her time girls *would* be girls: but now girls *will* be men.' Taken with the passionate female gendering of weapons – *Rosalie* and *Laura*, *die Braut des Soldaten* and *Dicke Berthe*, 'Mother' and 'Granny' (see p. 199) – in a male-monopolised environment of killing, we see the war dismantling the language of stable gender patterns.

The Pall Mall Gazette published this court report, 14 June 1916:

Man in Woman's Clothing

At Highgate Police Court this morning, fashionably dressed in a long blue navy coat, with college cap and veil, and white kid gloves, Frederick Wright, aged twenty-two, a valet, was brought up on remand charged with being an idle and disorderly person, clad in female attire, with giving a false description when registered as a lodger, and with being a deserter. Defendant lodged in the house of a Belgian lady, and gave the name of Katherine Woodhouse. The Bench ordered him to be handed over to a military escort.

In contrast to the formal terminology of the charge and the coded 'handed over to a military escort', with its hidden promise of retribution and correction, the details of Wright's clothing stand out as the 'real story': the colours, and the assessment as 'fashionable'. Note also the syntactic differences in the two lists, the charges being merely repetitive. Wright made no compromise in his presentation in court, despite being on remand, and for both him and the journalist, his presentation as female was arresting, as he both appears in court, and is previously charged with being, 'clad in female attire'.

the message from George to Mrs Dawson, presumably his wife, the photograph showing a woman in underwear sitting on a wall with her legs over the shoulders of a man in French uniform, he facing away from, but looking up at her. Another shows a man in British uniform about to embrace a woman in underclothes; 'If you love me prove me it', is the message in what was probably not the copywriter's first language. The same team had a slightly better result with 'It is the moment to sign the alliance'. Many British postcards display the gap between the reality of sex during wartime and the desire, innuendo and visual puns framing misogynist fantasies as jokes or infantilism, the billeting officer asking a female householder 'how many can you take?', or the dog looking up a female police officer's skirt with the caption 'under police protection'. Alongside the bravado there is a wistfulness in the message on the back of the card showing a French soldier (with helmet) rushing eagerly towards an enthusiastically undressed young woman: 'Well old dear, This makes him smile somewhat. Roll on when I get treated like it. Cheer up. Life is gay.' Significantly, few of these cards show postmarks, so their survival in England indicates that they were probably sent in envelopes, perhaps to avoid embarrassment. There was certainly a fear of being found dead in possession of pornographic material, as the soldier's effects were sent home when possible; Horace Stanley tells of burning the porn collection of a recently killed young officer as an act of generosity to the family.[456]

Being so problematic, any relationship between men and women was surrounded by codes. Brophy and Partridge report the term 'square-pushing' for men accompanying nannies on walks with a pram (see Williamson above), while naval slang had the wonderfully bizarre 'poodle-faking' for walking out with a young woman, possibly based on the idea that the young man would be a substitute for a poodle. A postcard to a corporal in the BEF from 'Gadget' gives what might be a coded homosexual message: 'have picked up a dear little chicken so hopes of having a go time'.[457] A discourse of infantilism was manifested in a culture of 'cute infants' picture postcards, in which the war was defused by portraying soldiers and sweethearts as fat rosy-cheeked children, sexualised nevertheless; they are simultaneously infants and adults, female genitalia provocatively hidden by towels, or in one postcard blanked out by an imagined censor. 'Can you see the spot?' asks a boy-adult holding a ladder and looking up the dress of a girl-adult at the top of the ladder and holding a telescope; the text of the card, sent On Active

Service, is in French and English. Occasional survivors from the war are items of correspondence or other communications which continue this into baby-talk. VAD Grace Pulvertaft's notebook for 12 July 1916 shows a cartoon drawn by a wounded soldier with a naked Mabel Lucie Attwell type girl holding a towel in front of her, the names of the '"5 teasers" of Roberts Ward' and the caption 'Oh! Did-ems did-ems do it?'; even within the pseudo-mother/child relationship of the hospital ward it is discomfiting, as much as the baby-talk of the private letter going from or to the Front. A letter sent in June 1917 disconcertingly uses baby-talk when talking about combat: '. . . all my dearest love to you darling & heaps of kisses from your dear little treasure who says daddy's gone to fight the naughty shermans & she wont love em'.[458] Earlier the same letter states that 'poor Harry Saville . . . was shot on the 10th and died of his wounds on the 15th . . .'.

There was, however, a strong female presence in all the combat zones where English was used, in the names of weapons. How are we to interpret the gendering of the names given to large guns, shells, mines, tanks, even the bayonet and rifle? 'Minnie' obviously derived from the German *Minenwerfer*, and 'Big Bertha' derived from the German 'Dicke Bertha', derived from the name of Bertha Krupp von Bohlen und Handbach.[459] But other names carried no clear female connection; Fraser and Gibbons record 'Asiatic Annie', 'Gentle Annie', 'Jericho Jane', 'Coughing Clara', and the shells 'Lazy Eliza' and 'Silent Susan' while Brophy and Partridge record the use of 'Emma' as 'a favourite German name for a cannon', and 'Kathe' was the name given to a German tank;[460] conversely the French named the 75-mm gun, (known to English-speakers as *soixante-quinze*) 'Eugène'.[461] There were also the names 'Stuttering Lizzie' given to a machine gun,[462] and 'Mournful Mary' or 'Mournful Maria' for the air-raid siren at Dunkirk.[463]

Not all names given were female – there were the shells 'Creeping Jimmy',[464] 'Whistling Percy/Walter/Willie/Rufus'[465] and of course, 'Jack Johnson' (the name was also given to the gun firing the shells); the guns at the Dardanelles, 'Artful Archie', 'Morbid Montmorenzi', 'Morose Montmorenzi', 'Spiteful William', and 'a big Asiatic "Jack Johnson"';[466] near Ypres there was 'Perishing Pavey'[467] (possibly a reference to the Flemish cobblestones), and 'Belching Billy'.[468] The largest guns were given male names: the German *Langer Max* became 'Long Fritz' in English, while Fraser and Gibbons record 'Long Tom' as the name for the British 60-pounder gun early in the war, the name originating from a Boer gun

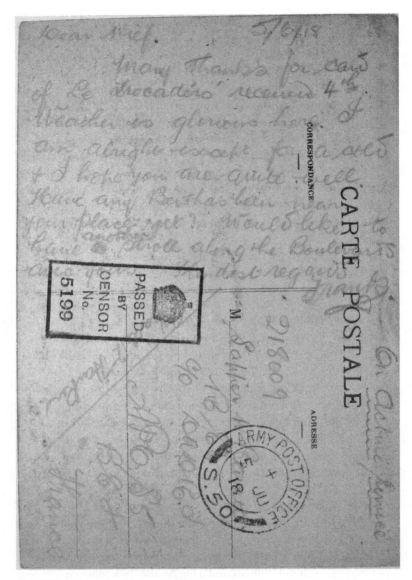

FIGURE 3.8 Postcard sent 'On Active Service', 5 July 1918. The image shows a view of a hospital, the location information scratched out. The writer asks Sapper Wilf Barrett, 'have any Berthas been near your place yet?'

used at Ladysmith. Alliteration played a large part in this, another aspect of the propensity of the English language to provide opportunity for wordplay, dating back to Old English poetry and riddles.

But the preponderance of female names and references remains uncomfortable. There was in the French and German armies a tradition of female association with the rifle; for Germans soldiers the rifle was *Braut des Soldaten*, 'the soldiers' bride',[469] while Partridge records 'Laura' and 'Karline', with 'Kusine' and 'Tante' adopted from French[470]. The French had 'Ma'm'selle Lebel' for their rifle, from the name of the inventor.[471] French nicknames for the bayonet were 'Josephine' and 'Rosalie', though there was resistance to the latter because of its known civil and literary origin; Partridge believed that nevertheless it prospered.[472] The British army during the war, despite the venerability of the name 'Brown Bess', did not develop a personal nickname for the rifle or bayonet. However, the terms 'Granny', 'grandmother' and 'mother' were used for larger guns. Fraser and Gibbons give the names 'Granny' and 'Grandmother' for the first British howitzer used in the fighting, in April 1915, the names being used later for other large guns – one of the captions for the film *The Battle of the Somme* reads 'Operating the 15-inch howitzer ("Grandmother") ...'. Both terms featured in the list put together by members of *The Times* staff who had served,[473] with 'Granny' as specifically a 9.2-inch gun, though Partridge later assigned it to a shell.[474] 'Mother', the name given to the first tank,[475] was also used for a gun: the *Daily Mirror* reported a correspondent talking to a soldier on leave, telling 'his stories in a language full of the slang of the trenches, newborn phrases that will soon be part of every story of soldier life. ... "Mother" is a pleasant, very effective gun of ours, a heavy and far-reaching piece of artillery that the Germans don't like a little bit. It takes good care of our infantry and comforts them considerably – hence the name.'[476] This is rather too comfortable, fitting the needs of journalism; a more appropriate connotation might be the idea of 'delivering', fitting the cynical worldview of the trenches. There are antecedents for this female association, going back a long way: the fifteenth-century siege gun at Edinburgh Castle, 'Mons Meg' (from its place of manufacture), is well known, but current thinking is that the origin of the word 'gun' itself derives from the Scandinavian woman's name 'Gunna', extended to 'Gunnilda', the suffix carrying the meaning of 'war'. A gun called 'Domina Gunilda' is mentioned in the munitions accounts of Windsor Castle for 1330–1.[477]

Place

'The Front' was a new expression in August 1914, and for the military a verbal response to the sudden development of a stationary rather than a mobile campaign, even though trench warfare had been a common feature of the Crimean and American Civil Wars. There was surprise at the sense of a barrier, though the speed with which newspapers reported the areas of confrontation between the German, French and British armies (from September 1914) meant that the terms 'Western Front' and 'Eastern Front' (though the Eastern Front changed much more) appeared within a week of the opening of hostilities between Britain and Germany.[478] 'The Front' was very quickly a term established in the public consciousness as a place – newspaper readers were told to expect 'news from the front' and 'letters from the front' in August 1914.[479]

While the trench warfare of the 19th century and beforehand had been often to do with besieging cities, the battlefield stasis of 1914 required a quick shifting of terminology. Andrew Clark observed how *The Scotsman* applied the word 'siege' to the kind of warfare, 'No longer a battle', along a 'hundred miles of front ... consisting of old forts and disused quarries. Bomb-proof shelters, formed of bags of cement, and subterranean passages ...'.[480] Lynda Mugglestone's examination of Clark's documentation of terminology at this time[481] shows the change towards the pre-eminence of the trench, as both physical and symbolic expression of the limit of movement. Though 'siege war' and 'siege warfare' continued in use – 'a regular siege war has been in progress for two days',[482] and 'siege warfare on the Aisne'[483] – soldiers were reported as digging trenches in mid-September 1914, and 'digging ourselves in' on 21 September,[484] the Germans having already been 'digging themselves in' by this time.[485]

What soon developed was the awareness of the pre-eminence of the trench, with its own growing culture and its status in the perception of the war. Its terminology became widespread – 'parapet', 'firestep', 'parados', 'supports', 'dug-out', 'communication trench' – while other terms – 'firing line', 'front line' – changed or assumed different meanings. Though there was terminology for attacking or defending – 'over the top', 'hop over the bags', 'a jumping-out trench', 'hold your trench' – the predominance of the phrase 'in the trenches' emphasises the static nature of the experience. 'In the trenches' rather than 'in a trench', pointing to the constant movement of men and supplies, the area rather than the single line being where the soldier was, and indeed where the artillery was directed; for the prime role of the infantry was to be shelled, and not to break. 'In a trench' is seen rarely, in a letter to 'Arthur' from T. Harold Watts dated 18 June 1915, or the song 'Living in a Trench' by Parsons and Woodville (published 1917), but overwhelmingly the expression was 'in the trenches'. It was in the UPS journal *The Pow-Wow* by December 1914[486] and its later form *The Gasper;*[487] in advertisements – 'In the trenches – Symingtons Soups (so easy to "fix up")';[488] and 'a watch I can depend on in the trenches';[489] in postcards – 'We are in the trenches fighting at present'[490] and 'Dan has been in the trenches';[491] in newspaper articles – 'after the spell in the trenches',[492] and 'the same kind of spirit as the men in the trenches';[493] it appeared in French as 'Dans les tranchées',[494] including in British soldiers' French – 'I have not been "dans les tranchées" for about a fortnight'.[495] Soldiers would 'go to the trenches', 'leave for the trenches', and on arrival 'take over trenches';[496] 'I am going in the trenches again' writes Henry on 26 May 1915 in the British Mediterranean Expeditionary Force.[497] And they 'only came out of the trenches last night',[498] or 'have come out of the Ts well'.[499] There were occasional variations: 'Relieved infantry in trenching' shows an early form from September 1915;[500] and the specific term 'in supports', for support trenches.[501]

Other phrases show how terms changed or merged, particularly when describing the forwardmost trench: George Williams writes in his diary that he is 'still on rations for 1st line',[502] while Stephen Hewett writes 'Here in the Fire-trenches'.[503] 'The firing line' was misunderstood in an early postcard which shows 'German officers on the Firing Line' standing conspicuously in a field; a more feasible image is seen in a cigarette card by Gallahers from 1915 showing 'Shelters Behind the Firing Line', with soldiers hiding beneath tarpaulins. A 1918 postcard showing a soldier and his sweetheart with the caption 'In the Firing Line' indicates that the phrase had changed from meaning 'where you shoot from' to 'where you are shot at'.[504] 'The front line' was easily and frequently shortened to 'the line' – soldiers spoke of 'going into the line' (see postcard Figure 2.3, p. 58), and there were variations 'the fire trench' and 'the firing trench'. For the general area of the Front there were a number of terms: for example 'the war zone',[505] 'the fighting line',[506] or 'the fighting zone'.[507]

The depth of the trench, deep enough for men to pass along without the risk of receiving a head-shot from a sniper, meant that being in the trenches was very much a case of being below ground-level. Thus being in the trenches was often described as 'being in'. In an undated letter from after Neuve Chapelle (March 1915) E. W. Bratchell writes 'we have been "in" since the 8th';[508] therefore 'we came out, after four days in',[509] 'we are about to come out for a few weeks',[510] and 'they have had no bacon since they came out'.[511] 'In' and 'out' reflect the vertical nature of the battlefield, with soldiers reporting seeing nothing but the sides and base of the trench and the slice of sky above. Hiding from aeroplanes above, under tarpaulins in shell craters, or in dug-outs, was essential in daylight hours, adding to the sense of being 'in'; and for those involved in mining activities, they were very much 'in' Flanders or France. This phraseology naturally merged with 'being in it', in the sense of being 'in the fighting', employing the language of avoidance. 'We shall soon be in it', wrote Major F. Crozier in December 1914,[512] while 'the odds would be against us coming out' implied 'coming out of the battle alive'.[513]

No man's land, between the two front lines, emerged as a military term around 1907/8, though the term in the sense of 'waste land' is medieval; yet despite its familiarity the written record shows people putting the term in inverted commas long after the war, and with even such an iconic expression there was no consensus as regards its written presentation. In August 1917 it was presented in provincial newspapers, variously as 'No Man's Land', 'No Man's Land', 'no man's land', and 'No man's land'.[514] W. H. Harris has it as 'No Man's Land',[515] *The Sphere* has it as 'No-man's-land' and 'No-Man's-Land',[516] Henry Williamson has it as 'Noman's-land',[517] and *A Month at the Front* has it as 'no mans land'.[518] James Addison in *The Story of the First Gas Regiment* (1919) has 'No Man's Land' (p. 28) and without inverted commas (p. 101), while Eric Hiscock has 'Nomansland'.[519] Lighter's *Slang of the AEF* gives three instances of the variation 'Nobody's Land',[520] while one American soldiers' English–French phrasebook translates the term as *Pays de mort*.[521]

By the end of 1914 the trench had become a clear locus of terminology, with the word in use as a suffix in terms such as 'trench cooker',[522] 'trench cap',[523] as commercial advertising recognised the value of associating products with the trench, both in terms of attractiveness to people buying items for soldiers, and in terms of patriotism by association. While 'British Warm' was widely used for heavy coats (Aquascutum),[524] the first use of 'Trench Coat' appeared in *Punch* 23 December 1914 in an advertisement for Thresher and Glenny ('Wind, Wet and Mud resisting'). A number of variations were available, some which retained the term 'trench coat', some adapting or modifying it, and others avoiding it. Aquascutum advertised a 'Field coat', Burberry advertised the 'Trench-warm',[525] and there was the 'Studdington waterproof trencher'.[526] Trench coats were advertised widely and regularly throughout the war, with variations – '25 shilling Ladies Trench Coats' were advertised in the *Daily Express,*[527] and 'ladies' trench-proofs' in the *Liverpool Echo.*[528] There were also the '"Carry-On" Trench Coat' made by Alfred Webb Miles & Co.,[529] Moss Bros' '"Moscow" trench coat',[530] the 'Trench "Dexter"',[531] the 'Zambrene "Triple-triple" proof coat',[532] and the Barker '"Kenbar" trench coat'.[533] The term disappeared after the war, a sign of the changing attitude to the conflict. Burberry, by Spring 1920, appeared to be avoiding the term: in *Punch* and the *Illustrated London News* they advertised 'the Guards' Burberry', 'the Monte B', 'the Urbitor', 'the Rusitor' and 'the Race Weatherall', but no trench coat, and by 1922 it was hard to find trench coats advertised anywhere.

Other trench-clothing was advertised throughout the war: Manfield advertised 'Officers' war boots' and 'trench boots',[534] and 'trench jackets' were also available; there was the army issue 'trench hat' 'commonly called a "Gor Blimey"',[535] and, from the AEF, the 'trench derby' ('tin hat').[536] Commercially available were the Wyse 'famous trench pipe',[537] 'trench pillows' and 'trench socks',[538] and 'trench waistcoats'.[539] Cramped and static posture and prolonged exposure to water in the trenches (Kipling recorded an order to the Irish Guards that men were 'not to stand in the water for more than twelve hours at a time'[540]) led to 'swollen feet', in 1915, which eventually became 'trench feet'[541] (sometimes 'trench foot'); there was 'trench fever',[542] and what was described by the sister of a military hospital ward in Alexandria as 'trenchitis', 'collapse after a month in the fighting line, owing to want of rest and food'[543] (an alternative 'disease', which could also be cured by rest, was 'sniper's rash'[544]); a propos of the trope of food remembered but not provided in the trenches, it is notable how many projectiles were given food names as nicknames – 'sausages', 'pine-apples', 'toffee-apples', 'eggs', 'plum-puddings', 'jam-pots', and even the associated 'potato-mashers'.[545]

'Trench language'[546] embraced clothing, objects and states of health. *The Listening Post* 10 August 1918 published a glossary of 'trench terms and their meanings', but as early as 31 March 1915 *The Times* had offered its readers a column on 'trench slang';[547] the term 'trench French' appeared in jokes in newspapers, but it is not known whether the copywriters had tried to say this aloud.[548] The idea that the view of trench language changed after the Armistice is seen in a cartoon in *Comic Cuts* 18 September 1919 which shows a wasp stinging a mask and remarking that the supposed face had not 'even used a trench word', with the implication that soldiers' slang was seen now as merely swearing. The *Daily Mail* headlined an article based on a soldier's letter with the words 'Trench Types' in which various models of attitude and behaviour are given,[549] while Lancelot Spicer quotes a song from a 'trench songster'.[550] Trench names, apart from the information they give about attitudes to home, the progress of the war, and the predominance of London in the soldiers' consciousness, show how the soldiers managed language: when British soldiers took over a French-controlled trench they changed its name from French to English, when English troops took over from Scottish troops place names were replaced, and on trench maps names were transcribed in non-Latin characters to aid Indian troops.[551]

If the trench was the focus of the Front, then mud has lasted as the defining characteristic of the trench, though the variations in soil type, seasons and weather produced great variations of humidity and water retention in the soil; the prevalence of comments about mud would indicate that it was the most annoying characteristic of the landscape. *The Gasper* described a trench as 'water surrounded by mud',[552] and Stephen Hewett wrote 'we live in a labyrinth of mud, which cakes us from hands to feet';[553] it was 'difficult to exaggerate',[554] – 'they say the mud is terrible at the front'.[555] There were different types of mud: 'deep viscous mud',[556] 'gruelly mud',[557] 'Mud, mud, nothing but mud mud without any bottom',[558] 'foul slime',[559] and the memorably sticky 'Wipers mud'.[560] Away from the Western Front there was 'very soft black Mesopotamian mud',[561] on the Italian Front there were mountain paths 'extremely narrow, . . . often from one to two feet deep in greasy mud',[562] and on the Eastern Front the 'history of the war is written in mud and battered roofs'.[563]

It was taken over by anglophone soldiers, possibly from Frank Reynolds' cartoon in Punch showing 'a Prussian household having its morning hate', so that the dawn bombardment became the 'morning hate', with frequent examples of 'evening hate' and 'night-time hate'.

In August 1916 Lancelot Spicer wrote home that he was 'supposed to be suffering from what the *Daily Mail* calls Trench Fever',[564] raising the question of how much of this was generated at the Front and how much in Britain or elsewhere. The relationship between the language used 'at home' and 'out there' is one of the strongest markers of the different experiences, attitudes and desires during the period; it is evident in the phrase 'out there' – 'there isn't any more "Out there" with us now. It's "Out here."'[565] Soldiers were strongly aware of how the press both misreported the situation at the Front and were fascinated by soldiers' slang, to the point of becoming over-involved in it. Soldiers had a range of views as regards newspapers, from their being the only way soldiers could get an idea of the progress of the war to parody of war-reporting in trench journals. While a middle view is given in a postcard from the Front dated 24 March 1918 – 'you can give some idea of what it is like here now by the papers but not all'[566] – what is very clear is how soldiers took home-generated expressions and mockingly adapted them for use at the Front. The 'Hymn of Hate',[567] a poem by Ernst Lissauer attacking Britain, first appeared in translation in British newspapers at the end of October 1914, and was a gift to satirists. It was taken over by anglophone soldiers, possibly from Frank Reynolds' cartoon in *Punch* showing 'a Prussian household having its morning hate', so that the dawn bombardment became the 'morning hate', with frequent examples of 'evening hate' and 'night-time hate'. This developed into 'Fritz sending his

FIGURE 3.9 Frank Reynolds' cartoon of a Prussian family engaged in their morning hate, published in *Punch*.

daily hate over',[568] 'spasms of intense hate',[569] or 'more hate this morning',[570] all with slightly different nuances. As the original poem had been sung by German schoolchildren its musical aspect also transferred into slang, as a bombardment became 'an evening serenade'.[571] The expression was also carried across to Gallipoli, where Aubrey Herbert felt 'a beautiful dawn [was] defiled by a real hymn of hate from the Turks'.[572] While this downgrading was a way of managing fear, it was also edged with a knowledge that the German press and public opinion had in the period around 1914 stirred up intense hatred against Britain, which may have been diluted in the first two years of the war at the Front, but which was a strong aspect of the fighting from mid-1917 onwards.

HATE

Ernst Lissauer's *Hymn of Hate* provided cartoonists with rich material for satire. Frank Reynolds' drawing, which appeared in the 24 February 1915 issue of *Punch*, captioned 'Study of a Prussian household having its morning hate', was one of many that made fun of the idea. The parents, the patriarch very much resembling Hindenburg, with three children and a dog, all frowning, grimacing, clenching hands round the table in a dark and heavily curtained parlour, typified the propagandists' model of futile bombast. While the phrase engendered the belittling descriptions of artillery barrages as 'the morning hate' or 'the evening hate', George Orwell's later use of the term in *1984* carries a much more sinister sense of manufactured hysteria in the post-Second World War period, closer to the original usage in Germany in 1914:

Before the hate had proceeded for 30 seconds, uncontrollable exclamations of rage were breaking out from half the people in the room. In its second minute the hate rose to a frenzy. People were leaping up and down in their places and shouting at the top of their voices. The horrible thing about the two minutes hate was not that one was obliged to act a part, but that it was impossible to avoid joining in.

'Frighfulness' too was taken up mockingly by the troops, Fraser and Gibbons describing the process thus: 'the word "Frightfulness" was so persistently used in the Press in England and Allied countries in the early part of the War that it became a word of jest in the Services, being used in all sorts of connections, and of anything, however trivial. A man, for instance, appearing for the first time with an incipient moustache, or wearing a new pair of trousers, or with anything at all unusual in his appearance or get up, would be chaffingly told that he was displaying "frightfulness"'.[573] By 1917 'frightfulness' was being parodied in the pages of the press itself, a cartoon advertisement for Ensignette Cameras giving tips for avoiding 'photographic frightfulness'.[574] Attempts to 'gift' slang words by the press met with mixed success; 'Rosalie', the French name for a bayonet invented in an erotic song by Théodore Botrel in 1914, was equally energetically dismissed by Henri Barbusse in *Le Feu*, translated as a phrase for 'padded luneys' [looneys?] in Fitzwater Wray's 1917 translation (p. 124). Fraser and Gibbons state that 'Cuthberts' (for those who attempted to avoid being sent to the trenches by getting desk-jobs) was invented by a cartoonist at the *Evening News*, but this was definitely taken up by the troops, as was 'Sammy', the American equivalent of 'Tommy', offered by *Punch* on 13 June 1917 – though there was a view that 'American soldiers hate being called "Sammies". They do not know what the word means'.[575] The famous "Arf a 'mo, Kaiser' catchphrase, popular with civilians, who bought plates and prints showing the picture, never caught on with soldiers, and does not feature in either Brophy and Partridge or Fraser and Gibbons.

'Hate' and 'frightfulness' show language change happening in a transference from home to the Front, but more recognised at the time was the process happening in the other direction: 'soldiers bring [new words] into vogue, and the public gets to know them from the letters which are published in the newspapers and joyfully adopt them'.[576] When presented by the press to the public these words were given as 'new slang', as in the case of 'flying pigs',[577] or 'Toot the sweet' (straightaway), a forces adaptation of the French *tout de suite*, whose development, 'and tooter the sweeter', appeared in a *Punch* cartoon in December 1917, under the heading 'The New Language': Eric Partridge dated its use among troops to two years earlier.[578] *The Iodine Chronicle* noted 'toot sweet' as 'a hackneyed saying' in December 1915. Developments of meaning or usage at the Front meant that there was a potential for delay in transference, so that a phrase might mean one thing at the Front and another at home. An example of this is 'over the top', 'the top' being the highest level of the parapet at the front of the trench. 'To go over the top', or 'go over', meant 'to leave one's own trench and join in the attack on the enemy', this usage being widely known at home from 1916. The 'top' was also the open ground between the trenches; hence by 1916 troops were using 'over the top' to mean 'in trouble',[579] and a glossary in the trench journal *Aussie* defines 'hopover', from 'hop over the bags' (i.e. the parapet) as 'the first step in a serious undertaking'.[580] After the war there appears to have been an occasional reversion to unfamiliarity with the usage. On 25 April 1919 the *Yorkshire Post and Leeds Intelligencer* felt the need to use quotation marks again in reporting the last action of a tank being used as a memorial – the tank was to be located in Hartlepool, going over an obstacle: 'and the tank will "go over the top" for the last time'. The sense of 'excessive' or 'extreme' was evident from 1919: on 26 June 1919 the *Hull Daily Mail* reporting on a trench re-enactment wrote 'the culminating spectacle is an "over the top" affair'. But there was an emerging use of the phrase as metaphorical: the same newspaper reported that the Archbishop of York 'urges the Welsh Church to go "over the top" on March 31st for a living wage for the disendowed clergy'.[581] The *Illustrated London News* on 4 October 1919 showed an image of people running to board a tram during the train strike with the caption: '"Over the top" on the Thames Embankment: suburban travellers struggling to get home'.

> *While slang may have insulated the army against civilian encroachment, soldiers could not equip themselves against direct questions that went to the heart of the inexpressibility of trench-warfare – 'what is it really like out there?' or 'the question, asked in letter after letter, "How many Germans have you killed?"'*

Language was a symptom and a driver of the distance troops felt between themselves and civilians in Britain. Graves wrote that 'the civilians talked a foreign language: and it was newspaper language'.[582] While slang may have insulated the army against civilian encroachment,[583] soldiers could not equip themselves against direct questions that went to the heart of the inexpressibility of trench warfare – 'what is it really like out there?',[584] or 'the question, asked in letter after letter, "How many

Germans have you killed?"'[585] As another trench journal put it in an article entitled 'Quaint questions asked by "Civvie"', 'one's language fails at such interrogations'.[586]

As much as uniting a nation, language could push services and civilians into separate camps. While 'baby-killers' and 'doing your bit' were occasionally used by soldiers, these were terms which originated in the civilian environment, as did 'pushing up daisies' and 'turd-walloper' (sanitary-fatigue man), both terms associated with the Front. Even 'Tipperary', the archetypal First World War song, was, according to F. T. Nettleingham, author of *Tommy's Tunes* (1917),[587] 'never "Tommy's" song'; Pte S. J. Levy stated emphatically of a regiment going to the trenches that 'they were not singing "Tipperary". No!'[588] Ernest Baker, writing to *The Athenaeum* post-war, proposed separate entities as creators of terms: 'carry on', 'get the wind up', 'going over the top' and 'to have cold feet' were army terms, while 'doing your bit', 'fed up', 'get a move on' were civilian inventions, 'deliver the goods', 'cut no ice' and 'keep doggo' were 'Yankee', and 'dazzle' a navy term. Unsurprisingly, civilian slang terms developed, which, indicative of how the First World War has been studied and remembered, have been totally overshadowed by soldier slang, or not thought of as, at the time, particular to the civilian – Edgar Preston, writing in the *National Review*, reckoned 'zepps' as civilian slang.[589] Specific fields produced their own slang: a 1916 *Daily Mail* article by Monica Cosens showed how the culture of the munitions factory was creating its own slang, including 'shell hands', 'mystic' (soap and water), 'basis' (the number of shells worked on before bonus work), a 'dump' (a shell needing reworking), and the 'cloaker' (cloakroom).[590] Though 'the Home Front' appeared only once during the war, in *The Times* in April 1917, there were terms to do with food-production: 'allotmenteer',[591] 'alloteer', and 'allotman', and 'grubber',[592] producers of the much-desired potato, itself also known as a 'U.S.' – for 'underground strawberry',[593] as at the Front the shortage of food produced imaginative lexis, though not necessarily what you would want to serve in December 1914 to invited soldiers at a 'Tommy party'.[594] At a society party, in a cartoon in *The Tatler*, 1 November 1916 (p. 131), the guests are bored to sleep by a 'social tank'.

4 THE HOME FRONT

Commerce and war language

The idea that commerce will always find a way was challenged by the mass of languages in use in France and Flanders, but trade quickly found ways of surviving and flourishing, with Flemish merchants picking up words of Chinese languages in order to sell to members of the CLC.[1] In Britain war terms were quickly put to the service of commerce. The vociferous patriotism in the press from August 1914 made it essential for advertisers to participate and associate with the soldier and the war effort; this took the form of declarations of patriotism, association with the war effort, particularly supporting soldiers, and using terminology from the war, particularly soldiers' slang. An advertisement for Swan pens in *The Sphere* October 1914 showed a soldier writing home, with the caption 'Tommy with his "little black gun" when a lull comes', an early instance of copywriters trying to create a slang expression. The jostling for position can be seen in an early spat between Waterman and Onoto in November 1914, concerning whether Austrian shareholders were receiving income from sales of Waterman's pens. Onoto's claim was that Waterman's pens were sold in the UK through an Austrian-controlled firm; Waterman's denied it, and Onoto re-affirmed their accusation. Onoto claimed that 'Every Waterman Pen sold, therefore, in this country means profit to the King's Enemies'.[2] Some practices and advertisements were frankly crude and exploitative: in January 1915 *The Lady* noted that 'everybody is ordering the newest biscuit produced by Macfarlane, Lang, and Co. They have named it the "Belgian," by way of a little compliment to our brave ally'.[3] An advertisement in the *Daily Sketch* in December 1914 states that 'It's a long, long way to Tipperary – but it doesn't seem a long way if you are wearing Wood-Milne rubber heels and tips'.[4] The *Portsmouth Evening News* carried an advertisement

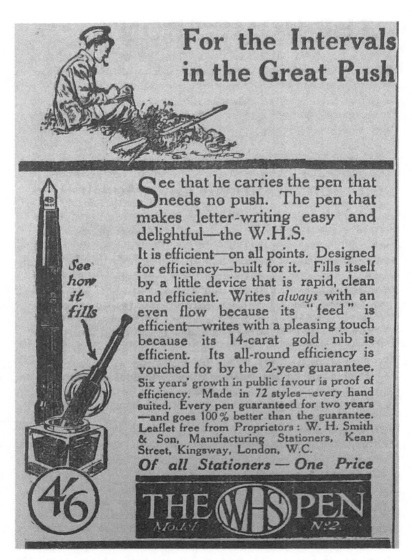

FIGURE 4.1 A typical use of war terminology in an advertisement in *Public Opinion*, 8 September 1916, p. 238, also exploiting the emotional links between the Home Front and servicemen and women, manifested in correspondence.

for 'Goldman for Uniform', in which the tailors challenged their competitors by saying 'we still hold our trenches and they will not take "Calais" if we can help it'.[5]

Punch in April 1915 emphasised its position by its use of trench slang, stating 'A future historian who takes no note of our soldiers making jokes about "Black Marias" in the trenches will fail to appreciate the spirit of our men who have fought so bravely against such mighty odds'.[6]

Advertisements for products of direct interest to soldiers – creams, soap, cigarettes, equipment – would target the soldier-readers, or more likely those who would buy in quantity to send out to soldiers. These made claims, verifiable or otherwise, that created a direct link between buyer and soldier through specifically identifiable phrases – 'Buy it for Your Soldier Friend ... On the March and in the Trenches it Prevents Thirst and Fatigue'.[7] Anecdotal reference to the Front might be included in an advertisement, though no direct link was made: Player's Country Life Cigarettes were advertised with an image of a military motorcyclist and the text 'Types of British Army – Motor Cycle Scout Carrying Despatches Under Fire'.[8] Or absurdly improbable anecdotes might be invented to sell a product – Pears Soap offered an image of 'Tommy' reaching out of a trench in daylight and saying 'Look here, someone's dropped a cake of Pears' Soap',[9] a suicidal gesture labelled as 'An Incident of the Trenches'. References to censorship occur frequently in advertisements; a Kenilworth Cigarettes advertisement reads 'For _____ somewhere in _____. Aren't you going to send him some?',[10] 'somewhere in ____' being immediately recognisable from soldiers' letters. The implication here is that the reader knows what is missing by virtue of being a recipient of soldiers' letters; a triangular link is set up between reader, 'soldier' and product, by implying that the reader knows the missing word. Puns inevitably are put into service: a Sunlight Soap advertisement[11] shows a wounded soldier being given a bar of soap by a woman, possibly a nurse, with the caption 'In France you called this "Savon", Tommy dear.... It's the SAVON that you SAVE ON, Tommy, dear'. Again the sub-text is that the reader knows the French words that British soldiers picked up; an inside group is created, of which the product is both symbol and reification.

Smoking was an area where the Navy was brought to the public's attention in advertising; Woodbines were very much an army cigarette – soldiers often asked for a Woodbine rather than a cigarette – but Player's Navy Cut tobacco and cigarettes were well-known and widely advertised.

Navy slang hardly featured in these advertisements, and in one advertisement, for Martins Cigarettes, where a soldier and a sailor are shown, the sailor, though taller, is verbally ignored: 'you can give happiness to the soldiers at – the – front – and in a personal way too. For each sixpence you spend the soldier gets a shilling's worth of tobacco and cigarettes'.[12] In 1916/17 Cavander's Cigarettes ran a series of advertisements for Army Club cigarettes in local newspapers with invented texts from British, Empire and Allied servicemen. An RNAS (Royal Naval Air Service) officer says, 'one of my college chums chips me [makes fun of me] whether the letters I have mean "Rather Naughty After Sunset" or "Really Not A Sailor"' referencing a widely-used re-interpretation game;[13] elsewhere 'The "Tank" Commander' says, 'They thought anything we produced was a "wash-out," but we caught them napping for once'.[14] Cavanders also used the persona of the American sailor, but the slang here is American rather than naval – 'But say, kid, *some* cigarette'.[15] Again, the knowledge of slang creates the link. 'Smokes' was used in the Weekly Dispatch Tobacco Fund campaign, along with the famous image of the soldier with his pipe and the caption ''Arf a mo, Kaiser', the use of 'smokes' allowing the inclusion of tobacco and cigarettes; but 'smokes' seldom appears in soldiers' letters.

Fictional anecdotes such as the Army Club personas were fairly harmless, but when actual events were used the use of identifying and linking slang to sell a product becomes more uncomfortable. An unidentified survivor of the loss of the *Hogue* (sunk 22 September 1914) is quoted as saying '[Oxo] made new men of us … we were all pretty nearly done for, I can tell you, but the crew were very good to us. They brought us round basins of hot **Oxo**, some with brandy in it, and it **bucked us up at once and made new men of us**' [underlining and bold font as in original].[16] On 17 November 1915 the hospital ship *Anglia* struck a mine and sank, with the loss of 164 wounded men, nurses, doctors and crew. *The Graphic* on 1 January 1916 carried an advertisement for Bovril (using the headline 'Gives Strength To Win') picturing the sinking of the ship, with rescued people being given cups of Bovril. 'Part of a letter written by a survivor of the "Anglia"' states 'We were just wondering how long it would be before we reached "Blighty". Someone said – "Oh, about half an …" The sentence was never finished.' The copy goes on to state that 'Bovril was a Godsend.' The use of 'bucked us up' and 'Blighty' puts the product at the centre of the action, but depends on the reader being familiar with these words.

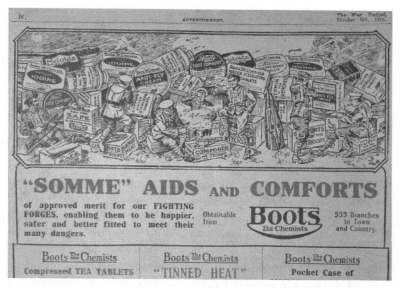

FIGURE 4.2 Boots advertisement in the *War Budget*, 5 October 1916.

Combining both pun and what to modern sensibilities seems an exploitative and callous topical reference, a Boots advertisement in the *War Budget*[17] depends on a pun on the Somme (the battle was still being promoted at home as a victory at this stage, despite the general knowledge of the extent of the casualties). The pun depends on the slang use of 'some' to mean 'noteworthy', in 1916 a fairly recent import from American slang. Nor was this an isolated example. In February 1917 *The Tatler* carried an advertisement for Gibbs's shaving soap with the headline: '"Somme" shave – It is really "some" soap, this Gibbs's.'[18]

An unnerving innocence is apparent in some of the early advertisements and naming of products, but the copywriters and marketers would surely have known what their products referred to: *The Rochdale Observer* in October 1914 carried an advertisement for fireworks that read:

Fireworks! Fireworks!
Ask for 'Black Maria' or 'Jack Johnson' shells.
Wholesale House: Edwards & Bryning Ltd [19]

and at least two newspapers in December 1914 carried an advertisement for a box of 100 toys marketed by the Allies Toy Co. in Brighton, which included a scenario described thus:

Boom! – Oom! – Om! – M! – Bang!!!

The 'Jack Johnson' great German Gun is at work. First 25 harmless shells explode with a bang, then the Red Cross Nurses and their white Tents appear on the scene to deal with the wounded.[20]

While many advertisements could claim that the use of war referencing was reasonable – a small ad in the *Liverpool Echo* reading 'Remember the Somme. Send our Boys some WILLIAMS'S "VELONA" TOFFEE'[21] is rather pushing at the boundary of this – some commercial use of war language was frankly gratuitous, slang or war-related terms having no intrinsic connection to the goods or services being offered. 'Tipperary' was used widely in this way in the early months: '"It's a Long Way to Tipperary" – Buy a Ford Touring Car, £125. Rowland Winn, M.I.A.E., Automobile Engineer, Leeds';[22] '"It's a Long, Long Way to Tipperary" But it's much nearer to Hyams and Son, 5 Bishopsgate, Stockton, for good British Furniture. The Very Best and so easy to buy …'[23] 'Are we downhearted? No!' was also quickly appropriated. The *Dundee Evening Telegraph* carried in the Miscellaneous Sales section of its small ads column: '"Are we downhearted?" – No, certainly not. "Bargains and Business as usual" at Farrell's pawnbroking salerooms, Brook St.';[24] while in December 1914 the *Surrey Mirror* carried an advertisement for H. Burton & Sons, wholesale and retail butchers of Redhill – 'Are we downhearted? No! Because we know that our cause is just and that we shall whack the Germans. Also that we shall keep up old customs by having as Happy a Christmas as possible with old friends at home'.[25] The large number of these apparently overtly exploitative advertisements argues a lack of awareness of the reality of the war, which itself argues a lack of the communication of that reality between Front and home. Did soldiers feel offended by texts such as 'It must be warm to be Under Fire. But warmth with comfort under one of our blankets. Frank Rowe & Co. Army and Navy Wool and Blanket Suppliers, North Devon',[26] did they not care, or did the apparent jingoistic blindness add to the communication gap between soldiers and civilians? The tailing off in the use of 'Are we downhearted?' as an advertising slogan during the war may indicate an abandoning of innocence (though it was still occasionally used in 1918),[27] but in its place the change of mindset at the Armistice was amply illustrated by tailors' advertisements using phrases such as 'from khaki to mufti'.[28] There was perhaps an attempt to compensate for the sudden loss of relevance of so many charged terms: an advertisement in the *Western Times* in January 1919 urged readers to consume 'Vi-Cocoa' to help deal with 'Peace Strain',[29] fortunately not a term which achieved wide circulation.

DORA and the control of words

The Defence of the Realm Act (DORA), passed on 8 August 1914, was short, and largely concerned with reasonable measures to ensure security, but one clause (21) set the tone for the general tone of pressure that extended through the six later amendments: 'No person in, or in the neighbourhood of, a defended harbour shall by word of mouth or in writing spread reports likely to create disaffection or alarm among any of His Majesty's Forces or among the civilian population.' Though there was a strong grass-roots movement against anyone who protested against the war,[30] it was not until October 1915 that anyone was arrested, this being the Scottish socialist John Maclean, for making statements that were considered 'prejudicial to recruiting'. The key offence governing the behaviour of civilians was doing anything, including talking, that might 'cause disaffection': 'Spreading, or possession without lawful excuse of, report or statement likely to cause disaffection.'[31] Effectively this tipped the scales in favour of the prosecution of the war according to the government's principles, and rendered mere questioning of this an offence, even an action likely to bring comfort to the King's enemies.

'Unpatriotic Language' was a frequently used headline heralding the spreading of disaffection; the *Manchester Evening News* on 18 February 1916 carried the story of Lewis Line, clerk, of 'Inthlingborough', who was sentenced to six months' imprisonment under the Defence of the Realm Act. After drawing parallels between deaths caused by air raids over England and deaths from starvation in Germany, Mr Line unhelpfully stated that the British Army and Navy were 'all scum'. 'Unpatriotic' was an accusation that was difficult to gainsay in wartime: the *Derbyshire Courier* reported on the 'bad language' used against the police by a man who had been caught 'with his arms around the wife of a soldier'.[32] 'The Bench expressed their disapproval of the defendant's unpatriotic and disloyal conduct' – the arresting police officer stated his belief that he deserved 'a good thrashing'. Earlier that month the *Newcastle Journal* had reported on the case of a miner in Melbourne who had refused to support 'a patriotic levy of 6d a fortnight' and had 'condemned workers taking their part in the war'; this rendered him 'an unpatriotic worker'.[33]

On 17 May 1916 *The Times* (p. 6) published a report about William Hedley Hawkins, 34, a clerk, who had been charged under the Defence of the Realm Act. The article was headlined:

£100 Fine for Disloyal Talk

William Hedley Hawkins, . . . who surrendered to his bail at Guildhall yesterday, was fined £100 with the alternative of three months' imprisonment for having made false statements calculated to prejudice recruiting.

The defendant, giving evidence on his own behalf, denied having made many of the statements attributed to him. Last November, he said, he applied for and obtained permission to attest, but domestic matters prevented him from doing so. He had waited till the Government made some provision for married men. His nickname in the office was 'Von Hawkins'. He certainly once made the absurd remark, 'We shall one day see the Germans marching up the Mile End-road,' and he also once said 'I suppose I shall have to head a deputation if the Germans come over here.' But that was mere chaff in reply to some bantering remarks. He urged that what he had said humorously had been taken seriously.

Men who were employed at the Smithfield goods depot said they had attested on the defendant's advice.

The *Pall Mall Gazette* for Thursday 29 June 1916 reported the appeal proceedings under the headline 'Alleged to be Pro-German'. Hawkins was alleged to have stated that:

'God made Germany the first country in the world, and put the Danube there to keep out the barbarians', that the King and Queen were secretly friends of Germany, and that the Russians were the scum of the earth; that the English have 'brought this war on themselves'; that he did not think the working classes should be made to pay for the war, and that he had in circulation circulars to repudiate the war loan. He also said that 'all soldiers are licensed murderers of the English Government', and that he would not willingly have them in his house.'

Hawkins was said to have commented on the typhus outbreak at the Wittenberg PoW camp 1914/15, in which it had been reported that guards and medical staff had abandoned their prisoners, who had previously been abused and allegedly tortured. Hawkins' alleged comment was that 'the British prisoners were not treated half so badly as the Germans in the English camp'.

Office chat and bullying may have had some part in this, but as the trial and appeal went on Hawkins' position became more difficult. Another clerk claimed Hawkins had said that 'the Germans were justified in sinking the Lusitania because it carried guns and ammunition'.[34] Hawkins claimed to have been wearing a moustache like the Kaiser's for six years before the war, and that his 'remarks about the Kaiser being a gentleman and a lover of peace were quotations from pre-war newspapers to show how opinions had changed in this country'.

On 1 July (p. 5) *The Times* reported on the upholding of both conviction and sentence; Hawkins was allowed 14 days for payment of the fine of £100, which was probably more than his annual salary, and the same amount of fine levied three weeks earlier on Bertrand Russell for publishing the leaflet *Two Years Hard Labour for Refusing to Disobey the Dictates of Conscience*. Hawkins' fine seems to have been an exemplary one, and what may have sealed his fate was the allegation by another clerk that he had said that 'he would rather fight for the Germans than the English, and when the Germans came he would go and meet them with a red flag'. Socialism was all too easily seen as 'unpatriotic', allowing newspapers to indulge in wordplay with the names of prominent socialists. *John Bull* altered Kier Hardie's name to 'Kur von Hardi',[35] the pun (on General Friedrich von Bernhardi) explained in rhyme by the *Western Mail*:

Fritz has his Hardi for his sins,
And so has John I fear;
The former's name with Bern begins,
The latter one's with Kier[36]

The Passing Show was still calling Ramsay MacDonald 'Herr Ramsay-und-Macdonald' after the Armistice.[37]

A different kind of patriotic pressure on language was seen in the case of Anzac-on-Sea. Early in 1915 Charles Neville set about purchasing several acres of land at Piddinghoe on the south coast of England and set up a company to develop this into a new town. Rather than advertising plots for sale through the usual process Neville placed advertisements for a competition to name the town; the first name selected was New

Anzac-on-Sea. Neville's scheme involved some shady practices – offering free plots as prizes, but with hefty conveyancing fees – which were exposed by the *Daily Express*, and the scheme was eventually wound up.

The original name had been chosen within an environment of celebrating the achievements of the Anzac forces, but as it quickly became entrenched in particularly Australian national identity, the word Anzac was felt to be a special case. Neville held a second competition to rename the town, Peacehaven being selected. A request by the governments of Australia and New Zealand led to the '"ANZAC" (restriction on trade use of word) Act, 1916', passed on 18 December, which made it illegal to use the word, 'or any word closely resembling that word', for any commercial purpose. The penalty for a first offence was a fine of ten pounds, with one hundred pounds for a second offence. The figures serve as a strong indicator of the severity of the punishment given to William Hawkins for defeatist talk.

While DORA undoubtedly matched the mood of the public early on, the growing number of cartoons portraying the act as an interfering elderly woman from 1917 onwards showed increasing public impatience. For Jennie Lee, aged 10 in 1914, the restrictions that forced her parents and other members of the ILP to hold anti-war meetings in the countryside were enforced by 'the local authorities and someone called DORA'.[38]

Outrage and the enemy within

The war's immediate impact against civilians, seen in the stories of refugees fleeing before the German advance into Belgium, the reprisals taken against *franc-tireurs* (the French term was used in German, a memory from the Franco-Prussian War of 43 years earlier), and later the stories brought by the Belgians arriving as refugees in Britain, provoked expressions of outrage. Britain's bringing in troops from its colonies,[39] and Belgium's apparently pointless refusal to allow German troops free passage, did the same in Germany. A tone of moral accusation was set early on, a propaganda that also assumed absolute moral justification, witnessed by the German belt-buckle motto '*Gott mit uns*' and the British myth of the 'Angels of Mons' in September 1914, itself an example of how fiction could become apparent fact.[40] The language of outrage pervaded any attack on civilians, non-military buildings, the destruction of heritage or property. Postcards sent home from the Front showed destroyed villages and damaged churches with captions such as 'after the passage of the barbarians', 'destroyed by the boches' or 'what's left of it'. The deliberateness of the process seemed inexplicable, and postcards emphasise the 'deliberate' or 'systematic' nature of shelling towns and villages. This was specified too in a still-standing plaque in Farringdon Road, London, which commemorates the fact that 'these premises were totally destroyed by a Zeppelin raid'. This was apparently not something that could be comprehended in a civilised continent; indeed the frequent use of 'barbarism', more common in French commentary on events (in a postcard view of Albert, 'les ruines après le passage des barbares'), indicated the breaking down of civilisation; 'civilisation' was 'caught napping' when the German army invaded Belgium.[41] The Germans were aware that 'barbarism' was being applied to them, and resented it.[42] For one British soldier at least civilisation was being abandoned by his own army: on 20 February 1917 George Lamb trained in taking a trench using bombs and bayonets, and wrote 'war has got to such a stage that we have to be a bit uncivilised at times'.[43] Such an approach to war was contextualised by locating it within a different kind of culture – 'Kultur', the German word being appropriated by the British to mean all that was seen in German attitudes as alien to civilisation. *Kultur* according to the Hong Kong Education Department 'is the name given by the Germans to their own form of education and government'.[44] 'Atrocity' and 'Kultur' were linked throughout the war: on 20 April 1918 the *Daily Mirror* reported on the shelling of Rheims Cathedral as 'German kultur has added another atrocity to its list of horrors' (p. 4). The vowel 'u' perhaps allowed a connection with 'Hun' – Walter Brindle wrote of 'Hunnish Kulture' in *France and Flanders*, which describes several acts of what are labelled 'useless destruction' such as smashing furniture and ruining buildings.[45] British propaganda proposed that 'kultur' was akin to a religious mission to infuse German ideals through the world, with a fanatical dedication to the Kaiser; the wording of some of the responses to this, such as 'the aim of Britain must be to drive her [Germany] into the wilderness, not for 40 years, but until she behaved herself and lived at peace with her neighbours'[46] seems bewilderingly naïve and arrogant. Masefield, interpreted rumours that German troops had eaten cats as 'It probably only means that the cats were killed as part of Kultur, or for not saluting, or for night-wandering ...'.[47] Vansittart's note to this states that 'kultur' means 'a compression of all the German civilised values, achievements, ideals and general superiority. When used by British and French writers, the tone is usually sardonic'. It certainly had scope for extension into satire or disdain: the Kaiser, as head of state, could thus be the 'great ruler of the Kulturists',[48] and a drawing of a soldier on a crowded railway platform, in *The Sphere*, has the caption '"Come and Look at the English swine" – A wounded prisoner is mocked by his "kultured" captors'.[49] But the term seemed to be easier to recognise than define: Weekley wrote that it was identical in origin, but not in sense, with 'culture',[50] though in an article published in the *Daily Mail* he stated that 'kultur' and 'savagery' were interchangeable[51]; the *Dundee People's Journal* described the German government as 'the squareheaded wild Indians of Berlin',[52] and the *Arbroath Herald* described them as 'squareheaded savages'.[53] It was clearly inimical to British geopolitical sensibilities and understanding of the attitude of a civilised state, and in this context the war, as spelled out on the servicemen and women's victory medals, could be morally justified as 'The Great War for Civilisation'.[54]

Of the major war glossaries, both Fraser and Gibbons and Brophy and Partridge omitted 'kultur' completely. Three of the dictionaries published immediately after the war offer definitions: 'the German system of intellectual, moral, aesthetic, economic and political progress, the characteristic of which is the subordination of the individual to the State, through the power of which kultur may ultimately be imposed on the rest of the world';[55] 'civilisation, culture and human progress in general, in accordance with Teutonic ideas and ideals';[56] 'German education; of which the chief doctrines were that the State should be supreme in Germany and Germany supreme in the world'.[57]

Attacks on civilians on home territory, particularly the naval attacks on the east coast, gave rise to terms such as Churchill's famous epithet 'baby-killers', used in his letter to the mayor of Scarborough in December 1914, and used again in the *War Budget* description of a Zeppelin raid; its crew were 'fire fiends' and ultimately 'victims of their own frightfulness'.[58] This term became a rallying-cry, even a banner to encourage recruiting: the east-coast raiders 'have undoubtedly done more to aid recruiting by their notorious frightfulness' and earned 'condemnation of wanton Frightfulness',[59] while the Zeppelins were seen as 'out for murder, not warfare'.[60] Atrocity reports in the press and in associated leaflets and booklets whipped up this portrayal of the German soldiers as unrestrained destroyers: *German Atrocities in France*, a translation of the official report of the French Commission,[61] published by the *Daily Chronicle* in 1915,

FIGURE 4.3 Reports of German atrocities in Belgium, and the shelling of English coastal towns, sparked a number of cottage industries producing pastiche iron crosses 'celebrating' the sites of conquest and the German mind-set, using the word 'Kultur'. The war established irony as a dominant rhetoric at all levels.

used the terms 'uncaged beasts', 'unbridled savagery', 'pitiless brutes' and 'abominable atrocities'. This language of sensationalist journalism, though it skirts around using the word 'rape' (the Germans 'gave themselves over to immorality and disgusting brutality ... unhappy women were vilely ill-treated ... violated' (p. 13)), was reflected back in the story of Kate Hume, a teenage girl who fabricated the story of her sister's death in Belgium. Allegedly Grace Hume, a nurse, had shot a German soldier while trying to rescue a wounded British soldier, had suffered mutilation, but managed to write a brief note before dying, the note being brought back by a supposed eye-witness.[62] The text included 'Hospital has been set on fire. Germans cruel. A man here had his head cut off. My right breast has been taken away', most of which would be familiar to anyone reading atrocity stories in the press in late 1914. The detail of breast mutilation itself became a long-lasting trope, along with soldiers cutting off children's hands. Arthur Ponsonby wrote in 1928:

> An amazing instance of the way atrocity lies may still remain fixed in some people's minds, and how an attempt may be made to propagate them even now, is afforded by a letter which appeared as recently as April 12, 1927, in the Evening Star, Dunedin, New Zealand. The writer, Mr. Gordon Catto, answering another correspondent on the subject of atrocities, wrote: 'My wife, who in 1914–15 was a nurse in the Ramsgate General Hospital, England, actually nursed Belgian women and children refugees who were the victims of Hun rapacity and fiendishness, the women having had their breasts cut off and the children with their hands hacked off at the wrists.'[63]

Notable is the way the form of words becomes a model – 'had their breasts cut off/had his head cut off' – adding to what Ponsonby proposed was a mythology of atrocity, and which depended largely on terms such as 'the crucified Canadian'. There is a grey area where received and passed-on propaganda met public hysteria and sensationalist journalism, where outrage provoked equally strong reaction in text. Note how a language of triumphalism greeted victories over Zeppelin raids: the memorial in Cuffley to Capt W. Robinson, who was the first to shoot down an airship over Britain (3 September 1916), describes how he 'sent it crashing to the ground as a flaming wreck'. As the casualty lists after the Somme devastated family after family a more sombre tone is noticeable. The memorial to the children killed by a bomb dropped on North Street

School, Poplar, on 13 June 1917 carries no outright condemnation, but relentlessly repeats after their names the ages of the victims: Louise A. Acompara aged five years, Alfred E. Batt aged five years, Leonard C. Bareford aged five years; and so on for the ages of the eighteen children.

As the Schlieffen Plan devolved into zero-tolerance of civilian action against the German army, the term *Schrecklichkeit* emerged to describe Germany's 'war of terror' against civilians. A disputed term in German, it has its own entry in the *Oxford English Dictionary*, with its first documentation being from January 1917. The quickly adopted English translation, frightfulness, was in use from the end of August 1914, but Brophy and Partridge propose that it was more a term used by the press and by officers than civilians and 'other ranks' soldiers. If the example in *The Pow-Wow*:

> The U.P.S. are quartered here.
> I feel as safe as safe can be,
> No Hunnish frightfulness I fear
> The U.P.S. are quartered here[64]

is typical of officer usage it is no surprise that among other ranks it was quickly deemed ripe for satire.

Sunlight Soap offered a counter to frightfulness, naïvely perhaps, in 'cheerfulness'; in several 1915 advertisements the nation was invited to 'take its cue from the Navy': 'Cheerfulness is uplifting. Frightfulness is a Millstone round the neck. Cheerfulness will overcome Frightfulness. Etc.', and inevitably 'Sunlight users are always cheerful'.[65] Even after the war the *Daily Mail* was proposing that 'Tommy' had won by being cheerful, and that the General Strike ('this war against the nation') could be overcome 'by smiling'.[66] The tone was revived in the propaganda of national optimism that characterised much of the public information output of the Second World War.

A lower level of outrage was expressed at those who were seen as an enemy within, those liable to be seen as damaging the supposed unity of the state in wartime. Strikers, shirkers and profiteers, as well as 'conchies', 'peace-bleaters', 'cuthberts' and even the apparently harmless 'knuts' (well-dressed young men) were at various times and in a wide range of forums vilified as unpatriotic; a soldier named Jack wrote to his sweetheart Floss on 13 December 1915: 'I see they are rounding the young men up now & serve them right if they love the country they are so proud of let them come out and fight for it'.[67]

Soldiers were understandably envious of those engaged in supposedly safe munitions work (the number of deaths from explosions was not high, but the threat was there, and some of the materials left a legacy of disease, radium in particular). In the circumstances of the 1915 shell crisis there was some pragmatic justification in this, and in the resentment felt against strikers. In verses by Sgt F. Walters of the Sussex Regiment, published in the *Sussex Agricultural Express* the 'men of Mother England' are told 'Don't feed the German papers with your strikes', showing an awareness of strikes' propaganda value to the enemy.[68] Rifleman H. V. Shawyer related how the mention of the word 'strike' alone turned a bar conversation between soldiers and munitions workers into a fight instantaneously: 'That one word had the same effect on the military as would a red rag to a bull'.[69] In a letter published in the *Sheffield Evening Telegraph* Driver George Hubbard RFA wrote 'for God's sake and for all our sakes tell your mates and friends not to strike'.[70] This was followed by a letter from Pte W. Storey of the Royal Engineers in which he pleaded with former colleagues in Sheffield 'to forget about union regulations . . . We have not time to say what we are or what we want to do, or if our union will allow it.' The same letter highlighted the types of men who had not yet enlisted: 'There are many "knuts" and "shirkers" who have not yet fallen in, so I say to them "Hurry up, and get a move on"'. Shirking could affect not just the shirker himself – the *Daily Mirror* reported that 'any employer who is convicted of giving work to a shirker' could be prosecuted.[71]

Shirkers, slackers and conscientious objectors seem at times to have overlapped; in a poem in the *Fifth Gloucester Gazette* the writer attacks any male 'in mufti', particularly '"pip-squeaks" inclined to "poodle-fake"'.[72] This poem is followed by another aimed at 'The "Conscientious" Shirker', who belongs to 'the Army Corps of cranks'. 'Peace-cranks and Shirkers, Look!' shouted the headline on the front page of the *Daily Sketch* on 26 January 1916, above an image of Serbian soldiers captured by the Austrian army. 'Cranks' was widely used: 'The I.L.P. conference at Norwich has been called a conference of cranks' claimed the *Dundee Courier*,[73] while the *Dublin Daily Express*, quoting the *Evening Standard*, labelled them as if they were zoological specimens undergoing taxonomy: 'too retiring to wish publicity; fears unpleasantness; poisonous, but not dangerous'.[74] 'Cranks' being insufficiently specific, they were more often 'peace-cranks', though once in context, the shorter form was common: *The Growler* headlined an article 'Intern Them! Father Bernard Vaughan on Peace Cranks', quoting the speaker as saying "The crank who dares to suggest our coming to terms with the enemy ...".[75]

'Conchies', 'peace-cranks' and 'pasty-faces' came in for a hard time, more from civilians than from some soldiers, who saw at first hand the work of organisations such as the Friends' Ambulance Unit (Quakers), who carried out relief work in Flanders. The Quakers were so identified with pacifism that the term 'quaker' was applied to any conscientious objector, Quaker or not.[76] But in combat stress lines emerged verbally – John Crofts noted the term 'conchies' being used by soldiers to describe their own comrades surrendering.[77] Politicians promoting a negotiated end to the war were called 'peace-bleaters'.[78] Soldiers' views of conscientious objectors, and the terms employed, act as markers of individual or group mentality, the reason of the individual and the sway of the group. *The Grey Brigade*, the camp journal of a number of territorial regiments, including the London Scottish, the Kensingtons, the Queen's Westminsters, and the Civil Service regiment, carried an article on 26 June 1915 asking questions about the nature of Quakers' pacifism in time of war, but finishes with a surprisingly generous text:

> The world needs no assurance that Quakers are not cowards, however. It is sometimes harder to clench one's teeth and turn away, than to deal the blow which would send the hated enemy staggering to the ground.
>
> The Friends stand for a principle which may be regarded, universally at any rate, as an untried adventure. To leave the righting of wrongs to the conscience of the wrong-doer, and to the hand of God has sometimes been a satisfactory solution of a difficulty. As far as we can see at present armed evil must be met by armed good, and we are leaving it to another generation to try the experiment of unarmed righteousness.
>
> But one thing is certain – they are brave men.

This was strong writing at a time when conscientious objectors were being physically attacked without much public sympathy; the same journal carried a report on 'peace cranks' on 2 October that year. *The War Illustrated* carried a photograph of Canadian soldiers 'executing' a banner seized from a 'peace meeting' in London, labelled '"Glad rag" trophies of the "Canada crowd"'.[79] Another party of Canadian soldiers rushed the platform at a meeting of the Union of Democratic Control on

29 December 1915 at the Memorial Hall, Farringdon, London; this was reported the following day in the *Daily Express* as 'Utter rout of the pro-Germans' (p. 2). The link between pro-peace activists and the enemy was repeated in the press through the war: 'Peace Cranks' New Plot',[80] 'Peace Cranks Routed – ILP Meeting stopped by Patriots',[81] 'It must have been very galling to peace cranks and friends of Germany ... to hear the ringing declaration of the chairman that Labour meant to get on with the war'.[82] In 1918 the perceived danger of a negotiated peace meant that peace activists were seen as the 'Pacifist Peril',[83] reporting a meeting at which Lord Beresford questioned the source of pacifists' income, implying that they might be funded from Germany, and that 'an enemy in our midst was more dangerous than one at the front'.

The *Fifth Gloucester Gazette* 15 June 1915 carried a spoof advertisement for an 'airy chateau in Northern France' 'suitable to Strike Leader or to Conchologist desirous of studying shells of every variety'. The extended joke includes references to gas supplies laid on, pollarded trees, etc. developing the 'conchie/conchologist/shell' pattern. Wordplay though often collapsed into name-calling, such as that in the *Western Mail* where an alphabet poem gives 'ink-slinging' as 'pacifists' delight' and calls C.O.s 'jelly-fish'[84] (this curious term appears again in the *Exeter and Plymouth Gazette* where the 'peace-party' are described as 'cosmopolitan jellyfish'[85]), or the *Western Times* headlined a short article 'Bishop of Liverpool and the Pasty-Faces', in which the bishop suggested that 'such people ... should leave the country'.[86]

The use of 'pasty-face' linked conscientious objectors physically to the enemy; pale skin was proposed as a German physical characteristic, seen in Hindenburg himself: Major-General Alfred Turner, having twice met the Field-Marshall, described him as 'a tall, stout, typical Hun, with a big, square, box-like head and pasty face ...'.[87] This supposed characteristic was around before the war: 'He was a German, with a large pasty face and a small moustache'.[88] A further link was that, like Germans, they wore glasses (the idea that Germans wore glasses was so fixed that it became a nationwide in-joke, 'Through German Spectacles' being used as a column heading from September 1914[89]). It was widely believed that unlike German soldiers, few British soldiers wore spectacles: 'the majority of German officers probably wear glasses. In the British Army, however, spectacles are as rare as beards'.[90] Though this was originally proposed as being down to some British recruits being rejected on grounds of poor eyesight, while German doctors prescribed glasses to make recruits more efficient, this was quickly taken up as evidence of poor German physique, and thus as a physiological link with British pacifists whose glasses became almost a badge of identity. At a peace-activist meeting the ILP politician F. W. Jowett 'glinted through his spectacles',[91] and though a group of pacifists on a labour-fatigue were described by Arthur Conan Doyle as 'working with a will' they were still 'half-mad cranks . . . neurotic and largely bespectacled'.[92]

The proposed peace conference in Stockholm (1917) offered more material for critics of the peace movement. Not unlike the 'he called me German and other rude names' sideswipe, a rare insult suggested that someone might 'go to Stockholm', while newspapers expressed their disdain for the project with articles such as 'Stockholm Again', which referred to the 'Stockholm palaver'.[93]

Pacifists aside, for the men at the Front there were many whose absence or apparent lack of input into the war effort were an affront; these included staff officers, conscientious objectors, munitions workers, 'blighters' ('A man who stays in Blightie when he ought to be at the Front'),[94] military instructors, and 'cuthberts'. Cuthberts were not just people who had landed in government jobs at home or staff jobs behind the lines, they were people who had deliberately sought these out through influence or excuses, to avoid going to the Front, and then took life easy. Partridge[95] describes a cuthbert as 'a slacker', a 'funk-hole' as a government office, indicating the degree of resentment felt. Fraser and Gibbons state that the name was coined by an *Evening News* cartoonist, 'Poy', who pictured cuthberts as frightened rabbits, presumably always living in fear of being called up, which explains why the term included 'men who deliberately avoided military service, Conscientious objectors, etc.' rather than just those who had managed to bag a safe desk job. Collinson describes them as 'limpets desirous of sticking to their government office or funk-holes'.[96] 'The Slacker' was the subject of a short story in the *Vivid War Weekly*, who only gets to woo the girl of his dreams ('Kiddie') by enlisting and becoming 'a man – a hero of heroes'.[97]

Profiteers caused lasting resentment[98] – Ernest Weekley in his *Etymological Dictionary* of 1921 turned his scorn on them in his entry for 'profit': ' "Profiteer" was coined, on "privateer", to describe those who levied blackmail on the nation's necessity by exacting inordinate prices for their commodities or labour'. To show that the phenomenon was not merely experienced in Britain he gives also the German *Kriegsgewinnler*. But there was a question as to the correct form of the word – 'profiteer' here described a person, but should that be the form for what that person does? The *Lancashire Evening Post* addressed this question on 9 August 1919 under the headline:

Not In The Dictionary

Sir Frederick Banbury's complaint that the new measure against 'profiteering' is directed against a deed without a name is hardly one of the more serious objections to it. I believe, though, that he is right in claiming that the word is not to be found in the dictionaries. The credit for inventing it belongs, I fancy, to the 'New Age,' [*New Age* magazine, February 1916] which applied it not to its present use, but to the operation of selling for any profit at all in a general indictment of the capitalist system. 'Profiting' would, perhaps, have met the case here, though 'profiteering' undoubtedly sounds more opprobrious. This method of suggesting odium by slipping in another syllable is not common in English. In Italian it is quite frequent. There are all sorts of philological puzzles suggested by the new word. Is a man who profiteers a profiteer? Or must he be called a profiteerer? The new term has come to stay, notwithstanding Sir Frederick's linguistic purism. I cherish a copy of Hansard in which the President of the Board of Education is credited with saying that children must be given the best education by which they are capable of 'profiteering'.

Was there some underlying need to have the '-eer' suffix fixed for verb or noun forms? If so, the earlier adoption of the verb 'commandeer', from the Dutch,[99] with 'pigeoneer' (American English, 'pigeon-handler') and 'munitioneer'[100] did not help. Weekley dated 'hoarder' to 1916 (it was much older, but became widely used in this year), but this was considerably less descriptive than its German counterpart *Hamstertante* (hamster-aunt).[101] Least dangerous, but among the most exasperating for those with jobs involving extreme pressure and fear, were those who talked. A hard-hitting editorial in *The Gasper* attacks 'blatherers' like Lord Buckmaster, then Lord Chancellor,[102] while John Masefield, base hospital orderly and later poet laureate and a sensitive writer of children's books, was driven to distraction by those who philosophised on the war, especially G. L. Dickenson, whose tract *The War and a Way Out* (1915) suggested a possible resolution, an idealistic one perhaps. Masefield's view was 'God deliver me from talkers'.[103]

Women and children

Women and children were enveloped in the language of the war from birth as they were given names like Somme or Poppy; their books were appropriated for satire (*Malice in Kulturland, Swollen-Headed William*) and their comics for anti-German propaganda; they became boy soldiers or munitionettes; elderly women provided a model for the caricature of DORA, the Defence of the Realm Act.

The linguistic record indicates that there was a long way to go before women would achieve a reasonable level of respect let alone equality. Women were belittled, mocked and judged: a soldier undergoing facial reconstruction was taken by a nurse to see the Walter Ellis play *A Little Bit Of Fluff*, a typical term for a young vivacious woman;[104] the frequently used term 'my best girl' to describe a close relationship carried an underlying verbal implication of comparison; female sexuality was mocked in postcards showing elderly women standing near placards announcing Kitchener wanting thousands of men, with the caption 'I only want one', or double-entendres to do with billeting ('How many can you take?'); the *Daily Mirror* gossip writer wrote an entry 'Women who annoy', listing four points, the last of which was 'talking inappropriately';[105]women's influence at high levels was castigated as 'petticoat influence'.[106] Even women who volunteered as nurses, if they were felt to be more concerned with 'doing their bit' than actually nursing, could find themselves described as 'useless amateur angels of pity'.[107]

Despite the extraordinary part played by women in the war, including fighting, munitions work and nursing, they were constantly verbally belittled. The enduring female images of the war, of women saying 'go', handing out lapel-flags or white feathers, or receiving telegrams, reflect a reality of secondary citizenship. In contrast, when men were incapacitated by shellshock they were seen as unmanned by hysteria,[108] while Father Eric Green wrote at Gallipoli of 'sights that would have unmanned anyone';[109] 'woman' itself was a term of abuse – Graves reports a staff-colonel referring to a colleague as 'a silly old woman',[110] while elsewhere a conscientious objector is referred to as 'Ethel' in Alfred Lester's 1915 review 'Round the Map', and Burrage refers to women in England as 'Old Tabbies'[111] (Fraser and Gibbons give 'tabby' for 'a girl'). And there was semi-official pressure on the position of women in the military context: Emily Galbraith wrote to Kitchener proposing that young women should be trained to serve as home guards, but received Kitchener's reply that 'he didn't approve of women fighting; it was the men's job to look after the women'.[112]

FIGURE 4.4 Undated postcard; the message reads 'Dear Eva, what do you think of the postcard – can you do anything for me as I thought I would send you one to see if you can put me up'.

FIGURE 4.5 Postcards sent in 1919 and 1918: the 'Granny-dears' card was printed in Britain, with a French translation to the caption, and with the message in French, sent to the writer's mother.

In this environment the use of the suffix '-ette', 'always belittling',[113] was pervasive. There were famously suffragettes and munitionettes, but also 'peacettes', 'conductorettes', and 'policettes',[114] even 'orderlettes'[115] and 'canteenettes';[116] *Punch* described the German Crown Prince's daughter as a 'burglarette', but it did not catch on.[117] The suffix '-ette' had been applied to several new (i.e. imitation) fabrics: 'leatherette' from 1880, 'silkette' and 'moirette' from 1895, and 'suedette' from 1915. The sense of 'imitating but less than' provided a model for occasional startling neologisms: *Woman's Weekly* in autumn 1914 ran a page of 'Husbands' Storyettes', while a writer to the *Derby Daily Telegraph* criticised an editorial by calling it a 'leaderette'.[118] As Lynda Mugglestone points out, '-ette' was not only belittling, but also indicative of the less authentic, and the less serious, and in this context, the less realistic.[119] The term 'flapper' had been applied to young women from the early 1900s, often with admiration, but after the outbreak of war it came to carry overtones of inappropriate frivolity: the flapper was 'a problem', teachers and social workers were told at a 1917 conference,[120] while 'Truth' in the *Daily Mirror* claimed that 'many

WORDS AND OLDER WOMEN

Just as the popular support for the war contributed to the wider acceptance of new army language, any failure to come to grips with the new phraseology, projected or real, was noticed, and highlighted; the group singled out more than any other for this linguistic disenfranchisement was older women. Countless cartoons appeared in magazines and on postcards with variations on: 'And were you wounded in the Dardanelles?' 'No miss, in the leg', or ridiculed older women as the butt of verbal jokes. Cartoons normalised voyeurism and jokes about female sexuality and stupidity. In the context of this casual misogyny, women of the older generation were cast as failures, stooges, jokes and outcasts in the new linguistic community, unable to recognise or use the new wartime slang.

The following article appeared on page 5 of the *Chelmsford Chronicle*, 14 September 1917:

Signs of the Times

In the war communiques we seem to be hearing considerable mention again of Ypres, which reminds me of the wounded soldier in hospital who, in the course of describing to a lady visitor a previous battle in that region, spoke repeatedly of 'Wipers.' Each time he mentioned the town the lady gently corrected his pronunciation by giving under her breath, the French rendering – and by that I do not mean the Anglo-French compromise, 'Eepray.' Afterwards he whispered to a nurse: 'What was the matter with that old girl? Every time I mentioned Wipers she went and hiccoughed.'

a soldier would far rather be lonely than have these forward and feather-brained girls perpetually worrying him.'[121] Disapprobation for flappers continued after 1918 – an article on the Bishop of London's severe disappointment at the 'disgraceful conduct of young women and girls and that of officers and men who in association with them had disgraced their uniform' was headlined 'The Flapper Problem',[122] but the word had already been extended into compounds, such as the 'flapper-bracket' on motorcycles.[123]

Alongside the portrayal of the resented Defence of the Realm Act as an elderly woman, elderly women generally were marked widely as failing to manage the current language, and in doing so they served to show the importance of language as marking membership of the group. Elderly women were mocked and criticised for their incorrect use of terminology, slang, or even for speaking to soldiers at all. Publicly in advertisements, press cartoons and postcards they were held up as the linguistic 'other'. *Punch* was a fertile ground for this kind of joke: in the issue for 14 April 1915 (p. 300) a woman displaying ignorance of ranks thinks a lance corporal is higher than a lieutenant. 'Welcome back to Blimey' is the greeting from a 'dear old lady' to a soldier on 8 January 1919 (p. 20). Another (8 January 1919, p. 27), asked if her husband is going to be released by the army, replies that 'he's got a fortnight before he goes back, but by that time 'e 'opes to be demoralised'. George Belcher created many cartoons of this type, published in *The Tatler*; in one an elderly woman says 'I think my boy Alf will be alright; they've put 'im in the Army Audience'.[124] Older women's failure with language here was an open admission of a break in the supposed unity between the forces and the Home Front, and can be seen in the context of 'language failure' proposed by the educational authorities (see page 9).

> *Elderly women generally were marked widely as failing to manage the current language, and in doing so they served to show the importance of language as marking membership of the group.*

A Reg Winter cartoon postcard used in 1918 shows a woman asking another: 'Is your son getting on alright in the army?'; 'Yes, I think so,' the other replies, 'He says he's in for a court martial.' Another postcard, singularly aggressive to modern sensibilities, shows an elderly hospital visitor being told to 'Oppitubitch', to which she replies 'Goodness, a Russian'. Elderly female hospital visitors were regularly mocked; Bagnold notes one 'old lady . . . at whom . . . it is the custom to laugh', noting that the soldiers followed the hospital staff in finding her 'comic'.[125] Queries as to the causes of injuries eliciting mocking responses usually involved elderly women. Swinton relates a typical story of 'Ginger', a hospitalised Australian, who is asked by 'a kind old lady' if he was 'hit in the Dardanelles' – 'No mum. I was hit in the leg'.[126] A humorous postcard shows an elderly woman visiting a wounded soldier – 'You weren't wounded at the Front, then?' she asks; the wounded soldier replies to the discomfited visitor 'No, lady! A shell exploded at the base, but the base happened to be mine'. She is embarrassed, while the soldier in the next bed is laughing. In others, an elderly woman talks to a sailor: 'I see the papers say you were stripped for action – I wonder you didn't catch your death of cold', or tells a soldier on crutches 'I know just what it must feel like, poor fellow – I had a corn plaster on all last week, and it's been somethink awful'. A postcard showing an old lady talking to a wounded soldier has her asking 'And what did you do when the shell hit you?' to which the soldier replies, 'Sent Mother a postcard to get the bed aired'; overleaf the message reads:

> Sorry to say, some people do like asking us silly questions. One asked me, if I should not like to live in France after the war! And if I was anxious to get home! Of course my answers were (1) Yes! (2) No! It pleased the dear old lady. Love, Ted[127]

Or there was simple leg-pulling – De L'Isle reports men telling a 'lady-visitor' that they were 'longing to get back to the firing-line'.[128] Or their questions might be dismissed totally: a repeatedly used advertisement for Ariston cigarettes shows a bed-ridden soldier turning to reach for a cigarette, the only thing to do 'If the dear old lady asks you what you think of the war ... in moments of exasperation, of embarrassment, of disquietude . . .'.[129] Enid Bagnold's *A Diary Without Dates* is scathing in its portrayal of women hospital visitors' tendency to say the wrong thing; introduced as 'the Visitors', the first of these has a tendency to say the wrong thing so much that the hospitalised soldiers 'treasure every item of [her] talk for future use'. A joke in *Tommy & Jack* runs:

> 'And how many times were you hit, my poor man?' said the kind lady who visited the hospital.

'Only once', groaned the weary patient.

'Only once!' echoed the lady.

'Why, 'ow many times would you like me to be 'it?' snapped the invalid. 'You old cannibal!'[130]

Memory of the phenomenon lasted well beyond the end of the war. An article in the *Aberdeen Journal* noted that 'it was ... faintly irritating during the war to hear the old lady talk serenely about the German "cannon"; it is nothing short of exasperating when she tells you some afternoon that you are a "masher"', 'masher' being very dated by then.[131] Helen Z. Smith's *Not So Quiet* has the VAD narrator responding to her wealthy mother's use of 'cushy' with the ironic 'How well up in war-slang is mother!'[132] And Brophy and Partridge associated the idea of troops talking derisively with 'imitating the style of a newspaper or a charitable old lady'.[133]

Children were involved fully in the language of the First World War, many from birth or before. Research done in 2016 at the National Archives and the Essex Record Office shows the number of children given names that commemorated battles, heroes or the wartime concepts of peace and victory.[134] This was not a new process, several children

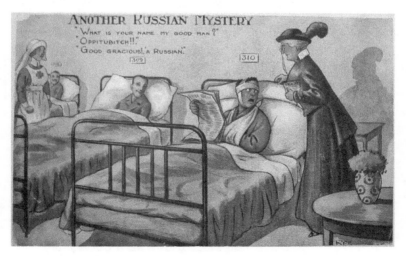

FIGURE 4.6 Postcard, not sent. The use of 'another' perhaps refers to the famous rumour of a secret Russian army supposed to have travelled from Scotland to the south coast by train overnight.

having been given names of battles during the Anglo-Boer War. What is curious is the fact that the most popular name used in Britain was not that of a battle in which the British forces were involved, but Verdun, and that it was extremely popular in South Wales. Ypres was far behind in the popularity stakes, with other battle names used including Mons, Dardanelles, Messines and Somme; non-battle, but otherwise relevant, names include Flanders and Louvain, Raida, and Cressy (after the ship sunk in 1914). Heroes commemorated included Beatty, Kitchener, Cavell and Haig, while 'end of war' names other than Peace and Victory included Poppy, and no doubt influenced the choice of Victor and Irene (goddess of peace). Some words were feminised for girls, Arras giving Arrasa and Arrasiny.[135] The motivations of these choices can be seen from website comments pages – commemoration of individuals or general empathy were factors – but topical incidents influenced choices too. Zeppelina Clarke, (later Zeppelina Williams) was born near the site of a Zeppelin crash, on 24 September 1914; the attending doctor suggested the name.[136] While *The Lady* wryly noted early in the war, 'The habit of naming children after great battles or other dated events is one that is often deeply resented by the unfortunate victims when they grow up', Mrs Williams carried the name through a long life.[137]

The *Aberdeen Evening Express* described this use of topical names as a 'craving';[138] it certainly seemed to risk going out of control. The article

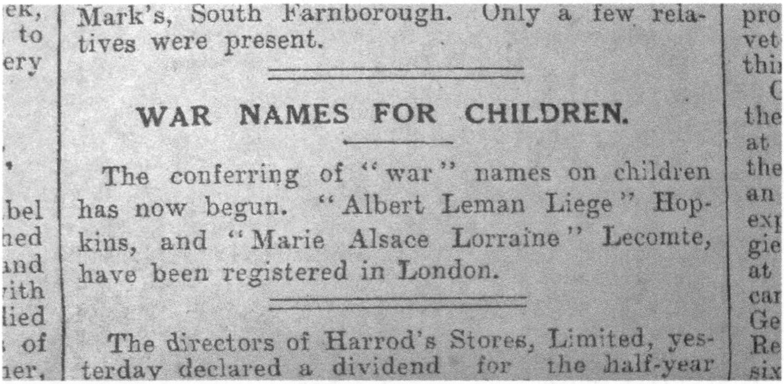

Mark's, South Farnborough. Only a few relatives were present.

WAR NAMES FOR CHILDREN.

The conferring of "war" names on children has now begun. "Albert Leman Liege" Hopkins, and "Marie Alsace Lorraine" Lecomte, have been registered in London.

The directors of Harrod's Stores, Limited, yesterday declared a dividend for the half-year

FIGURE 4.7 Giving children names relating to the war began very early, in this case eight days after the declaration of war on Germany. The text indicates that the phenomenon was expected as part of the process of war. *Daily Graphic*, 12 August 1914, p. 10.

FIGURE 4.8 Postcard sent on 28 August 1915.

showed that in the Abruzzi area of Italy, influenced by various factors, including non-standardisation of Italian, and probably lower literacy levels, there had been a sudden use of the name Firmato, meaning 'signed'. This phenomenon had developed following the wide dissemination of a communique from General Cadorno, with the words 'Firmato Cadorno' at the foot of the document. The *Yorkshire Post and Leeds Intelligencer* wondered reasonably whether anglicised place names had been used; would there be somewhere a 'Plugstreet Brown, or Wipers Jones, or Armenteers Robinson'?[139]

Children were early immersed in the terms and phrases of the war – *The Child's ABC of the War*, published in 1914, has for 'N':

N's for the 'No' that from lips roundly parted
Comes when we ask ourselves: 'ARE WE DOWNHEARTED?'[140]

Woman's Weekly carried a few pages for young children, including in 1914 a column 'For the Ti-nies'; on 3 October 1914 'Tom-my's Un-cle Har-ry' visits, 'in un-i-form', and Tommy cries 'Oh, I wish I could come to the war, Un-cle!'; on 7 November 'Er-ic's Dad-dy' has thought of a 'love-ly plan' by which Eric can support the war-effort – Eric starts saving his pennies and halfpennies 'and Dad-dy takes them and buys cig-ar-ettes for the sol-diers'.[141] Younger children's comics gradually acknowledged the war, and its terms; *The Rainbow* published a story on 3 July 1915 (p. 4) in which a boy's toy soldiers come to life, reveal themselves to have been made in Germany, are beaten back by his older brother's toy reinforcements, and are eventually 'interned . . . in a cupboard, there to remain until the war shall be over'.

Children adapted to changing linguistic circumstances as pragmatically as adults, and probably faster. French children quickly learned to use appropriate language ('jig-a-jig') to pimp their older sisters to British soldiers coming off troop-ships,[142] or to sell fruit 'crying in a monotonous sing-song, "Three apples – une pennee",[143] while Belgian refugees in Scotland were reported as quickly picking up the local accent.[144] Commonly documented are the incidences of children in France and Belgium either picking up or being deliberately taught slang, taboo words or other offensive language use, such as an incident involving a French girl shortchanging a British soldier, and responding to his complaint with 'Garn you fuckin long barstid'.[145] This linguistic influence did not impress some British soldiers.[146] A tone of didactic disappointment is seen in an article in the *Folkestone Herald*, where the potential for British children to pick up practice in a foreign language is noted as not being taken up – in this children's world the onus was clearly on the incomer to learn the language.[147] But the introduction to unfamiliar language where it could not be avoided brought potential for some dynamic expression. Gavin Bowd has shown how in German-occupied Belgium children exposed to the language of the soldiers created their own hybrid texts. When forced to collect berries instead of going to school they created a song:

Toujours toujours travailler.
Travailler *nicht gut.*
Toujours toujours marmelade.
Allemands malades.
Toujours toujours manger choucroute.
Allemands *kaput.*[148]

Children's written words showed how closely they observed events, in terms of both direct experience and the nature of the war. Following Zeppelin raids over London on 8 September and 13 October 1915 some of the pupils of Princeton Street Elementary School were given the task of recording their impressions;[149] the pattern of essay-writing after Zeppelin raids seems to have been well established, as C. W. Kimmins lecturing to the Child Study Society used evidence from 945 texts by children.[150] The descriptions combine observation of the sensation of the airship going over ('reverberating roar') with echoes of adventure-story writing ('like lions when they are hungry', the airship 'sheered off in a south-westerly direction', 'no sooner had I got out when . . .', 'I was sitting at my ease', 'a shell went screaming by on its errand of death'; one of the writers is disturbed from reading *Boys' Friend*, so for him the incident was closely linked to adventure-story writing). Previous experiences contribute to the impressions – women and children going into the tube tunnel at Holborn are described as looking like Belgian refugees, and there is no fear of reticence in graphic description in 'people say that lumps of flesh were found sticking to the walls and posts'. Immediate observations ('short sharp pieces of red flashing from the muzzle [of a gun]'), excitements ('As soon as one fire was under control another burst out undone all the firemen's work'), and later thoughts ('In Leather Lane there were a wife and two children killed of a policeman and he has gone silly'), show children using a range of expressive language to assess their changing world – one girl wrote that 'people were running about like mad bulls and the windows were falling out like rain'. J. McHenry and G. A. Rist use the word 'zep', and Rist writes that 'the guns were well on it' but otherwise these texts, possibly bearing in mind that they were school exercises, do not have slang expressions. C. W. Kimmins noted that 'the noise of firing bulked very largely in the essays', and the descriptions of the sounds of bombs and shells – 'Boom! Whiz!' or 'Boom – crash – boom' – echo transcriptions made by soldiers at the Front. There were expressions of anger against German spies noted in the words of ten-year-old girls, but fear did not feature in their accounts: 'Mother said she did not want to see or hear the Zeppelins again. I do.' Another 11-year-old girl, echoing the adult criticisms of how Germany waged war, wrote 'this kind of thing makes one realise what war is; and yet dropping bombs on harmless people is not war. That night I felt bitter towards the Germans. I felt I could fly to Germany and do the same thing to them.' Her words express the moral dilemma, implied but not resolved in the children's books below, that certain types of activity were unacceptable in the waging of war, but that there was an urge to exact revenge for those activities.

Even where there was not direct contact, children picked up foreign terms: On 7 September 1917 *The Cheltenham Looker-On* stated that the British soldier 'has an irresistible way with the children, who are growing up to speak a very quaint language. They live in an atmosphere of Tommy's slang. Their parents use it. Their big French or Belgian brothers on leave make use of some of the phrases'. The war as a tool for language learning was formalised in the Hong Kong Education Department, whose publication *War Stories in English and Chinese* was designed for 'Chinese boys who have been studying English for three to four years'. Setting out a series of short bilingual texts covering Edith Cavell, Capt Fryatt, Jack Cornwell, the *Lusitania*, with a familiar sense of outrage, the preface assured readers that 'all statements regarding the war herein contained have been carefully checked, as it is not desired to fight Germany with her own weapons',[151] the moral precepts being reinforced as part of learning the language.

Using the war as a case-study for moral teaching lies at the heart of Elizabeth O'Neill's *Battles for Peace: the story of the Great War told for children*. Written before the Armistice, O'Neill's final sentence states 'this, the last of all the wars, should be written down in history as the war for Peace'. Yet the book is loaded with condemnation of German attitudes, right up to the last pages,[152] which castigate Germans for night air raids, Edith Cavell, the *Lusitania*, killing women and children. Quoting 'an

English statesman' as saying 'there must be no next time', the clear message is stated that 'this war is a war to end war'. The phrase 'scrap of paper' is reiterated, to remind child-readers of the cause of the war, but the key contrast brings together war and sport: 'Only victory mattered. This is what the Germans believed and many of them said it . . . The only thing that matters, say the Germans, is to win'; in contrast, 'Almost every other nation believed that the *way* in which you do things matters most. In games it is a good thing to win, but the great thing is to play hard and fairly.' O'Neill's moral precepts for governing rules of engagement were in tune with the wider thinking about how Britain fought the war, often described as 'clean' or 'sportingly'. But her assessment of the Somme shows how children were exposed to propaganda: 'The Germans . . . suggested that they [the Allies] had wasted their men as they [the Germans] had done at Verdun. This was not true. The Allied losses were small except in places where the desperate courage of the men, as at Delville Wood and Guillemont, led to prolonged struggles for some coveted position'.[153] Edward Parrott's *The Children's Story of the War* engages 'us', with a slight delay from actual events, through its scores of parts gathered into ten volumes. There are distinct persons evident in the writing, the 'I' of the narrator – 'I have told you in these pages of scores of heroic deeds';[154] the 'we' of the British, imperial and colonial armies, and the 'you' of the reader – 'Thiepval, you will remember, was the one important point in the German second line which we had not yet taken'.[155] This structure frames the language teaching which goes on through the text which embraces the pronunciation of foreign words and some etymology. Maurepas is pronounced '*More-pah*';[156] 'poilu' has a footnote: '*Pwah-loo*, French privates; so called because most of them had let their beards grow'.[157] The end of the first volume includes a section on the organisation of the army, and a glossary of military terms. But through the narrative there are moral judgements made, as well as familiar references to sport as a moral paradigm. Parrott's assessment of the execution of Capt Fryatt for attempting to ram a German submarine with his packet boat, was that 'no fouler murder was ever committed'; he quotes the Prime Minister as saying 'this was an atrocious crime against the law of nations and the usages of war'. 'On the battlefield our soldiers grimly said, "We'll make the Germans pay for this"'. But within the same story Capt Müller of the Emden is described as 'an exceptional German. Most of his fellow-countrymen have not the slightest notion of how to "play the game"'.[158] As there was no easy way to steer round the moral judgements as to the conduct of war together with those surrounding the reasons for the war, sport, its rules and manners, from a rather public school background, provided a way of trying to bring to children, and adults, some meaning to what was happening.

The family

One of the most enduring texts of the war is the caption to the poster published in 1915, 'Daddy, what did you do in the Great War?' It implies that being involved also meant being able to look back at the conflict – essentially surviving it – and being a father. While probably more sons than fathers served in the forces the concept of the family was at the core of the experience of the war.

An important aspect of how family relationships were affected linguistically by the war is seen in the use of the word 'give'. People 'gave their lives', but more specifically parents, and especially mothers, 'gave' their sons. This took a number of forms, 'giving sons to the army' (or to 'the services', or occasionally to 'the king'), 'giving sons to fight', or just 'giving'; the tense of the verb may be significant. 'Bramley Family Give Four Sons' is the headline of an article about a family with sons in the Army and Navy,[159] while the *Manchester Courier* reported on a family with seven sons serving: 'the mother, Mrs Cundell, is naturally proud to give her sons for their country's service'.[160] 'Mrs Dyson ... has given her four sons to the army' begins an article in the *Burnley News*.[161] Not only families were involved – countries and towns 'gave' their sons, in a familial pattern: 'Dundee and Forfar Give Their Sons' stated a headline in the *Dundee Courier*.[162] The term was used for raising money to pay for the war, in advertisements which quoted the Chancellor of the Exchequer: 'Shall it ever be said that we were willing to give our sons, but we were not willing to give our money?'[163]

Employers were even put in a dubious position of 'giving' their employees: Lord Derby sent a letter to a recruiting meeting in Ormskirk suggesting that 'farmers [should] give their sons and labourers up to join the army'.[164] A writer in the *Fifth Gloucester Gazette* put the concept as: 'Some parents give their sons without / A murmur to the war'.[165] Difficulties arose as people examined the nature of the giving: in an article about the danger of alcoholism in the army, a mother is reported as saying 'I gave my son's body for the King, but not his soul!'[166] The presence of the past tense tends to indicate a deeper loss: 'Gave Her Sons' is the headline of an article about a French mother with three sons dead and the survivor a prisoner,[167] a widow 'gave her son for King and Country',[168] 'Mrs Roberts gave four of her sons to the army. One son . . . was killed early in the war, and another son . . . is missing.'[169]

> *Sybil Morrison, described as a pacifist and ambulance driver, wrote after the war: 'there was this attitude, "I have given my son", which always upset me – because nobody has the right to "give" somebody else and I think on the whole they did go willingly'.*

'Giving' meant something distinct if the 'given' person was killed: sacrifice, permanence, a present absence, compared to the sense of 'loan, with risk' for those who hoped, believed, assumed their sons would return. 'Giving your son to the army' could thus become 'giving your son'. 'A hardy veteran of the mine who had given his son for his country's sake' is typical of this term.[170] Sybil Morrison, described as a pacifist and ambulance driver, wrote after the war: 'there was this attitude, "I have given my son", which always upset me – because nobody has the right to "give" somebody else and I think on the whole they did go willingly'.[171]

Family letters and above all postcards from the Front tend to use a language that tries to affirm stability – 'Dear Dad, am going on alright', 'Dear Bro + Sis, Hoping you are both well as this PC leaves me in the pink', 'Dear Nell, Coming home in a day or two', 'Dear Mother, Will you please send 1 doz Gillette razor blades', 'Hope Father and George are working'. Often a soldier's letter to an older child reads like an exchange between equals: 'Dear Gwen, I received your letter and fags and was very pleased with them. I was glad to here (sic) you and Mum and Bert were quite well as I am the same in the best of health. The weather seems to be on the shift and nobody will be sorry to have it a little warmer. Good luck, your loving Dad'.[172] More uncomfortable to modern readers is correspondence between the child and the father in the forces, letters and cards which only rarely refer to combat. 'Dear Daughter, Received both your very welcome letters today, glad you are all first class, I am in the pink . . .', the string of clichés being relieved by the obvious and heartfelt 'I have nothing much to write about, only that I hope to be home with you both and all soon'.[173] This is more typical than when George Fairclough wrote home on 18 December 1914 with a message for his daughter: 'Tell Olive that Father Christmas will come next year for certain – he had to go to Germany this year as there are a lot of little girls who have no Daddy'.[174] In postcards or letters from father to child rare references to the war tend to maintain a cheerful tone: 'Jackie, Here are some German prisoners the French have captured. I often see them here. These lot look pleased they are captured. How are you going on? Being a good lad I hope!! Love Father'.[175] Endearments might make the war seem all but forgotten: 'My dear Rabbit, I have sent all the others a card so I had better send you one to avoid a row. How are your rabbits going on I am jolly anxious to see them'.[176] Awareness of the importance of obligations, despite the war, is evident in: 'Dear Olive, Just a line to say I am well hopeing (sic) you all are the same I should have sent what you asked for but we are having it rough now. Dad'.[177] Correspondence with a child allowed an adult to be momentarily somewhere else. Perhaps 2nd Lt Arthur Lamb's standard use of 'mummy' ('My goodness mummy dear, the cold!'[178]) in letters home referred to a reassuring memory of earlier years. Some normality could be suggested by sending postcards for a collection: 'One could spend a long time here as there are so many places of interest. I am just starting a series of 11 cards so look out for them. Love, Dad',[179] 'Dear Katie, Another card for your album. We have now left the fighting zone'.[180] Incidental tourism and its postcards allowed almost a semblance of holiday, the novelty of the foreign lifting the spirits of both sender and reader: 'Dear Ma, I have just had a feed of snails, not so bad. Arthur'.[181]

In the interest of reassuring the people back home, the possibility of never returning was less referred to, and the more shocking when it appears: an American postcard showing a doughboy on the step of a train, holding up a child, the caption beneath reading 'The Last Kiss From Papa?' (the message reads 'I hope I won't see this time'); or a British cartoon postcard of a family seeing off the soldier father at the station, with a tactless child saying 'I'll look fer yer name in the casualty lists.' In a community so brutalised by war that the notification of death had come through to humour, this equals any of the cynicism of the Front.

5 OWNING THE LANGUAGE

Class

In one of his essays on the slang of the armies of 1914 to 1918 in *Words! Words! Words!* Eric Partridge proposes that internal influence within a language would be 'always much stronger in a live and lively language than any external, i.e. virtually foreign, influences can be .... The mixing of the classes is more potent than the mixing of the nations'.[1] Clearly slang moved up and down the social scale in English during the war, particularly at the Front, but the influence of class on wartime language was more than just a case of working-class soldiers learning a little public school slang and officers learning the slang of the factory and the street; and Partridge believed that the 'educated' classes gained far more from the contact, in terms of vivid language, than the uneducated, who picked up little more than some journalese and officialese.[2] However, following Jean Aitchison's proposal that sub-dominant groups adopt the language of dominant groups,[3] the adoption of working class slang by the upper classes during the war indicates that the upper classes at some level recognised the working classes as socially dominant during this period, though cause and effect here may be difficult to unravel.

Like any profession, the Army has developed its own jargon, and still carries a general rank differentiation, between officers, holding commissions, and 'other ranks', denoting privates, guardsmen, troopers, gunners, riflemen, etc.; within the Army the term 'other ranks' carried, and carries, no sense of disrespect. But the use of 'other' in this verbal classification carried a risk of confusion, seen in a letter to the *Manchester Guardian* in which a former soldier remembered receiving notification of the impending arrival at an RAF HQ of '300 pigeons and 3 other ranks'.[4] A sense of social distinction *was* present in the term 'temporary gentleman' for the New Armies raised from 1914.[5] A. J. Dawson in the preface to A *"Temporary Gentleman" in France* writes that the German army claimed to have killed off all the British officers in France in 1914, and that no more were available;[6] certainly the more strongly visible designations of rank, later abandoned, did lead to a disproportionate number of British officers being killed in the early months of the war. The British Army did immediately set about training officers from among those who had had some experience in Officers' Training Corps (OTC) in public schools and universities, along with 'members of a University' and 'other Young Men of good general education',[7] and later built up Officer Cadet Battalions. The resulting officers were 2nd lieutenants, or 'temporary officers', temporary as they had enlisted not permanently, but according to the recruitment forms 'for a period of three years or until the war is concluded'.[8] The 'gentlemanly' status of previous officers led to these new officers being 'temporary gentlemen', a term that provoked some derision and perhaps some pride; Dawson's largely fictional main character (who gets promotion from lance corporal to 2nd lieutenant in December 1914), previously a South London estate agent, uses the term 'temporary gentleman' frequently in his letters home, without any sense of this being a derogatory term. There was even a possibility of apparent social improvement – William Cushing, Temporary 2nd Lieutenant, arrived for his medical examination to be told by the Medical Officer that 'we', i.e. officers and gentlemen, 'do not suffer from such defects [as hammer toes]'.[9] However, formal publications always reminded readers that many elevations were only temporary: *The War Dragon*, the regimental magazine of the East Kent Regiment, recorded '2nd-Lieut. (temp. Lieut.) W. A. MacFadyen to be Lieut., with precedence from 8th January, 1916'.[10] Though the exigencies of combat levelled the playing field, and as Stephen Graham wrote, 'the uniform of the King, whilst it enlarges and increases some, making "men" into "temporary gentlemen," does narrow and straiten others, making "gentlemen" to be temporarily "men"',[11] there were problems of adjustment post-war; a popular post-war comedy exploring this situation, *The Temporary Gentleman*, was subtitled 'A study in wartime snobbery',[12] and Brophy and Partridge labelled the term 'snob journalese'.[13] Emma Duffin turned the concept round, noting that she had a patient who was a 'gentleman ranker'.[14]

Recognition of the camaraderie of the trenches and the positive effects of the mingling of social classes was reflected in the decision by the Imperial War Graves Commission to lay aside rank in ensuring that uniform grave-stones were used for all ranks of service personnel in war cemeteries around the world, thus creating a long-lasting image of the First World War of equality in death; this was supported in a House of Commons debate, 17 December 1919, by a former officer, Trevelyan Thomson MP, who said 'we desired that if we fell we should be buried together under one general system and in one comradeship of death. . . . I think it would do much to undo the value of the comradeship that was cemented by the War if afterwards we had a considerable distinction made, measured by the wealth of those who remain behind rather than by the service given overseas'.[15] It was a long way from the beginning of the war, when the war diary of the 1st Life Guards could record on 30 October 1914: 'Missing – Captain Lord Hugh Grosvenor, Captain E. D. F. Kelly, Lieutenant Hon. Gerald Ward, Lieutenant J. Close-Brooks, 100 rank and file'.[16] But death in the war did not by any means indicate an end to the language of social stratification in the business of commemoration: the flowers carried by mourners past the Cenotaph and the grave of the Unknown Warrior in 1920 'were brought by men and women, old and young, principally of the humbler working class, many of whom must have travelled from the farthest parts of London'.[17]

> *While 'other ranks' suffered from shellshock or were diagnosed as 'hysterics', officers suffered neurasthenia.*

The linguistic distinction between officers and men sat alongside other distinctions: separate hospitals, the context of comfortable foreign travel for soldiers' phrasebooks, and the awareness that men, not officers, were 'Tommies'. While 'other ranks' suffered from shell shock or were diagnosed as 'hysterics', officers suffered neurasthenia.[18] The docility with which British soldiers accepted this, compared to the supposedly undisciplined Australians, or the allegedly brainwashed Germans, puzzled many contemporary observers; C. E. W. Bean put it down to the majority of private soldiers believing themselves to be 'inferior, socially and mentally, to their officers'.[19] This perhaps made possible a joke such as that in the *War Budget* in which disabled soldiers retraining as shoemakers are said to be 'entering the "upper" class'.[20]

Awareness of class was a given in pre-war British society. The middle classes were able to afford day-servants, railway carriages were labelled in three classes, and public houses, schools, churches, and places of entertainment were all segregated according to the economic status of their clientele. Wealth and deference were visible in the towns, and the wealthy and titled in the countryside enjoyed a dominance that was not distant from feudal;[21] Marwick's assessment shows the imbalance, 80 per cent of the population being working class, with an income less than a quarter of that of the salaried class.[22] Indicators of assumptions of superiority and privilege appear all through the incidental documentation of the period: an envelope from the Front, addressed simply to 'Messrs Harrods, London SW';[23] Ethel Bilbrough's diary entry, 'we met an extremely poor and common man, but excitement and danger make everyone equal';[24] VAD Enid Bagnold wretchedly realising that her English is practically incomprehensible to working-class soldiers.[25]

> Awareness of class was a given in pre-war British society. The middle classes were able to afford day-servants, railway carriages were labelled in three classes, and public houses, schools, churches, and places of entertainment were all segregated according to the economic status of their clientele. Wealth and deference were visible in the towns, and the wealthy and titled in the countryside enjoyed a dominance that was not distant from feudal; Marwick's assessment shows the imbalance, 80 per cent of the population being working class, with an income less than a quarter of that of the salaried class.

All of this was manifested in the first months of the war. When Britain was managing the distribution and accommodation of Belgian refugees care was taken to match the social status of guest and host – 'Everything is now being put in order for the reception of Ilford's visitors, who are all of the superior artisan class'.[26] Lancelot Spicer talks about enlisting in a 'public schools battalion of the Middlesex Regiment, the ranks of which were drawn from one's social contemporaries'.[27] 'We are in a Division of some fame, and a fine Battalion we are, full of the better-class men. It is the "first city of Birmingham Battalion", once half made up of gentlemen, and still full of clerks and educated folk', wrote Stephen Hewett in February 1916, noting that the officers in his company mess were all 'gentlemen', and later 'the officers happen to be gentlemen, which robs the life out here of the only terrors it ever had for me'.[28] The idea that fear of dealing with people outside one's own class could be worse than fear of the trenches was not a huge exaggeration. The same threat provided a strong theme in recruitment in 1914/15, in the creation of the Pals Battalions, and the sense of welcoming men into an environment they could trust, before sending them to kill and be killed. The social make-up of Kitchener's citizen armies ranged widely, from adventurers to former soldiers, shop-workers, factory hands and clerks, as 'all the recruiting offices are besieged by young and able-bodied men, many of them of the prosperous middle class'.[29] By the end of August 1914 prominent citizens were finding a role for themselves in recruiting locally, raising money to clothe and equip local young men, and wanting some recognition for their work in the identification of these units as locally created. Other groups came together via workplaces or clubs, such as the 10th (Stockbrokers) Battalion (1,000 men), who were in effect the first of the Pals Battalions.[30] The key idea in the success of the recruitment drive from the end of August was that men should be serving alongside people they felt comfortable with; Lord Derby's letter to the *Daily Post* on 27 August 1914 proposed that men would be willing to enlist 'if they felt assured that they would be able to serve with their friends and not be put in a battalion with unknown men as their companions'; the concept 'amongst friends' is repeated in the next sentence, but more bluntly F. C. Stanley reported the *Liverpool Post*'s observation that the day's recruiting on 31 August 1914 had made up the full number in an hour, with 'no undesirables'.[31] With woollen khaki in short supply, local access to cloth enhanced the ability of recruiting committees to supply their own battalions, at the same time increasing the sense of identity, often bolstered by badges, uniform designs, hats, which in turn supported the idea that units could be made up to suit any area, profession, class or interest. Battalion names such as the Artists' Rifles, the Arts and Crafts Battalion, the Church Lads Brigade, or Grimsby Chums indicate people enlisting together; Hull had a Commercials Battalion, a Tradesmen's Battalion, a Sportsmen's Battalion, and by the end of 1914 a fourth battalion with no specific identification, known as the Hull T'Others. Class was the key to recruiting: 'surely Leeds can furnish with ease from its offices and warehouses the thousand young fellows, all of the middle-class, that are required for a battalion';[32] 'I am sure there are many hundreds of middle class young married men (twenty-five to thirty-five years), earning from £200 to £400 per year … who are most anxious to join Kitchener's Army'.[33] 'Middle class', 'better class', 'friends', all indicated people looking over their shoulders nervously at those worse off, while 'tradesmen' looked up – the Hull 'Tradesman' Pals were mostly manual workers;[34] there was recruiting in Leeds in September 1914 for two 'Workers Pals Battalions', but recruitment was slow and the Workers Battalions were rather overshadowed by the 'Leeds Pals', officially the 'City of Leeds Battalion of Businessmen'.[35] While the Leeds Pals were undergoing their medicals on 10 September '60 young men of the artisan class enrolled their names' for the 'new workers' "Pals" battalions'.[36] The recruits were mostly from manual trades, with a few clerks; by the following evening 400 men had come forward. By 15 September recruitment for the Workers Pals had fallen to around 60 a day,[37] making a total of about 1,200 by 18 September, half the number desired. On 22 September the *Yorkshire Evening Post* expressed the hope of Leeds sending 13,000 soldiers to the army, including '1,200 Leeds "Pals" Battalion, 2,500 Leeds Workers' Battalions'.[38] On 26 September recruitment for the Leeds Workers' 'Pals' Battalions was closed, 1,200 short of the hoped for number.[39] It seems likely that the preferential recruitment of the battalion of businessmen in Leeds, excluding artisans and manual workers, led to increased class tension, compounded by a huge crowd at the railway station, cheering the Leeds Pals as they went off to training.[40]

Education was one of the signifiers of class status, and it continued to be manifested during the war, with the UPS Battalions' trench journals decorated with literary and classical allusions and Latin quotations; Latin aphorisms were regular sights on the pages of *The Pow-Wow*, and *Dum spiro spero* (while I breathe I hope) was not out of place in an officer's postcard home.[41] Literary ambition became apparent on thousands of pages of trench journals, and something of a joke, according to the *Morning Rire* (2nd Irish Guards), whose 'What We learnt in London' column included: 'That all the publishers want to take 2nd Lieutenant Lynch into partnership'. But a huge gulf in both education and speech between officers and men became apparent to Stephen Graham:

> I found that no one knew anything of literature. Our national glories of the word were naught to my mates. They were deaf to the songs which should thrill and inspire. Shakespeare was a mere name. Tennyson and

Browning and Keats were unknown. If you quoted to them from Keats you must explain that a man called Keats wrote it. If the soldiers opened the books they could not grasp what the poems were about. Our prized language when used in a noble way was like a foreign tongue. If you spoke to them in normal correct English they did not quite understand and you had to re-express yourself in halting working man's English, full of 'you see' and 'it's like this' and expletives and vulgarisms, or the working man would be rather offended at the way you spoke and imitate you in a drawl when your back was turned.[42]

The men responded by imitating officers' accents – still known as 'talking Rupert'.

This raises questions about the social locus from which so many memoirs and contemporary collections of letters were written. Christopher Dowling, in 1980 Keeper of Education and Publications at the Imperial War Museum, starts his preface to George Coppard's *With a Machine Gun to Cambrai* ([1968] 1986) with: 'Of the scores of military reminiscences of the First World War, almost all are the work of officers or of men, who, though serving in the ranks, by education and upbringing belonged to the officer class'; the back cover blurb describes it as 'almost unique in that it was written by a private soldier'.

Slang too carried class labels, regardless of rank; the Swansea *Cambria Daily Leader* noted that 'class slang of all kinds is interesting to most people . . . none is more so than that common to officers and men of the Fleet'.[43] But small comments indicate class associations: a private writing the *9th Royal Scots Active Service Diary* for 13 to 15 April 1915 wrote about stumbling over a railway in the dark, 'that put (in vulgar phrase) the tin hat on it';[44] the *Glamorgan Gazette* created a glossary from 'the letter of a sailor on board His Majesty's ship Caroline':[45] some examples – 'Stripey' for sergeant of marines, 'grub-spoiler' for cook, 'crusher' for ship's policeman, 'oily' for engineer – indicate that this was coming from a rating rather than an officer. Curiously this glossary does contain the word 'matloes', from the French, but generally officers and educated men slipped French into their writing, and presumably their speech, more naturally; typical of Masefield's letters home are 'My friend has gone to dejeuner' and 'often a plusiers reprises till the cart would shog to one side'.[46] Tommy French was often identified as specifically not officer slang: Edmund Blunden stated that 'Ocean Villas' was the form of Auchonvilliers used by 'my batman and a large number of his cronies',[47]

and Lancelot Spicer writes home, 'That was meant to be the idea –
Compree, as Tommy says when he thinks he's speaking French'.[48]

If speaking French properly was seen as typical of the officer class,
then certain slang expressions or speech mannerisms were seen as 'officer
slang'. Some of this might still be recognisable as upper class slang – 'Hang
it all', used by the Officers' Training Corps cadet,[49] or the P. G. Wodehouse
style of 'just as the working party comes in and gets under cover, she
['Minnie' – Minenwerfer, the trench mortar] lets slip one of her disgusting
bombs, and undoes the work of about four hours. It was a joke at first, but
we are getting fed up now. That's the worst of the Bosche. He starts by
being playful; but if not suppressed at once, he gets rough; and that, of
course, spoils all the harmony of the proceedings'.[50] There were playful
uses of French and German – 'degommy' for *dégommé* (sacked, of
officers), 'der tag' for anything much desired. There was the slumming use
of street slang – for example *The Gasper*, used as the title of the UPS
Battalions' magazine. Old Army slang was taken forwards – 'stellenbosched'
(sent home in disgrace), from the Boer war, and 'mufti'; terms from
officers' tasks, such as 'comic cuts' for memoranda, and 'propaganda' for
rumours, were noted as officer slang terms.[51] Brophy and Partridge also
note 'battle bowler', 'stopping a blast' (being shouted at), 'as you were' and
'jump to it' as officer slang. Officer slang could be part of a studied ease,
almost a decadence: the *Daily Express* in June 1918 reported on
convalescing officers relaxing at the seaside, their 'indolence ... almost
epicurean; their slang is subtle super-slang'.[52]

A particularly difficult aspect of the war is the way that so many
people writing at the time, especially those who had been
through the public school system, seemed to try to apply the
moral rules of sport to warfare.

A particularly difficult aspect of the war is the way that so many people
writing at the time, especially those who had been through the public
school system, seemed to try to apply the moral rules of sport to warfare:
fight fair, as you would play fair, according to rules; be decent to the
surrendering enemy; be chivalrous in victory and uncomplaining in
defeat. How much of this actually took place is difficult to know – no

doubt sometimes it was the case, and it was a useful myth. As Brophy and Partridge put it, 'decent men cloaked the nature of war on every possible occasion with their own, quite irrelevant, sentiment and unkindliness'.[53] It was not just officer-speak: 'Jerry is no sportsman', wrote a Birmingham soldier to his parents;[54] and, at least early in the conflict, British sportsmanship was recognised by the Germans: 'The English act and behave like proper sportsmen'.[55] 'Sportsman' and 'gentleman' closely overlapped, part of the recognised expectations of behaviour of the upper-middle classes in both Britain and Germany – in October 1914 it was deemed acceptable to leave a wounded comrade 'in the hands of the Saxons who are known to be gentlemen'.[56] Generally though, the distinction was clear:

> Given half a chance, the natural inclination of our men is to wage war as they would play cricket—like sportsmen. You've only to indicate to them that this or that is a rule of the game—of any game—and they're on it at once. And if you indicated nothing, of their own choice they'd always play roughly fair and avoid the dirty trick by instinct. But the Boche washes all that out. Generosity and decency strike him as simply foolishness. And you cannot possibly treat him as a sportsman, because he'll do you down at every turn if you do.[57]

Occasionally there appears a sense that, especially early on in the conflict, this was some kind of game, employing the language of the fairground: one nurse in November 1914 was given the opportunity to fire a large gun: 'The Major looked down at me and said, "Would you like to have a shot at the Boches?" and I said "Rather!"'

It is not easy at this distance to take these terms with the gravity that applied to them at the time: a report in March 1916 tells the story of a French battery destroying a hidden German battery and the German artillery taking revenge by destroying a French village. Clearly the motives and the deliberated revenge are imagined, but the process is given as 'one that reveals the callous and unsporting side of the detestable character of the Hun'.[58] But how seriously in 1915 did people take some of the advice in *War-Time Tips*: 'It is not "etiquette" for a soldier to try to shoot the commander of a force unless he unnecessarily exposes himself to fire. It is permissible to try to take him prisoner, however.' 'If, by any chance, your company or detachment should be forced to surrender, you must not discard your arms and slip away. It is against the rules.'[59] Occasionally there appears a sense that, especially early on in the conflict, this *was* some kind of game, employing the language of the fairground: one nurse in November 1914 was given the opportunity to fire a large gun: 'The Major looked down at me and said, "Would you like to have a shot at the Boches?" and I said "Rather!"'[60] Even as late as 1917 *The Tatler* was running a regular series of group photographs of officers with the headline 'Engaged in "The Great Adventure"'.[61]

Despite the change of attitude at the Front, particularly in 1918, when fear turned to grim pragmatism, sportsmanship was still being put out as moral propaganda: E. B. Osborn wrote in his preface to an anthology of poetry, *The Muse in Arms* (1918), 'The Germans, and even our Allies, cannot understand why this stout old nation persists in thinking of war as sport; they do not know that sportsmanship is our new homely name, derived from a racial predilection for comparing great things to small, for the *chevalerie* of the Middle Ages'.[62] Synonymous with 'being a sportsman' was 'playing the game': 'The Germans have played the game in that they have buried many of our men here'.[63] The imagery continued post-war: General Plumer's speech in Torquay, reported in the *Daily Mail* 6 May 1919, praised the Allied forces, who had 'played together for the side'.

'Sport' meant different things to different people. The Sportsmen's Battalion raised in September 1914 was one for 'upper and middle class men, physically fit, and able to shoot and ride'; applicants were assessed on their ability to 'shoot, ride, and walk well'.[64] After some debate over the question of whether professional football should continue, a Footballers' Battalion was formed, comprising professional players and fans. But these sportsmen were overshadowed by the obsession for playing football at the Front. British soldiers were perceived as being football mad: there was the term *Fussballinadianer* used by the Germans, and liaison officers were driven distracted trying to borrow land from French farmers for what they called 'le foolball'.[65] Bavarian soldiers in 1914 were described as being 'puzzled' by the British soldiers' use of football cries: in a bizarre episode 'the Germans were shot and bayoneted to such cries as "On the ball," "Mark your man," and "Here's for goal"'.[66] Charles Douie recorded a football match being relocated outside Albert to escape shelling: 'The game was terminated, without definite result, owing to a battery opening fire with shrapnel. This disregard of the decencies on the part of the German Army was the subject of much unfavourable comment'.[67] Yet a captured German officer suggested that his own soldiers might have picked up the habit of playing football behind the trenches from seeing British soldiers in the distance doing the same thing.[68] A curious footnote to this is the fact that out of the 10,000 names given to trenches on the Allied side of the Front, only two referenced football grounds, Aston Trench and Villa Trench;[69] perhaps a kind of truce was in operation.

'Sport' also meant betting, and this indeed was common in the trenches;[70] in 1914 the use of the word 'sport' to mean hunting typified another area of speech that showed class differences within English, as the metaphor of hunting was applied to combat. At its most direct this is seen in the phrase 'boche-hunting' or 'potting the Hun' or 'Taube-shooting from French covers';[71] Neil Tytler's 1922 memoir *With Lancashire Lads* makes no apology for treating war as anything other than 'the employment to their fullest extent of the machinery of death already prepared', but the simplicity and directness of the hunting analogy can still surprise: 'Just after dawn and the hour after sunset are my happy hunting hours, which usually yield the best sport'[72] (especially as on the same page he describes shooting partridges, with a dog, in no man's land). A day spent shelling 'Hunland' is described as 'a tiresome and difficult shoot'.[73] But connecting this to metaphors of 'cleansing' and 'vermin', a newspaper reference to 'ratting' did not find favour with one soldier: 'newspapers in the UK wrote of tremendous victories and killing Germans as a sport similar to ratting. We could laugh aloud at these reports, plagued by lice ...'.[74] The extended metaphor of hunting, the 'bag', allowed some distancing, and was often applied to taking prisoners rather than killing: Capt R. J. Trousdell described in his diary for 9 April 1917 'the total bag for the Corps about 3,000',[75] while the *Dublin Daily Express* reported on an officer who described the Germans ('Huns') as 'the mad dogs of Europe' with the headline '22 Germans bagged with an empty revolver'.[76] But the term was also used of killing: Major Cowan of the Royal Engineers in 1917 described laying mines which would 'make a decent bag',[77] and H. M. Stanford, a gun observer at the Somme, wrote 'I believe I made a bag of about 20 Huns with one round'.[78] 'Up' in the hunting sense of 'disturbed into flight'[79] was used too, but transferred from quarry to predator: the beaters' cry of 'Bird up!' was carried over into the trenches, as 'Minnie up!',[80] 'Aeroplane up!'[81] and the Canadian and American 'Heinie up!'[82]

Our language

On 18 November 1921 *The Times* posted a note about the current issue of *Notes and Queries*, which continued a discussion about 'Army Slang in the War'.[83] One contributor had sent in a list of words which he described as 'the most typical expressions of general Army slang as he heard it: Buckshee, lash-up, all cut, head-worker, hard skin, wangle, lit, talking wet, napoo, san-fairyann, the duration, soaked, stiff, touch-out, blighty, windy, click, cushy, win, jam on it, swinging the lead, oojar, scrounge, stunt, umpteen, wash-out, go west, cold feet, strafe, work your ticket, where are you working, soft job, some lad, issue, muck in, sweating, and the gear.' The list has some rare inclusions ('head-worker', 'hard skin', 'touch-out', 'soft job'), but where are 'lousy', 'whizz-bang' and 'Fritz'? The concept of assessing the language of the war was present before November 1918, particularly a kind of ranking of importance or liking, no doubt influenced by what people found the most stimulating in their own environment. Generally these display few surprises but on 12 September 1915 the *Manchester Guardian* proposed that 'the commonest words' were 'cushy, blikey, charpawnee, pozzy, rotey'; even allowing that 'blikey' may have been a typo, few commentators would have reckoned the last three words as 'most common'. Post-war assessments include 'J.E.E.'s statement that 'gaspirator', 'knife-rests', 'concertina', 'elephant', 'baby elephant', 'baron' [army commander] were 'in daily use in France';[84] Brophy and Partridge's assessment of 'San Fairy Ann' as 'an extremely popular phrase', and 'shit' as 'very widely used for mud, and for shells and shelling';[85] E. B. Osborn's claim that 'napoo' was 'indispensable and inevitable' and 'to be heard a hundred times a day';[86] and De V. Payen-Payne's note that '"napoo" has become classic'.[87] There was also awareness of change: the language collector Andrew Clark noted in his diary for 10 July 1918 that 'A little while ago *Na pooh* was the great expression among the soldiers – it was *Na pooh* for everything. Recently "swinging the lead" has taken its place, as also a "cushy Blighty" as a popular slang-term for a slight wound.'

Not just words, but sayings were subjected to assessment. *The Iodine Chronicle*, trench journal of the 1st Canadian Field Ambulance unit, in December 1915 printed a list of 'ten hackneyed sayings', which included 'Any more for any more?' (No. 1), 'Say, I hear there's a war on' (No. 3), and 'toot sweet' (No. 8). Mottoes and catchphrases – 'Gott strafe England', 'mort pour la patrie', 'are we downhearted' – served as group identifying speech acts for different communities in the conflict, many of them securely fixed in the respective languages by their rhythmic pattern. In English certain phrases repeat the same phonic stress pattern: 'Are we downhearted?', 'Brave little Belgium', 'ladies from hell', 'backs to the wall', 'over the top', 'Kitchener's men', 'somewhere in France', 'lest we forget'. In fitting to common speech stress patterns these phrases were more likely to be repeated or fixed in the mind. Even an anglicised French phrase that for many commentators was one of the most common phrases of the war, 'san fairy ann', fits the model, as does 'après la guerre'. The point should not be laboured too far, but with this in mind we should look to the slow vowels of 'the Great War', and its predecessor 'the Great World War', with additional vowel clusters, as giving immediate gravitas.

> *Given that there were extremely limited ways for the men at the Front to express themselves (trench art, though creative and reactive, was made by limited numbers), language was the means by which people could interpret and give meaning to their war.*

'Napoo' was certainly one of the most frequently documented terms of soldiers' speech; 'cushy', 'in the pink', 'scrounge', 'fag', 'bully', 'grousing', 'whizz-bang', 'lousy', 'fed up', 'san fairy ann', 'Fritz', 'windy', 'minnie' (trench mortar), 'strafe', 'Jerry', 'stunt', 'no man's land', 'over the top', 'wash out', and 'Blighty', together give a loose picture of the experience of the war, uncomfortable, frightening, dirty, unrewarding, and socially reassuring. Given that there were extremely limited ways for the men at the Front to express themselves (trench art, though creative and reactive, was made by limited numbers), language was *the* means by which people could interpret and give meaning to their war. The language that came to be recognised as that of the war was opportunistic, creative, exploitative, scavenging and ruthless: it pounced on the weakness of the politician's phrase 'a certain liveliness', it blasted authority, even the authority of the overwhelming weapon, with withering scorn – 'nail-scissors' for the crossed swords on a general's cap, 'plum-pudding' for a trench mortar bomb; it somehow suggested paternalism or shared culture while mocking – 'makee learn' (officer under instruction), 'brass hats' (senior officers); it shrugged off the foreign – 'Rude Boys' for Rue de Bois, 'japan' (*pain*), 'compree' – and was sentimental and frightened in the soldier's hope for 'a blighty wound'. The best of it instantly exploited what was happening – 'Jack Johnson' for a bomb giving off black smoke, within hours of the breaking of the story of the black heavyweight boxer's arrest; and played with words – 'saucebox' for a tank serving with the Worcestershire Regiment – in a tradition of English wordplay dating back to Anglo-Saxon poetry.

Humour was undoubtedly a major part of this, but of necessity, much of it was gallows humour, the laughter of the survivor of disaster: 'we saw the grim humour of it, and laughed and pulled ourselves together, thankful that we were still in the land of the living'.[88] Paul Fussell's *The Great War and Modern Memory* begins by pitching the conflict as a massive irony, 'a hideous embarrassment' to prevailing moral thought. From the initial irony of the outbreak of the war itself at a time when people in Britain were expecting conflict in Ireland, to Philip Gibbs' comments on the irony that all the creative processes of the nineteenth had found expression in destruction,[89] irony was the overwhelming structure of the war, leading up to the supreme irony of the first day of the Somme.[90] The disillusion after November 1918, the silence of the veterans after the expenditure of so many words, the mistrust of the newspapers by those in the trenches who had read them to find out 'who's winning',[91] all added to an ambience of irony and cynicism, that characterised the verbal legacy of the war. Unknowing irony frames the utterances of chivalry, gallantry, sportsmanship, just as knowing irony frames the soldiers' slang, and the literary understatement of the officers' talk, the trench journal of the City of London Rifles, *The Castironical*. Eric Partridge proposed that the characteristics of Tommy slang were that, compared to the slang of 'Poilu' and 'Jerry', it was 'the most direct, the most obvious and the best humoured',[92] and later that 'irony or sarcasm, or a typically British understatement occurred in almost every third word or phrase'. Given the situation men found themselves in there was a choice between despair, gung-ho chivalry ('Who's afraid of a few dashed Huns?' and 'Tell them I died happy, loving them all' – the last recorded words of Francis Grenfell, 1915[93]), or irony and cynicism. The 'ambience of mortal irony'[94] locates the particular mindset of dark optimism that developed the throw-away lines 'we're winning', or 'thank God we've got a navy'; they evidence a sense of failure faced in the light of moral superiority, stared down using the only available means of expression, even in the use of 'asquith' for an unreliable match (from the Prime Minister's catchphrase 'wait and see'). Despite everything, the Brits believed they would muddle through, because they did, always had, and ultimately would, though slipping badly in the competition for the bragging rights after the American Expeditionary Force's initials matched the phrase 'After England Fails'. But this hardly touched the nation's self-belief – 'the war will go on until we have muddled through', as the editorial of the trench journal *The Pow-Wow* put it in February 1916. If fear was ubiquitous, group dynamics meant that it was seldom admitted; even the class relationships and age differentials of the trench meant that it was essential for leadership that fear should be controlled: 'For months . . . the fear I had that dominated my waking moments was not will I be afraid, but will I be able to control my fear. I was always afraid I would be afraid'.[95] Charles Edmonds dealt with a seventeen-year-old in terror waiting to attack, by assuming his 'martinet voice', reassuring the boy, and saying 'Come along, now, jump to it'; this restores his own spirits (and he remarks that he is only two years older than the boy). A few moments later during the attack he finds himself on the parapet, shouting 'Come on lads, over the top'; 'something in me that was cynical and cowardly looked down in a detached way at this capering little figure posing and shouting unrepeatable heroics at the men below', as even fear and heroism become ironic. Later, having captured an empty German trench, he and a colleague squabble over a souvenir German helmet.[96]

Partridge's assessment of soldier slang is that it was a combination of apparent opposites – 'tolerantly contemptuous' to civilians and military superiors, or 'with a bitterness that was usually ironical, sometimes even playful'.[97] Philip Gibbs noted of black humour that 'the more revolting it was, the more [people] shouted with laughter';[98] the strongest ironic statements matched these incongruities and apparent unmatchables – 'permanent rest camp', for a cemetery,[99] 'wooden overcoat' for coffin,[100] 'you're holding up duration',[101] 'shock absorber' for the observer, seated at the front of a plane.[102]

Partridge also believed that one result of the war expressions becoming so widely disseminated was that there was a more direct speech in writing after the war, this being seen in the work of those who went through the war, and also those who 'mixed freely with the survivors'.[103] The movement of language from Front to Home, and vice versa, provoked the question of who created the terms, who took them up, and whether there was any sense of ownership. W. Courthorpe Forman, writing in *Notes and Queries* in 1918, stated that 'many so-called "new" words are the individual slang of some particular schools, and, being often most expressive, have been eagerly snapped up and adopted by the Tommies who have heard them used',[104] while a writer to *The Gazette of the 3rd London General Hospital* criticised rhyming slang as lazy: 'the New Army's slang seems to me to be of a poorer mint, and its swift spread is regrettable'.[105] It has generally been felt that the movement of slang was from the Front to the Home Front, along the lines described by Ward Muir – 'the men go home [from the training camps and the various fronts] carrying to their native places slang which would never, in ordinary circumstances, have penetrated there'.[106] This was to be posed as problematic when language suggestions came from the Home Front to the combat zone ('Rosalie', dismissed by Barbusse; *The Cheltenham Chronicle*'s suggestion of a new title for the *Fifth Gloucester Gazette*;[107] *Punch*'s 'Sammy', which many American soldiers hated). Not all such terms were rejected by soldiers: Fraser and Gibbons note terms coming from newspapers, e.g. 'mad minute', 'cuthbert', and being taken up at the Front; Partridge felt that 'Rosalie' was successful in being taken up by French soldiers.[108] Others, e.g. 'do your damnedest', and 'Big Willlie' and 'Little Willie', were invented by the press and taken up by civilians.[109]

> there persisted during and after the war, matching the wartime enthusiasm for soldiers' slang, the idea that 'real slang' came from, and belonged to, the soldier in the field, and that it was more authentic the closer it was to the combat zone.

But there persisted during and after the war, matching the wartime enthusiasm for soldiers' slang, the idea that 'real slang' came from, and belonged to, the soldier in the field, and that it was more authentic the closer it was to the combat zone. 'A.H.B.' in the correspondence column of *The Athenaeum* wrote: 'May I ask Dr Baker [Ernest Baker, who had initiated the discussion in May 1919] to allow the soldier's undoubted right to be "fed up"? He has been so and has said he was so in those same words, as far back as my memory of army life extends, a period of some twenty years, and doubtless he had been so for many years before that. The civilian is welcome to take the soldier's words and make them his own; but if he does, then it may be well to remind him at the beginning of this new era that though these words may be slang they are none the less of proud origin, that it was the soldier who coined the expression "to get a move on" as well as that of "to carry on" and that he does both in spite of numerous and legitimate "grouses" . . .'.[110] No matter that the claims for both terms are unsustainable, the claim is that the soldier, by virtue of originating the term, has rights of association. Further on in the same correspondence Frederick Nettleinghame, the respected compiler of *Tommy's Tunes*, wrote that he did not believe it was possible to distinguish between soldier slang and civilian slang, purely because the vast majority of the soldiers essentially were civilians; and through the process of coming into contact with and using terms previously avoided as vulgar, the civilian soldiers had given these terms '"tone" and so helped in the addition of four hundred odd words and phrases to the common speech of the people'.[111] But it was not all so simple: 'bus' as a term for an aeroplane, was originally RAF slang, then picked up by civilians, seen by airman as hackneyed, and then as bad form. An article in the *Yorkshire Evening Post* claimed that 'soldiers' slang has readily been adopted in the munitions factories', citing 'Hill 60' for a rock bun, 'doorsteps' as teacakes, and 'submarines' as sausage-rolls, though these may not have been widespread.[112]

6 LETTING GO

Losing the language of war

The end of the war was discussed from the moment it began, as enlisting men were told that employers 'will keep their places open till the war is over'.[1] The familiar phrase 'over by Christmas' did not vanish at the end of 1914, but carried over into 1915. 'I expect to be home for Christmas', wrote Pte W. Astbury in 1914,[2] but on 3 December 1915 L. D. Spicer wrote home 'I only wish your rumour, which is said to emanate from the War Office were really the truth, and that the war were really going to be over by Christmas'.[3] Unlike wars at the end of the twentieth century, the conflict was formed in discourse as an event, with a beginning and end: 'There's a war on' stated newspapers[4] regularly, emphasising this start-happen-stop aspect;[5] and at the Front soldiers described shelling in the same way – 'bombardment on for 1 hour', wrote George Williams of the E. Yorks Regiment in his diary on 27 July 1916.[6] And while journalists, strategists and song-writers cried 'on to Berlin', to become more familiar in a later war, the men at the Front couched this sentiment in the rather less jubilant 'finish the job'.[7] Mostly they wished for it to be 'over': 'My brother Arthur is quite well and safe at present I hope he will remain so till this terrible war is over which I hope and trust won't be long', wrote Charlie while 'On Active Service', to Miss Bessie Camp on 30 October 1917. The two views are combined in a letter home from Rifleman Fred Walker in which he writes 'let's hope that this job will soon be over'.[8]

For many the hopes of an imminent armistice were balanced with imaginings of a war extending far into the future; Dormer in Mottram's *The Crime at Vanderlynden's* (1926) reckoned that the British Army would take 180 years to reach Berlin,[9] Charles Edmonds wrote that 'in 1917 the war seemed likely to go on for ever'.[10] While Mabel Lethbridge, who had worked in a munitions factory, remembered in 1964 this feeling of 'it can't go on';[11] others, such as the French servicemen discussing 'the old topic' with John Masefield, agreed that it was more likely than not that the war would go on for a long time;[12] Jack, writing home on 13 December 1915 expressed his approval of conscription, 'then we might begin to think about the end then'.[13] Trench journals, in typically caustic style, proposed that the war might stretch far into the future. *Fall In* reprinted a story from *The Tatler* on Christmas Day 1915 (p. 22) suggesting the war would still be in progress in 1956, though at a very much slower rate, with 'grand old men, veterans from the long war – the only British manhood' waiting for the results of 'Germany's turn to fire'; *The Listening Post* reckoned 1967 as 'the limit of frightfulness'.[14] Lt John Nettleton, after the Armistice, described it as 'the war that had been going on since the beginning of time',[15] while Dan Todman notes that this sense of the war going on for ever is proposed in the way that *Oh! What a Lovely War*, the theatre production by Joan Littlewood, written by Charles Chilton in 1963, gives 'no hint that the war itself ever came to a conclusion'.[16]

When the fighting stopped on 11 November 1918 the reaction at the Front could not have been more different from the public reaction in the streets of Britain. In France and Flanders there was suspicion, resentment, but most of all bewilderment and a sense of weariness. Charles Douie described it as a curious switch of the noise balance – suddenly it was quiet at the Front while 'the civil population remembers Armistice Day for the most part in terms of noise'.[17] Journalist Webb Miller, reporting from the front line, noted that 'the war just ended', while Cpl R. Hume remarked that 'you could stand up and not be shot'.[18] Margaret Mercer, working with the French army, noted the same mix of anti-climax and awareness of the core of the situation – *on ne se tue pas* (the killing has stopped). The process of demobilisation was a source of massive resentment, leading to riots in some camps in 1919. In places a kind of verbal sorting was involved, described by Charles Douie,[19] almost surreal in its application: he found himself waiting for the demobilisation train with two jockeys, who he realised were there because, as 'students of form', they had managed to be described as 'students', while a farm labourer, put down as 'farm asst.', found himself demobilised early as a chemist.

The realisation that the Armistice meant the end of the war led to immediate calls for the abandoning of DORA, or at least for her to loosen up – an American journalist wrote 'An Open Letter to Dear Dora' in the *Daily Mirror* indicating that she had previously managed to bypass regulations by pretending to be Canadian.[20] In a cartoon in *Punch*[21] '1919' is shown as a winged child carrying a sword marked 'Liberty' approaching 'John Citizen' who is tied up and being sat on by the elderly 'Dora' and a male 'Bureaucracy'. DORA was still being used as a catch-all term for bureaucratic control at the end of the 1920s,[22] and though the Act was due to expire at the end of hostilities, MPs were still asking, on 23 June 1921, when this would happen.[23] The end of DORA appeared to slip past unnoticed: Arthur Nall-Cain MP asked on 23 November 1931 when the restrictions set out in DORA would be finally repealed, and was told by the Home Secretary that the last of the regulations set out in DORA had been repealed over ten years previously.[24] Fraser and Gibbons's 1925 comment on DORA is telling: the Act 'gave the Government despotic powers over everybody and everything during the War'.[25]

'Napoo' was in many ways an ideal candidate for the iconic word of the war, the perennial shortage of anything except killing at the Front, the attempts to create something both new and homely in a foreign land, and the need to communicate surmounting barriers of language and hostility. Civilians and soldiers emerged from the darkness with the words 'Guerre Fini! Boche napoo!',[26] but the word was to become napoo itself within a short time. 'This year – to use a common language – motor touring in France to the south of Paris is *narpoo*' appeared in *The Times* 25 March 1919, but the word was not seen there again until in a letter in 1932. It is not found in the *Manchester Guardian* after 1919, until Robert Kee's 1965 review of Brophy and Partridge's *The Long Trail – Soldiers' Songs and Slang 1914–18*, which noted how 'squiffy' and 'napoo' were used as historically evocative markers in *Oh! What a Lovely War*. Odd occurrences include its use as a poignant message impressed into wet concrete in 1923[27] necessitating a translation, as a headline in 1926,[28] and in 1932, again with an explanation that it meant 'nothing doing'.[29] Some terms persisted for a while – Pratt's Tours advertised a trip to Lowestoft past where 'a "Zep" was brought down in 1916'[30] (note the use of inverted commas). But the review of Fraser and Gibbons's book in 1925 in the *Daily Mail* described the whole subject as 'Quaint War Slang',[31] and when some slang was revived in September 1939 it was described as 'banter'.[32]

Throughout the war there had been comments in the press suggesting that army slang should be used by soldiers and not the general populace, particularly not those in positions of power;[33] but there are also suggestions that in the third year of the war slang was no longer as exciting or uplifting as it had been: 'the new Whitehall officialdom is far sunk in the generally adopted colloquialisms of Canada and the States'.[34]

The press and its readership was getting tired of war slang,[35] with comments that it had been less beneficial to the language than at first proposed. This turning against the association with the military culture, albeit a citizen–military culture, marks perhaps a beginning of the return to the normalisation of the army's place in the peacetime state, to be cheered or avoided as circumstances demanded. Commercial users of language, the advertising profession, were less inhibited, retaining many expressions into the early twenties, or using 'from 'khaki to mufti' as a way of getting the best of both worlds. Burberry advertised 'Mufti kit' in January 1919,[36] while Moss Bros headed their *Bystander* advertisement on 3 September 1919, '1914–1919 Khaki to Mufti'.

As the locus of war slang slipped away from France and Flanders the reason for the use of anglicised place names quickly disappeared. Those with particular or fond memories, Pop (Poperinghe, site of Toc H, the all-ranks rest centre),[37] Wipers and Plugstreet,[38] survived longer than the rest, but soon acquired the inverted commas or bracketed references to their actual names that indicated a move away from the forefront of public consciousness. The Michelin *Guide to the Battlefields – Ypres and the Battle of Ypres*, published in 1920, mentions none of the three slang place names. This distancing can also be seen happening in the press less than a year after the Armistice, with 'Wipers', seldom previously appearing in inverted commas, appearing thus in a letter to the *Manchester Guardian*, 21 September 1919.

The press evidence indicates that in the case of 'Plugstreet', less than a year after the Armistice, where the text is not primarily directed at veterans, inverted commas and explanations are used; where veterans are the expected audience no inverted commas are used, till the mid-1920s, after which there is a gradual shift to using inverted commas or brackets with explanations, indicating that the term has lost familiarity. Inverted commas tend to be omitted after the late 1920s only when the expected audience is veterans. Later, in the 1930s, explanations were usually deemed necessary: the *Manchester Guardian* 10 May 1936 has 'Ploegsteert (the Plugstreet of the war days)', and the publication *The Great War – I was there* (1938–9) has, for example, 'Plugstreet' twice (Section 8, p. 299), but also on the same page, 'Ploegsteert'. The *Lancashire Evening Post* has 'WAR MEMORIES REVIVED – Ploegsteert, or Plug-street as our Tommies renamed it',[39] and 'it was in the muddy trenches of "Plugstreet Wood" that Old Bill first saw the light of day';[40] but the Plugstreet War Memorial was conventionally known as such. The sheer number of soldiers who fought near Ypres and Ploegsteert, and later the number of soldiers buried there, meant that the names Wipers and Plugstreet were perpetuated through the 1920s and 30s, even being proposed as models for language change after September 1939; 'wherever the scene may be we shall have the same corruption of foreign place names. "Wipers" and "Plugstreet" must again become reconciled to such comments as "San fairey ann" …'.[41] After the Second World War an explanation was necessary: 'in a short space of time we were in the front line at Ploegsteert (known to all the troops as Plugstreet)';[42] 'we were holding the line at Ploegsteert, familiarly known to the troops as "Plugstreet".'[43]

The Ypres Times, a veterans' journal, seems to have avoided using wartime anglicisations, and certainly sticks to 'Ypres';[44] a comment in a letter from a veteran following a 1922 visit to Ypres starkly delineates the changing identity of the place as it moved on from being a graveyard to a site of commerce and entertainment – apparently abandoning the identity of 'Holy Ground' it was 'Not our Ypres'.[45] Despite the massive numbers of personnel who were at the Salient, by 1925 it was felt that the connection between the actual name and the slang name had to be made explicit: 'Between 1914 and 1915 almost every soldier in the British Army fought at Ypres ("Wipers")'.[46] Memoirs retained the place names, an indication perhaps of veterans as the expected readership, but inverted commas functioned as an inclusive gesture to readers who had not been 'out': Holmes has '"Wipers" hadn't been any garden of roses,'[47] Aubrey Smith has 'Ploegsteert, commonly called "Plug Street"',[48] and R. H. Mottram has 'Pop' in his *A Personal Record*.[49] Reviews of books and films retained Plugstreet and Wipers, usually without explanation, but more frequently with inverted commas as time passed: Plugstreet in a book review in *The Scotsman* September 1919; Wipers in a film title or subtitle in *The Times*, including documentary films of visits by the Prince of Wales, 1925; 'Plugstreet' in a book review in the *Manchester Guardian* 27 March 1929; 'Plugstreet' in a review of Churchill's *Thoughts and Adventures* in *The Times* 10 November 1932. The anglicised place names of France and Flanders were enthusiastically collected by post-war scholars of war slang as indicators of the supposed irrepressible spirit of the Tommies, seeing them as creative slang, slightly disparaging to the French. Through the later 1920s they became familiar to readers of war memoirs. But hoteliers and tour guides in the areas of the former battlefields, speaking more to relatives and friends than veterans, had little use for them.

Some slang changes were more obvious than others: the *Illustrated London News* used inverted commas on the caption to a photograph of '"Enemy" War Graves' on 26 April 1919 to signify a change in attitude; the familiar note on postcards home, 'Somewhere in France', disappeared almost completely (the demise of its variants was celebrated by Eric Partridge in 1933[50]), until it was suddenly revived in 1939. Selective lexicography gave official sanction to some terms but not others – 'Beachcomber' looked in vain for 'doings', 'binge' and 'oojah' in the supplement to the latest edition of the *Chambers Dictionary*,[51] though all three were to feature in Fraser and Gibbons. For some the abandonment of war-slang terms was deliberate, driven by a need to mark the end of an experience to be set aside or a respect for the dead. On 27 October 1919 the *Sheffield Evening Telegraph* (p. 6) began an article on the inclusion of army slang in Cassell's latest edition of its English dictionary with:

> Will the war words which have passed into the dictionary live? It is a question raised by an observant ex-soldier, who says he handed in his army language on the day he surrendered his kit to the quartermaster's store. It no longer gives him any mental relief to use the comic words of the Army.
>
> If he is weary at the end of the day's work, he does not say he is fed up, but simply and more truthfully, 'I am tired.'

This is followed by several examples of words to be abandoned by this soldier, including 'char', 'umpteen' and 'Blighty'. Canadian soldiers were encouraged to abandon swearing at the end of the war, with formalised 'purity pledges' being given to officers and NCOs in one division.[52] G. K. Chesterton wrote in the *Illustrated London News* 14 December 1918:

> Surely it might be suggested that the rapid transference of the terms of the Great War to the General Election is a little lacking in dignity, and even in decency. It was really ridiculous enough when party politicians used the terms of war in times of peace. It was absurd even then when comfortable candidates and vote-pullers should talk perpetually about raising the banner and routing the enemy, about storming the breach and breaking the battle-line. It was bad enough when it was said quite hastily and heavily, by political hacks who had never raised anything but taxes and never broken anything but promises. It is intolerable that these things should be said in the very presence of real things; that

politicians should talk thus about losing their seats to men who have lost their legs and arms; that they should decorate their sham fight with the tattered colours of the genuine fight. It is intolerable that some wealthy person when he has consented to accept a post and a salary should announce with a beaming smile that he has decided 'to go over the top'. Doubtless he desires to be on the top, but not in the sense of going over it. It is intolerable that some oligarchal official, having shuffled and equivocated from the Front Bench for half-an-hour at Question Time, should describe himself as having been 'under fire'. Everyone knows that such fire is merely fireworks. These things are not only matters of public dignity but of private tragedy; and we do not want charlatans plucking their flowers of rhetoric from the garlands on the graves of the dead.

Chesterton's observations on what would now be seen as non-pc language mark a moral suppression of language use, but also raise a question of ownership: if it was not appropriate for non-veterans to use these terms, was it 'appropriate' for veterans to do so? If the soldier gained 'mental relief' from war slang during the conflict, what might be lost or gained by abandoning its use after the Armistice? And how did this suppression of war slang, in which the country had been encouraged to participate, sit with the rise of the language of commemoration?

The sacred and the remembered: places and names

As early as 1915 the awareness that people would want to go to the battlefields was being discussed in the public domain. Battlefield tourism has a long history in Europe, and there was little new in the cartoon published in *The Bystander* on 24 February 1915, entitled 'In Europe – some day', with its images of relic/souvenir sellers and veterans showing parties of 'sightseers' around a landscape through which rows of charabancs convey visitors while two young lovers sit on a gun, in an echo of exactly what was to happen a few years after the war. In 'What We Find In The German Trenches' a post-war French farmer is imagined fencing off a crater, 'erect[ing] a tea-house . . . not forgetting the ticket-office. He might . . . make a huge collection of Boche mementoes, and sell them to the visiting public'.[53] Souvenir-hunting by civilians was recorded in 1914,[54] and in March 1915 Thomas Cook's announced that they would not be running battlefield tours until the cessation of hostilities,[55] though Michelin began to publish their guides to the battlefields in 1917. Among the reasons why people wanted to visit the battlefields was 'morbid curiosity', the assessment of A. J. Norval's 1936 report on tourism,[56] with a description of people 'rushing to the scene of war' implying an unseemly haste, typical of one stream of criticism of tourism during the post-war period; Norval felt that 'never has the atmosphere been more saturated with morbidity than during the first decade after the war'. However, an opposing view was that people should go as quickly as possible 'for tomorrow it will be gone'.[57] 'Morbid curiosity' was the term used in a criticism of 'battlefield tours' in an article in October 1914, which castigated 'souvenir hunters' as 'little better than looters'.[58] In a rerun of the reporting of war, battlefield tours were described as a 'continental invasion' by the *Dundee Courier* in May 1920.[59] The arguments over civilians going to the battlefields continued decades after its end. Different views of the reason to go to France and Flanders as a pilgrim emerged: to see a marked grave, to walk in the path of a lost loved one, to be in an associated place if no grave was known, to marvel at the battlefields and see the ruination of the landscape, or just to try to get some idea of what it was like. Given the thousands of picture postcards of ruins sent home by soldiers, the Gothic appeal of the ruin drew many, including 'hundreds of Belgians' who went to see 'how badly Ypres is ruined',[60] almost following the instructions of the German sign at Péronne, *Nicht ärgern, nur wundern*. When President Wilson went to Ypres in June 1919 the *Western Daily Press* headlined the story with 'Beauty of the Ruins'.[61]

> The lexical parameters were set for a Christian ecclesiastical model for the bereaved particularly, and the survivors generally, to conduct their emotions, perceptions and actions after the war.

It seems likely that the wartime process of Flanders becoming 'sacred' through acts of sacrifice generated the idea of post-war pilgrimage. Areas where there had been large loss of life became sacred in the public mind: 'SOIL SACRED TO THE BRAVE AUSTRALIANS' was the headline of an article about Gallipoli in the *Liverpool Daily Post*, 4 November

1915,[62] while the *Aberdeen Evening Express* headed an article 'Somme's Sacred Ground'[63] on 29 July 1916. Journalists were making 'a pilgrimage to the front' already in 1917,[64] and the Maharajah of Patiala made 'a special pilgrimage to the spot where his troopers fought finely in 1914'.[65] Newspapers began to talk about Ypres being consecrated around the same time that wartime memoirs and collections of letters began to use the idea:[66] on 29 April 1916 the *Daily Record* (Lanarkshire) mentioned 'the lines around Ypres already consecrated by British valour',[67] while on 8 September 1916 the *Leeds Mercury* wrote that 'the whole neighbourhood of Ypres is sacred ground to the British Army and the British nation'.[68] Combined with the employment of the word 'sacrifice', as in 'THE GREAT SACRIFICE. HOW A HULL HERO DIED',[69] the lexical parameters were set for a Christian ecclesiastical model for the bereaved particularly, and the survivors generally, to conduct their emotions, perceptions and actions after the war. Beatrix Brice wrote of the Ypres salient that 'the earth on which we stand is literally the very substance of man's sacrifice',[70] the bodies of the soldiers transubstantiated into the land they fought on and for; Rowland Fielding was outraged by the thought of an American sightseer spitting and 'saturat[ing] the ground that has been soaked with the blood of our soldiers'.[71]

Post-war language confirmed this model with visits to the battlefields, particularly Ypres (as Lord French said, 'What Verdun means to the French, Ypres means to us'[72]), being irrevocably presented as pilgrimages to holy ground, consecrated ground or sacred ground.[73] The expectations of the pilgrimage were extended into expectations of the behaviour of pilgrims, as visitors to the Grange Tunnel under Vimy Ridge saw a notice which asked them not to leave graffiti: 'these walls are sacred to the memory of those who inscribed them during the occupation of the war. Please omit yours'.[74] A due state of mind was mandatory, Kipling writing to *The Times* in December 1919 requiring that the places visited be not 'overrun with levity'.[75] The wrong sort of person being there provoked a sense of sacrilege: 'sacrilege at the idea of our battlefields being visited by a tourist', the view of the *Aberdeen Weekly Journal*,[76] invoked the sense of both expectation and possession. Guidebooks to the battlefields castigated signs of commerciality: Beatrix Brice wrote of Hill 60 in the Ypres Salient, 'this hill of heroic memory is now desecrated . . . by horrible erections of booths and shanties',[77] posing a Biblical contrast between the sacred and commerce. The difficulty was that there was a financial incentive for making the battlefields available and safe to visitors, which inevitably sanitised them, making the visitors tourists rather than pilgrims to sites of devastation. Postcard packs showed tidied up versions of the trenches, with rows of neat sandbags and clean duckboards, while visitors to Vimy Ridge in 1928 found 'machine guns and trench mortars have been mounted in little concrete emplacements on the actual spots in which they were employed by the rival armies'.[78] Comparison between tourism and pilgrimage provoked ideas of status: David Lloyd makes the point that sacrifice and the sense of obligation to the dead privileged the bereaved and the veteran,[79] but equally this would privilege certain emotions and states of mind over others. Activities too could be judged by this yardstick: the *Illustrated London News* in January 1919 showed a picture of some well-dressed people having a picnic in a former dug-out in France: 'the roads traversing the former battlefields of France to-day swarm with motors bringing parties of sightseers to visit the scenes of fighting. Among them are some who view the sights with more serious eyes'.[80] Inevitably questions of class and vulgarity, or worse, arose in some critics' objections: for Rowland Fielding it was 'horrifying to see this sacred ground desecrated' by military sightseers in December, made worse by the prospect of 'the cheap tripper let loose'.[81] How long would it go on? Charles Douie wrote in 1928 that 'the time must come when the travellers are seen no more',[82] but the use of 'must' indicates a wish as much as a prediction. Super-quick tours trivialised the experience, though a *Manchester Guardian* article pointed out that 'there is something sound in the notion that one can see the battlefields in a day; the repetition would give no new tone, but intrinsically the same impression'.[83] To counter any of this the archaic language of the Church sermon was employed to bring in the gravitas of established religion: *The Daily Telegraph* stated that Ypres was 'a shrine at which to chasten pride and cast out all thoughts but those of pure service to humanity';[84] for Ethel Richardson the soldiers' sacrifices 'will . . . find at last in God's good time, their due and meet reward';[85] the caption to the photograph of pilgrims tracing a name from the Lone Pine Cemetery in Gallipoli describes this as a 'carven name'.[86] Unsurprisingly, many veterans were avoiding such trips; during the war soldiers had discussed returning after hostilities, but 'it was the common verdict of the man in the mud-hole that, once "out of it," Wipers and he could be best of friends – at a distance'.[87] For another veteran, W. G. Shepherd, the experience was too much: 'I would not go to that place [Plugstreet] again, or to any other place where I have seen battle, except by force . . . For young men who were in the war of all the lonely places on earth the loneliest and the awfullest, the place of all places on earth not to go, is a battlefield where they have been in war.'[88]

If the business of the pilgrimage privileged the bereaved as much as or more than the veteran, the bereaved woman, mother, sweetheart or widow, was privileged within this group. Ian Hay wrote that those with graves to visit were 'pilgrims proper',[89] and the *Northern Whig* described the women as the 'Pilgrim Mothers'.[90] David Lloyd proposes that there was an underlying assumption of the special role of women to mourn the dead,[91] and the 1928 British Legion book underlined their gender with the term 'pilgrimess'.[92]

Much of the discourse of the pilgrimage continued or revived that of the war. Returning to wartime sites often provoked feelings of time loops such as that experienced by R. H. Mottram while reporting on the 1928 pilgrimage in Ypres; watching from a first-floor window he 'could not feel easy where I sat, fifty paces from the Menin Gate, with my back to the German guns'.[93] More obviously The Salvation Army and the YMCA facilitated the pilgrimages, as they had assisted soldiers during the war; the title of *The Ypres Times*, the magazine of the Ypres League, echoed the *Wipers Times* and the *Ypres Times and Tombstones Journal* (trench journal published by the Royal Marines from 1916). The 1928 pilgrimage showed clear verbal echoes of the war, the organisation of the event echoing army organisation, with Party leaders, Deputy Party Leaders, Accommodation Officers, Transport Officers, and the pilgrims divided into 'parties' and 'companies'.[94] This created the parameters for the re-use of wartime language: *The Yorkshire Post* reported a pilgrim in an estaminet ordering drinks with the words 'Toot sweet, and the tooter the sweeter … not spoiled by the fact that the waiter understood wartime "French"';[95] the Prince of Wales 'wore mufti';[96] a homage trench journal, *The Pilgrim*, was published for the 1928 pilgrimage; pilgrims gave each other nicknames;[97] 'Are We Downhearted' was shouted and responded to by different groups;[98] the pilgrims ate 'iron rations'.[99] The large number of pilgrims facilitated this, but it was not new: in the book on the earlier pilgrimage to Salonika pilgrims are 'reported present and correct by bedtime'.[100]

The separation between those who had been at the Front and those who had not, up till November 1918, continued after the war, particularly implicit in some of the language emanating from the experience of the pilgrimages. The motive for many veterans visiting was to re-experience some of the 'comradeship' felt during the war, the aim of the Ypres League being to maintain the comradeship of the war experience.[101] Nostalgia for the wartime landscape, even though at the time some felt they were in 'these dead countries',[102] was easy to construct at a safe distance in time from the war, but there was an awareness of difference: 'what there is paints in very false colours the Ypres of war', wrote Beatrix Brice in 1929.[103] Rowland Fielding was feeling nostalgia as early as 3 February 1919: 'the better kind of men who have lived in [the trenches] will look back upon them hereafter with something like affection'.[104] The sense of disappointment with change, felt by many, was often expressed in terms of ownership: as Ypres began to be rebuilt it became 'Not My Ypres'[105] (in the January 1922 issue it was 'Not "Our" Ypres', p. 15); 'Our War, the War that seems the special possession of those of who are growing middle-aged . . .'.[106] Perhaps the parameters for this mentality had been established casually much earlier on: in a letter home to Canada sent on 9 October 1916 Armine Norris wrote, 'Just set your mind, Mother, on meeting me in England, say next September, (apres la guerre, of course) and then we'll see together the places I have told you of but could not name, and I'll show you some of our battlefields'.[107]

Wartime reality clashed with memory of events so extreme that they were, of necessity, more real than the everyday of post-war life. 'Remember' and 'forget' were words often encountered during the war: 'Remember' or 'Remember me', frequent mottoes on silk postcards; 'Lest we forget' badges, available via the *Navy and Army Magazine*, 20 March 1915; 'Remember Belgium', 'Remember the Lusitania', as battle cries. Commemorating the dead after the war relied much on the concepts of knowing people who had served, and preventing the forgetting of them, seen in statements such as 'a soldier of the Great War known to God', 'the Unknown Warrior', 'lest we forget',[108] 'At the going down of the sun and in the morning, We will remember them', 'The Not Forgotten Association'.[109] The 'necessary art of forgetting'[110] together with the obligation to remember, in order to give meaning to the sacrifice and the grief, necessitated the constant interplay of remembering and forgetting. Essential to this was the role of the name: the individual's name took on massive significance during the war since the army and the circumstances, as John Brophy saw it, 'rarely allowed a private soldier to be an individual'.[111] Indeed the name was the only point at which the army sanctioned the existence of the individual private soldier, who was often otherwise denoted without reference to the human: 'At the end, I told them I had asked for 95,000 fresh rifles';[112] French temporary graves for unnamed soldiers identified the soldier as '*Nr de la Baionnette*'. The importance of the name is seen in the 'dog-tag' identity disc, introduced in the British Army in 1907, in the daily publishing of casualty lists and rolls of honour from September 1914, in the determination to mark soldiers' graves, however temporary, with a name, in the superstition against mentioning dead comrades' names,[113] and in the constant reiteration of the name in In Memoriam newspaper columns. The idea of the name featured in the mythology of the bullet 'having your name on it', in the disgrace of 'losing your name' (being charged or noted for punishment), and in the extensive culture of naming guns, weapons and shells.

Post-war the name took on even greater national significance, in the phrase 'Their name liveth for evermore', in the King's injunction, again in archaic language, 'See to it, ye that come after, that their names be not forgotten', and in the seemingly endless names, embracing individuality and uniformity in death, on the great memorials to the missing and the cemeteries in France and Flanders. In Britain every city, town, village, school and institution marked its own communal loss with a memorial bearing the names of its fallen, and in the Scottish National War Memorial in Edinburgh Castle 100,000 names were placed in a steel chest; Henry Benson, writing about memorials in the *Western Morning News* creates a hypnotic repetition of the word 'names': 'Loos (20,700 names), Le Touret (13,480 names), Vis-en-Artois (9,893 names), Pozières (14,707 names), Arras (35,000 names), and Thiepval (72,000 names)'.[114] The Admiralty and the War Office issued well over a million memorial plaques and scrolls with the names of soldiers and nurses who died in or as a result of the conflict; the plaque showed the individual's full name, even when for some this was a single name, such as 'Abdulla', 'Gama' or 'Nadar'. Every combatant's name was also recorded on the rim of his or her British War Medal, a total of 6.5 million medals. Individual acts of remembrance included a bereaved mother in Salonika tracing the name of her loved one from a memorial,[115] and an elderly Scottish woman who was reported kissing her grandson's name on the war memorial at King's Cross Station,[116] pilgrims in Gallipoli '[writing] down names and [taking] photographs of the headstones to bring comfort to the many who had not been able to accompany them',[117] while dedications of war memorials and remembrance services included reading the names of the war dead throughout the 1920s.[118]

For Jay Winter the reiteration of the name, either through publicly reading or privately touching the name on the memorial, combined both forgetting and remembering;[119] the reverential enshrining of the name allowed a distancing to take place, allowing people to move on while still maintaining contact with the dead.

Silence

'Daddy, what did you do in the Great War?' asks the child in the poster. The father does not look at the child, or engage in conversation, but looks out at us almost in the way that later came to be known as the 'thousand-yard stare'. The poster itself had an existence after the war, as the Imperial War Museum website points out:

> This British recruiting poster was produced in 1915 and has since become infamous for its use of emotional blackmail to urge men to enlist with the British Army. Produced by the London printers Johnson Riddle & Co., it was conceived from the director Arthur Gunn's own feelings of guilt at having not volunteered himself. Seeing the persuasive potential of a child's awkward questions to a shirking father in peacetime, Gunn commissioned a poster picturing such a scene. Although Gunn joined with the Westminster Volunteers shortly after the poster's publication, the poster became the source of much bitter trench humour on the Western Front. Such was the resentment towards it in post-war Britain that its creator, Savile Lumley, a children's book illustrator, is said to have disowned it.[120]

If the poster's implication at the time was that the father should enlist, in order to be able to answer the question, in the post-1918 world it becomes, 'Having been there, what should I tell them?' And indeed, 'what experience should I protect them from?' The poster text projects into the future, asking from there a question about the past; this manipulation of time invites further manipulation: if, as the Imperial War Museum states, the poster was the source of bitter humour, and thus being thought about by soldiers, it would presumably have challenged those soldiers in the trenches to consider, at the time, how *they* would mediate their experience in the future.

'He was in the war, but he never spoke about it'. An unwillingness to talk about the war, expressed in this familiar sentence, sums up its horror, stoicism, and inexplicability. As the culture of the war then and since has been so much a verbal culture, this absence of words needs to be considered. Was the silence engendered by the soldiers themselves, was there pressure on them to remain silent, or was there a drift into leaving it all behind? And was it indeed as widespread an experience as later generations have believed? Diane Athill, born in 1917, summed up the experience as, 'Killing certainly did affect the minds of those exposed to it by the First World War. It shocked most of them into silence. Many of the men who survived the fighting never spoke of it. And I think it had the same effect on most of those the men returned to. It was too dreadful. They shut down on it'.[121] The phenomenon was observed by Graves early in the war while training at Wrexham in 1915; of two wounded officers who survived the retreat from Mons he writes, 'Neither would talk much of his experiences'.[122] But there is a wealth of evidence for people who did talk. Matthew Wright's *Shattered Glory*, about the experiences of the New Zealand forces, begins with 'Joe Gasparich never tired of discussing Gallipoli with my grandfather';[123] Lancelot Spicer wrote home, 'I'll be able to tell you a lot more about that [the bombing of Le Touquet] when I do come on leave – afraid the censor might object at present';[124] Sybil Morrison remembered that though the wounded men did not want to talk about their experiences, it did come out – she says 'I think we had a lot of information first-hand';[125] Hallie Miles in December 1914 got from a relative on leave details of the soldiers' despair at being unable to help wounded comrades lying in no man's land.[126] When she was a child Barbara Rosser's father told her a lot about conditions in the trenches,[127] but others realised they might have to wait: Florence Cottle wrote to her husband that a neighbour's brother-in-law had told her some things that were 'terrible . . . I know I shall never hear anything from you, at least not until long after the war'.[128] For others, finding out what the war had been like came through other pathways, the post-war visits to France and Flanders[129] and the war-discourse that blossomed in the cinema.

> Erich Maria Remarque *wrote of home in* All Quiet on the Western Front *(1929): 'I do not belong here any more, it is a foreign world'.*

There were certainly a variety of reasons for veterans not to speak about the experience of the war. Much of it had been boring, or repetitive routine tasks, with a lot of waiting, looking, dozing, or wasting time. As well as being painful and terrifying, a vast amount of it was boring and apparently pointless. There was also the huge gap between the Front and the Home Front, illustrated by much of what has gone before. For Robert Graves 'home was awful because you were with people who didn't understand what this was all about':[130] in particular he noted that the level of noise at the Front was incommunicable. Cpl J. Bemner writes in his diary, three days after his return from England to the Front: 'I am beginning to feel all right again after leave' (6 August 1915).[131] A poem, 'On Leave', in the *Depot Review* No.5, begins:

I wanter get back from the war news
I wanter get back to the Hun;
I wanter retreat from the chaps in the street
'Oo know how the war should be won . . .

Erich Maria Remarque wrote of home in *All Quiet on the Western Front* (1929): 'I do not belong here any more, it is a foreign world'.[132] Those who had not been at the Front could not possibly understand what it was like, and 'talked a foreign language'.[133] It was in a sense pointless to try to communicate this environment because it was so alien, so particular, and so vividly experienced by those who had been there, so impossible for those who had not, to realise.

If we think of the post-war silence as an act of self-censorship, a direct continuity from wartime becomes apparent. During the war a culture of control over communication stretched across Britain and the theatres of conflict. Troops knew their letters and postcards were being censored, the press knew that their access to the Front was controlled, and numerous amendments to the Defence of the Realm Act left people unsure of what they could legitimately say, while knowing that dissent was a punishable offence. The familiarity of the phrase 'Somewhere in France', and the fact that people were prepared to joke about it, the ubiquity of the Field Service Postcard, the constant use of clichés such as 'in the pink', 'hoping this finds you as it leaves me', shows how censorship, and particularly self-censorship, as acts of security and paternalist protection against distress, became mainstream. In this light the extension of this beyond the end of the war, to protect people against unpleasant truths, seems fairly straightforward.

Also to be considered is the language of combat. The evidence clearly shows that swearing was in most environments at the Front more or less the norm. Evidence also indicates that for many soldiers this was not the norm for their home environments, that they had to learn to become accustomed to swearing. If swearing had become effectively the standard means of spoken expression for the frontline, how was this environment to be described and narrated without swearing? How could the soldier who had seen such extreme situations mediate them to sisters, mothers, aunts, children, neighbours when the primary means of expression was unavailable? In a domestic environment, where saying that 'my mate was blown to buggery' would cause a breakdown in communication, few soldiers were equipped to find words that would meaningfully convey the experience without offending. While the surge in graphic description in memoirs ten years after the conflict showed that there was a written language that could do this, during and immediately after the war few people wrote books or letters that matched the 'war-porn' of the late 1920s. There were exceptions of course: the letters of Guardsman Boorer, published as *A Place Called Armageddon* included a description of a captured trench with descriptions such as 'dead men hanging over the trenches, blown almost inside out';[134] Masefield in March 1917 wrote home a description of a crater 'with dirty water at the bottom, & German corpses and hands & skulls & books & rags all littered down the sides'.[135] Generally the tone was more 'concerning their actual killing exploits the men were absurdly reticent' from *Troddles in the Trenches* by R. Andom, printed for *Newnes' Trench Library* (1919), rather than 'a Mills bomb would blow seven men to rags' from Charles Edmonds' *A Subaltern's War* ten years later. Probably the most frequent description of the Front was that it defied description: it was 'beyond description',[136] 'utterly indescribable'.[137]

Reticence, phlegm, sangfroid were recognised aspects of male self-control which developed through the nineteenth century, particularly through the public school educational system. In metaphors that appear now absurd – the battlefield as playing field – control was employed and no doubt felt particularly among officers – 'nothing makes you feel madder than being fired at when doing a job that has to be done slowly and carefully, such as insulating the wire after baring the cable and joining the ends. A man who has been fouled at footer has the same feeling', wrote C. W. Langley in *Battery Flashes*.[138] Rudyard Kipling, devastated in private by the death of his son at the Front, mentioned his name in passing in one sentence in *The Irish Guards in the Great War* (1923). Sister J. Calder remembered seeing wounded soldiers whose limbs could have been saved with prompt treatment: 'We felt terribly sorry for them but we had to try to not show our feelings, because it would never have done'.[139] To what extent this reticence was reflected back to the self as bravery is hard to comprehend at this distance of time, but it is likely that the social parameters providing models for emotional response may have helped some people, as the suppression of emotions by silence did to varying extents manage to suppress those emotions. To pursue this further, a specific form of rhetoric that has been discussed earlier can be seen as continuing beyond the Armistice. The avoidance of mentioning something to make it less real was manifested in the number of ways of not saying 'death', 'kill', 'die', and so on, replacing them with 'copping it', 'becoming a landowner in France', 'napooing', and so on. One way to deal with the experience of suffering, of inflicting pain on others, and of witnessing death and injury on such a scale, so new and different for many men and women serving, was by removing it from speech entirely: just as speaking about it made it real, not speaking about it contained it, made it unreal. When Paul Bäumer's father in *All Quiet on the Western Front* wants him to talk about his experiences Paul realises that 'it is too dangerous for me to put these things into words. I am afraid they might then become gigantic and I be no longer able to master them'.[140] This placatory silence suited the medical treatment of stress, particularly shellshock. Shellshock during the war was generally treated as a malingerers' attempt to avoid service, despite the unavoidable nature of its effects, verbal as well as physical and mental – one soldier treated at Manchester had been buried by a shell explosion, and during treatment switched between Lancashire and West Country accents.[141]

In many cases shellshock was seen as an affront to manliness. Manliness here was seen as the condition of a truly integrated being, one in whom self-control was manifested in a controlled body and a controlled mind. Failure at self-composure was manifested in the moving body, one who could not keep still, facially or muscularly, symptoms then seen as typical of the outsider, racially or socially, the Jew, the criminal, the lunatic.[142] Thus stillness, parade-ground physical control if necessary to the point of loss of consciousness, keeping one's ground, not flinching, were all held out as examples of manliness, character, courage. The phrase 'stiff upper lip' implies not moving and, specifically, being seen not to speak. These ideals survived the war, and despite the slow change in some people's view of shellshock during the conflict, notably Lord Moran, and *The Times* editorial on the day of the publication of the report still couched the subject in terms of strength and weakness as regards being able to 'maintain command' of oneself.[143] During the war few doctors, notable exceptions being W. H. Rivers and Arthur Brock at Craiglockhart Hospital, used the possibilities of the verbal exploration of trauma; the norm was to not talk about the experience of shelling or combat. One of Rivers' patients said 'that it was obvious to him that memories such as those he had brought with him from the war could never be forgotten. Nevertheless, since he had been told by everyone that it was his duty to forget them he had done his utmost in this direction'.[144]

As has been shown above, various linguistic and other markers signalled how people were thinking about the end of the war: the 'change from khaki to mufti', the abandonment of slang expressions, jokes about demobilisation. This move towards closure was seen also in cartoons celebrating the abandonment of the Defence of the Realm Act, together with the War Office's stance of putting shellshock behind it in the Committee of Enquiry report of 1922; the words of war were being put away. The official closure on the unseen effects of war, particularly the word 'shellshock' itself, which had been only reluctantly tolerated,[145] together with the onus on disabled soldiers to prove that their injuries had been caused by the war, sent out a message that the establishment 'did not want to talk about it'. Advertisements caught this mood: one in the *Pall Mall Gazette* (8 May 1919) read: 'So bury all those unpleasant memories in Dora's waiting grave . . . and get your Austin Reed straw hat to signalise the event', while another, for Kenilworth cigarettes, in *Punch* in April 1919 reads, 'You've seen it through! You don't want to talk about it. You don't want to think about it. You just want to lean back and feel that the day you've been dreaming about since that first August of 1914 has come at long last'.[146] In effect veterans were told not to talk about the war.

Much discussed in study of First World War memoirs is the phenomenon of the ten years' delay: why did so many memoirs appear ten years after the Armistice, and why did people wait? And how to interpret the graphic nature of much of the material? There was certainly some extremely graphic war-literature published and read before 1918: Henri Barbusse's account of trench life, *Le Feu* (1916), translated as *Under Fire* (1917), was widely read on both sides of the Front, with a reviewer in the *Manchester Guardian* noting that generally 'the "horrors of war" are taken for granted but . . . mercifully concealed.' But the majority of the best-known novels and memoirs that verbally explored the body's destruction were not published until 10 years after the Armistice: the translation of Remarque's *All Quiet on the Western Front* (1929), Robert Graves's *Goodbye to All That* (1929), *Three Personal Records of the War* (R. H. Mottram, John Easton, Eric Partridge, 1929), Charles Edmonds' *A Subaltern's War* (1929), Henry Williamson's *The Patriot's Progress* (1930), Helen Z. Smith's *Not So Quiet* (1930), Frederic Manning's *Her Privates We* (1930), A. M. Burrage's *War is War* (1930), Siegfried Sassoon's *Memoirs of an Infantry Officer* (1930) are a few of over sixty books on the war that were published in these two years, provoking some complaint that the only story being told now was that of the horror of war.[147] For Graves, *Goodbye to All That* was, as the title states, an attempt at closure, the 1929 text stating: 'once this has been settled in my mind and written down and published it need never be thought about again'. The interim silence seemed to be as much about 'holding on' as 'holding back'. But there appears to have been a consensus for a period of literary silence, broken after a decade with a tumult of descriptions of violent death. Herbert Reed, reviewing the translation of *All Quiet on the Western Front* in 1929, felt that what was happening was the mind 'dismissing the debris of its emotional conflicts until it feels strong enough to deal with them'.[148] By extension this could be applied to the nation's collective mind, Fussell's sense of a shift towards irony and a crisis in language, indicating that for the period 1918 to 1928 the mind and the means of expression together combined to shut the story down. While Fraser and Gibbons published their work on wartime slang in 1925, Brophy and Partridge's more critical study was published in 1930, in the environment of the war memoir boom.

Dan Todman's study of the changing attitudes to the war in *The Great War* (2005) notes how the BBC television series *The Great War* in the 1960s catalysed a great outpouring of reminiscence from people who were moving into old age.[149] He notes that a request for information brought tens of thousands of responses, with the implication that this period might mark the end of the silence. A new context of respect and amazement, in what Todman describes as 'an interaction between younger Britons and their grandparents about what they had done in the war',[150] perhaps echoing the poster caption, created a new frame for telling. This sense of being brought back into the mainstream should be considered as contextualising the horrific evidence related to researchers such as Lynn MacDonald; reminiscences such as those in *They Called it Passchendaele* rival and exceed the worst to be found in the memoirs of 1929 to 1931.[151] Todman points out that Martin Middlebrook's research for his project on the Somme involved taking notes during interviews rather than voice-recording veterans, to avoid them 'declaiming',[152] raising again the question of different kinds of mediation. All telling of the war is mediated in different ways, but in these cases people were speaking rather than writing – we should note that the wording used in the statement is not 'he never wrote about it', but 'he never talked about it', or 'he never spoke about it'.

Returning to the period of the war, on considering the different theatres of war and the varying degrees to which forces personnel acquired local terms, a kind of cultural pragmatism becomes apparent. France and Egypt were culturally closer to Britain, through reasons of association or empire, than the Eastern Mediterranean or Greece. The term 'Mesopolonica' summed up the way that the average Briton did not know where these places were, and did not much care. In Macedonia troops hardly picked up any of the local language; Capt J. R. Wilson of the RFC, stationed in Salonika, used no local words in his diary, but on moving to Egypt used 'backsheesh', 'garry' (Anglo-Indian word for a carriage) and 'Gyppies'.[153] The environment generated the words, and once the environment changed, the language changed. Typical of the act of remembering the war were lapses into silence, the 'vacant look' characterised by absence of communication. Absence and silence, cenotaphs and archway memorials with central open spaces, over time became the defining manifestation of the aftermath of the war, as the 'empty space in the centre' became the lasting motif of memorialising the war. The end of the extreme and very different wartime environment quite naturally led to a loss of language, the immediate and most appropriate means of expression being removed. For example, 'napoo', reckoned by many to be the most common slang expression of the war, disappeared fairly quickly after 1918. The loss of language would have reinforced the idea that the stories of that language might equally be abandoned.

Looking again at the poster, the implication is that this conversation would go on between generations, that those who fought would tell their children, as a way of keeping alive the importance of the war. But did people actually want to hear? While relatives needed details of time and place in order to make meaning out of their loss, did they want to know that the bodies of their uncles or brothers, fathers and husbands had been blown apart or lain rotting until only their clothes were recognisable? W. H. Rivers noted the 'natural tendency to repress, being in my experience almost universally fostered by . . . relatives and friends'.[154] As Paul Fussell pointed out, 'the real reason is that soldiers have discovered that no one is very interested in the bad news that they have to report'.[155] We might have a prurient interest in 'war-porn', but it is, as the wealth of published material shows, well suited to writing if not speech. If, as Fussell suggests, the question is one of rhetoric and manners rather than language, we can find that we accept as literature material that is too shocking for us to be told face to face, or, even more so, to read in a letter.

We cannot know how many, and in what terms, conversations took place in the interwar years between veterans in British Legion bars; commemoration of the more positive aspects of the war were clearly visible, but we do not know whether or for how long after 1918 there was a sharing of reminiscences similar to those which emerged in the 1960s and 70s. We do have the testimony of veterans such as John Brophy, who wrote in 1965: 'for the men who survived it, it became in retrospect an experience to be thrust out of memory most of the time, an experience impossible for the mind to digest, and, for many, tolerable only when some of the less distressing events were selected for recall and dressed up with sentimental emotions'.[156]

Post-war study

Wartime word-collecting and glossaries had served purposes of popularisation of and identification with soldier culture, with certain related specific roles, such as Lorenzo Smith's *Lingo of No Man's Land* (1918), intended for recruitment support. Post-war collecting attempted to find a way to preserve the camaraderie of the Front, to retain some of the creative culture of the war.[157] In providing a locus for pooled information, it devolved into competitiveness in some cases, as it showed possibility of becoming an area for academic as well as martial reputation. For Brophy and Partridge it provided second-phase ironical enjoyment, just as language itself had done at first hand for many soldiers during the conflict.

In the last year of the war academics began to take a greater interest in slang; Dauzat's *L'Argot de la Guerre* was published in Paris, Ernest Weekley's *Daily Mail* article appeared in January, and the Bodleian Library acquired a manuscript glossary of trench slang compiled by a Royal Field Artillery soldier.[158] Discussion of war slang appeared in the pages of *Notes and Queries* in the same month as the Armistice, with Archibald Sparke's article 'War Slang: Regimental Nicknames'.[159] Sparke rather invited reaction by beginning 'Quite a large number of new words have come into common use ...'; R. C. Temple, who had called for a compilation of war slang, responded with further information on Hindi words in Sparke's list showing that they were by no means new to the British Army.[160] The January 1919 issue brought further correspondence widening Sparke's definition of 'scrounge', and the March issue brought one comment that Sparke's list was 'good, but there are two words at least from which he has not extracted the full service meaning', and another that 'fed up' was from the Boer War,[161] to which Sparke in the June 1919 issue responded 'J.R.H. is perhaps correct in his impression ...' (followed by citations from 1904 and 1900 which would seem to indicate that there was no 'perhaps' about it).[162] The correspondence at that point moved over to the pages of *The Athenaeum*, with an article by Ernest Baker enthusing at change and the range of new words in the language, including newly invented scientific terms for explosives – 'ballistite', 'triona', and 'filite'; officialese – 'embus', 'liaison officer'; military terms – 'depth-charge', 'star-shell' (likened to the Anglo-Saxon 'war-gear' and 'heath-stepper'); and, new medical terms such as 'coagulen' and 'hypnoid'.[163] Baker continued in the 11 July issue, pointing out that many of the words 'classed as vulgarisms or slang' – 'dud' and 'stunt' for example – were not new, but suddenly apt; Baker roved enjoyably over the whole field, taking up 'Dora' and 'Anzac', 'conchy' and 'cuthbert', 'in dock' and 'buckshee', 'strafe', 'Fritz' and 'umteen'.[164] The first respondent, a week later, was the novelist and soldier Boyd Cable, whose corrections were in turn modified the following week by Henry Bush,[165] and the correspondence became a weekly series of modifications and additions involving among others Eric Verney, Frederick Nettleingham, author of *Tommy's Tunes*, and Archibald Sparke. Claim and counter-claim had been succeeded by a more generous attitude by November 1919 – 'I am happy to oblige Mr Nettleinghame', wrote H. Lonsdale[166] – when Eric Verney surveyed the correspondence as having produced 288 words and phrases, of which 100 were 'definitely war slang', 65 'definitely pre-war slang', 62 'Old Army slang' (of which 15 were 'of Indian etymology'), 11 'American and Colonial', and 50 'period of origin doubtful'.[167]

At this time Ernest Weekley was compiling his *An Etymological Dictionary of Modern English* (1921), not a book specifically of war slang, but one in which the war, and its language, has an overwhelming presence.

Weekley's citations show a lexicographer introducing new terminology, some of which would be classed as slang:

Scrimshaw
Also *scrimshander*. Cf. *scrimshanker*, shirker, of later appearance. Origin unknown.
　'It was the army that gave us "strafe" and "blighty" and "napoo" and "wind-up" and "scrimshanker"'.
Saturday Review Aug 11, 1917

But Weekley was deeply affected by the war, selecting citations which indicate a lasting resentment against the recent enemy:

Frazzle
To unravel, etc
　'The Allies have to beat Germany to a frazzle'.
Referee, May 27, 1917

Napoo
Regarded by Mr Atkins as a current French phrase closing a discussion in indefinite fashion. Fr *il n'y en a plus*. Cf. the German war word *naplü*, cognac.
　'Not the napoo victory ensuing from neutral pressure and semi-starvation, but the full decisive military victory'.[168]
Pall Mall Gazette Feb 15, 1917

Wartime terms began to appear in newly published dictionaries and glossaries, such as the *New English Dictionary on Historical Principles* fascicle Si-St and Su-Th (1919), which included a citation for 'stunt' from *Blackwoods Magazine* April 1916 – 'You remember it is time to get up, for there is a "stunt on"'; and 'strafe', which included a citation of a mother threatening to strafe her child, in acknowledgement of the processes by which the word had come from German to British soldiers, and then on to British civilians. Blackie produced a *Compact Etymological Dictionary* (1920) with an appendix of 'Terms of Special Note in Modern Warfare', and *Brewer's Dictionary of Phrase and Fable* (1923) included the words 'napoo', 'to get the wind up','brass hats' and 'over the top'. *Blackie's Standard Dictionary* (no date, but before 1925), had a section on 'War Words and Words Recently Introduced', which included 'soixante-quinze', 'strafe', 'Tommy', and 'Taube'.

The first post-war book specifically on army slang was *Digger Dialects*, by W. H. Downing (1919), Downing having served in Egypt and France. The book was published while he was a student, having returned to Australia, and is by no means limited to Australian-originated terms, its second part containing a passive Australian vocabulary of words encountered via British/Asian contacts, Papuan Pidgin, Russian and Italian. The work acquired major political importance in terms of the war's underlining of Australia's growing identity, to the extent that it provoked some criticism for its inclusion of terms originating outside Australia or the Anzac experience.[169] Downing's work provided about a third of the material that made up the *Glossary of Slang and Peculiar Terms in Use in the A.I.F.* (1921–4),[170] compiled by librarians at the Australian War Memorial library.

The compiling of *Soldier and Sailor Words and Phrases* (1925) was carried out by Edward Fraser and John Gibbons at the behest of the Imperial War Museum, starting with an announcement in *The Times* in October 1921 that the journal *Notes and Queries* would be collecting material. A comment that some of the terms might not be 'fit for polite conversation' pointed the way for the sending in of terms that would reflect the language of the soldiers rather than that of readers of *The Times*. Sieveking, since his appointment as librarian of the Imperial War Museum had been working on forces slang, also collecting French and German army slang. His first article in *Notes and Queries*, on 29 October 1921, offered a discussion of slang as part of the development of language, a supporting statement for the idea of collecting slang from Henry Bradley, editor of the *New English Dictionary* (later the *Oxford English Dictionary*), a discussion of the words 'poilu' and 'boche', which showed many of the extensions shown above (see p. 95), and a glossary, made up from contributions by members of the staff of *The Times*, former soldiers all. A fortnight later the challenges appeared: '"Base-wallah" can scarcely be described as of Hindu origin', and 'Acdum. From Hindustani *Ek dam*', from H. Wilberforce-Bell; and 'No 9 "An aperient pill". Not slang but a definite compound in the Military Pharmacopoeia';[171] and 'Scoff – This is omitted in the list – a very old Army term for "eating"', from 'Constant Reader'.[172] Sieveking offered another list the following week 'compiled from words kindly supplied to us' by five contributors, including Archibald Sparke. Further lists appeared on 10 December 1921, 7 January 1922 (specifically Russian, supplied by Lonsdale Deighton), and on 18 March 1922 (Indian words supplied by R. C. Temple and L. M. Anstey).

This was followed by an article on 'Wipers' and the anglicisations of other Flemish and French place names, on 22 July 1922. The *Notes and Queries* correspondence seems to be more generous-spirited than the *Athenaeum* correspondence, which had been typified by statements such as Boyd Cable's 'I have just read in your current issue the article on "Slang in Wartime", and I am the more anxious to point out a number of inexact and incorrect statements because with the authority of such a journal behind them, they may in future years come to be accepted as authoritative and correct',[173] and 'A.H.B.'s '"Gadget" is not a war word'.[174] If reactions were sharply worded, this may have been an indication of how much the subject mattered to people; by the time of the 1921/2 correspondence academics seem to have been more willing to accept other people's views on usages and etymologies.

Despite their obvious enthusiasm for the subject in their seminal work, these discussions on slang featured neither Edward Fraser, a military history writer, nor John Gibbons, who went on to write travel books, and for whom *Soldier and Sailor Words and Phrases* was his first published work. Julie Coleman notes that 'much of what is in this dictionary is official terminology rather than slang', and that 'this dictionary was based on written material, which would necessarily over-represent the language of more educated individuals', which, together with the extensive sections on battle honours and regimental nicknames, leads to the view that the book was compiled more from a military than a linguistic viewpoint.[175] But a sense of fun and irony is apparent in their definitions of 'Mesop' (Mesopotomia – also Mess-Up) and 'doing savage rabbits' (lying in wait), neither of which appear in Brophy and Partridge's book.

Eric Partridge served in Egypt, Gallipoli and France, returning to Australia to finish his studies, and eventually setting up the press which published *Three Personal Accounts* (1929), and in 1930 publishing with John Brophy, another ex-soldier, *Songs and Slang of the British Soldier: 1914–1918*. The first sentence of its preface states that time was running out and that as time passed the songs would be more difficult than the slang to record and find. While acknowledging a debt to Fraser and Gibbons, their view was that their own work was different, specifically based on their personal experience as former soldiers, and deliberately trying to make a 'record-by-glimpses of the British soldiers' spirit and life.'[176] For them Fraser and Gibbons's 'excellent compilation' was 'wider in scope ... but written in less detail'. Looking back at the preface to Fraser and Gibbons's work, their awareness of their own fallibility and the acknowledgement that it was 'the only book on the subject published' sits well with their hope that the book is 'interesting and entertaining' – noteworthy is the positioning opposite the title page of a Bairnsfather cartoon mocking GHQ messages about supplies. While Fraser and Gibbons state their first intention was to make 'a Dictionary of War Slang at the instance of the authorities of the Imperial War Museum using materials contributed by officers and men',[177] for Brophy and Partridge this meant the book was written 'from a more or less "official" standpoint'.[178] Brophy and Partridge were equally insistent that their work had been made by 'consulting men of different ranks and widely varying experience',[179] though their primary aim was to collect and publish songs before slang.

> Clearly before the end of the decade there had grown a sense that there was 'good' war slang and 'bad' war slang; the sense that certain terms might give offence, and should therefore be laid aside, may be considered an early form of 'politically correct language'.

In 1933 Partridge published *Words! Words! Words!*, a collection of previously published essays, including essays on 'British Soldiers' Slang with a Past', 'German Army Slang', and 'The Slang of the *Poilu*', together with a new essay on the 'Soldiers' Slang of Three Nations'. The last of these iterates Partridge's assessment that class mixing in the stress of the Front changes slang more than foreign influences do, despite foreign contributions being 'very much more picturesque and interesting'. As he saw it, the winners in this were not the working classes, who acquired some grandiloquent and officialese phrases, but the educated classes, whose language, in danger of becoming 'effete, pretty-pretty or wire-drawn', became much more robust.[180] The same year saw the publication of his *Slang To-day and Yesterday*, with sections on sailors' slang and soldiers' slang, where he discusses the 1922 doctoral dissertation of Hans Ehlers, *Farbige Worte im England der Kriegszeit* (Colourful Words in England during Wartime). For Partridge the difficulty with this work was that Ehlers had not distinguished sufficiently between 'the jargon rife in the Press' and soldiers' slang,[181] and that it raised the ghosts of the civilian vituperation of Germany and Germans in slang. Partridge quotes

Collinson's assurance to Ehlers that 'the worst expressions he has gathered' were moribund, a curious position given Partridge's obvious enthusiasm for the subject. W. E. Collinson's *Contemporary English, A Personal Speech Record* (1927), included a section on 'War Words' in which Collinson referred to material gathered by Ehlers: 'My reading of his work was not unaccompanied with a certain amount of grim and bitter amusement at the merciless showing-up of some of the more distressing symptoms of that war-psychosis, which afflicted us ...'.[182] Collinson felt that some of the 'most rabid' terms had been lost or acquired a 'playful or teasing significance', terms such as 'mad dog', 'mailed fist', 'frightfulness', 'steam-roller', 'somewhere in France'. Clearly before the end of the decade there had grown a sense that there was 'good' war slang and 'bad' war slang; the sense that certain terms might give offence, and should therefore be laid aside, may be considered an early form of 'politically correct language'.

The late 1930s saw continuing German interest in English war slang. Herbert Hiddeman's doctoral thesis in 1938, *Investigation into the Slang of the English Army in the World War*, was a thorough exploration of expressions found in dictionaries such as Fraser and Gibbons, Brophy and Partridge, and in war memoirs and novels. Referencing the *Athenaeum* correspondence, Collinson, the *Wipers Times* and similar contemporary publications, it surveys the period's language well, occasionally missing nuances that exist almost exclusively in the oral register: 'Sweet F.A.', for example, is given as the short form of 'Sweet Fanny Adams' without a mention that this was also the shortening of 'sweet fuck all'.[183]

Rolf Greifelt's *Der Slang des englischen Soldaten im Weltkrieg 1914–1918* (English Soldiers' Slang in the 1914–18 World War), written as his doctoral dissertation in 1937, gives a view into how British (and some other English-speaking) soldiers' slang was being recorded and analysed nearly a generation after the conflict. The work investigates the nature of slang, English soldiers' slang and its position and meaning within slang generally, the methods of creating and the forms of spoken soldiers' slang, the content and forms of words, the experience of war in speech, and the distinction between English, German and French soldiers' speech. The final section contains some observations on the influence of soldiers' slang on post-war English and an extensive glossary, in several sections. Greifelt's work includes studies of rhyming slang and its shortenings – 'china' from 'china plate'/'mate' – and back slang (he notes 'Can't Manage A Rifle' for RAMC). He even nearly gets round the nonsense word 'hoojamakloo' (as 'hooga ma kloo'), manages 'oojiboo', and his transcription of 'skiboo, skiboo, skibumpity-bump-skibboo' is impressive. In an echo of the trilingual wordplay of the war (n'y a plus/narpoo/naplü), Greifelt presents anglicisations of place names such as 'Moo-Cow Farm', 'Arm in tears' and 'Ocean Villas', and his inclusion of expressions such as 'to tank up' – *sich volltanken* (get drunk) and 'Blind' – *Blindgänger* (dud shell) show the close relation between the German and British mediations of the experience of the Front. Greifelt taught American English at Marburg and Heidelberg, before moving to Darmstadt. He died in March 1945.

The year of the outbreak of the Second World War saw the publication of T. Werner Laurie's *The Soldier's War Slang Dictionary*. Laurie had published a *Soldiers' English-French Conversation Book* in 1914, followed by a *Soldiers' English–German Conversation Book* in 1915; the 1939 24-page glossary, possibly published with an eye to a new war creating a revival of interest in the subject, contained a larger proportion of Russian terms than most glossaries gave, and some rarer terms, such as 'begnet' (Scots for 'bayonet'), 'jimmy' (a salute), and 'hot-cross bun' (Red Cross ambulance).

The resurgence in the 1960s of interest in the conflict brought back to remembrance the rich and colourful language of 1914 to 1918. Robert Kee, writing in *The Observer* in 1965 on the re-issue of Brophy and Partridge's *The Long Trail – Soldiers' Songs and Slang 1914–18* took issue with Brophy's apparent prudishness, feeling that the senseless repetition of obscenity was one of the most dynamic aspects of military slang, and that the 'surrealist use of obscenity' brought a 'near-poetic value' to the language.[184] But the appreciation of 'napoo' and 'squiffy' as 'as nostalgic as any book of photographs' – historically evocative, as was the use of such words in Joan Littlewood's theatre production *Oh! What a Lovely War* (1963) – recreated the language, as authentic, for a third generation (though the First World War song was titled 'Oh! It's a Lovely War'). The contrast between Brophy's attitude towards obscenity, rooted in the distance between the language of the home and that of the Front, and Kee's 1960s enthusiasm for swearing serves as another indicator of successive generations' differing viewpoints and uses of the material. For Collinson some of it was an embarrassment, for Brophy also, but for different reasons, while for Kee it was how history could be made to come to life. For 'Through German Spectacles', the regular wartime column heading of the *Daily Express*, read 'Through Changes of Spectacles'. The following decade brought Fussell's seminal study of the war, the language of literature, and its lasting effect on the twentieth century, and Jonathan Lighter's collection of American slang from the war, *The Slang of the American Expeditionary Forces in Europe 1917–1919* (1972). Described by Jonathon Green as 'the outstanding example of its kind'[185] this glossary was drawn from a wide range of sources, its harshness matching the cynicism of the Vietnam period. Dan Todman's discussion of the possible 'end of relevance' of the war, published in 2004, missed how anniversaries create both marketing opportunities and opportunities to re-examine convenient if arbitrary blocks of history. Anniversaries do, by the power of a number, concertina time, and the run up to 2014 produced a massive resurgence in family history research and shelfloads of books on the war, including studies of the English language during the conflict, alone and in combination with other languages, and, tellingly, in comparison with the English language as used by the British Army in Afghanistan.[186]

Then and now

A bundle of pens and pencils sits in a beaker on the desk; the beaker was made 'to commemorate PEACE – The Great European War – 1914–1919'. At the time of its most recent purchase, for it had probably gone through several hands before it arrived here in 2013, website-compilers were discussing whether to use the form 'First World War', or 'World War One'. Though the first form was in use from September 1914, there would be a difference in meaning depending whether the stress was on 'First' or 'World'; stress on the first word would emphasise an order, on the second would emphasise the extent of the fighting. The form 'World War One' appeared when it was clear there would be a World War Two, Brophy stating that while it was happening it was 'the war'.[187] Though it is not difficult to find references to the war as a 'great war', the conflict was being described in the press as 'The Great War' by early September 1914.[188]

Paul Fussell listed in *The Great War and Modern Memory* a number of ways in which the war lived on – pub closing hours, cigarette-smoking, distrust of the press, wrist-watches,[189] but also noted how the re-use of First World War terms in the Second World War gave the impression of 'one Great War running from 1914 to 1945'.[190] He begins the final section, 'Survivals', of the chapter 'Oh What a Literary War' with the proposal that 'nobody alive during the war, whether a combatant or not, ever got over its special diction and system of metaphor';[191] the persistence of ironical wordplay, the sense that officialdom mocks itself through its own language use, the idea that persistent use of taboo words could shift them into the mainstream, would argue that certain facets of wartime language, and changes brought about as a result of the First World War have anchored themselves into English language usage. But the origin of these usages should be contextualised in a language which now sounds in many ways different from present English. The point can be derived from another observation by Fussell, the use of 'quite' as an intensifier in the Field Service Postcard statement, 'I am quite well'; for Fussell this is 'egregious', a use of 'quite' which in the early twenty-first century seems odd: an advertisement which promotes Four Crown Whisky as 'quite good'[192] looks absurd now, but shows that the phrase 'I am quite well', appearing on countless soldiers' postcards home, is more enthusiastic than it now appears.

Occasional differences in meaning between then and now create a sense of otherness, a distinction in sensibilities. When a billet gets shelled the soldiers 'just turn out, stand behind the wall and put on a pipe [light a pipe]';[193] a sentry standing by Robert Graves tells him 'Keep still, sir, and they can't spot you. Not but what a flare is a bad thing to fall on you'[194] – 'not but what' meaning 'nevertheless'; James Hope Moulton in 1915 wrote 'German scholarship and science are naturally being canvassed vehemently in Britain today', 'canvassed' meaning 'attacked';[195] Fraser and Gibbons include the term 'give it best', as in 'That'll do, I've had enough, I'll give it best', to mean 'to admit defeat'.[196] There are terms used which now seem utterly inappropriate – 2nd Lt Arthur Lamb describing a gas attack as 'bally awful',[197] while *The War Illustrated* headlined a page of photographs of curiosities as 'New Year Novelties of the Ever-Wonderful War';[198] others that sound just slightly different – 'Am going on alright';[199] and others – 'to get off with' (see p. 193) – which survived and seem surprisingly un-old-fashioned. Particularly, 'fed up' was a lot stronger then than now: Pte James Jones wrote in his diary that 'a box of cigs from Madge . . . really saved my life, as I was about fed up'.[200]

Other usages seem shocking to us a hundred years on: the Bovril advertisement using as a setting the loss of the *Anglia* hospital ship (see p. 216), the Boots advertisement using the pun on the word 'Somme', the war toys and fireworks advertised in 1914 using fictionalised anecdotes of the battlefield. The cynicism of 'gassed' meaning 'drunk' is difficult now, as we view with some reverence the pain of the soldiers, though the term had been in use for years beforehand, deriving from the use of gas as an anaesthetic; its unacceptability to us is partly due to the way that gas has been considered as such an icon for the horror of the war for so many decades. Were these usages clumsy or cynical, did they distress people at the time? If there was any reaction against them it was overshadowed by the enthusiasm – certainly in the case of the use of the 'Somme/some' pun – with which they were copied and re-used by others, including soldiers. Though the verbal irony and cynicism that emerged from the war lasted long afterwards it is difficult for us at this distance to feel comfortable with seeing it at its source, or to accept such tactless innocence. But the deadening of mind produced, such that anyone could create the phrase 'Anzac soup' for a water-filled crater with the bodies of soldiers in it, is exactly why the First World War made such a difference, and continues to matter.

Apart from the obvious terms still in use – 'trench-coat', 'over the top', 'dug-out', 'cushy', 'lousy', 'crummy', 'bumf', 'wangle', 'A1', 'cop it' – which originated in or were popularised by the war, the English language still retains an ear for the officialese that so many were exposed to: London Underground passengers still 'entrain' or 'detrain', or occasionally 'disentrain'; we instantly recognise 'towels, swimmers for the use of' as military officialese; 'no man's land' and 'the Front' are still signifiers of combat in the modern era. And terms are still being developed from them: 'over-the-topness' and 'trench-talk'. A second generation of terms – 'lions led by donkeys' and 'Oh, what a lovely war' – ensures the survival of the mythology of the war. As much as anything the war gave to English a ready-made language for war, both for the military and the Home Front, as can be seen in the way that terms from 1914 to 1918 were re-used in 1939;[201] 1915 was echoed in 2015, with 'Terry Taliban' not far from 'Johnny Bulgar', nor 'Lash Vegas' and 'Camp Butlins' from 'Eddesburg' or 'Eat Apples'.[202]

Partridge, critiquing Dauzat's interpretation of the developments in French slang during the war, proposes an idea for the pattern of survival of newly-acquired slang. Dauzat looks at the four chief military sources of slang: the languages of foreign soldiers fighting in France, the German occupation of Northern France, the French corps in Salonika, Gallipoli and Italy, and the prisoners of war in Germany; but these exert less influence on soldier slang than transformations in Parisian slang, the pre-war vocabulary of the army, and changes, metaphors and puns occurring in standard French. Generalising from this, and implicitly comparing it with English, Partridge proposes that externally-originating terms 'may seem to be more interesting than, but they are rarely so long-lived as, the continuous graftings of the domestic stock'.[203] At a distance of a century we are in a position to feel that 'dekko', 'cushy', 'pukka', 'wallah', and 'gone phut', all of which have been in English usage for much longer than 100 years, and which were popularised by the war, can claim to be as domestic as centuries' worth of adoptions from French, and are surely as entrenched in the language as 'wangle', 'cop it' and 'bumf'. 'Napoo', 'sanfairyann', 'tooter the sweeter', 'compree' have all gone now, as have 'Blighty', 'pozzy' and 'gippo', all pre-war. But 'ersatz', 'ace', 'souvenir', 'morale', sound as comfortable to English-speakers as 'dig in', 'pillbox' and 'wash-out'. Why was language so dynamic during this period, and why does it continue to fascinate? Eric Partridge proposed that the soldier's speech was characterised by terms that were 'brutally cynical yet inherently courageous'.[204]

'Anzac soup' is horrific because it is funny, and funny because it is horrific. 'Bert' both acknowledges the foreign and demands the familiar. 'Fanny Durack' makes a game of war, as 'camelry' makes a game of language. 'Archie', 'woolly bear' and 'coal-scuttle' belittle that which overcomes us. 'After England Fails' builds the self at the expense of the other; the French response to seeing US troops with what appeared to be Boy Scout hats, and calling them 'the Second Children's Crusade', did the same. When the American army took delivery of Chauchat machine-guns they were renamed 'hot cats', a knowing de-exoticising. 'Whizz-bang' is about learning survival skills. Naming a child after a battle says 'these things matter, carry it into the future'. Bairnsfather's post-war cartoon of Ole Bill seeing a tin of plum and apple jam, with the caption 'Alas, poor Yorick', is about knowing how culture creates us and gives us the material with which we continuously recreate ourselves. 'No man's land' is about the fragility of civilisation. 'Blighty' starts by acknowledging the gaze of the other, and makes it the ultimate object of the gaze of the self. 'Plonk' tells us that we want simple creativity to come out of industrialised destruction. 'Napoo' takes an expression of nothingness and turns it into a wealth of different meanings of nothingness. 'Rainbow', the name for a recruit arriving just after a battle, is about as good as irony gets, it hurts as it amuses.

Taken as a whole the overwhelming impression is of people using language as play, a deadly game in cases of propaganda, but creative nevertheless. Seeing the subject in this light offers no simple resolution, no underlying answer, but a conflicting complexity as people tried to understand a situation that, at anything beyond the simplest level, could not be comprehended: as one of the most long-lasting of the songs of the war offered – 'we're here because we're here'.

NOTES

Introduction

1 E. Partridge, *Slang of the British Soldier 1914–18*, in *Twenty Years After*, E. B. Swinton, (ed.), (London: Newnes, 1936–38), Vol. 3, p. 52.

2 Ibid. p. 59.

3 Lord Moran, (see under C. Wilson) *Anatomy of Courage*, (London: Constable & Co., [1945] 1987), 1987 edn, p. 143.

4 D. Todman, *The Great War*, (London: Hambledon, 2005), p. 26.

5 http://research.gold.ac.uk/16713/1/Grayson%252c%20R.pdf accessed 2 April 2016.

6 *War-Time Tips for Soldiers and Civilians*, (London: C.A. Pearson, 1915), p. 62.

7 'Among the fragments of leather and helmets were a number of scraps of letters and postcards, . . .' G. Young, *From the Trenches*, (London: T. Fisher Unwin, 1914), p. 49.

8 *Fifth Gloucester Gazette*, (Gloucestershire: Alan Sutton Publishing, [1915–1919] 1993), February 1917; E. Baker, *The Athenaeum*, (London: J. Lection, 1830–1921) 11 July 1919, p. 583.

9 L. D. Spicer, *Letters from France, 1915–1918*, (London: Robert York, 1979), 3 December 1915.

10 P. Fussell, *The Great War and Modern Memory*, (Oxford: Oxford University Press, [1975] 1977), 1977 edn, pp. 228–30.

11 *The Attack/The Estaminet, (Memories of France –)*, [sound dramatisation], (England): 78 rpm disc, R517, Parlophone, 1920s; CD41-001, *Oh! It's a Lovely War*, Vol. 1, CD41 Publishing Ltd, 2001).

12 Major A. E. Rees, dir., *In the Trenches*, [sound dramatisation], (England): 78 rpm disc, R2796 B, Columbia, 1917; CD41-001, *Oh! It's a Lovely War*, Vol. 1, CD41 Publishing Ltd, 2001).

13 T. Cook http://research.gold.ac.uk/11325/1/AngelsofMonspapersocieties-04-00180.pdf accessed 15 February 2016.

1 Language, Dialect and the Need to Communicate

1   e.g. Nelson (Edinburgh 1844), Simms & M'Intyre (London 1854) (see Walker, J. in the bibliography).

2   J. Walker, *A Critical Pronouncing Dictionary and Expositor of the English Language*, (Edinburgh: Thomas Nelson & Sons, 1844), p. 17.

3   H. Alford, *A Plea for the Queen's English*, (London: Strahan, 1864), p. 280.

4   AQA GCSE examination in Geography, May 2010.

5   The Board of Education, *The Teaching Of English In England*, (London: The Board of Education, 1921), p. 60.

6   Pp. xvi–xvii, quoted in G. Knowles, *A Cultural History of the English Language*, (London: Arnold, 2005), p. 147.

7   A. M. Burrage, *War is War*, (Barnsley: Pen & Sword Military, [1930] 2010), 2010 edn, p. 99.

8   R. Holmes, *Tommy*, (London: Harper Collins, 2004), p. 149.

9   Quoted in R. Van Emden, *Tommy's War*, (London: Bloomsbury, 2014), p. 168.

10 P. Doyle and R. Schäfer, *Fritz and Tommy*, (Stroud: The History Press, 2015), p. 49.

11 B. Cable, 'The Blighty Squad', in F. Treves, (ed.), *Made in the Trenches*, (London: George Allen & Unwin, 1916), p. 15.

12 Todman, *The Great War*, p. 123.

13 M. MacDonald, *Under the French Flag*, (London: Robert Scott, 1917), p. 164.

14 'The Sergeant's Langwidge', *Yorkshire Evening Post*, 16 September 1916, p. 4.

15 *Punch*, 7 February 1917, p. viii.

16 *Burton Daily Mail*, 26 March 1917, p. 2.

17 Spicer, *Letters from France*, 15 March 1916.

18 *The Bystander*, 8 January 1919, p. iv.

19 *The Sphere*, 3 June 1916, pp. 211, 213.

20 In a letter from 'a Bradford soldier' published in the *Plymouth and Exeter Gazette*, 3 November 1916, p. 1.

21 R. D. Holmes, *A Yankee in the Trenches*, (Boston: Little, Brown & Co., 1918), p. 200.

22 Pte E. Roe in Doyle and Schäfer, *Fritz and Tommy*, p. 43.

23 *The War Illustrated Album De Luxe*, 1918, Vol. 6, p. 2072.

24 W. Spencer, *War Letters 1914–1918; From a Young British Officer at the Western Front during the First World War*, (WarLetters.net, 2014), 2 February 1915.

25 J. Crofts, *Field Ambulance Sketches*, (London: John Lane, 1919), pp. 97, 98.

26 W. Brindle, *France and Flanders*, (Saint John: S. K. Smith, 1919), p. 53.

27 H. Harvey, *A Soldier's Sketches under Fire*, (London: Sampson, Low, Marston & Co., 1916), p. 36.

28 *The Lady*, 13 August 1914, p. 274.

29 *Home Notes*, 22 August 1914, p. 345.

30 A. Smith, *Four Years on the Western Front*, (London: Odhams Press, 1922), pp. 163, 153.

31 G. Barker, *Agony's Anguish*, (Manchester: Alf Eva, 1931), p. 28.

32 Anon, *A Sunny Subaltern*, (Toronto: McClelland, Goodchild & Steward, 1916), p. 140.

33 'One of the Jocks', *Odd Shots*, (London: Hodder & Stoughton, 1916), p. 37.

34 J. Graystone, *Diary,* 1 August 1916, Private papers held by Imperial War Museum.

35 J. E. Parrott, *The Children's Story of the War*, (London: Thomas Nelson & Sons, 1915–19), p. 103.

36 E. Duffin, T. Parkhill, (eds), *The First World War Diaries of Emma Duffin*, (compiled in 1919), (Dublin: Four Courts Press, 2014), pp. 64, 74, 121, 116.

37 E. Bilbrough, *My War Diary 1914–1918*, (London: Ebury Press, 2014), 7 October 1915.

38 Smith, *Four Years on the Western Front*, p. 3.

39 G. W. Broadhead, *Diary*, 3 December 1916, Private papers held by Imperial War Museum, – he had previously used the same word without inverted commas, 4 July 1916, so presumably was unsure of it.

40 E. Stuart, letter (undated), National Archives (RAIL 253/516).

41 I. Hay, *The First Hundred Thousand*, (Edinburgh: William Blackwood, 1916), p. 269.

42 E. W. Bratchell, undated letter, National Archives (RAIL 253/516).

43 Burrage, *War is War*, 2010 edn, p. 17.

44 *Daily Sketch*, 25 January 1916, p. 10.

45 Ibid., 10 December 1914, p. 10.

46 *Illustrated London News*, 7 August 1915, p. 187.

47 E. Partridge, 'Frank Honywood, Private', in *Three Personal Records of the War*, (London: Scholartis, 1929), pp. 322, 385, 304.

48 Ibid., p. 312.

49 J. R. Pinfold, (ed.), *A Month at the Front: the diary of an unknown soldier*, (Oxford: Bodleian Library, 2006), p. 39.

50 *9th Royal Scots (T.F.): B Company on active service; from a private's diary*, 13 April 1915.

51 C. Dawson, *Living Bayonets*, (London: John Lane, 1919), 20 June 1918.

52 Duffin, *Diaries*, p. 70.

53 Every time these terms appear in the *Illustrated London News*, 10 October 1914, it is in inverted commas.

54 *Weekly Dispatch*, 11 July 1915, p. 10.

55 *Daily Sketch*, 23 October 1914, p. 9.

56 *Aberdeen Evening Express*, 15 November 1918, p. 3.

57 Private collection, 24 November 1918.

58 Duffin, *Diaries*, pp. 74, 50, 138.

59 http://encyclopedia.1914–1918-online.net/article/warfare_1914–1918_ belgium accessed 5 February 2017.

60 M. McDonald, '*We Are Not French!': language, culture and identity in Brittany*, (London: Routledge, 1989), p. 136.

61 M. Bloch, (ed.), *Écrits de Guerre*, 1914–1918, (Paris: Colin,1997), p. 146.

62 L. Barthas, *Poilu: the World War I notebooks of Corporal Louis Barthas, barrelmaker, 1914–1918*, trans. E. Strauss, (New Haven: Yale University Press, 2014), p. 145.

63 A. Clement, letter to *Liverpool Daily Post*, 23 June 1917, p. 7.

64 S. Gibson, *Behind the Front*, (Cambridge: Cambridge University Press, 2014), p. 148.

65 *Dundee Courier*, 6 April 1916, p. 2.

66 R. H. Mottram, *Journey to the Western Front*, (London: G. Bell & Sons, 1936), p. 20.

67 P. Vansittart, (ed.), *John Masefield's Letters from the Front 1915–17*, (London: Constable & Co., 1984), 29 March 1915, p. 80.

68 C. Douie, *The Weary Road*, (London: John Murray, 1929), p. 54.

69 http://herolettersww1.blogspot.co.uk/2008/12/ymca-during-wwi-with-photos.html accessed 13 November 2016.

70 A. Kennedy and G. Crabb, *The Postal History of the British Army in World War One*, (Epsom, Surrey: G. Crabb, 1977), p. 12.

71 E. Greenhalgh, *The French Army and the First World War*, (Cambridge: Cambridge University Press, 2014), p. 66.

72 MacDonald, *Under the French Flag*, p. 56.

73 D. Omissi, *Indian Voices of the Great War*, (Basingstoke: Macmillan Press, 1999), letter, Raja Khan, 17 October 1917.

74 Ibid., letter, Signaller Nattha Singh, 8 December 1915.

75 Vansittart, *John Masefield's Letters*, p. 65.

76 Spicer, *Letters from France,* 9 November 1915.

77 L. Karvalics, 'Crosspoints of information history and Great War', in L. Karvalics, (ed.), *Information History of the First World War*, (Paris: L'Harmattan, 2015), p. 9.

78 *War Budget*, 24 August 1916, p. 1.

79 Barthas, *Poilu*, p. 5.

80 R. Graves, *Goodbye to All That*, (London: Penguin, [1929] 1960), 1960 edn, p. 177.

81 B. Nevill, *Billie*, (London: MacRae, 1991), p. 109, quoted in Holmes, *Tommy*, p. 270.

82 T. Ashworth, *Trench Warfare 1914–1918: the live and let live* system, (London: Macmillan, 1980), pp. 34–5.

83 Holmes, *Tommy*, p. 270.

84 *Daily Gazette for Middlesbrough*, 29 October 1914, p. 2.

85 *Liverpool Daily Post*, 29 January 1915, p. 7.

86 R. Van Emden and S. Humphries, *All Quiet on the Home Front*, (London: Headline, 2003), p. 53.

87 Spicer, *Letters from France*, 21 October 1915.

88 A. Herbert, *Mons, Anzac, and Kut*, (London: Hutchinson & Co., [1919] 1930), 1919 edn, p. 98.

89 Spicer, *Letters from France*, 1 October 1915.

90 *Aberdeen Evening Express*, 2 December 1914, p. 3.

91 *Liverpool Daily Post*, 29 January 1915, p. 7.

92 Holmes, *Tommy*, pp. 370–1.

93 D. Gill and G. Dallas, *Unknown Army*, (London: Verso, 1985), p. 59.

94 *The Times*, 16 November 1962, p. 14.

95 L. MacDonald, *Somme*, (London: Penguin, 1993), p. 270.

96 Quoted in Van Emden, *Tommy's War*, p. 149.

97 Vansittart, *John Masefield's Letters*, 6 May 1917, p. 273.

98 Gnl Sir Ian Hamilton, *Gallipoli Diary*, (London: Edward Arnold, 1920), p. 121.

99 *Newcastle Journal*, 1 January 1916, p. 3.

100 V. Noakes, *Voices of Silence: the alternative book of First World War poetry*, (Stroud: Sutton, 2006), p. xi.

101 E. B. Osborn, *The Muse in Arms*, (London: John Murray, 1918), p. v.

102 G. Seal, *The Soldiers' Press: Trench Journals in the First World War*, (Basingstoke: Palgrave Macmillan, 2013), p. 2.

103 The front page of *The Ghain Tuffieha Gazette*, February 1916, announces that its editor is Colonel G. T. K. Maurice, CMG, RAMC.

104 http://encyclopedia.1914–1918-online.net/article/soldier_newspapers accessed 13 November 2016.

105 Seal, *The Soldiers' Press*, p. 92; *Eyewash*, August 1918, was edited by Sapper R. Fitzpatrick '(who is responsible to the Commanding Officer for the

conduct of this magazine)', while *The Maple Leaf*, No. 7 1917, was 'Passed by Press Bureau'.

106 *Illustrated London News*, 27 February 1915, p. 276.

107 *Home Chat*, 10 October 1914, p. 66.

108 J. Winter, *Sites of Memory, Sites of Mourning*, (Cambridge: Cambridge University Press, 1998), p. 113; T. Walter, 'War grave pilgrimage', in T. Reader and T. Walter (eds), *Pilgrimage in Popular Culture*, 1993, p. 72, quoted in Todman, *The Great War*, p. 69.

109 *South Shields Daily Gazette*, 31 January 1916, p. 2.

110 Herbert, *Mons, Anzac, and Kut*, 1919 edn, p. 144.

111 Duffin, *Diaries*, p. 133.

112 *Report of the Central Register of Belgian Refugees*, 1919, p. 62.

113 *Western Mail*, 19 October 1914, p. 3.

114 Presumably taken during a trench raid, or from a captive. Author's collection.

115 Herbert, *Mons, Anzac, and Kut*, 1919 edn, p. 119.

116 P. Chasseaud, *Rats Alley*, (Staplehurst: Spellmount, 2006), pp. 180, 91.

117 *Daily Express*, 21 June 1918, p. 2.

118 *Cambridge Independent Press*, 6 September 1918, p. 6.

119 *Daily Mirror*, 16 January 1915, p. 5.

120 See R. Fogarty 'We did not speak a common language: African soldiers and communication in the French Army, 1914–1919' in J. Walker and C. Declercq (eds), *Languages and the First World War: communicating in a transnational war*, (London: Palgrave Macmillan, 2016), pp. 44–58.

121 G. Trevelyan, *Scenes from Italy's War*, (London: T. C. & E. C. Jack, 1919), p. 103.

122 Omissi, *Indian Voices*, letter, Kachahaf, 9 March 1918.

123 Herbert, A., *Mons, Anzac, and Kut*, 1919 edn, p. 61.

124 S. H. Hewett, *A Scholar's Letters from The Front*, (London: Longmans, Green & Co., 1918), p. 14.

125 Spicer, *Letters from France,* 2 June 1918.

126 *9th Royal Scots, Diary*, 1916, p. 15.

127 *The Fuze*, October 1916, p. 2.

128 Sgt F. Compton, in Doyle and Schäfer, *Fritz and Tommy*, p. 133.

129 MacDonald, *Somme*, p. 197.

130 Duffin, *Diaries*, p. 133.

131 *Ghain Tuffieha Gazette* (Malta), March 1917; under the title 'Corporal Atkins at Boulogne', in the *Navy and Army Magazine*, 28 November 1914, p. iii.

132 *Surrey Mirror*, 22 January 1915, p. 7.

133 MacDonald, *Under the French Flag*, pp. 100–1.

134 Author's collection.

135 *Northern Mudguard*, April 1917, p. 14; *Fifth Gloucester Gazette*, reported in *Chelmsford Chronicle*, 8 September 1916, p. 5.

136 J. Jones, *The First World War Diary of James Gilbert Jones*, (Welshpool: Montgomeryshire Genealogical Society, 1998), 3 February 1917.

137 *Exeter and Plymouth Gazette*, 13 January 1915, p. 4.

138 Adèle De L'Isle, *Leaves from a V.A.D.'s Diary*, (London: Elliot Stock, 1922), p. 20.

139 Omissi, *Indian Voices*, letter, Badshah Khan, 26 July 1915.

140 https://davinaatkin.wordpress.com/2014/08/29/28th-july–1914/ accessed 12 December 2016.

141 J. Lighter, 'The Slang of the American Expeditionary Forces in Europe 1917–1919: an historical glossary', in *American Speech*, Vol. 47, (Tuscaloosa: University of Alabama Press for the American Dialect Society, [1972] 1975), p. 103.

142 In Van Emden, *Tommy's War*, p. 110.

143 Gibson, *Behind the Front*, p. 149.

144 *Publishers' Circular*, 26 September 1914, p. 265.

145 Ibid., 30 January 1915, p. 79.

146 *Daily Mail*, 13 January 1915, p. 8.

147 *Home Chat*, 21 November 1914, p. 297.

148 *War-Time Tips*, p. 46.

149 Noticeable here too is the way English is manipulated to as much as possible match French syntax and vocabulary – Où se procure-t-on des billets? & À quelle heure le bureau de la poste ferme-t-il?

150 *What a British Soldier Wants to Say In French*, 1914.

151 *English–Flemish Military Guide*, (Poperinge: Drukk, 1915).

152 Gibson, *Behind the Front*, p. 155.

153 Doyle and Schäfer, *Fritz and Tommy*, p. 71.

154 *Dundee Courier*, 19 November 1914, p. 2.

155 *Belfast Weekly News*, 12 November 1914, p. 10.

156 H. Williamson, *The Patriot's Progress*, (London: Geoffrey Bles, 1930), p. 144.

157 Mottram, *Journey to the Western Front*, p. 16.

158 *9th Royal Scots*, *Diary*, 1915, p. 17.

159 *Manchester Guardian*, 22 February 1922, p. 5.

160 Gibson, *Behind the Front*, pp. 148–52.

161 Smith, *Four Years on the Western Front*, p. 19.

162 H. Stanley, *Grandad's War*, (Cromer: Poppyland Publishing, 2007), p. 22.

163 In Treves, *Made in the Trenches*, p. 72.

164 Author's collection, printed in Britain.

165 Spicer, *Letters from France*, 31 December 1915.

166 Both sent On Active Service, author's collection.

167 Author's collection.

168 Diary of Cpl R. D. Doughty, http://www.thekivellfamily.co.nz/military_history/ralphs_diaries/transcribes/diary_five_p3.html accessed 14 December 2016.

169 Diary of Walter Shuttleworth, 22 August 1917, http://www.klewis.org.uk/Diary/August accessed 12 December 2016.

170 Diary of C. B. Spires, 2 May 1917, http://www.bertspires.co.uk accessed 14 December 2016.

171 Quoted in L. MacDonald, *Voices and Images of the Great War*, (London: Penguin, [1988] 1991), 1991 edn, p. 48.

172 L. MacDonald, *They Called it Passchendaele*, (London: Penguin, [1978] 1993), 1993 edn, p. 114.

173 R. H. Mottram, 'A Personal Record', in *Three Personal Records of the War*, (London: Scholartis, 1929), p. 99.

174 D. McNair, *A Pacifist at War: military memoirs of a conscientious objector in Palestine, 1917–1918*, (Much Hadham: Anastasia, 2008), p. 9.

175 In Van Emden, *Tommy's War*, p. 111.

176 Graves, *Goodbye to All That*, 1960 edn, p. 93.

177 C. Douie, *The Weary Road*, p. 39.

178 Burrage, *War is War*, 1930 edn, p. 43.

179 Williamson, *The Patriot's Progress*, pp. 43, 52.

180 Author's collection.

181 Diary of C. B. Spires, 2 May 1917, http://www.bertspires.co.uk accessed 14 December 2016.

182 Harvey, *A Soldier's Sketches*, pp. 105–6.

183 *Punch*, 26 June 1918, p. x.

184 Vansittart, *John Masefield's Letters*, 28 March 1915, p. 79.

185 Gibson, *Behind the Front*, p. 156.

186 Douie, *The Weary Road*, p. 198.

187 Vansittart, *John Masefield's Letters*, 28 March 1915, p. 79.

188 Smith, *Four Years on the Western Front*, p. 11.

189 A. Dauzat, *L'Argot de la Guerre*, (Paris: Armand Colin, [1918] 2007), 1918 edn, p. 120.

190 E. Partridge, *Words! Words! Words!*, (London: Methuen, 1933), p. 169.

191 F. Déchelette, *L'Argot des poilus*, (Paris, 1918).

192 *Nottingham Evening Post*, 27 October 1917, p. 2.

193 *The Times*, 9 May 1916, p. 3.

194 Hay, *The First Hundred Thousand*, p. 302.

195 Partridge, *Words! Words! Words!*, pp. 178–9.

196 Account of Red Cross work with Russian prisoners of war in Germany, 1919, Imperial War Museum.

197 G. Nobbs, *Englishman, Kamerad!: Right of the British line*, (London: William Heinemann, 1910), p. 143.

198 *Liverpool Daily Post*, 14 August 1916, p. 6.

199 He became a Doctor of Economics; quoted in MacDonald, *Voices and Images*, 1991 edn, p. 192.

200 De L'Isle, *Leaves from a V.A.D.'s Diary*, p. 92.

201 *Daily Express*, 25 September 1916, p. 5.

202 *Liverpool Daily Post*, 3 November 1916, p. 5.

203 Duffin, *Diaries*, pp. 101, 114.

204 Herbert, *Mons, Anzac, and Kut*, 1919 edn, p. 86.

205 Quoted in Doyle and Schäfer, *Fritz and Tommy*, 2015, p. 13.

206 Smith, *Four Years on the Western Front*, p. 188.

207 Duffin, *Diaries*, p. 162.

208 Graves, *Goodbye to All That*, 1960 edn, p. 145.

209 *Derbyshire Courier*, 29 July 1916, p. 2.

210 In Van Emden, *Tommy's War*, p. 86.

211 *The Times*, 13 December 1916, p. 13.

212 H. Lake, *In Salonica with our Army*, (London: Andrew Melrose, 1917), pp. 185–6.

213 'Anzac Slang' in Treves, *Made in the Trenches*, p. 78.

214 In H. Jones, 'Imperial captivities: colonial prisoners of war in Germany and the Ottoman Empire, 1914–1918', in S. Das, (ed.), *Race, Empire and First World War Writing*, (Cambridge: Cambridge University Press), 2011, p. 186.

215 J. Brophy and E. Partridge, *The Long Trail – Soldiers' Songs and Slang 1914–18*, (London: Sphere, [1965] 1969), p. 105.

216 Duffin, *Diaries*, p. 58.

217 Fraser and Gibbons note that this phrase was 'pronounced according to ability'.

218 Pte W. C. Brock, Private papers held by Imperial War Museum.

219 Holmes, *Tommy*, p. 296.

220 Barker, *Agony's Anguish*, p. 58.

221 *The Times*, 20 April 1917, p. 5.

222 *Punch*, 25 April 1917, no page number.

223 In Van Emden, *Tommy's War*, p. 111; Gibson, *Behind the Front*, p. 151.

224 *Punch*, 23 October 1918, p. xi.

2 Language at the Front

1 W. Muir, *Observations of an Orderly*, (London: Simpkin, Marshall & Co., 1917), p. 223.

2 *The White Band*, (Officer Cadet Battalions, Crookham, 1917), April 1916.

3 *Manchester Guardian*, 'Miscellany' section, 5 September 1917, p. 30.

4 *Yorkshire Evening Post*, 7 August 1917, p. 2.

5 *Birmingham Gazette*, 31 May 1915, p. 4.

6 *Burnley News*, 12 January 1916, p. 2.

7 *The Times*, 19 June 1918, p. 6.

8 Partridge, *Words! Words! Words!*, p. 135.

9 *Illustrated London News* already on 22 August 1914 was advertising the *Illustrated War News* as 'the only album ... dealing with ... The Great War'.

10 M. Moynihan, (ed.), *A Place Called Armageddon – Letters from the Great War*, (Newton Abbott: David & Charles, 1975), p. 26.

11 H. M. Denham, *Dardanelles: a midshipman's diary 1915–16* (London: Murray, 1981), 14 May 1915.

12 Doyle and Schäfer, *Fritz and Tommy*, pp. 94, 109.

13 *Fifth Gloucester Gazette*, February 1917.

14 Kit Dodsworth, quoted in L. MacDonald, *The Roses of No Man's Land*, (London: Papermac, [1980] 1984), 1980, p. 98.

15 E. Weekley, *Words Ancient and Modern*, (London: John Murray, 1926), p. 105.

16 *The Cornishman*, 19 August 1915, p. 4.

17 *The Sporting Times*, 4 August 1917, p. 1.

18 L. Strange, *Recollections of an Airman – Diary*, (London: John Hamilton, [1933] 1935), 30 September p. 64, (*OED*).

19 Brophy and Partridge, *The Long Trail*, 1969 edn, p. 66.

20 Partridge, *Slang of the British Soldier*, p. 59.

21 *The Athenaeum*, 29 August 1919, p. 822.

22 *The Observer*, 23 March 1919, p. 6.

23 Notably Hazelden in the *Daily Mirror*.

24 F. Manning, *The Middle Part of Fortune/Her Privates We*, (London: Serpent's Tail [1929–30] 2013), p. 104.

25 *Notes and Queries*, March 1919, p. 79.

26 *The Athenaeum*, 29 August 1919, p. 823.

27 Denham, *Dardanelles*, 9 May 1915.

28 De L'Isle, *Leaves from a V.A.D.'s Diary*, p. 23.

29 *Poverty Bay Herald*, 19 October 1916, p. 8; *Evening Post*, 8 July 1915, p. 2.

30 *Morning Bulletin* (Rockhampton), 16 July 1923, p. 6.

31 Both in W. Downing, *Digger Dialects*, (Melbourne; Sydney: Lothian Book Publishing Co., 1919).

32 'Vang-blong' was given as a pronunciation guide in the phrasebook, D. Rees, *The Briton in France*, (London: Leopold B. Hill, 1906, 1918), 1918 edn, p. 57.

33 *Register News-Pictorial* (Adelaide), 31 October 1927, p. 26.

34 *The Athenaeum*, 29 August 1919, p. 822.

35 J. Randerson, *The Origin of the War Term No Man's Land as Applied to the World War*, (Albany: Privately published, 1922), p. 12.

36 https://www.theguardian.com/stage/2015/dec/18/chitty-chitty-bang-bangs-not-so-pretty-origins & https://www.theguardian.com/film/2015/dec/21/chitty-chitty-bang-bang-goes-another-ian-fleming-theory accessed 5 February 2017.

37 *Sheffield Independent*, 23 August 1914, p. 4.

38 *Huddersfield Daily Examiner*, 29 September 1914, p. 3.

39 The *Western Mail*, 19 October 1914, p. 3, reports on the distributing of French, Flemish and English glossaries.

40 *The Sphere*, 28 November 1914, p. 214.

41 *Yorkshire Post*, 8 October 1914, p. 4.

42 *West Briton and Cornwall Advertiser*, 3 April 1916, p. 4.

43 *Huddersfield Daily Examiner*, 29 September 1914, p. 3; *Hendon and Finchley Times*, 15 January 1915, p. 7; *Liverpool Echo*, 16 March 1915, p. 4; *Portsmouth Evening News*, 19 March 1915, p. 3; *Newcastle Journal*, 6 October 1915, p. 3; *The Times*, 12 July 1916, p. 10.

44 *Leamington Spa Courier*, 21 March 1919, p. 4.

45 *Evening Despatch*, 19 December 1917, p. 3.

46 *Yorkshire Evening Post*, 16 October 1916, p. 5.

47 *Daily Mail*, 1 February 1916, p. 4.

48 *Derry Journal*, 25 September 1918, p. 2.

49 *War Budget*, 23 March 1916, p. 179; *Reading Mercury*, 1 April 1916, p. 4.

50 *The Times*, 31 March 1915, p. 7.

51 *The Gasper*, 8 January 1916, p. 5.

52 *The Gasper*, 28 February 1916, p. 2.

53 *B.E.F. Times*, 15 August 1917, p. 7.

54 *Poilu*, October 1916, p. 3.

55 'Rest – time dedicated to manoeuvres, parades, night marches, etc.'

56 T. O'Toole, *The Way They Have in the Army*, (London: John Lane, 1916), pp. 38–44.

57 M. Mügge, *The War Diary of a Square Peg*, (London: George Routledge and Sons Ltd, 1920), pp. 217–224.

58 Muir, *Observations of an Orderly*, p. 231.

59 *Illustrated London News*, 27 October 1923, p. 778.

60 *Notes and Queries*, 29 October 1921, p. 343.

61 Reported in *Hull Daily Mail*, 31 December 1921, p. 1.

62 *Irish Times*, 6 October 1921, p. 4.

63 J. Brophy, *The Soldier's War: a prose anthology*, (London: Dent, 1929), p. 263.

64 Brophy and Partridge, *The Long Trail*, 1969 edn, p. 12.

65 *Derby Daily Telegraph*, 25 September, p. 6.

66 *War Budget*, 13 April 1916, p. 261.

67 *Hull Daily Mail*, 10 November 1914, p. 8.

68 *The Gasper*, 1 April 1915.

69 G. H. Malins, *How I Filmed the War*, (London: Herbert Jenkins, 1920), p. 129.

70 Williamson, *The Patriot's Progress*, p. 167.

71 *Hull Daily Mail*, 20 September 1917, p. 3.

72 *Manchester Guardian*, 1 May 1916, p. 6.

73 Denham, *Dardanelles*, 21 March 1915.

74 'jollies', used for the Marines, in the *Vivid War Weekly*, 16 October 1915, p. 173, dated back to the 17th century.

75 Fraser and Gibbons.

76 Of these four Fraser and Gibbons say they were originally naval slang; Brophy and Partridge, both former soldiers, say this only for 'gadget'; 'bully-beef' may though derive from 'bull-beef', described in *The Newlanders Cure* (1630) as appropriate food for 'Labourers and Hindes' (manual workers) p. 18.

77 *Daily Express*, 2 August 1918, p. 2.

78 *Pearson's Weekly*, 13 February 1915, p. 722; *Abergavenny Chronicle*, 4 August 1916, p. 2; *Daily Mail*, 5 May 1917, p. 2; *Diss Express*, 21 June 1918, p. 3.

79 *Folkestone Herald*, 10 August 1918, p. 9.

80 E. Partridge, *Dictionary of R.A.F. Slang*, (London: Pavilion, [1945] 1990), Introduction p. 4.

81 *The Athenaeum*, 23 May 1919, p. 360.

82 *The Athenaeum*,1 August 1919, p. 695.

83 E. Partridge, *Slang To-day and Yesterday*, (London: Routledge & Kegan Paul, [1933] 1970), p. 259.

84 *Daily Chronicle*, 1 May 1915, p. 4.

85 *John Bull*, 22 January 1916, p. 9.

86 *Yorkshire Evening Post*, 5 February 1917, p. 3.

87 *Yorkshire Evening Post*, 1 September 1917, p. 5.

88 *The Athenaeum*, 12 December 1919, p. 1350.

89 *Cheltenham Looker-On*, 10 October 1914, p. 14.

90 *Dundee Courier*, 24 December 1917, p. 2.

91 *Liverpool Daily Post*, 15 November 1915, p. 7.

92 *Yorkshire Evening Post*, 6 September 1916, p. 6.

93 *Birmingham Gazette*, 2 October 1915, p. 5.

94 *Belfast News-letter*, 17 November 1916, p. 6.

95 *Sunderland Daily Echo*, 23 September 1916, p. 3.

96 Spicer, *Letters from France,* 20 February 1916.

97 Letter, author's collection.

98 P. MacGill, *The Great Push*, (London: Herbert Jenkins, 1916), p. 113.

99 Postcard, On Active Service, 30 March 1918, author's collection.

100 McNair, *A Pacifist at War*, p. 51.

101 In Fraser and Gibbons.

102 Postcard, On Active Service, 19 April 1918, author's collection.

103 http://encyclopedia.1914–1918-online.net/article/censorship accessed 20 December 2016.

104 India Office Records, IOR/L/MIL/5/825/1, 20 March 1915.

105 For a study of this see H. Foottit, 'Poetry, parables and codes: translating the letters of Indian Soldiers' in Walker and Declercq, *Languages and the First World War: communicating*, pp. 115–27.

106 Omissi, *Indian Voices*, letter, unnamed Afridi Pathan soldier, 14 February 1915.

107 Ibid., letter, Lance Naik Ram, May 1915.

108 ap Glyn, I., '"Dear Mother, I am very sorry I cannot write to you in Welsh ...""; censorship and the Welsh language in the First World War', in Walker and Declercq, *Languages and the First World War: communicating*, p. 128.

109 ap Glyn, 'Dear Mother ...', in Walker and Declercq, *Languages and the First World War: communicating*, p. 139.

110 Brock, Private papers, 30 September 1918.

111 Williamson, *The Patriot's Progress*, p. 37.

112 Letter, author's collection.

113 Quoted in MacDonald, *Voices and Images*, 1991 edn, p. 141.

114 Letter in the *Sheffield Evening Telegraph*, 18 August 1915, p. 3.

115 Spicer, *Letters from France,* 6 October 1915.

116 Pinfold, *A Month at the Front*, p. 46.

117 Broadhead, *Diary*, 15 December 1916.

118 Postcard, On Active Service, 27 October 1917, author's collection.

119 Postcard, On Active Service, 26 March 1916, author's collection.

120 Letter, 25 April 1915, quoted in Doyle and Schäfer, *Fritz and Tommy*, p. 127.

121 Letter, On Active Service, 31 October 1917, author's collection.

122 Quoted in MacDonald, *Voices and Images*, 1991 edn, p. 137.

123 Nobbs, *Englishman, Kamerad!*, p. 71.

124 *Vivid War Weekly*, 16 October 1915, pp. 162, 163.

125 Postcard, On Active Service, author's collection.

126 15 September 1915, quoted in J. Wadsworth, *Letters from the Trenches*, (Barnsley: Pen & Sword Military, 2014), p. 27.

127 Postcard, On Active Service, 30 March 1918, author's collection.

128 Postcard, 4 December 1918, author's collection.

129 Letter, On Active Service, 27 April 1916, author's collection.

130 Diary, 6 November 1914, http://www.bobbrookes.co.uk/DiaryCH2.htm accessed 21 December 2016.

131 Vansittart, *John Masefield's Letters*, 15 May 1917, pp. 281–2.

132 *Hull Daily Mail*, 9 September 1914, p. 4.

133 *Western Daily Press*, 15 September 1914, p. 6.

134 Diary, George Williams, 30 April 1916, http://www.europeana1914–1918.eu/en/contributions/17242 accessed 7 October 2016.

135 *Burnley Express*, 24 July 1915, p. 9.

136 *Daily Mail*, 1 October 1919, p. 2.

137 J. Boraston, (ed.) *Sir Douglas Haig's Despatches, (December 1915–April 1919)*, (London; Toronto: J. M. Dent & Sons, 1919), 1917, p. 142.

138 Lt Col E. Cook, *War Diary of the 1st Life Guards, 1914–15*, (England, 1915), p. 109.

139 Hay, *The First Hundred Thousand*, p. 269.

140 Broadhead, *Diary*, 15 September 1916.

141 Mottram, *A Personal Record*, p. 36.

142 *Diary of a Nursing Sister on the Western Front, 1914–15,* (Edinburgh London: William Blackwood & Sons, [1915] 1930), 1915 edn, p. 179. Kateluard.co.uk/category/kate-luards-diaries.co.uk accessed 30 January 2015.

143 A. Niceforo, *Le Génie de l'Argot,* (Paris, 1912), p. 245.

144 E. Partridge, '"Slang", Society for Pure English', Tract LV, 1948, in *The English Language: essays by linguists and men of letters 1858–1964,* W. F. Bolton and D. Crystal, (eds), Vol. 2, 1969 edn, p. 188, (Cambridge: Cambridge University Press, [1940] 1969).

145 D. Jones, *In Parenthesis,* (London: Faber & Faber Ltd, [1937] 1969), p. 146.

146 Fussell, *The Great War,* 1977 edn, p. 176.

147 Spencer, *War Letters,* 28 January 1915, 16 February 1915.

148 *Manchester Guardian,* 13 January 1915, p. 5.

149 D. Jones, *In Parenthesis,* 1969 edn, pp. 67, 107.

150 S. De Loghe, *The Straits Impregnable,* (London: John Murray, 1917), p. 164.

151 In Walker and Declercq, *Languages and the First World War: communicating,* p. 203.

152 D. Jones, *In Parenthesis,* 1969 edn, p. 103.

153 Quoted in M. Arthur, *We Will Remember Them,* (London: Weidenfeld & Nicholson, 2009), pp. 130, 157.

154 'I have not seen him since and I am afraid he went under', Burrage, *War is War,* 2010 edn, p. 114.

155 D. Walker, *With the Lost Generation,* (Hull: A. Brown & Sons Ltd, 1970), p. 33.

156 Major F. P. Crozier, quoted in MacDonald, *Voices and Images,* 1991 edn, p. 53; Brophy and Partridge also have 'to get 'em', in which 'them' refers to shaking fits (J. Brophy and E. Partridge, *Songs and Slang of the British Soldier: 1914–1918,* (London: Eric Partridge Ltd, 1930), p. 127).

157 Jones, *In Parenthesis,* 1969 edn, p. 35.

158 Brophy and Partridge, *The Long Trail,* 1969 edn, p. 135.

159 Fussell, *The Great War,* 1977 edn, p. 178.

160 I. Hay, *All In It: K1 carries on,* (Toronto: Briggs, 1917), p. 160.

161 E. R. Hepper, *Captain E. Raymond Hepper's Great War Diary 1916–19,* (Kirkby Stephen: Hayloft Pub., 2011), 18 October 1917.

162 Crofts, *Field Ambulance Sketches,* p. 36.

163 G. B. Manwaring, *If We Return,* (London; New York: 1918), p. 79.

164 *The Gasper,* 8 January 1916.

165 Lighter, *Slang of the AEF,* p. 63.

166 Denham, *Dardanelles,* 1 May 1915.

167 Hewett, *A Scholar's Letters,* p. 39.

168 'Liveliness' in this sense was first used in a letter from Admiral Lord Fisher to Winston Churchill, 8 November 1914, to describe fighting in the North Sea.

169 De L'Isle, *Leaves from a V.A.D.'s Diary*, p. 65.

170 G. Pulvertaft, *Reminiscences of a V.A.D.*, (Great Britain: John Brunsdon, 2014), 29 October 1918.

171 Dawson, *Living Bayonets*, p. 183.

172 Laugesen A, *Glossary of Slang and Peculiar Terms in Use in the A.I.F.* http://andc.anu.edu.au/australian-words/aif-slang/annotated-glossary accessed 6 February 2017.

173 Fraser and Gibbons.

174 Spicer, *Letters from France*, 12 and 20 February 1916.

175 Quoted in Vansittart, *John Masefield's Letters*, 6 September 1916, p. 125.

176 Pulvertaft, *Reminiscences*, 29 October 1918, p. 84.

177 Brindle, *France and Flanders*, pp. 54–5.

178 Graves, *Goodbye to All That*, 1960 edn, pp. 192–3.

179 G. Coppard, *With a Machine Gun to Cambrai*, (London: Papermac, [1979] 1986), 1986 edn, p. 108.

180 Burrage, *War is War*, 2010 edn, p. 107.

181 French, Sir J., 8th Dispatch to War Office, 15 June 1915.

182 Graves, *Goodbye to All That*, 1960 edn, p. 150.

183 Spicer, *Letters from France*, 6 October 1915.

184 Gas not having been brought into use till several months after the retreat from Mons.

185 Sadly one of the fatalities caused on Armistice Day was a soldier who was in fact gassed in 1918 at Mons: *Western Times*, 29 November 1918, p. 5.

186 C. Edmonds, *A Subaltern's War*, (London: Peter Davies, 1929), p. 136.

187 Mottram in *A Personal Record* speaks of 'the utter inconsequence of infantry in modern warfare', p. 43; *The Pow-Wow* 9 December 1914 editorial states 'the present war being essentially an artillery war'.

188 G. Apollinaire, *Letters to Madeleine: tender as memory*, trans. D. Nicholson-Smith, L. Campa, (ed.), (Chicago: Chicago University Press, 2010).

189 Crofts, *Field Ambulance Sketches*, p. 65.

190 A. Copping, *Souls in Khaki*, (London: Hodder & Stoughton, 1917), p. 118.

191 Doyle and Schäfer, *Fritz and Tommy*, p. 126.

192 *Thirty Second News*, November 1918, p. 5.

193 *The Castironical*, March 1916.

194 *Thirty Second News*, November 1918, p. 17.

195 Rabbi Stephen Wise, reported in *The Times*, 7 June 1918, p. 5.

196 *Daily Express*, 18 June 1918, p. 2.

197 Partridge, *Words! Words! Words!*, p. 157.

198 Brophy and Partridge, *The Long Trail*, 1969 edn, pp. 94–5.

199 Quoted in Doyle and Schäfer, *Fritz and Tommy*, p. 75.

200 Brophy and Partridge, *The Long Trail*, 1969 edn, p. 101.

201 *Notes and Queries*, 29 October 1921, p. 345.

202 *War Budget*, 30 March 1916, p. 195.

203 *The Cornishman*, 9 August 1915, p. 4.

204 In postcards, On Active Service, 4 November 1916, author's collection.

205 Dawson, *Living Bayonets*, p. 183.

206 *Yorkshire Evening Post*, 16 October 1916, p. 5.

207 Williamson, *The Patriot's Progress*, p. 167.

208 *The Athenaeum*, 7 November 1919, p. 1163; the AEF had 'hobnail express' for fast marching.

209 Lt R. Macleod, quoted in MacDonald, *Voices and Images*, 1991 edn, p. 65.

210 *Yorkshire Evening Post*, 16 October 1916, p. 5.

211 Muir, *Observations of an Orderly*, p. 222.

212 Partridge, *Words! Words! Words!*, pp. 181–207.

213 *Notes and Queries*, 1921, p. 342.

214 In MacDonald, *Voices and Images*, 1991 edn, p. 92.

215 *The Fuze*, October 1916, p. 5.

216 *Notes and Queries*, 1921, p. 384.

217 Hamilton, *Gallipoli Diary*, Vol. 2, 1918, p. 120.

218 Cook, *War Diary*, 26 October 1914.

219 *The Story of an Epic Pilgrimage*, (England: The British Legion, 1928), p. 98.

220 Graves, *Goodbye to All That*, 1960 edn, p. 79.

221 Spicer, *Letters from France*, 9 November 1915.

222 Brophy and Partridge, *The Long Trail*, 1969 edn, p. 136.

223 De Loghe, *The Straits Impregnable*, p. 159.

224 Cook, *War Diary*, 13/14 October 1914, p. 17.

225 Ibid., 25 August 1914.

226 Denham, *Dardanelles*, 25 February 1915.

227 *War-Time Tips*, p. 55.

228 General Birdwood claimed to have invented it in 1915; the *Warwick and Warwickshire Advertiser*, on 7 August 1915 (p. 8), stated that 'Anzac appeared on Wednesday for the first time'.

229 *Menin Gate Pilgrimage*, (London: St Barnabas Society, 1927), p. 8.

230 *Sunderland Daily Echo*, 13 June 1917, p. 2.

231 Percy Bryant, (RFA gunner), Imperial War Museum interview, [sound recording, 1975].

232 H. McBride, *The Emma-Gees*, (Indianapolis: Bobbs Merrill Co., 1918), p. 62.

233 Brophy and Partridge, *The Long Trail*, 1969 edn, p. 165.

234 *Sunderland Daily Echo*, 11 January 1915, p. 5.

235 H. Clapham, *Mud and Khaki*, (London: Hutchinson & Co., 1930), p. 36.

236 E. Partridge, *Quarterly Review*, (London: John Murray, 1931), Vol. 256, p. 356.

237 *Taunton Courier*, 18 Nov 1914, p. 1; *Sheffield Weekly Telegraph*, 16 June 1917, p. 3; *Biggleswade Chronicle*, 9 August 1918, p. 1; though the general proportion of 'Ypres' to 'Wipers' was about 50:1.

238 *Nottingham Evening Post*, 2 November 1914, p. 3; *Birmingham Daily Post* 24 December 1914, p. 3; *Sheffield Evening Telegraph*, 19 February 1915, p. 4.

239 *Nottingham Evening Post*, 14 November 1914, p. 2.

240 Ibid., 15 October 1914, p. 1.

241 *Newcastle Journal*, 26 April 1915, p. 6.

242 *Berwickshire News*, 14 March 1916, p. 5.

243 *Yorkshire Evening Post*, 16 February 1915, p. 3.

244 Ibid., 7 November 1914, p. 2.

245 *Sheffield Evening Telegraph*, 16 November 1914, p. 2.

246 *Liverpool Echo*, 11 February 1915, p. 4.

247 *Aberdeen Journal*, 24 August 1916, p. 4.

248 *Birmingham Daily Post*, 2 December 1914, p. 6.

249 *Motherwell Times*, 30 October 1914, p. 6.

250 *Portsmouth Evening News*, 6 July 1915, p. 2.

251 Mottram, *Journey to the Western Front*, p. 101.

252 http://1914–1918.invisionzone.com/forums/index.php?showtopic=217500 accessed 12 September 2016.

253 *The Literary Digest*, (New York: Funk & Wagnalls Co., 1918), 5 October 1918, p. 29.

254 Fraser and Gibbons, 'The nickname of a big gun in action on the Arras sector in 1917'.

255 Ibid., 'The nickname given to a Turkish big gun, and its shell, at the Dardanelles'.

256 Van Emden, *Tommy's War*, p. 163.

257 C. MacArthur, *A Bug's-eye View of the War*, (United States: privately published, 1919), p. 74.

258 Spencer, *War Letters*, 2 February 1915.

259 W. Merrill, *A College Man in Khaki*, (New York: George H. Doran, 1918), p. 227.

260 J. Kilpatrick, *Atkins at War, as Told in His Own Letters*, (London: Herbert Jenkins, 1914), p. 30.

261 Capt E. Gore-Booth, quoted in Noakes, *Voices of Silence*, p. xii.

262 Quoted in Doyle and Schäfer, *Fritz and Tommy*, p. 130.

263 M. R. Kelley, 'But Kultur's Nar-poo in the Trenches', in *Art In America*, June 2014, New York. http://www.artinamericamagazine.com/news-features/magazine/but-kulturs-nar-poo-in-the-trenches/ accessed 13 April 2017.

264 A. Marwick, *The Deluge*, (Basingstoke: Macmillan, [1965] 1991), 1991 edn, p. 33.

265 *Grey Brigade*, (Dorking: 1915), 18 September 1915.

266 *The Kemmel Times*, 3 July 1916.

267 *Dublin Daily Express*, 20 October 1917, p. 9.

268 *Fall in*, 25 December 1915, p. 22.

269 *The Ghain Tuffieha Gazette*, March 1917.

270 *The Gasper*, 28 February 1916.

271 Partridge, *Slang of the British Soldier*, p. 60.

272 *John Bull*, 9 January 1915, p. 3; *Manchester Courier*, 8 October 1914, p. 2; *Sunderland Daily Echo*, 23 September 1916, p. 3.

273 *Hull Daily Mail*, 25 March 1922, p. 1.

274 Malins, *How I Filmed the War*, p. 238.

275 *The Story of an Epic Pilgrimage*, p. 97.

276 Kilpatrick, *Atkins at War*, p. 29.

277 Partridge, *Slang To-day and Yesterday*, 1970, p. 263.

278 Dawson, *Living Bayonets*, p. 49.

279 *The Athenaeum*, 8 August 1919, p. 728.

280 Lighter's documentation for 'meat-grinder' dates from 1967; frequently used of campaigns such as Verdun or The Somme, it appears to be a term used of, rather than during, the war. But 'a French soldier' quoted in Julien Bryan's *Ambulance 464* (1918, p. 152) describes the (mythological) German 'corpse factory' as employing 'a big machine like a sausage grinder'.

281 All in Downing, *Digger Dialects*.

282 Smith, *Four Years on the Western Front*, p. 11.

283 Quoted in Van Emden, *Tommy's War*, p. 157.

284 Quoted in MacDonald, *Voices and Images*, 1991 edn, p. 141.

285 J. Brophy, 'After Fifty Years', in J. Brophy and E. Partridge, (eds), *The Daily Telegraph Dictionary of Tommies' Songs and Slang*, (Barnsley: Pen & Sword Military, 2008), p. 16.

286 Quoted in MacDonald, *Voices and Images*, 1991 edn, p. 188.

287 Brophy and Partridge, *Songs and Slang of the British Soldier*, p. 193.

288 E. Partridge, *A Dictionary of Slang and Unconventional English*, (London: Routledge and Kegan Paul, [1937] 1974), 1974 edn, p. 842.

289 Quoted in MacDonald, *Voices and Images*, 1991 edn, p. 118.

290 Advertisement in *The Boot and Shoe Retailer*, 11 September 1914, p. 2.

291 *The War Illustrated*, 10 June 1916, p. 397. The same trick is applied in a short story series in *The Strafer* November 1916, p. 7.

292 *Yorkshire Evening Post*, 8 April 1915, p. 4.

293 *Derby Daily Telegraph*, 2 August 1916, p. 3.

294 *Newcastle Journal*, 10 June 1915, p. 2.

295 *The Bystander*, 24 November 1915, p. xxiv.

296 *War Budget*, 1 June 1916, p. ii.

297 *The Leadswinger*, 4 September 1915, p. 1.

298 Coppard, *With a Machine Gun to Cambrai*, 1986 edn, p. 88.

299 De L'Isle, *Leaves from a V.A.D.'s Diary*, p. 27.

300 Pte J. Gray, 'A linesman's Gallipoli', in W. Wood, *In the Line of Battle*, (London: Chapman & Hall, 1916), p. 49.

301 J. Agate, *L. of C. (Lines of Communication)*, (London: Constable and Company, 1917), p. 102.

302 *Notes and Queries*, 29 October 1921, pp. 343–4.

303 *Cairns Post*, 12 March 1918, p. 7.

304 *Yorkshire Evening Post*, 25 August 1917, p. 4.

305 *The Huns' Handbook*, (London: The Echo and Evening Chronicle, 1915), pp. 3, 46.

306 H. Buller, *The Soldiers' English–German Conversation Book*, (London: T. Werner Laurie Ltd, 1915), p. 50.

307 *Fifth Gloucester Gazette*, 12 March 1916, p. 70.

308 *The B.E.F. Times*, 1 December 1916, p. 6.

309 In Treves, *Made in the Trenches*, p. 63.

310 *Fifth Gloucester Gazette*, February 1916, p. 63.

311 *The Gasper*, 28 February 1916, p. 4.

312 *The Athenaeum*, 1 August 1919, p. 695.

313 Brophy and Partridge, *Songs and Slang of the British Soldier*, pp. 16, 17.

314 Jones, *In Parenthesis*, 1969 edn, p. xii.

315 Omissi, *Indian Voices*, letter, J. N. Godbole, 18 March 1915.

316 16 October 1916, quoted in Wadsworth, *Letters from the Trenches*, p. 59.

317 1916, quoted in MacDonald, *Voices and Images*, 1991 edn, p. 164.

318 Douie, *The Weary Road*, p. 57.

319 RSM Harry Atkin Cheshire Regt https://davinaatkin.wordpress.com/2014/08/29/28th-july-1914/ accessed 6 February 2017.

320 Shoeing Smith C. H. Williams, 1916, quoted in MacDonald, *Voices and Images*, 1991 edn, p. 188.

321 G. Maxwell, in T. Cook, 'Fighting words: Canadian soldiers' slang and swearing in the Great War', in *War in History*, (2013), Vol. 20 issue 3, p. 336.

322 *Falkirk Herald*, 14 March 1917, p. 3.

323 *Birmingham Daily Post*, 9 August 1915, p. 5.

324 Cpl George Mitchell, in S. Palmer and S. Wallis, *A War in Words*, (London: Pocket Books, [2003] 2004), 2004 edn, p. 123.

325 *The Times*, 15 August 1918, p. 3.

326 *Sheffield Evening Telegraph*, 11 March 1919, p. 3.

327 E. L. M. Burns, quoted in Cook, 'Fighting Words', p. 335.

328 MacDonald, *Somme*, pp. 143–4. One of the Church Lads Brigade is quoted as taking off his boots and socks after a march and saying 'Those bloody fucking bastards'.

329 Burrage, *War is War*, 1930 edn, p. 35.

330 G. Goodchild, 'The Sensitive Plant', in Treves, *Made in the Trenches*, pp. 49, 50.

331 Graves, *Goodbye to All That*, 1960 edn, p. 81.

332 Dawson, *Living Bayonets*, pp. 43–8.

333 Cook, 'Fighting Words', p. 326.

334 Ibid., p. 340.

335 Pte W. Ogilvie quoted in ibid., p. 340.

336 in 1914 G. B. Shaw noted that it was 'a class word': Hughes, G., *Swearing*, 1998, p. 187; E. L. M. Burns noted it as 'the "bloody" of the English workingmen' – Cook, 'Fighting Words', p. 335.

337 Douie, *The Weary Road*, p. 95.

338 Dawson, *Living Bayonets*, letters 20 June 1918, 22 August 1918.

339 McNair, *A Pacifist at War*, pp. xix, 48.

340 Duffin, *Diaries*, p. 91.

341 *A Red Triangle Girl in France*, (New York: George H. Doran, 1918), p. 125.

342 William James Newton, Imperial War Museum interview, [sound recording, 1975].

343 C. Savage, quoted in Cook, 'Fighting Words', p. 336.

344 MacDonald, *Somme*, p. 208.

345 A. Clark, *Echoes of the Great War: the diary of the Reverend Andrew Clark*, J. Munson (ed)., (Oxford: Oxford University Press, [1985] 1988), 1988 edn, 2 September 1916, p. 154.

346 *Carry On: The Trotters' Journal*, New Year 1916, p. 3.

347 In Treves, *Made in the Trenches*, p. 196.

348 Barker, *Agony's Anguish*, p. 11.

349 A. Hale, in Cook, 'Fighting Words', p. 342.

350 Graves, *Goodbye to All That*, 1960 edn, p. 80.

351 J. Maclean, in Holmes, *Tommy*, p. 292.

352 Douie, *The Weary Road*, pp. 62, 63.

353 Brophy and Partridge, *The Long Trail,* 1969 edn, pp. 20, 21.

354 Graves, *Goodbye to All That*, 1960 edn, p. 206.

355 MacDonald, *Somme*, p. 143.

356 Jones, *In Parenthesis*, 1969 edn, pp. 15, 48.

357 For 'blooming/bloomin'' see *The Fuze*, 1916 Vol. 1, No.1, p. 2, and Taft, G., *Reminiscences of a V.A.D.*, 2014, 8 September 1916; for 'blinking/blinkin', see Rifleman B. Eccles in a letter to his mother, 16 April 1917, in MacDonald, *Voices and Images*, 1991 edn, p. 205, and *On the Road to Kut: a soldier's story of the Mesopotamian campaign*, London: Hutchinson & Co., 1917, p. 207; for 'ruddy' see Holmes, *A Yankee in the Trenches*, p. 185, and *The Fuze*, 1916 Vol.1, No.1, p. 4; for 'bloody well' see Coppard, *With a Machine Gun to Cambrai*, 1986 edn, p. 107; for 'gore blimey' (as the soldier's cap) see the *Fifth Gloucester Gazette* June 1917, p. 211.

358 In MacDonald, *Voices and Images*, 1991 edn, p. 26.

359 J. Winter and B. Baggett, *1914–18*, (London: BBC Books, 1996), p. 292.

360 Holmes, *A Yankee in the Trenches*, p. 210.

361 *Daily Mirror*, 26 November 1917, p. 10.

362 http://www.britishnewspaperarchive.co.uk/search/results/1919-01-01/1919-12-31?basicsearch=blimey&somesearch=blimey&sortorder=score&exactsearch=false&page=2 accessed 2 November 2016.

363 In Treves, *Made in the Trenches*, p. 66.

364 Ibid., p. 71.

365 Smith, *Four Years on the Western Front*, p. 21.

366 Graves, *Goodbye to All That*, 1960 edn, p. 100.

367 *The Athenaeum*, 1 August 1919, p. 695.

368 *The White Band*, April 1916, p. 7.

369 Graves, *Goodbye to All That*, 1960 edn, p. 81.

370 Jones, *In Parenthesis*, 1969 edn, p. 53.

371 Brophy and Partridge, *The Long Trail,* 1969 edn, p. 74.

372 *Punch*, 29 May 1918, p. x.

373 Denham, *Dardanelles,* 14 August 1915.

374 In MacDonald, *Voices and Images*, 1991 edn, p. 85.

375 *In the Hands of the Huns: being the reminiscences of a British civil prisoner of war, 1914–1915,* (London: Simpkin, Marshall & Co., 1916), p. 20.

376 Coppard, *With a Machine Gun to Cambrai*, 1986 edn, p. 47.

377 Ibid., p. 47.

378 T. Johnson quoted in Cook, 'Fighting Words', p. 337.

379 *Punch*, 15 May 18.

380 *Yorkshire Evening Post*, 1 December 1919, p. 7.

381 S. Graham, *A Private in the Guards*, (London: Macmillan, 1919), p. 205.

382 Cyril Jose's account of a charge made it clear they were not http://www.pollingerltd.com/bookshop/martin_body/2nd-devons-somme.pdf accessed 6 February 2017.

383 Smith, *Four Years on the Western Front*, p. 11.

384 Mottram, *A Personal Record*, p. 95.

385 Clark, *Echoes of the Great War*, 1988 edn, 2 September 1916, p. 242.

386 Graves, *Goodbye to All That*, 1960 edn, p. 268.

387 Quoted in Van Emden and Humphries, *All Quiet on the Home Front*, p. 30.

388 Smith, *Four Years on the Western Front*, p. 166.

389 The *Western Chronicle*, 6 August 1915, p. 7.

390 Spicer, *Letters from France,* 15 March 1916.

391 Letter, On Active Service, author's collection.

392 Douie, *The Weary Road*, p. 165.

393 N. F. Tytler, *With Lancashire Lads and Field Guns in France*, (Manchester: John Heywood, 1922), p. 76.

394 *Weekly Freeman's Journal*, 17 October 1914, p. 2.

395 Harvey, *A Soldier's Sketches*, p. 139.

396 H. Quigley, *Passchendaele and the Somme*, (London: Methuen & Co., 1928), p. 84.

397 *Derry Journal*, 7 July 1915, p. 6.

398 Pte G. Howard, *The Berwick Advertiser*, 8 June 1917, p. 4.

399 Edmonds, *A Subaltern's War*, p. 142.

400 Graves, *Goodbye to All That*, 1960 edn, p. 110.

401 The *Western Chronicle*, 6 August 1915, p. 7.

402 Douie, *The Weary Road*, p. 115.

403 Spicer, *Letters from France,* 5 July 1916.

404 A Goole gunner, quoted in the *Hull Daily Mail*, 4 June 1915, p. 7.

405 Vansittart, *John Masefield's Letters*, 25 September 1916.

406 A soldier's letter in the *Walsall Advertiser*, 20 March 1915, p. 5.

407 Winter and Baggett, *1914–18*, p. 191.

408 Vansittart, *John Masefield's Letters*, 25 September 1916.

409 Quoted in Holmes, *Tommy*, p. 405.

410 Highland Regiment officer, *Warwick and Warwickshire Advertiser*, 9 October 1915, p. 5.

411 Lt A. Behrend, in Holmes, *Tommy*, p. 405.

412 Quoted in Doyle and Schäfer, *Fritz and Tommy*, p. 114.

413 Coppard, *With a Machine Gun to Cambrai*, 1986 edn, p. 26.

414 Graves, *Goodbye to All That*, 1960 edn, p. 115.

415 Jones, *In Parenthesis*, 1969 edn, p. 35.

416 Fraser and Gibbons.

417 S. Beames, quoted in Cook, 'Fighting Words', p. 333.

418 Lt F. J. Sleath in the *Whitby Gazette*, 4 October 1918, p. 10.

419 Brindle, *France and Flanders*, p. 69.

420 *The War Illustrated Album De Luxe,* 1918, Vol. 9, p. 3114.

421 MacDonald, *Voices and Images*, 1991 edn, p. 168.

422 *Chelmsford Chronicle*, 19 March 1915, p. 10.

423 Graves, *Goodbye to All That*, 1960 edn, p. 222.

424 http://www.europeana1914–1918.eu/en/contributions/17242 accessed 7 October 2016.

425 Pte F. Russell, in MacDonald, *Somme*, p. 180.

426 Smith, *Four Years on the Western Front*, p. 166.

427 *Birmingham Mail*, 4 August 1915, p. 6.

428 May 1916, quoted in Wadsworth, *Letters from the Trenches*, p. 31.

429 C. W. Langley, ('Wagger'), *Battery Flashes*, (London: John Murray, 1916), p. 101.

430 Brophy and Partridge, *The Long Trail*, 1969 edn, p. 49.

431 Burrage, *War is War*, 1930 edn, p. 78.

432 Graves, *Goodbye to All That*, 1960 edn, p. 97.

433 Edmonds, *A Subaltern's War*, p. 49.

434 Williamson, *The Patriot's Progress*, pp. 132, 158, 161.

435 Smith, *Four Years on the Western Front*, pp. 16, 42, 48.

436 Barker, *Agony's Anguish*, p. 28.

437 Coppard, *With a Machine Gun to Cambrai*, 1986 edn, p. 93.

438 Pte J. Hodson, 'The "Sure-To-Be-Hit" Feeling' in Treves, *Made in the Trenches*, p. 182.

439 MacDonald, *Voices and Images*, 1991 edn, p. 131.

440 Rifleman N. Hains, letter quoted in *Hull Daily Mail*, 2 September 1916, p. 4.

441 *Birmingham Gazette* 29 December 1914, p. 4.

442 *Burnley News* 26 October 1918, p. 7; *Birmingham Gazette* 25 October 1916, p. 4.

443 Williamson, *The Patriot's Progress*, p. 169.

444 Pte L. Sanders, quoted in Van Emden, *Tommy's War*, p. 118.

445 A soldier's letter in the *Portsmouth Evening News*, 22 October 1915, p. 3.

446 A. West, *The Diary of a Dead Officer*, (Llandogo, Monmouth: Old Stile Press, 1919), 7 December 1915.

447 *Yorkshire Evening Post*, 14 July 1915, p. 3.

448 Cpl F. Gillman, in *Birmingham Daily Gazette*, 15 May 1915, p. 4.

449 E. Liveing, *Attack: an infantry subaltern's impressions*, (New York: The Macmillan Company, 1918), p. 53.

450 Hewett, *A Scholar's Letters*, p. 43; *Evening Dispatch*, 4 September 1915, p. 6.

451 Spicer, *Letters from France,* 15 October 1915; Graves, *Goodbye to All That*, 1960 edn, p. 98.

452 Hewett, *A Scholar's Letters*, p. 43.

453 Nobbs, *Englishman, Kamerad*, p. 101.

454 *Evening Dispatch*, 4 September 1915, p. 6.

455 Letter from Pte Mabbott in the *Nottingham Evening Post*, 19 May 1915, p. 5.

456 *Marlborough Express*, 21 October 1916, p. 2.

457 Van Emden, *Tommy's War*, p. 118.

458 Smith, *Four Years on the Western Front*, p. 48.

459 E. P. Williams, diary, 25 April 1915, in M. Wright, *Shattered Glory: the New Zealand experience at Gallipoli and the Western Front*, (Auckland, New Zealand: Penguin, 2010), p. 20.

460 *9th Royal Scots, Diary*, 23 April 1915, p. 17.

461 9th *Royal Scots, Diary*, 1915, pp. 61–2; *Kirkintilloch Herald*, 31 July 1918, p. 8.

462 *Birmingham Daily Gazette*, 17 July 1916, p. 1.

463 *Kirkintilloch Herald*, 31 July 1918, p. 8.

464 Manwaring, *If We Return*, p. 123.

465 *Daily Record*, 20 April 1915, p. 6.

466 Spicer, *Letters from France*, 15 March 1916.

467 Pte L. Sanders, quoted in Van Emden, *Tommy's War*, p. 118.

468 *The Gasper*, 8 January 1916, p. 6.

469 *The Champion* (boys' comic), (London, England, 1922–), 9 May 1925, which terms a machine-gun as 'Stuttering Lizzie'.

470 Pte H. Baverstock, in MacDonald, *Voices and Images*, 1991 edn, p. 170.

471 Spicer, *Letters from France*, 5 July 1916.

472 Williamson, *The Patriot's Progress*, p. 169.

473 Cpl T. North, in MacDonald, *Voices and Images*, 1991 edn, p. 32.

474 *Letters to Madeleine*, 2010, 6 Oct 1915, p. 257.

475 Vansittart, *John Masefield's Letters*, 7 March 1915, p. 57.

476 H. Grimm, *Schlump*, trans. J. Bulloch, (London: Vintage Books, [1928] 2014), 2014 edn, p. 100.

477 Smith, *Four Years on the Western Front*, p. 48.

478 Williamson, *The Patriot's Progress*, p. 169.

479 Ibid., p. 113.

480 *Perthshire Advertiser*, 18 April 1917, p. 4.

481 A. Caseby, *Diary*, Private papers held by Imperial War Museum.

482 Edmonds, *A Subaltern's War*, p. 44.

483 On Active Service, 29 May 1915, author's collection.

484 Pte H. Baverstock, in MacDonald, *Voices and Images*, 1991 edn, p. 170.

485 Sgt G. Dunn, *Liverpool Echo*, 20 October 1914, p. 5.

486 *9th Royal Scots, Diary*, p. 54; 2nd Lt A. Stanley-Clarke, quoted in Doyle and Schäfer, *Fritz and Tommy*, p. 149.

487 Douie, *The Weary Road*, p. 121.

488 *Daily Mirror*, 22 February 1916, p. 10.

489 Barker, *Agony's Anguish*, p. 39.

490 *Hull Daily Mail*, 4 August 1915, p. 2.

491 http://www.pbenyon.plus.com/Scapa_Diary/Jul_17.html accessed 12 October 2016.

492 *Hull Daily Mail*, 11 November 1914, p. 1.

493 Edmonds, *A Subaltern's War*, pp. 59–60.

494 Holmes, *Tommy*, p. 423.

495 E. Edwards, in *Yorkshire Evening Post*, 14 July 1915, p. 3.

496 9th *Royal Scots, Diary*, 23 April 1915.

497 In Van Emden, *Tommy's War*, p. 132.

498 *Derry Journal*, 25 September 1918, p. 2.

499 Philip Gibbs in the *Hull Daily Mail*, 12 July 1916, p. 1.

500 *The Times*, 7 September 1917, p. 7.

501 Ibid., p. 7 ('a private in France').

502 Spicer, *Letters from France*, 5 July 1916.

503 Jones, *In Parenthesis*, 1969 edn, p. 47.

504 Pte H. Baverstock, in MacDonald, *Voices and Images*, 1991 edn, p. 170.

505 Smith, *Four Years on the Western Front*, p. 48.

506 In Noakes, *Voices of Silence*, p. 206.

507 Lighter, *Slang of the AEF*, p. 88; Boyd Cable, *The Athenaeum*, 18 July 1919, p. 632.

508 Merrill, *A College Man in Khaki*, p. 227.

509 Downing, *Digger Dialects*, p. 34.

510 Williamson, *The Patriot's Progress*, p. 64.

511 Douie, *The Weary Road*, p. 95.

512 Pte L. Sanders, quoted in Van Emden, *Tommy's War*, p. 118.

513 MacDonald, *Voices and Images*, 1991 edn, p. 189.

514 *The Somme Times*, 31 July 1916.

515 Grimm, *Schlump*, 2014 edn, p. 108.

516 Brophy and Partridge, *The Long Trail,* 1969 edn, p. 73.

517 *Hull Daily Mail*, 9 September 1914, p. 1.

518 Douie, *The Weary Road*, pp. 156–7.

519 D. Walker, *Lost Generation*, p. 18.

520 Smith, *Four Years on the Western Front*, p. 91.

521 Tytler, *With Lancashire Lads*, p. 262.

522 Edmonds, *A Subaltern's War*, p. 58.

523 Lighter, *Slang of the AEF*, p. 118.

524 Grimm, *Schlump*, 2014 edn, p. 73 – 'und die Splitter fauchten auseinander wie tausend Katzen, und manche klagten und heulten wie verflughte Geister'.

525 *The Times*, 29 May 1916, p. 9.

526 Langley, *Battery Flashes*, 1916, p. 168; Lighter, *Slang of the AEF*, p. 113.

527 *Daily Telegraph*, 25 January 1916, p. 3.

528 *Daily Telegraph*, 11 July 1916, p. 5.

529 Brophy and Partridge, *The Long Trail,* 1969 edn, p. 157.

530 D. Walker, *Lost Generation*, p. 26.

531 *Hull Daily Mail*, 25 May 1915, p. 4.

532 F. Hitchcock, *Stand To: a diary of the trenches 1914–1918*, (London: Hurst & Blackett, 1937).

533 Lighter, *Slang of the AEF*, p. 109.

534 Ibid., p. 54.

535 Pte L. Onions, 24 October 1916, p. 4.

536 Pte S. McFarlane, *Burnley Express*, 11 December 1915, p. 4.

537 Postcard, On Active Service, 29 May 1915, author's collection.

538 Moynihan, *A Place Called Armageddon*, letter home, 2 October 1914.

539 Kilpatrick, *Atkins at War*, p. 50.

540 *German Atrocities in France*, translation of the official report of the French Commission, published by the *Daily Chronicle*, 1915, pp. 4, 10, 13, 19.

541 2nd Lt A. Stanley-Clarke, quoted in Doyle and Schäfer, *Fritz and Tommy*, p. 118.

542 *Diary*, 12 October 1916, http://www.firstworldwar.com/diaries/rlm1.htm accessed 22 December 2016.

543 Dawson, *Living Bayonets*, p. 101.

544 Spicer, *Letters from France,* 11 February 1918.

545 See E. Jones, 'The psychology of killing', *Journal of Contemporary History*, Vol. 41, No. 2, (London, 2006), p. 244.

546 A. Cornet-Auquier, *A Soldier Unafraid*, trans. E. Stanton (Boston: Little, Brown & Co., 1918), p. 78.

547 Vansittart, *John Masefield's Letters*, 17 May 1917.

548 Douie, *The Weary Road*, p. 129.

549 *Diary*, Capt C. May, 6 April 1916 http://www.express.co.uk/news/world-war-1/489831/Charlie-May-s-War-Secret-diary-WWI-officer accessed 27 December 2016.

550 W. Wood, *In the Line of Battle*, (London: Chapman & Hall, 1916), p. 38.

551 Spicer, *Letters from France,* 20 February 1916.

552 West, *The Diary of a Dead Officer*, 26 February 1916.

553 E. H. Shears, *Active Service Diary*, (Liverpool: Henry Young & Sons Ltd, 1919), 18 February 1917.

554 Quoted in Wadsworth, *Letters from the Trenches*, p. 147.

555 *Manchester Guardian*, 4 January 1919, p. 6.

556 Brophy and Partridge, *The Long Trail,* 1969 edn, p. 23.

557 Burrage, *War is War*, 2010 edn, p. 144.

558 In E. Weekley, *An Etymological Dictionary of Modern English*, (1 New York: Dover Publications, 1921), col. 783, 'Archie talking to Jerry' (*Daily Chronicle*, 13 July 1918).

559 West, *The Diary of a Dead Officer*, 29 September 1916.

560 Smith, *Four Years on the Western Front*, pp. 159, 166.

561 Jones, *In Parenthesis*, 1969 edn, p. 143; A. Bluett, *With Our Army In Palestine*, (London: Andrew Melrose, 1919), p. 248.

562 *The Gasper*, 28 February 1916; Edmonds, *A Subaltern's War*, p. 137; if its effect lasted it was a 'souvenir', Sgt F. Woodhouse, quoted in Wadsworth, *Letters from the Trenches*, p. 32.

563 Spicer, *Letters from France*, 30 August 1916.

564 Quoted in MacDonald, *Voices and Images*, 1991 edn, p. 170.

565 F. Sandes, *Autobiography of a Woman Soldier*, (London: H. F. & G. Witherby, 1927), p. 20.

566 Duffin, *Diaries*, p. 96.

567 *Diary Of A Nursing Sister*, 1915 edn, p. 156.

568 Partridge, 'Frank Honywood', p. 323.

569 William Henry Early, https://www.theguardian.com/world/2016/aug/11/shakespeare-hut-london-first-world-war accessed 20 August 2016.

570 *Yorkshire Evening Post*, 21 July 1917, p. 5.

571 P. Gibbs, *The Soul of the War*, (London: William Heinemann, 1916), p. 357.

572 Partridge, *Words! Words! Words!*, p. 195.

573 Quoted in Doyle and Schäfer, *Fritz and Tommy*, p. 237.

574 *Yorkshire Evening Post*, 17 August 1917, p. 4.

575 E. Stride, quoted in Wadsworth, *Letters from the Trenches*, p. 101.

576 *Portsmouth Evening News*, 19 March 1915, p. 3.

577 J. Beck, *A Diary of Armistice Days*, (Philadelphia: printed for private circulation, 1923), p. 43.

578 D. Walker, *Lost Generation*, p. 33.

579 *B.E.F. Times*, 1 December 1916.

580 *The War Illustrated*, 1 April 1916, p. xxviii.

581 Lighter, *Slang of the AEF*, pp. 20, 24, 66, 72.

582 *The Great War Interviews*, recorded 1964, [BBC televison programme], http://www.bbc.co.uk/iplayer/group/p01tbj6p accessed 7 February 2017.

583 Pte R. Price, quoted in Doyle and Schäfer, *Fritz and Tommy*, p. 255.

584 Partridge, *Words! Words! Words!*, p. 151.

585 W. Blackledge, *The Legion of Marching Madmen*, (London: Sampson Low, Marston & Co., 1936), p. 44.

586 Fraser and Gibbons.

587 Brophy and Partridge, *The Long Trail*, 1969 edn, p. 126.

588 Pte S. Carson, quoted in MacDonald, *Voices and Images*, 1991 edn, p. 106.

589 MacDonald, *Voices and Images*, 1991 edn, p. 107.

590 Smith, *Four Years on the Western Front*, p. 155.

591 Caption to *The Battle of the Somme*, [film], G. H. Malins and J. McDowell, British Topical Committee for War Films, 1916.

592 MacDonald, *Under the French Flag*, p. 167.

593 Tytler, *With Lancashire Lads*, p. 132.

594 E. M. Remarque, *All Quiet on the Western Front*, trans. A. W. Wheen, (London: Putnam, 1929), p. 236.

595 Ibid., p. 115.

596 *Yorkshire Evening Post*, 21 July 1917, p. 5.

597 *Huddersfield Daily Examiner*, 29 September 1914, p. 3.

598 Dawson, *Living Bayonets*, p. 183.

599 *War Budget*, 5 September 1914, p. 14.

600 Rees, *In the Trenches,* [sound dramatisation].

601 Surgeon-Major Cowie, *War Diary of the 1st Life Guards. First year, 1914–1915,* (England), 31 October 1914.

602 Coppard, *With a Machine Gun to Cambrai*, 1986 edn, p. 26.

603 Wright, *Shattered Glory*, 2010, p. 205.

604 Bernard Livermore, quoted in Holmes, *Tommy*, p. 342.

605 Graves, *Goodbye to All That*, 1960 edn, p. 220.

606 De Loghe, *The Straits Impregnable*, p. 160.

607 Quoted in Palmer and Wallis, *A War in Words*, 2004 edn, p. 127.

608 J. Easton, 'Broadchalk, a chronicle', in *Three Personal Records of the War*, (London: Scholartis, 1929), p. 248.

609 Lighter, *Slang of the AEF*, p. 107.

610 Lt Col R. Fielding, quoted in Doyle and Schäfer, *Fritz and Tommy*, p. 229.

611 http://www.pollingerltd.com/bookshop/martin_body/2nd-devons-somme.pdf accessed 20 March 2015.

612 Herbert, *Mons, Anzac, and Kut*, 1919 edn, p. 162.

613 MacDonald, *Voices and Images*, 1991 edn, p. 75.

614 Quoted in Vansittart, *John Masefield's Letters*, 28 March 1915, p. 78.

615 MacDonald, *They Called it Passchendaele*, pp. 100, 108, 118, 123.

616 Holmes, *Tommy*, pp. 151, 265.

617 MacDonald, *Voices and Images*, 1991 edn, p. 170.

618 Pte J. Bowles, quoted in MacDonald, *Voices and Images*, 1991 edn, p. 181.

619 *9th Royal Scots, Diary*, p. 56.

620 Douie, *The Weary Road*, p. 105.

621 Quoted in Vansittart, *John Masefield's Letters*, 18 March(?) 1915, p. 70.

622 Graves, *Goodbye to All That*, 1960 edn, p. 227, though of course he survived.

623 Duffin, *Diaries*, p. 101.

624 Quoted in MacDonald, *Voices and Images*, 1991 edn, p. 105.

625 Quoted in Vansittart, *John Masefield's Letters*, 27 March 1915.

626 Smith, *Four Years on the Western Front*, p. 170.

627 Coppard, *With a Machine Gun to Cambrai*, 1986 edn, p. 26.

628 Douie, *The Weary Road*, p. 200; Douie describes this as 'in the parlance of the trenches'.

629 Lighter, *Slang of the AEF*, p. 82.

630 *Portsmouth Evening News*, 19 March 1915, p. 3.

631 Gill and Dallas, *Unknown Army*, p. 36.

632 Holmes, *Tommy*, pp. 400, 402.

633 From May 1915, 'a British officer' quoted in Wadsworth, *Letters from the Trenches*, p. 135.

634 Cpl A. Howard, quoted in Doyle and Schäfer, *Fritz and Tommy*, p. 229.

635 *Diary*, Capt C. May, 6 April 1916 http://www.express.co.uk/news/world-war-1/489831/Charlie-May-s-War-Secret-diary-WWI-officer accessed 27 December 2016.

636 *A War Nurse's Diary*, 1918 edn, p. 56.

637 A. Smith, *The Second Battlefield: women, modernism and the First World War*, (Manchester: Manchester Unviersity Press, 2000), p. 33.

638 June 1917, officer's letter quoted in Wadsworth, *Letters from the Trenches*, p. 122.

639 Quoted in Winter and Baggett, *1914–18*, p. 169.

640 Ernest West, quoted in Wadsworth, *Letters from the Trenches*, p. 51.

641 Sgt Fairclough, quoted in ibid., p. 17.

642 Stanley Goodhead, quoted in ibid., p. 37.

643 Brophy and Partridge, *The Long Trail*, 1969 edn.

644 Sgt Fairclough, quoted in Wadsworth, *Letters from the Trenches*, p. 18.

645 Sapper George Clayton, quoted in Arthur, *We Will Remember Them*, p. 173.

646 *Public Opinion*, 8 September 1916, p. 224; E. La Motte, *The Backwash of War: the human wreckage of the battlefield as witnessed by an American hospital nurse*, 1916; Stereoview photograph V18837, 'Human Wreckage in No Man's Land', Keystone View Company, c.1917.

647 Burrage, *War is War*, 2010 edn, p. 81.

648 Holmes, *A Yankee in the Trenches*, p. 162.

649 Moran, *Anatomy of Courage*, 1987 edn, p. 62.

650 Graves, *Goodbye to All That*, 1960 edn, p. 269.

651 Todman, *The Great War*, p. 20.

652 L. Napper, 'The Battle of the Somme (1916)', in M. Hammond and M. Williams (eds), *British Silent Cinema and the Great War*, (New York: Palgrave Macmillan, 2011), p. 35.

653 Edwin Wood, quoted in Wadsworth, *Letters from the Trenches*, p. xiii.

654 Tytler, *With Lancashire Lads*, p. 49.

655 Edmonds, *A Subaltern's War*, p. 55.

656 Lt J. Glubb, quoted in Holmes, *Tommy*, p. 452.

657 J. Tarbot, *Jerry Tarbot, the Living Unknown Soldier*, (New York: Tyler Publishing Co., 1928), p. 58.

658 Vansittart, *John Masefield's Letters*, 29 March 1917.

659 H. Stewart, *From Mons to Loos*, (Edinburgh; London: W. Blackwood and Sons, 1916), p. 117.

660 *Lancashire Evening Post*, 3 March 1917, p. 2.

661 Western Gazette, 20 October 1916, p. 10.

662 Spencer, *War Letters*, 22 December 1914.

663 Vivian Stevens, letter On Active Service, 3 April 1916, author's collection.

664 Kilpatrick, *Atkins at War*, p. 53.

665 Capt O. Flowers, quoted in MacDonald, *Somme*, p. 220.

666 E. W. Perogoe (NCO), *Hastings and St Leonards Observer*, 10 July 1915, p. 6.

667 D. Fallon, *The Big Fight*, (London: Cassell & Co., 1918), p. 148.

668 Vansittart, *John Masefield's Letters*, 12 March 1915, p. 65.

669 Douie, *The Weary Road*, p. 128.

670 Cpl F. Kelling, quoted in Van Emden, *Tommy's War*, p. 159.

671 Cpl W. Hartley, quoted in the *Sheffield Evening Telegraph*, 18 August 1915, p. 3.

672 R. Tobin, *The Great War Interviews*, recorded 1963–4, [BBC television programme], http://www.bbc.co.uk/iplayer/group/p01tbj6p accessed 7 February 2017.

673 Cpl G. Mitchell, quoted in Palmer and Wallis, *A War in Words*, 2004 edn, pp. 128–9.

674 Omissi, *Indian Voices*, letter, unnamed wounded Punjabi Rajput soldier, 29 January 1915.

675 *Punch*, 24 January 1917, p. ix.

676 *Lancashire Evening Post*, 3 March 1917, p. 2.

677 Brophy and Partridge, *The Long Trail*, 1969 edn.

678 A. J. Dawson, *A "Temporary Gentleman" in France*, (London: Cassell, 1917), p. 173–4.

679 Graham, *A Private in the Guards*, p. 8.

680 'Cheeriboy's Warisms', in *Derbyshire Advertiser and Journal*, 20 September 1918, p. 5.

681 *The Gasper*, 8 January 1916, p. 2.

682 *Grantham Journal*, 2 November 1918, p. 7.

683 *Lancashire Daily Post*, 7 March 1919, p. 5.

684 *Western Times*, 7 March 1919, p. 12.

685 *Lancashire Daily Post*, 8 March 1919, p. 2.

686 *Essex Newsman*, 8 March 1919, p. 1.

687 *Derby Daily Telegraph*, 16 April 1919, p. 3.

688 *Yorkshire Evening Post*, 6 November 1918, p. 4.

689 *Sunderland Daily Echo*, 17 April 1920, p. 6.

690 *Manchester Guardian*, 13 February 1930.

691 Letter to *The Times*, 11 March 1982.

692 J. Winter, *The Experience of World War I*, (Oxford: Equinox, 1988), p. 159.

693 Todman, *The Great War*, pp. 336, 114.

694 Amalgamated Engineering Union quoted in B. Waites, *A Class Society at War*, (Leamington Spa: Berg, 1987), p. 72.

695 Ibid., p. 73.

696 *War-time Tips*, p. 44.

697 Burrage, *War is War*, 2010 edn, p. 96.

698 Graves, *Goodbye to All That*, 1960 edn, p. 161.

699 Holmes, *Tommy*, p. 414.

700 Driver Frank Woodhouse, May 1916, quoted in Wadsworth, *Letters from the Trenches*, p. 27.

701 Tobin, *The Great War Interviews*.

702 Rees, *In the Trenches*, [sound dramatisation].

703 Postcard, 18 August 1918, author's collection.

704 Moran, *Anatomy of Courage*, 1987 edn, p. 75.

705 Quoted in Holmes, *Tommy*, p. 336.

706 MacDonald, *Voices and Images*, 1991 edn, p. 183.

707 Hay, *The First Hundred Thousand*, p. 36.

708 Lighter, *Slang of the AEF*, p. 64.

709 General Routine Order No. 1796, Gill and Dallas, *Unknown Army*, p. 42.

710 MacDonald, *Voices and Images*, 1991 edn, p. 183.

711 Graves, *Goodbye to All That*, 1960 edn, p. 250.

712 Edmonds, *A Subaltern's War*, pp. 41, 63, 133.

713 Moran, *Anatomy of Courage*, 1987 edn, pp. 127, 139.

714 Postcard, On Active Service, 26 July 1917, author's collection.

715 E. M. Arthur Rhind, 25 April 1915, in Wright, *Shattered Glory*.

716 M. Brown, diary, 9 August 1915 in Smith, *The Second Battlefield*, p. 37.

717 P. Nash, letter, 16 November 1917, quoted in D. F. Jenkins, *Paul Nash, The Elements*, (London: Scala, 2010), p. 58.

718 Omissi, *Indian Voices*, letter, Dilawar Chand, 28 December 1917.

719 J. H. Benn, quoted in Doyle and Schäfer, *Fritz and Tommy*, p. 215.

720 Cpl H. White, letter in *The Boot and Shoe Retailer*, 4 December 1914, p. 30.

721 Omissi, *Indian Voices*, letter, Luddar Singh, 1 July 1915.

722 *Birmingham Mail*, 15 January 1915, p. 3.

723 *Birmingham Daily Post*, 3 February 1915, p. 6.

724 *Derry Journal*, 9 July 1915, p. 2.

725 *Cheshire Observer*, 16 October 1915, p. 8.

726 *Hull Daily Mail*, 21 May 1915, p. 3.

727 *The Observer*, 21 January 1917, p. 6.

728 Ibid., 15 November 1914, p. 8.

729 *Manchester Guardian*, 19 November 1914, p. 12.

730 Marwick, *The Deluge*, 1991 edn, p. 175.

731 J. Hendrie, n.d., *Letters of a Durisdeer Soldier*, (Edinburgh: 1917), p. 84, quoted in Marwick, *The Deluge*, p. 189.

732 L. Housman, *War Letters of Fallen Englishmen*, (London: Victor Gollancz, 1930), p. 30, quoted in Marwick, *The Deluge*, 1991 edn, p. 189.

733 *The Great War Interviews*, recorded 1964, [BBC television programme], http://www.bbc.co.uk/iplayer/group/p01tbj6p accessed 7 February 2017.

734 Burrage, *War is War*, 2010 edn, p. 67.

735 *Manchester Guardian*, 17 September 1917, p. 3.

736 Graves, *Goodbye to All That*, 1960 edn, p. 269.

737 Quoted in Vansittart, *John Masefield's Letters*, p. 294.

738 Field Marshall D. Haig, quoted in Doyle and Schäfer, *Fritz and Tommy*, p. 222.

739 Duffin, *Diaries*, p. 100.

740 Fussell, *The Great War*, 1977 edn, p. 170.

3 Us and Them

1   E. Hobsbawm, *Nations and Nationalism since 1780*, (Cambridge: Cambridge University Press, 1992), p. 133.

2   O. Roynette, in C. Declercq and J. Walker, *Languages and the First World War: representation and memory*, (London: Palgrave Macmillan, 2016), pp. 22–3.

3   O. Leroy, *A Glossary of French Slang*, (London: Harrap & Co., [1922] 1924), 1924 edn, p. 5.

4   Published by the National Security League, NY City, 1918.

5   Speech given 20 November 1918.

6   *The War Illustrated Album De Luxe*, 1915, Vol. 1, p. 57.

7   *Yorkshire Evening Post*, 19 August 1914, p. 2.

8   T. Scheer, 'Habsburg languages at war: "The linguistic confusion at the Tower of Babel couldn't have been much worse"', in Walker and Declercq, *Languages and the First World War: communicating*, pp. 62–78.

9   *Daily Express*, 10 February 1915, p. 5.

10 Fogarty in Walker and Declercq, *Languages and the First World War: communicating*, pp. 44–61.

11 *A War Nurse's Diary*, 1918, p. 57.

12 *The Story of an Epic Pilgrimage*, p. 103.

13 *Picture Fun*, 25 December 1914, pp. 4–5.

14 De L'Isle, *Leaves from a V.A.D.'s Diary*, p. 35.

15 Lighter, *Slang of the AEF*, p. 8.

16 *Yorkshire Post and Leeds Intelligencer*, 9 March 1918, p. 7.

17 Ibid., 7 August 1914, p. 3.

18 Graves, *Goodbye to All That*, 1960 edn, p. 193.

19 *Daily Record* (Lanarkshire), 23 August 1915, p. 4.

20 *Hull Daily Mail*, 10 June 1915, p. 4.

21 *Newcastle Journal*, 2 February 1917, p. 5.

22 *Dublin Daily Express*, 31 August 1917, p. 3.

23 *Dundee Evening Telegraph*, 7 November 1917, p. 1.

24 *Aberdeen Evening Express*, 27 May 1918, p. 3.

25 *Yorkshire Evening Post*, 9 April 1918, p. 4.

26 *The Times*, 2 September 1914, p. 7.

27 *Liverpool Daily Post*, 10 February 1916, p. 8.

28 E. Armstrong, *The Crisis of Quebec*, (New York: Columia University Press, 1937), Foreword, p. ix.

29 Ibid., pp. 90, 91.

30 *Peterhead Sentinel*, 25 January 1902, p. 5.

31 *Birmingham Daily Post*, 30 September 1914, p. 8.

32 *Derry Journal*, 5 August 1914, p. 6.

33 *Sunderland Daily Echo*, 10 May 1902, p. 3.

34 *Western Times*, 15 June 1901, p. 2.

35 *South Wales Daily News*, 6 June 1900, p. 4.

36 *Bexhill on Sea Observer*, 24 October 1908, p. 16.

37 *Manchester Courier*, 1 December 1906, p. 10.

38 *Dundee Courier*, 25 June 1914, p. 4.

39 *Rochdale Observer*, 26 September 1914, p. 4.

40 *Coventry Evening Telegraph*, 5 September 1914, p. 2.

41 *Manchester Courier*, 1 September 1914, p. 4, 17 August 1914, p. 4.

42 *Newcastle Journal*, 30 September 1914, p. 8.

43 *Huddersfield Daily Examiner*, 11 November 1918, p. 2.

44 Speech given by King George V, 20 Nov 1918.

45 Omissi, *Indian Voices*, letter, J. N. Godbole, 18 March 1915.

46 Ibid., letter, Isat Singh, 1 May 1915.

47 P. Stanley '"He was black, he was a White man, and a dinkum Aussie": race and empire in revisiting the Anzac legend', in Das, *Race, Empire*, p. 220.

48 Omissi, *Indian Voices*, letter, Dunjibhoy Chinoy, mid-July 1915.

49 *Ypres Times*, July 1922, p. 106.

50 *The Times*, 11 September 1914, p. 7.

51 *Vivid War Weekly*, 16 October 1915, p. 167.

52 R. Stumpf, *War, Mutiny and Revolution in the German Navy*, trans. D. Horn, (New Brunswick: Rutgers University Press, 1967), p. 51.

53 *Yorkshire Post and Leeds Intelligencer*, 8 October 1917, p. 5.

54 Jones, 'Imperial captivities', p. 178.

55 See William Barnes for the nineteenth-century move to substitute Latin-based words with Old English-based words.

56 C. Dawson, letter, 14 February 1912, quoted in M. Russell, *Piltdown Man*, (Stroud: Tempus, 2003), p. 149.

57 *The Times* 5 September 1914, p. 10.

58 Ibid., 14 September 1914, p. 3.

59 C. Sarolea, *How Belgium Saved Europe*, (London: William Heinemann, 1915), p. 196.

60 MacDonald, *Somme*, p. 185.

61 *The Times*, 3 September 1914, p. 8.

62 Manwaring, *If we Return*, p. 23.

63 *Melbourne Bulletin*, 6 April 1916, p. 7.

64 J. Beck, (US Solicitor General), speech, Savoy Hotel, 28 November 1918, *Diary of Armistice Days*, p. 38.

65 Le Naour J-Y, 1998, 'Les désillusions de la libération d'après le contrôle postal civile de Lille (octobre 1918–mars 1919)', in *Revue du Nord*, tome LXXX, Vol. 325 (April–June), quoted in G. Bowd, 'From Hatred to Hybridization: the German language in occupied France, 1914–1918', in Walker and Declercq, *Languages and the First World War: communicating*, p. 204.

66 C. Calwell, *Experiences of a Dug-Out 1914–1918*, (Constable & Co., 1920), p. 20.

67 In Vansittart, *John Masefield's Letters*, 2 April 1915.

68 In Treves, *Made in the Trenches*, p. 158.

69 *The Story of an Epic Pilgrimage*, p. 65.

70 *Evening Despatch*, 12 October 1915, p. 3.

71 S. Hedin, *With the German Armies in the West*, trans. De Walterstorff, (London: John Lane, 1915), p. 30.

72 *Exeter and Plymouth Gazette*, 16 January 1918, p. 2.

73 *Folkestone Herald*, 2 May 1917, p. 7.

74 *Sunday Post* (Lanarkshire), 1 December 1918, p. 2.

75 *Derby Daily Telegraph*, 30 December 1918, p. 3.

76 *Western Daily Press*, 17 December 1918, p. 4.

77 *The Times*, 7 September 1914, p. 9.

78 *Pan-Germanism*, R. Usher, in advertisement in *The Times*, 15 September 1914, p. 12.

79 Stumpf, *War, Mutiny and Revolution*, 1967 edn, p. 106.

80 Quoted in MacDonald, *Voices and Images*, 1991 edn, p. 52.

81 *Newcastle Journal*, 10 June 1915, p. 2. The suggestion that they were 'taking in one another's washing' is hopefully a journalistic metaphor.

82 *Yorkshire Post*, 24 July 1915, p. 8.

83 J. Dunn, *The War the Infantry Knew*, (London: Abacus, [1938] 2004), p. 113.

84 *Illustrated London News*, 9 January 1915, p. 50.

85 Lord Northcliffe, (see under Harmsworth), *At The War*, (London: Hodder & Stoughton, 1916), p. 198.

86 Har Dayal, *Forty-four months in Germany and Turkey*, (London: P. S. King & Son, 1920), p. 29. Germans were also 'the unspeakable Hun', *John Bull*, 10 June 1916, p. 18.

87 Hamilton, *Gallipoli Diary*, Vol. 2, 1918, pp. 43, 140, 252.

88 Har Dayal, *Forty-four months*, pp. 31, 32.

89 Hamilton, *Gallipoli Diary*, Vol. 2, 1918, p. 258.

90 J. H. Brittain, quoted in *Rochdale Observer*, 4 December 1915, p. 7.

91 *The Times*, 16 September 19, p. 9.

92 *Daily Gazette for Middlesbrough*, 23 September 1915, p. 5.

93 R. Long, *Colours of War*, (New York: Charles Scribner's Sons, 1915), p. 152.

94 *Dundee Evening Telegraph*, 9 October 1912, p. 1.

95 'A Scottish soldier', letter to *Berwickshire News and General Advertiser*, 23 May 1916, p. 4.

96 *Sussex Agricultural Express*, 20 April 1917, p. 4.

97 *Dundee Evening Telegraph*, 25 October 1918, p. 5.

98 *Banbury Advertiser*, 6 May 1915, p. 5.

99 Mottram, *A Personal Record*, p. 102.

100 '*La guerre actuelle est la lutte des Welsches contre les Boches.*' Dauzat, *L'Argot de la Guerre,* 1918 edn, p. 59. For Dauzat 'Boche' implied 'not just a people, a race, with the pejorative nuance with which the mob views "the other", enemy or not'.

101 J. Grimm and W. Grimm, *Deutsches Wörterbuch* (Leipzig: Verlag von S. Hirzel, 1922).

102 Reprinted in *Huddersfield Daily Examiner*, 26 June 1916.

103 In J. Röhl, *Wilhelm II: into the abyss of war and exile 1900–1941*, (Cambridge: Cambridge University Press, 2014), p. 933.

104 Ibid., p. 921.

105 In Röhl, *Wilhelm II: into the abyss*, p. 922.

106 Stumpf, *War, Mutiny and Revolution*, 1967 edn, p. 263.

107 C. Koller, 'Representing Otherness: African, Indian, and European soldiers' letters and memoirs', in Das, *Race, Empire*, p. 129.

108 In Röhl, *Wilhelm II: into the abyss*, p. 1129.

109 From the work of Cesare Lombroso and Carl Mittermaier.

110 MacDonald, *Under the French Flag*, 1917, p. 157.

111 Fraser and Gibbons.

112 *Yorkshire Post*, 31 May 1917, p. 4.

113 *Chester Chronicle*, 25 December 1915, p. 2.

114 *Sevenoaks Chronicle*, 7 August 1914, p. 5.

115 Northcliffe, *At the War*, p. 198.

116 B. Millman, *Polarity, Patriotism and Dissent in Great War Canada, 1914–19*, (Toronto; Buffalo: University of Toronto Press, 2016), p. 53.

117 *Evening Dispatch*, 22 August 1917, p. 4.

118 *In the Hands of the Huns*, p. 12.

119 Wright, *Shattered Glory*, p. 20.

120 Duffin, *Diaries*, p. 94.

121 *The Kit-bag*, August 1918, p. 63.

122 *Dundee Courier*, 24 October 1919, p. 5.

123 *Weekly Despatch*, 17 January 1915, p. 1.

124 G. Yerta, *Six Women and the Invasion*, (London: Macmillan & Co., 1917), p. 106.

125 Herbert, *Mons, Anzac, and Kut*, 1919 edn, p. 120.

126 *Yorkshire Post and Leeds Intelligencer*, 19 May 1915, p. 5.

127 *Ruhleben Camp Magazine*, August 1916, p. 22.

128 *War Budget*, 27 September 1914, p. 27.

129 Robert Houston, MP, http://hansard.millbanksystems.com/commons/1916/oct/11/statement-by-prime-minister accessed 7 February 2017.

130 23 September 1916, p. 6.

131 British Newspaper Archive search, 29 October 2016, http://www.britishnewspaperarchive.co.uk/search/results/1916–01–01/1916–12–31?basicsearch=negro&somesearch=negro&exactsearch=false&sortorder=score&page=0.

132 *Gloucestershire Echo*, 20 September 1915, p. 4.

133 *Nottingham Evening Post*, 19 December 1914, p. 1.

134 See concerns expressed by R. Seton-Watson, reported in *Diss Express*, 7 April 1916, p. 3.

135 R. Munro, *From Darwinism to Kaiserism*, (Glasgow: J. Maclehose & Sons, 1919), p. xii.

136 Ibid., p. 151.

137 Ibid., p. 152.

138 Ibid., e.g. 'No ethical creed, divine or human, homologates the extinction of a smaller race, merely to give greater scope to a larger one', p. 151.

139 *The Times*, 7 September 1914, p. 9.

140 Har Dayal, *Forty-four months*, p. 102.

141 Naoko Shimazu, 'The racial equality proposal at the 1919 Paris Peace Conference', doctoral thesis, Oxford University, 1995.

142 *Daily Express*, 10 February 1915, p. 5.

143 See M. Beyen on Jeroom Leuridan, 'Linguistic syncretism as a mark of ethnic purity? Jeroom Leuridan on language developments among Flemish soldiers during the First World War', in Walker and Declercq, *Languages and the First World War: communicating*, p. 228.

144 *Die Sprache gegenüber den uns feindlichen Staaten kann hart sein. Eine beschimpfende, den Gegner unterschätzende Tonart aber ist kein Zeichen von Kraft. Die Reinheit und Größe der Bewegung, die unser Volk erfaßt hat, erfordert eine würdige Sprache.* "The language we employ towards our enemies may be harsh. However, a tone that insults and underestimates the enemy is not a sign of power. The purity and greatness of the movement that has seized our people requires a dignified language."
Richtlinien der Zensur (censorship guidelines), 1914. (Letter of the Prussian War Ministry to the Army commanders) Übermittlung und Erläuterung der Ergänzungen des Merkblattes für die Presse, 9. November 1914, Bundesarchiv/Militärarchiv, Freiburg i. Br., MA/RMA, Nr. 2049, XVII. 1. Mai 1933, Bd. 1, Abschrift. Supplied by Robin Schäfer.

145 Partridge, *Slang To-day and Yesterday*, 1970, p. 261.

146 Doyle and Schäfer, *Fritz and Tommy*, p. 87.

147 Partridge, *Slang of the British Soldier*, p. 52.

148 Brophy and Partridge, *The Long Trail*, 1969 edn, p. 102.

149 *Notes and Queries*, 29 October 1921, p. 342.

150 *Manchester Guardian*, 17 November 1914, p. 5.

151 In Vansittart, *John Masefield's Letters*, 3 April 1915, 5 April 1915.

152 Dauzat, *L'Argot de la Guerre*, 2007 edn, p. 93.

153 Déchelette, *L'Argot des Poilus*, p. 9.

154 The spelling 'Bosche' was used in a number of newspapers, e.g. *Manchester Courier and Lancashire General Advertiser*, 19 October 1915, p. 8; *Sussex Agricultural Express*, 14 September 1917, p. 1; *Birmingham Daily Post*, 1 August 1918, p. 5; *Derbyshire Advertiser and Journal*, 31 October 1919, p. 8.

155 A. Hunter-Weston, *Private War Diary*, add. MS 48355–48368, British Library, p. 57.

156 E. Hulse, *Letters written from the English Front in France, 1914–15*, (privately printed, 1916), p. 32.

157 Capt F. B. Parker, letter, 18 October 1915, Private papers held by Imperial War Museum.

158 The spelling 'Boche' was used in French.

159 *Illustrated Evening News*, 29 November 1915, p. 2, and 11 September 1915, p. 322, respectively.

160 *Daily Mirror*, 14 July 1915, p. 10.

161 *Sheffield Evening Telegraph*, 25 May 1916, p. 2.

162 Barker, *Agony's Anguish*, p. 56.

163 Hewett, *A Scholar's Letters*, p. 46.

164 Spicer, *Letters from France*, 22 May 1918.

165 Caseby, *Diary*.

166 Hepper, *Great War Diary*, 18 October 1917.

167 Spicer, *Letters from France*, 5 July 1916.

168 R. Cude, *Diary*, Private papers held by Imperial War Museum.

169 Barker, *Agony's Anguish*, p. 68.

170 *The Attack/The Estaminet*, [sound dramatisation].

171 Broadhead, *Diary*.

172 Quigley, *Passchendaele and the Somme*, p. 131.

173 Malins, *How I Filmed the War*, p. 130.

174 *The Times*, 21 September 1914, p. 7.

175 Pte F. Dunn, quoted in Arthur, *We Will Remember Them*, p. 6.

176 *Illustrated London News*, 23 November 1918.

177 *Stars & Stripes*, 15 February 1918, p. 1, quoted in Lighter, *Slang of the AEF*, p. 19.

178 *Manchester Guardian*, 5 December 1918, p. 6.

179 S. Haasmann, *Deutsch–Englischer Soldaten-Sprachführer*, (Leipzig: Verlag Hachmeister & Thal, 1914), p. 3.

180 *Manchester Guardian*, 21 July 1921, p. 9.

181 *New York Times*, 6 January 1923, p. 7.

182 *Daily Mail*, 17 December, 1919, p. 4.

183 *The Times*, 13 May 1919, p. 11.

184 *Nottingham Evening Post*, 27 July 1921, p. 1.

185 *The Ypres Times*, October 1924, p. 97.

186 *The Letters of Rudyard Kipling*, T. Pinney, (ed.), *1931–36*, (Basingstoke: Macmillan, 2004), p. 158.

187 Though in September 1917 Flying Sgt E. A. Boyd was sentenced to a year in internal prison as a PoW for referring to his captors as 'the Hun' – *Manchester Guardian*, 13 December 1918, p. 12.

188 Trench journal of the No. 1 Canadian Field Ambulance.

189 No actual claim was made by Wilhelm II, http://germanhistorydocs.ghi-dc.org/sub_document.cfm?document_id=755 accessed 17 October 2016.

190 *The Pow-Wow*, 9 December 1914.

191 For *Huns Ancient and Modern* see the widely used *Hymns Ancient and Modern*.

192 *John Bull*, 2 January 1915, pp. 2, 14.

193 Ibid., 13 February 1915, p. 16.

194 Ibid., 23 January 1915, p. 3.

195 *John Bull*, 15 September 1917, p. 4, of a vicar who urged his congregation to think about a negotiated end to the war.

196 *Manchester Guardian*, 13 January 1915, p. 5.

197 http://www.bobbrookes.co.uk/DiaryCH2.htm accessed 10 October 2016.

198 R. James, letter, 10 August 1915, National Archives (RAIL 253/516).

199 Spicer, *Letters from France*, 12 February 1916.

200 *Fall In*, (journal of the Duke of Cambridge's Regiment) 15 January 1916, p. 60.

201 Cpt A. A. Emmett in *The Middlesex Chronicle*, 1 September 1917, p. 6.

202 E. Shears, *Active Service Diary*, 17 February 1917.

203 Caseby, *Diary*.

204 Tytler, *With Lancashire Lads*, p. 132.

205 *Manchester Guardian*, 29 November 1918, p. 4.

206 Cpt A. A. Emmett in *The Middlesex Chronicle*, 1 September 1917, p. 6.

207 *Illustrated London News*, 12 September 1914, pp. 5, 6.

208 *Leeds Mercury*, 3 March 1918, p. 2; the German aeroplane the Taube, with fluted wings swept back at the end, was known as 'the bird'.

209 Walker, *Lost Generation*, p. 18.

210 *Huns Ancient and Modern*, (London: Skeffington & Son Ltd, 1918), pp. 12, 13.

211 A. Ponsonby, *The Crank*, (London: Headley, 1916), p. 9 (the Merchant's view).

212 *Vivid War Weekly*, October 1915, pp. 167, 170.

213 *Dundee Courier*, 13 November 1914, p. 2.

214 *Huddersfield Daily Examiner*, 13 November 1914, p. 2.

215 Spicer, *Letters from France*, 4 April 1917.

216 *Manchester Guardian*, 25 November 1918, p. 3.

217 Robert Smillie quoted in the *Manchester Guardian*, 7 December 1918, p. 8.

218 Labour politician Ben Tillett, speech quoted in the *Taunton Courier*, 7 March 1917, p. 4.

219 Though it does not appear in *Slang of the AEF* or *Digger Dialects*.

220 *A War Nurse's Diary*, 1918, p. 66.

221 Brindle, *France and Flanders*, p. 31.

222 Bilbrough, *Diary*, 29 March 1916.

223 *In the Hands of the Huns*.

224 'The cussed Huns have got my gramophone', *Punch*, 15 May 1918.

225 *Manchester Guardian*, 22 January 1919, p. 5.

226 *The Athenaeum*, 12 December 1919, p. 1350.

227 Edmonds, *A Subaltern's War*, p. 79.

228 Ibid., p. 37.

229 *The Comet*, 23 January 1917, p. 2.

230 Broadhead, *Diary*.

231 Manwaring, *If We return*, p. 128.

232 Pte W. H. Harris, *Private papers*, Imperial War Museum, 13 April 1917.

233 Déchelette, *L'argot des Poilus*, p. 104.

234 William Jesse Stanley, Headquarters Co., 150th Field Artillery, 42nd (Rainbow) Div., Grant County, Indiana http://www.wwvets.com/42ndDivision.html accessed 28 October 2016.

235 Quoted in Holmes, *Tommy*, p. 248.

236 I. Hay, *Carrying On: after the first hundred thousand*, (Edinburgh London: William Blackwood and Sons, 1917), p. 288.

237 *Illustrated London News*, 23 February 1918, p. 2.

238 Northcliffe, *At the War*, 1916, p. 146.

239 Broadhead, *Diary*.

240 Rifleman F. Walker, letter, 15 September 1918, author's collection.

241 E. Judge, quoted in Wadsworth, *Letters from the Trenches*, p. 61.

242 Manwaring, *If We Return*, p. 79.

243 *The Gasper*, 8 January 16, p. 7.

244 *Birmingham Daily Post*, 26 February 1915, p. 4.

245 *Newcastle Journal*, 14 April 1916, p. 5.

246 Hay, *Carrying On*, p. 230.

247 *Western Times*, 22 September 1916, p. 12.

248 Spicer, *Letters from France*, 6 December 1915; Cpl T. Keale in Arthur, *We Will Remember Them*, p. 26.

249 Doyle and Schäfer, *Fritz and Tommy*, p. 43.

250 Cpl B. Thomson, in MacDonald, *Somme*, p. 126, but NB this is in an interview from the early 1980s.

251 Crofts, *Field Ambulance Sketches*, p. 129.

252 Percy Bryant, Imperial War Museum interview.

253 H. M. Tomlinson, *All Our Yesterdays*, (London: William Heinemann, 1930), p. 448.

254 Duffin, *Diaries*, p. 156.

255 *Comic Cuts*, 25 August 1917.

256 MacDonald, *Voices and Images*, 1991 edn, p. 195.

257 Broadhead, *Diary*, 26 April 1916, 19 May 1916, 29 July 1916, etc.

258 *The Listening Post*, 10 August 1917, 1 December 1917.

259 *Leeds Mercury,* 31 August 1922, p. 6.

260 *Aberdeen Journal,* 28 June 1927, p. 5.

261 MacArthur, *A Bug's-eye View,* p. 30.

262 Dawson, *A "Temporary Gentleman",* p. 125.

263 *Liverpool Echo,* 8 July 1915, p. 3.

264 *Portsmouth Evening News,* 24 July 1915, p 2.

265 *Daily Mirror,* 14 July 1915, p. 10.

266 Soldier's letter, *Coventry Herald,* 1 January 1915, p. 7.

267 *Gloucester Echo,* 21 April 1915, p. 5 (Cheltenham soldier serving with a Canadian unit).

268 Soldier in the South Wales Borderers, *Coventry Evening Telegraph,* 7 April 1915, p. 3.

269 Pte W. Thomson, Black Watch, *Sussex Agricultural Express,* 21 April 1916, p. 8.

270 *Folkestone Herald,* 30 March 1918, p. 3.

271 *Exeter and Plymouth* Gazette, 3 November 1916, p. 1 – also NB the combination of terms – '"That's true, ain't it Fritz?" and the Boches gave a nod.'

272 *Newcastle Evening Chronicle,* 20 September 1915.

273 *32nd News* (American trench journal), November 1918, pp. 4, 15.

274 Saxons 'are known to be gentlemen', *War Diary of the 1st Life-Guards,* 22 October 1914.

275 *Huns Ancient and Modern,* p. 13.

276 *War Budget,* 29 August 1914, pp. 3, 17; 5 September 1914, p. 21.

277 Meaning 'military imperialism'; Ponsonby, *The Crank,* p. 10.

278 J. H. Moulton, *British and German Scholarship (Papers for Wartime),* No. 31, (Oxford: Oxford University Press, 1915), p. 11.

279 *Daily Chronicle,* 26 July 1917, p. 2.

280 In Treves, *Made in the Trenches,* p. 20.

281 *Punch,* 26 February 1919, p. 155.

282 *In the Hands of the Huns,* p. 55.

283 Holmes, *Tommy,* p. 270.

284 Kilpatrick, *Atkins at War,* p. 110.

285 H. Wheeler, *Daring Deeds of Merchant Seamen in the Great War,* (London: G. G. Harrap & Co., 1918), pp. 70, 48.

286 Crofts, *Field Ambulance Sketches,* p. 140.

287 In MacDonald, *Voices and Images,* 1991 edn, p. 129.

288 Partridge, *Words! Words! Words!,* p. 221.

289 K. Bergmann, *Wie der Feldgraue Spricht*, (Giessen: Töpelmann, 1916), p. 26.

290 e.g. 'Hans was at last convinced of the futility of further effort', F. Coleman, *With Cavalry in 1915*, (London: Sampson Low & Co., 1916), p. 7.

291 See for example MacDonald, *They Called it Passchendaele*, which 'has of necessity been compiled from the recollections of old people', author's foreword, p. xiii.

292 Graham, *A Private in the Guards*, pp. 328–9.

293 Fraser and Gibbons.

294 Brophy and Partridge, *The Long Trail*, 1969 edn.

295 *The Great War Interviews*, recorded 1964, [BBC television programme], http://www.bbc.co.uk/iplayer/group/p01tbj6p accessed 7 February 2017.

296 Herbert, *Mons, Anzac, and Kut*, 1919 edn, p. 171.

297 Wright, *Shattered Glory*, p. 126.

298 *The Leadswinger*, 16 October 1915, p. 20.

299 Spicer, *Letters from France*, 23 March 1916.

300 Partridge, *Words! Words! Words!*, pp. 220–1; *pointus* may have been in part a counterbalance to *poilus*.

301 Bergmann, *Wie der Feldgraue Spricht*, p. 26.

302 Smith, *Four Years on the Western Front*, p. 85.

303 Quoted in Wadsworth, *Letters from the Trenches*, p. 86.

304 Duffin, *Diaries*, p. 62.

305 Barker, *Agony's Anguish*, p. 59.

306 *The Champion*, 23 May 1925, p. 500.

307 Pte W. Nixon, quoted in MacDonald, *Voices and Images*, 1991 edn, p. 105.

308 *Rochdale Observer*, 20 May 1916, p. 6.

309 *Sheffield Evening Telegraph*, 24 September 1914, p. 10.

310 *Sunderland Daily Echo*, 5 January 1917, p. 6.

311 *Edinburgh Evening News*, 24 November 1917, p. 4.

312 *Punch*, 4 November 1914, p. iii.

313 e.g. *The Gasper*, 28 May 1915.

314 e.g. the spy in *Special Constable Smith*, with an obviously anglophone actor as a German spy trying to put on an English accent, [sound dramatisation], (Regal 6842, 1915; CD41–003/2, *Oh! It's a Lovely War*, Vol. 2, 2001).

315 Coldstream officer quoted in Holmes, *Tommy*, p. 338.

316 *Home Chat*, 28 November 1914, p. 324.

317 Coppard, *With a Machine Gun to Cambrai*, 1986 edn, p. 51.

318 *The Pow-Wow*, 25 November 1914, p. 2.

319 *The Bystander*, 17 February 1915, p. 215.

320 Hay, *The First Hundred Thousand*, p. 227.

321 *The Switchboard*, September 1916.

322 Nobbs, *Englishman, Kamerad!*, p. 120.

323 *Punch*, 2 October 1912, p. 283, and 12 February 1912, p. 91.

324 Fraser and Gibbons.

325 Burrage, *War is War*, 2010 edn, p. 143.

326 In Treves, *Made in the Trenches*, p. 29.

327 *Le Poilu*, February 1916.

328 *Le Mouchoir*, 25 October 1916, p. 1, though Partridge (*Slang To-day and Yesterday*, 1933 edn, p. 179) gives 'kamerad'.

329 *German Atrocities in France*, translation of the official report of the French Commission, published by the *Daily Chronicle*, 1915, p. 15.

330 *Northern Mudguard*, November 1915, p. 8.

331 *Nottingham Evening Post*, 27 October 1917, p. 2.

332 *The Auckland Star*, 2 February 1918, p. 15.

333 Jones, *In Parenthesis*, 1969 edn, p. 72.

334 Smith, *Four Years on the Western Front*, p. 7.

335 Hay, *The First Hundred Thousand*, p. 227.

336 De L'Isle, *Leaves from a V.A.D.'s Diary*, p. 64.

337 *Aberdeen Weekly Journal*, 6 June 1919, p. 4.

338 *The Leadswinger*, 16 October 1915, p. 17.

339 Smith, *Four Years on the Western Front*, p. 153.

340 Douie, *The Weary Road*, pp. 170–1.

341 *The Times*, 17 November 1915, p. 7.

342 *The Comet*, 5 February 1917.

343 Chasseaud, *Rats Alley*, p. 93.

344 Douie, *The Weary Road*, p. 140.

345 H. Greenwall, *Scoops*, (London: Stanley Paul & Co., 1923), p. 175.

346 De L'Isle, *Leaves from a V.A.D.'s Diary*, p. 22.

347 *Fall In*, 15 January 1916, p. 66.

348 Malins, *How I Filmed the War*, p. 132.

349 Duffin, *Diaries*, p. 40.

350 *The Growler*, 1 January 1916, p. 3.

351 R. Kipling, *The Irish Guards in the Great War*, (Garden City, New York: Doubleday, Page & Co., 1923), p. 38.

352 Ibid., p. 64.

353 In the *Aberdeen Evening Express*, 11 January 1917, p. 2.

354 Graves, *Goodbye to All That*, 1960 edn, p. 81.

355 Crofts, *Field Ambulance Sketches*, p. 105.

356 Smith, *Four Years on the Western Front*, p. 50.

357 Hay, *Carrying On*, p. 230.

358 Quoted in Holmes, *Tommy*, p. 306.

359 Quoted in ibid., p. 384.

360 Duffin, *Diaries*, p. 212.

361 *The Fuze*, Vol.1, Issue 2, pp. 1, 5.

362 T. Baggs, *Back from the Front*, (London: F. and C. Palmer, 1914), p. 92.

363 Mottram, *Journey to the Western Front*, p. 24.

364 Chasseaud, *Rats Alley*, pp. 96, 141, 158.

365 *Daily Express*, 18 June 1918, p. 2.

366 *Birmingham Mail*, 4 September 1915, p. 3.

367 Osborn, *The Muse In Arms*, pp. ix–x.

368 *Yorkshire Evening Post*, 28 July 1914, p. 4.

369 J. Coleman, '"Extraordinary cheeriness and good will": the uses and documentation of First World War slang', in Walker and Declercq, *Languages and the First World War: communicating*, p. 261.

370 See Todman, *The Great War*, p. 17.

371 Jones, *In Parenthesis*, 1969 edn, p. xii.

372 Partridge, *Words! Words! Words!*, p. 165.

373 *Daily Express*, 25 September 1914, p. 2.

374 Greenwall, *Scoops*, p. 174.

375 Muir, *Observations of an Orderly*, p. 224.

376 Crofts, *Field Ambulance Sketches*, p. 34.

377 J. Nicholson, *The Folk Speech of East Yorkshire*, (London: Simpkin, Marshall & Co., 1889), p. 1.

378 Gill and Dallas, *Unknown Army*, p. 35.

379 Omissi, *Indian Voices*.

380 Mottram, *A Personal Record*, p. 85 notes the bewilderment of regular army staff officers faced with French and Flemish, compared to the 'various Indian tongues' they had a little knowledge of.

381 Chasseaud, *Rats Alley*, p. 91.

382 *The War Illustrated*, 5 February 1916, p. c.

383 *The Story of an Epic Pilgrimage*, p. 85.

384 *Derry Journal*, 30 November 1917, p. 3.

385 Holmes, *Tommy*, p. 153.

386 See ap Glyn, 'Dear Mother . . .' in Walker and Declercq, *Languages and the First World War: communicating*, pp. 128–42.

387 P. Doyle, *Kitchener's Mob*, (Stroud: The History Press, 2016), p. 152.

388 Gill and Dallas, *Unknown Army*, p. 45.

389 ap Glyn, 'Dear Mother . . .', in Walker and Declercq, *Languages and the First World War: communicating*, p. 132.

390 MacDonald, *Under the French Flag*, p. 125.

391 Vansittart, *John Masefield's Letters*, 5 April 1915.

392 Pulvertaft, *Reminiscences*.

393 *Liverpool Daily Post*, 26 July 1916, pp. 3–4.

394 *Birmingham Mail*, 4 September 1915, p. 3.

395 Capt Keith Duce, Imperial War Museum interview, [sound recording c.1975].

396 M. McDonagh, *The Irish on the Somme*, (London: Hodder & Stoughton, 1917), p. 126.

397 L. W. Crouch, *Duty and Service: letters from the front by Captain Lionel William Crouch*, (London; Aylesbury: printed for private circulation, 1917), quoted in K. Cowman, '"The . . . 'parlez' is not going on very well 'avec moi': Learning and Using "Trench French" on the Western Front', in Walker and Declercq, *Languages and the First World War: communicating*, p. 30.

398 *Rochdale Observer*, 20 May 1916, p. 6.

399 *Daily Gazette for Middlesbrough*, 17 December 1915, p. 3; the *Leeds Mercury*, 22 June 1915, p. 2, and the *Stonehaven Jornal*, 27 December 1917, p. 3, used the term without inverted commas.

400 Weekley, *Words Ancient and Modern*, p. 78.

401 Brophy and Partridge, *The Long Trail*, 1969 edn, p. 155.

402 E. Bagnold, *A Diary Without Dates*, (London: Heinemann, 1918).

403 2nd Lt Claude Sisley, writing in *The Athenaeum*, 1 August 1919, p. 695, confirmed this.

404 Partridge, *Words! Words! Words!*, p. 163.

405 Brophy and Partridge, *The Long Trail*, 1969 edn, p. 133.

406 MacDonald, *Under the French Flag*, pp. 103, 104, 114.

407 Leroy, *A Glossary of French Slang*, 1924 edn, pp. 30–31.

408 H. Wyatt, *Malice in Kulturland*, (Richmond: The Car Illustrated, [1914] 1917), p. 37.

409 In Stanley, '"He was black . . .", in Das, *Race, Empire*, p. 213.

410 *Menin Gate Pilgrimage*, p. 13.

411 *War Budget*, 3 February 1916, p. 377.

412 *The Lady*, 12 November 1914, p. 712.

413 Partridge, *Words! Words! Words!*, pp. 151, 189.

414 Ibid., p. 137.

415 *Fifth Gloucester Gazette*, 5 May 1915.

416 Barker, *Agony's Anguish*, p. 64.

417 Lighter, *Slang of the AEF*, p. 52.

418 *The Times*, 18 May 1915, p. 6.

419 Quoted in Wadsworth, *Letters from the Trenches*, p. 146.

420 Edmonds, *A Subaltern's War*, p. 127.

421 Barker, *Agony's Anguish*.

422 Kilpatrick, *Atkins at War*, p. 42.

423 Brindle, *France and Flanders*, p. 79.

424 *The Scotsman*, 23 July 1917, p. 6.

425 *Western Daily Press*, 29 May 1915, p. 9.

426 Stereoview postcard caption, author's collection.

427 Stereoview postcard caption, author's collection.

428 Cpl W. Shaw, quoted in MacDonald, *Voices and Images*, 1991 edn, pp. 155–6.

429 *Punch*, 2 December 1914, p. xiii.

430 Duffin, *Diaries*, and D. Walker, *Lost Generation*.

431 Letter quoted in *Menin Gate Pilgrimage*, p. 39.

432 Ibid., p. 15.

433 Florence Billington in Van Emden and Humphries, *All Quiet on the Home Front*, p. 19.

434 Bagnold, *Diary Without Dates*.

435 For example McDonagh, *The Irish on the Somme*, p. 126.

436 Partridge, *Words! Words! Words!*, p. 223; Leroy, *A Glossary of French Slang*, 1924 edn, p. 11.

437 'Oh la la' Partridge notes as being used by Germans and Americans to the French, 'Dee-donk' by Americans only: Partridge, *Words! Words! Words!*, p. 222.

438 Partridge, *Words! Words! Words!*, p. 157.

439 *Yorkshire Evening Post*, 15 November 1918, p. 5.

440 *The Athenaeum*, 25 July 1919, p. 664. It is surprising to see this in this publication; perhaps the writers did not recognise the implication.

441 Coppard, *With a Machine Gun to Cambrai*, 1986 edn, p. 16.

442 Smith, *Four Years on the Western Front*, p. 71.

443 Mottram, *Journey to the Western Front*, p. 45.

444 Burrage, *War is War*, 2010 edn, p. 90; he uses 'souvenir' to mean a baby fathered by a Canadian soldier.

445 C. Makepeace, 'Soldiers, masculinity and prostitutes in WW1', in J. Arnold and S. Brady (eds), *What is Masculinity?*, (London: Palgrave Macmillan, 2011), p. 416.

446 Ibid., p. 420.

447 Palmer and Wallis, *A War in Words*, 2004 edn, p. 227.

448 Williamson, *The Patriot's Progress*, p. 133.

449 Makepeace, 'Soldiers, masculinity and prostitutes in WW1', p. 418.

450 Graves, *Goodbye to All That*, 1960 edn, p. 116.

451 See Smith, *The Second Battlefield*, p. 78.

452 Williamson, *The Patriot's Progress*, p. 136.

453 Rees, *In the Trenches*, [sound dramatisation].

454 E. Southard, *Shellshock And Other Neuropsychiatric Problems*, N. Fenton and C. Mills (eds), (Boston: W. M. Leonard, 1919), p. 212.

455 *Fun*, 25 December 1915, tenth page (unpaginated).

456 Stanley, *Grandad's War*, p. 53.

457 Postcard, 24 May 1919, author's collection.

458 Quoted in J. Marlow, *The Virago Book of Women and the Great War*, (London: Virago Press, [1998] 2005), 1998 edn, p. 219.

459 The name was given by German troops grateful that they would not have to charge the Belgian forts in August 1914.

460 Karl Schrever, quoted in Doyle and Schäfer, *Fritz and Tommy*, p. 226.

461 Also the name '*soixante-quinze*' was given to a cocktail invented in 1915.

462 *The Champion*, 9 May 1925, p. 425, in a boys' serial story.

463 Fraser and Gibbons.

464 *The Wellington Times* (NSW), 24 January 1918, p. 9.

465 Brophy and Partridge, *The Long Trail*, and Denham, *Dardanelles*, April–May 1915.

466 Denham, *Dardanelles*, April–May 1915. Denham wrote 'we gave all the enemy howitzer guns nicknames', 27 April 1915.

467 Hepper, *Great War Diary*, 30 November 1917.

468 *Manchester Guardian*, 4 October 1914, p. 5.

469 Doyle and Schäfer, *Fritz and Tommy*, p. 57.

470 Partridge, *Words! Words! Words!*, p. 185.

471 Ibid., p. 186.

472 Ibid., p. 163.

473 *Notes and Queries*, 29 October 1921, p. 344.

474 Partridge, *Slang of the British Soldier*, p. 58.

475 D. Miller, *The Illustrated Directory of Tanks of the World*, (London: Salamander, 2000), p. 302.

476 *Daily Mirror*, 30 November 1914, p. 12.

477 *Oxford English Dictionary*.

478 *Sheffield Independent*, 7 August 1914, p. 5 ('Western front'); *Dublin Daily Express*, 24 August 1914, p. 3 ('Eastern front').

479 *Dublin Daily Express*, 12 August 1914, p. 6; *Aberdeen Press and Journal*, 25 August 1914, p. 4.

480 *The Scotsman*, 23 September 1914, p. 8.

481 L. Mugglestone, *States of Siege*, December 2014. https://wordsinwartime.wordpress.com accessed 26 November 2016.

482 *Aberdeen Evening Express*, 2 September 1914, p. 3.

483 *Birmingham Daily Post*, 25 September 1914, p. 5.

484 *Western Mail* (et al.), 21 September 1914, p. 5.

485 *The Scotsman*, 18 September 1914, p. 3.

486 *The Pow-Wow*, 16 December 1914, pp. 3, 4.

487 *The Gasper*, 8 January 1916, p. 7.

488 *Daily Sketch*, 25 January 1916, p. 10.

489 *Daily Record*, 27 September 1915, p. 1.

490 Postcard dated 31 March 1915, On Active Service, author's collection.

491 Postcard dated 17 April 1915, On Active Service, author's collection.

492 *Leeds Mercury*, 31 August 1917, p. 6.

493 *Dundee* Courier, 30 September 1918, p. 2.

494 Postcard, On Active Service, 1 July 1915, author's collection.

495 Spicer, *Letters from France*, 16 March 1916.

496 Diary of George Williams, 1 April 1916, 30 June 1916, 31 August 1916. http://www.europeana1914–1918.eu/en/contributions/17242 accessed 7 October 2016.

497 Postcard, On Active Service, author's collection.

498 Postcard dated 1 July 1915, On Active Service, author's collection.

499 Postcard dated 23 October 1915, On Active Service, author's collection.

500 Cook, *War Diary*, 15 September 1914.

501 Rifleman F. Walker, *Diary*, 6 October 1918, author's collection.

502 Diary of George Williams, 1 April 1916, http://www.europeana1914–1918.eu/en/contributions/17242 accessed 7 October 2016.

503 Hewett, *A Scholar's Letters*, p. 40, written before July 1916.

504 Postcard dated 9 September 1918, author's collection.

505 *Manchester Evening News*, 8 March 1915, p. 2.

506 *Sheffield Evening Telegraph*, 18 August 1915, p. 3.

507 Postcard dated 23 December 1915, On Active Service, author's collection.

508 Letter, National Archives (RAIL 253/516).

509 Lt R. Palmer, 24 April 1915, quoted in Van Emden, *Tommy's War*, p. 120.

510 Spicer, *Letters from France*, 23 August 1917.

511 Amy Shield, letter, 23 February 1916, p. 4, author's collection.

512 Quoted in MacDonald, *Voices and Images*, 1991 edn, p. 53.

513 Capt G. Horridge, 1917, quoted in ibid., p. 215.

514 *Gloucestershire Echo*, 22 August 1917, p. 1; *Birmingham Daily Post*, 27 August 1917, p. 3; *Burnley News*, 15 August 1917, p. 4; *Yorkshire Post*, 23 August 1917, p. 6.

515 Harris, *Private papers,* 13 June 1916.

516 *The Sphere*, 3 June 1916, pp. 211, 213.

517 Williamson, *The Patriot's Progress*, p. 61.

518 *A Month at the Front*, p. 39.

519 Quoted in Holmes, *Tommy*, p. 286.

520 Lighter, *Slang of the AEF*, p. 82.

521 F. Vizetelly, *The Service Soldier's Dictionary of English and French Terms*, (New York: Funk & Wagnalls Co., 1917), p. 94.

522 *Falkirk Herald*, 23 October 1915, p. 8.

523 Ibid., 29 January 1916, p. 10.

524 *The Daily Telegraph*, 2 November 1914, p. 7.

525 *Punch*, 21 February 1917, p. x.

526 Ibid., 17 May 1916, p. iv.

527 *Daily Express*, 20 April 1918, p. 4.

528 *Liverpool Echo*, 31 August 1917, p. 4.

529 *Punch*, 9 May 1917, p. xv.

530 Ibid., 10 April 1918, p. iv.

531 Ibid., 8 May 1918, p. iv.

532 Ibid., 28 February 1917, p. ix.

533 *The Bystander*, 3 April 1918, p. 3.

534 *The Daily Telegraph*, 3 November 1914, p. 7.

535 *The Gasper*, 28 February 1916, p. 2.

536 Lighter, *Slang of the AEF*, p. 67.

537 *Punch*, 24 April 1918, p. ix.

538 *St Andrews Citizen*, 4 November 1916, p. 1.

539 *Daily Record*, 13 December 1916, p. 2.

540 Kipling, *The Irish Guards*, p. 55.

541 *Sporting Times*, 20 January 1917, p. 7.

542 *Aberdeen Evening Express*, 19 October 1915, p. 4.

543 *Chelmsford Chronicle*, 8 October 1915, p. 2.

544 *Army and Navy Gazette*, 16 January 1915, p. 4.

545 In the other direction there were 'Zeps in a cloud' (sausages and mash), and 'shrapnel', 'dum-dum' and 'handgrenades' (grape-nuts, beans and meatballs, all US slang).

546 *Weekly Freeman's Journal*, 12 May 1917, p. 4.

547 *The Times*, 31 March 1915, p. 7.

548 *Evening Dispatch*, 6 January 1917, p. 2; *Sunday Mirror*, 25 February 1917, p. 7.

549 *Daily Mail*, 16 December 1915, p. 4.

550 Spicer, *Letters from France*, 3 December 1915.

551 Chasseaud, *Rats Alley*, p. 91.

552 *The Gasper*, 8 January 1916, p. 3.

553 Hewett, *A Soldier's Letters from The Front*, p. 39.

554 R. Vernède, *Letters To His Wife*, (London: W. Collins, Sons & Co., 1917), p. 32.

555 *A Red Triangle Girl in France*, p. 19.

556 Hewett, *A Soldier's Letters from The Front*, p. 46.

557 Langley, *Battery Flashes*, p. 163.

558 MacBride, *The Emma-Gees*, p. 77.

559 2nd Lt A. Lamb, quoted in Doyle and Schäfer, *Fritz and Tommy*, p. 239.

560 *Aberdeen Weekly Journal*, 5 July 1918, p. 2.

561 *On The Road To Kut*, p. 25.

562 Trevelyan, *Scenes From Italy's War*, p. 52.

563 Long, *Colours of War*, p. 128.

564 Spicer, *Letters from France*, 2 August 1916.

565 Dawson, *A "Temporary Gentleman"*, p. 7.

566 Postcard On Active Service, 24 March 1918, author's collection.

567 '*Haßgesang gegen England*'.

568 Broadhead, *Diary*, 28 November 1916.

569 Tytler, *With Lancashire Lads*, p. 22.

570 Wright, *Shattered Glory*, p. 243.

571 Lighter, *Slang of the AEF*, p. 97.

572 Herbert, *Mons, Anzac, and Kut*, 1919 edn, p. 92.

573 Fraser and Gibbons.

574 *Punch*, 23 May 1917, p. iv.

575 *Sheffield Evening Telegraph*, 12 March 1918, p. 5; E. T. Cook in *Literary Recreations,* (London: Macmillan & Co., 1918), p. 154, noted that the New York *Sun* urged that the American soldier's nickname 'must be *Teddy*'.

576 'Our Own Correspondent', 1915, quoted in Coleman, '"Extraordinary cheeriness and good will"', in Walker and Declercq, *Languages and the First World War: communicating*, p. 263.

577 *Daily Mirror*, 11 August 1916, p. 12.

578 Partridge, *Dictionary of Slang and Unconventional English*.

579 Ibid.

580 *Aussie*, January 1918, p. 10.

581 *Hull Daily Mail*, 24 November 1919, p. 1.

582 Graves, *Goodbye to All That*, 1960 edn, p. 237.

583 Cook, 'Fighting Words', p. 343.

584 F. A. Voigt, *Combed Out*, (London: Jonathan Cape, [1920] 1929), p. 193.

585 *The Gasper*, 8 January 1916, p. 2.

586 *Fall-In*, 29 January 1916, p. 70.

587 Fraser and Gibbons.

588 *Daily Mail*, 26 November 1914, p. 8.

589 Reported in the *Hull Daily Mail*, 31 December 1921, p. 1.

590 *Daily Mail*, 3 March 1916, p. 4.

591 *Liverpool Echo*, 2 February 1918, p. 4.

592 All suggestions sent in to the *Hull Daily Mail*, 8 June 1917, p. 1.

593 *Manchester Guardian*, 17 April 1917, p. 3.

594 *Daily Express*, 15 December 1914, p. 4.

4 The Home Front

1 D. Dendooven, '"Fake Belgium": linguistic issues in the diary of Father Achiel Van Walleghem (1914–1919)', in Declercq and Walker, *Languages and the First World War: representation*, p. 51.

2 *The Daily Telegraph*, 11 November 1914, p. 11. Lyons' Tea had already in September taken legal action against Lipton Ltd to prevent them from claiming that some of the directorate of Lyons were Germans.

3   *The Lady*, 21 January 1915, p. 69.

4   *Daily Sketch*, 10 December 1914, p. 13.

5   *Portsmouth Evening News*, 20 November 1914, p. 1.

6   *Daily Telegraph*, 11 November 1914, p. 11.

7   Wrigleys Chewing Gum, *Daily Mirror*, 14 October 1914, p. 11.

8   *Nottingham Evening Post*, 18 May 1915, p. 6.

9   *Bath Chronicle and Weekly Gazette*, 1 January 1916, p. 3.

10 *Punch*, 3 May 1916, p. vii.

11 *War Budget*, 1 June 1916, p. ii.

12 *The Times*, 10 September 1914, p. 4.

13 *Yorkshire Evening Post*, 31 October 1916, p. 5.

14 Ibid., 18 December 1917, p. 3.

15 *Punch*, 20 November 1918, p. x.

16 *The Times*, 7 October 1914, p. 3.

17 *War Budget*, 5 October 1916, p. iv.

18 *The Tatler*, 21 February 1917, p. 253.

19 *The Rochdale Observer*, 31 October 1914, p. 1.

20 *Western Gazette*, 11 December 1914, p. 5; *Daily Sketch*, 3 December 1914, p. 13; toys and games continued to appear, *John Bull* carrying on 15 January 1916 (p. 30) an advertisement for 'The "Strand" War Game', offering 'the most fascinating pastime for the dull evenings . . . Soldiers and sailors all agree it is the best game of the war'.

21 *Liverpool Echo*, 3 November 1916, p. 5.

22 *Yorkshire Evening Post*, 26 November 1914, p. 4.

23 *Daily Gazette for Middlesbrough*, 27 November 1914, p. 1.

24 *Dundee Evening Telegraph*, 13 October 1914, p. 4.

25 *Surrey Mirror*, 18 December 1914, p. 8.

26 *North Devon Journal*, 1 October 1914, p. 1.

27 'G.C. Dean, The Tailor' – 'Are we downhearted? A dozen times no! Then go in for a good blue serge suit or a nice Scotch Tweed, while you have the chance . . .' *Tamworth Herald*, 20 April 1918, p. 2.

28 *The Bystander*, 8 January 1919, p. 58.

29 *Western Times*, 3 January 1919, p. 11.

30 See C. Pennell, *A Kingdom United*, (Oxford: Oxford University Press, 2014), pp. 90–91, for examples of actions against individuals and meetings.

31 Regulation 27/113 https://archive.org/stream/defenceofrealmma00grearich/defenceofrealmma00grearich_djvu.txt accessed 12 September 2016.

32 *Derbyshire Courier*, 23 September 1916, p. 5.

33 *Newcastle Journal*, 9 September 1916, p. 12.

34 *Pall Mall Gazette*, 30 June 1916, p. 5.

35 *John Bull*, 9 January 1915, p. 2.

36 *Western Mail*, 15 April 1915, p. 4.

37 *The Passing Show*, 18 January 1919, p. 461.

38 J. Lee, *To-morrow is a New Day*, (London: The Cresset Press, 1939), p. 38, quoted in Pennell, *A Kingdom United*, p. 90.

39 Koller, 'Representing Otherness . . .', pp. 128–9.

40 P. Doyle and J. Walker, *Trench Talk: words of the first World War*, (Stroud: The History Press, 2012), pp. 193–4. Fraser and Gibbons described the short story as 'a piece of realistic fiction'.

41 *Vivid War Weekly*, 16 October 1915, p. 167.

42 Doyle and Schäfer, *Fritz and Tommy*, pp. 83, 242.

43 Quoted in Wadsworth, *Letters from the Trenches*, p. 133.

44 Hong Kong Education Department, *War Stories in English and Chinese*, (Hong Kong, 1918), p. 8.

45 Brindle, *France and Flanders*, p. 6.

46 Liberal–Labour political meeting, reported in the *Portsmouth Evening News*, 1 May 1915, p. 5.

47 Vansittart, *John Masefield's Letters*, p. 230, 27 March 1917.

48 *Fall In*, 15 January 1916, p. 66.

49 *The Sphere*, 6 March 1916, p. 297.

50 Weekley, *An Etymological Dictionary*, col. 812.

51 *Daily Mail*, 7 January 1918, p. 2.

52 *Dundee People's Journal*, 9 September 1916, p. 1.

53 *Arbroath Herald*, 29 November 1918, p. 7.

54 An ongoing subliminal sense of the language of justification can be seen in advertisements such as that for Tremol Treatment (Bad Legs Cured) *Daily Express*, 2 August 1918, p. 2, with its subheading 'The Reason Why'.

55 Cassell, *New English Dictionary*, (London: Cassell, 1919).

56 Macmillan, *A Modern Dictionary of the English Language*, (London: Macmillan, 1922).

57 *Blackie's Compact Etymological Dictionary*, c.1920.

58 *War Budget*, 17 February 1916, pp. 16–17.

59 *The Sphere*, 26 December 1914, p. 306.

60 A. Fell, letter to *The Times*, 20 April 1915, p. 11.

61 *Commission instituée en vue de constater les actes commis par l'ennemi en violation du droit des gens.*

62 *The Times*, 29 December 1914, p. 3.

63 A. Ponsonby, *Falsehood in War-time: propaganda lies of the First World War*, (London: George Allen & Unwin, 1928), Ch. 23.

64 *The Pow-Wow*, 25 November 1914, p. 3.

65 *Burnley Express*, 24 July 1915, p. 9.

66 *Daily Mail*, 1 October 1919, p. 2.

67 Letter sent On Active Service, author's collection.

68 *Sussex Agricultural Express*, 1 October 1915, p. 5.

69 1916, quoted in MacDonald, *Voices and Images*, 1991 edn, p. 145.

70 *Sheffield Evening Telegraph*, 18 August 1915, p. 3.

71 *Daily Mirror*, 27 March 1917, p. 10.

72 *Fifth Gloucester Gazette*, 12 March 1916.

73 *Dundee Courier*, 7 April 1915, p. 2.

74 *Dublin Daily Express*, 17 July 1915, p. 2.

75 *The Growler*, 1 January 1916, p. 9.

76 Both Brophy and Partridge, (*The Long Trail*, 1969 edn), and Fraser and Gibbons note this.

77 Crofts, *Field Ambulance Sketches*, p. 124.

78 The *Daily Express*, 10 February 1915, p. 5.

79 *The War Illustrated*, 15 January 1916, p. 519.

80 *Daily Express*, 5 October 1915, p. 2.

81 *Western Mail*, 11 November 1916, p. 6.

82 *Dundee Courier*, 27 June 1918, p. 2.

83 *Birmingham Daily Mail*, 9 May 1918, p. 2.

84 *Western Mail*, 6 April 1918, p. 4.

85 *Exeter and Plymouth Gazette*, 11 November 1915, p. 3.

86 *Western Times*, 23 May 1916, p. 8.

87 *Western Times*, 24 April 1917, p. 6.

88 From E. P. Oppenheim, *The Missing Delora*, serialised in the Portsmouth *Evening News*, 15 October 1913, p. 1.

89 *Yorkshire Post*, 14 September 1914, p. 10.

90 *Western Daily Press*, 3 September 1914, p. 5.

91 *Western Mail*, 11 November 1916, p. 6.

92 *Liverpool Daily Post*, 13 June 1916, p. 5.

93 *Dundee Courier*, 20 August 1917, p. 2.

94 *The Gasper*, 28 February 1916, p. 2.

95 Partridge, *Slang of the British Soldier*, p. 52.

96 W. E. Collinson, *Contemporary English: a personal speech record*, (Leipzig; Berlin: G. B. Teubner, 1927), p. 102.

97 *Vivid War Weekly*, 16 October 1915, pp. 175–6.

98 Bovril was still in 1922 arguing its case against accusations of profiteering, (*The Bystander*, January 1920).

99 *Birmingham Gazette*, 1 December 1914, p. 4.

100 *The Athenaeum*, 1 August 1919, p. 695.

101 *The Times*, 28 January 1918, p. 5.

102 *The Gasper*, 28 February 1916, p. 2.

103 Vansittart, *John Masefield's Letters,* p. 59, 8 March 1915.

104 De L'Isle, *Leaves from a V.A.D.'s Diary*, p. 90.

105 *Daily Mirror*, 27 March 1916, p. 10.

106 *The Tatler*, 17 January 1917, p. 72; *The Times*, 20 April 1918, p. 6.

107 De L'Isle, *Leaves from a V.A.D.'s Diary*, p. 60.

108 E. Showalter, quoted in D. Poynter, 'A study of the psychological disorders of nurses and female V.A.D.s who served alongside the B.E.F. and Allied Forces during the First World War', doctoral thesis, 2008, p. 34.

109 Quoted in MacDonald, *Voices and Images,* 1991 edn, p. 73.

110 Graves, R., *Goodbye to All That*, 1960 edn, p. 153.

111 Burrage, *War is War*, 2010 edn, p. 107.

112 Quoted in Van Emden and Humphries, *All Quiet on the Home Front*, p. 19.

113 Margaret Darrow, quoted in N. Khan, *Women's Poetry of the First World War*, (Lexington: The University Press of Kentucky, 1988), p. 15.

114 *The Era*, 19 September 1917, p. 23.

115 Treves, *Made in the Trenches*, p. 152.

116 *The Leadswinger*, 16 October 1915, p. 3.

117 *Punch*, 14 April 1915, p. 281.

118 *Derby Daily Telegraph*, 15 September 1916, p. 3.

119 L. Mugglestone, *Pacifists, peace-plotters, and peacettes,* [online] 16 May 2015. https://wordsinwartime.wordpress.com accessed 25 September 2016.

120 *Evening Dispatch* 21 May 1917, p. 3.

121 *Daily Mirror*, 5 June 1916, p. 5.

122 *Aberdeen Journal*, 28 March 1919, p. 6.

123 'I'll take my Susie for a ride / Upon the flapper bracket' Chairman cigarettes advertisement, *Hull Daily Mail*, 26 March 1919, p. 6.

124 *The Tatler*, 28 February 1917, p. 271.

125 Bagnold, *A Diary Without Dates*.

126 Swinton, *Twenty Years After,* Vol. 3, p. 217.

127 Postcard, 9 December 1917, author's collection.

128 De L'Isle, *Leaves From a V.A.D.'s Diary*, p. 21.

129 *Punch*, 16 May 1917, p. viii; 5 September 1917, p. viii; 5 December 1917, p. viii.

130 *Tommy & Jack*, 1916, p. 8.

131 *Aberdeen Journal*, 1 July 1922, p. 4.

132 H. Smith, *Not So Quiet*, ([1930] 1988), 1988 edn, p. 182.

133 Brophy and Partridge, *The Long Trail*, 1969 edn, p. 155.

134 http://www.essexrecordofficeblog.co.uk/the-battle-babies-of-essex/ accessed 19 April 2016, http://blog.nationalarchives.gov.uk/blog/battle-babies/?utm_source=The%20National%20Archives&utm_medium=email&utm_campaign=6724312_FWW%20update%20February&dm_i=MAN,404IG,AD27MM,EGQQE,1 accessed 19 April 2016.

135 http://www.royalleicestershireregiment.org.uk/archive/journals/green-tiger–2015-spring-present/2015-autumn/592921 accessed 19 April 2016.

136 http://www.nancy.cc/2012/06/21/baby-girl-named-zeppelina/ accessed 8 September 2016.

137 *The Lady*, 29 October 1914, p. 639.

138 *Aberdeen Evening Express*, 19 August 1916, p. 1.

139 *Yorkshire Post and Leeds Intelligencer*, 29 October 1936, p. 6.

140 G. Whitworth, *The Child's ABC of the War*, (London: George Allen & Unwin, 1914).

141 *Woman's Weekly*, 3 October 1914, p. 582; 7 November p. 718.

142 Graves, *Goodbye to All That*, 1960 edn, p. 93.

143 Douie, *The Weary Road*, p. 39.

144 *Exeter and Plymouth Gazette*, 13 January 1915, p. 4.

145 Pte A. J. Abraham, quoted in Holmes, *Tommy*, p. 339.

146 See Gibson, *Behind the Front*, pp. 152, 156.

147 *Folkestone Herald*, 7 November 1914, p. 3.

148 P. Lotterie, *Un village ardennois pendant les deux guerres mondiales*, (privately published, 1981), p. 52, quoted in Bowd, 'From Hatred to Hybridization', p. 199.

149 https://www.bl.uk/collection-items/impressions-airship-raids-over-london-schoolchildren#sthash.RHecNbj1.dpuf accessed 26 September 2016.

150 *The Times*, 10 December 1915, p. 11.

151 Hong Kong Education Department, *War Stories*, preface.

152 E. O'Neill, *Battles for Peace: the story of the Great War told for children*, (London: Hodder & Stoughton, 1918), pp. 214.

153 Ibid., p. 143.

154 Parrott, *The Children's Story of the War*, Vol. 2, p. 170.

155 Parrott, *The Children's Story of the War*, Vol. 6, p. 102.

156 Ibid., Vol. 2, p. 100.

157 Ibid., Vol. 2, p. 170.

158 Ibid., Vol. 2, pp. 110–12.

159 *Leeds Mercury*, 2 July 1915, p. 4.

160 *Manchester Courier*, 15 August 1914, p. 6.

161 *Burnley News*, 18 September 1915, p. 5.

162 *Dundee Courier,* 9 September 1914, p. 2.

163 *Luton News and Bedfordshire Chronicle*, 8 February 1917, p. 4; the 'give' motif can be seen also on 'tank-banks' and on a German fund-raising medal of 1914 – *Gold gab ich zur wehr Eisen nahm ich zur ehr* (Gold I give for War, Iron I take for Honour).

164 *Liverpool Echo*, 10 August 1915, p. 8.

165 *Fifth Gloucester Gazette*, 12 March 1916.

166 *Fifeshire Advertiser*, 5 January 1918, p. 4.

167 *Western Daily Press*, 26 November 1915, p. 3.

168 *Hendon and Finchley Times*, 6 August 1915, p. 8.

169 *Arbroath Herald*, 9 August 1918, p. 3.

170 Unattributed, quoted in Wadsworth, *Letters from the Trenches*, p. 173.

171 Quoted in Arthur, *We Will Remember Them*, p. 178.

172 Postcard, On Active Service, 15 February 1917, author's collection.

173 Postcard, On Active Service, 19 November 1918, author's collection.

174 Quoted in Wadsworth, *Letters from the Trenches*, p. 20.

175 Postcard, On Active Service, 24 March 1917, author's collection.

176 Postcard, On Active Service, 5 November 1917, author's collection.

177 Postcard, On Active Service, 20 September 1916, author's collection.

178 Quoted in Doyle and Schäfer, *Fritz and Tommy*, p. 113.

179 Postcard, On Active Service, 15 July 1917, author's collection.

180 Postcard, On Active Service, 'Somewhere-on-Sea', 15 December 1915, author's collection.

181 Postcard, On Active Service, 28 November 1917, author's collection.

5 Owning the Language

1 Partridge, *Words! Words! Words!*, p. 167.

2 Partridge, *Slang of the British Soldier*, p. 50.

3   J. Aitchison, *The Language Web*, (Cambridge: Cambridge University Press, 1997), p. 15.

4   *Manchester Guardian*, 19 December 1919, p. 5.

5   The counterpart to the 'temporary gentleman', was the 'gentleman ranker', the title of a play current in November 1914 (*East Ham Echo*).

6   Dawson, *A "Temporary Gentleman"*, p. 8.

7   War Office recruiting advertisement, 10 August 1914.

8   Recruiting advertisement, 'A Call To Arms', 8 August 1914.

9   Quoted in MacDonald, *Voices and Images*, 1991 edn, p. 29.

10 *The War Dragon*, September 1916.

11 Graham, *A Private in the Guards*, p. 347.

12 *The Era*, 11 June 1919, p. 13.

13 Brophy and Partridge, *The Long Trail*, 1969 edn, p. 153.

14 Duffin, *Diaries*, p. 72.

15 http://hansard.millbanksystems.com/commons/1919/dec/17/imperial-war-graves-commission#S5CV0123P0_19191217_HOC_411 accessed 5 December 2016.

16 Cook, *War Diary*, p. 57.

17 *Aberdeen Press and Journal*, 13 November 1920, p. 5.

18 Winter and Baggett, *1914–18*, p. 212.

19 C. Bean, *The Official History of Australia in the War of 1914–1918*, 1983, in Gill and Dallas, *Unknown Army*, p. 39.

20 *War Budget*, 24 February 1916, p. 36.

21 Marwick, *The Deluge*, 1991 edn, p. 62.

22 Ibid., p. 63.

23 From Field Post Office, 19 February 1917, author's collection.

24 Bilbrough, *Diary*, 13 October 1915.

25 Bagnold, *Diary Without Dates*, Ch. 3.

26 *Ilford Recorder*, 6 November 1914, p. 5.

27 Spicer, *Letters from France*, p. xi.

28 Hewett, *A Scholar's Letters*, pp. 18, 17, 19.

29 *Western Mail*, 10 August 1914, p. 2.

30 Doyle, *Kitchener's Mob*, p. 93.

31 F. Stanley, *History of the 89th Brigade 1914–1918*, (Liverpool: Daily Post, 1919), p. 8.

32 *Yorkshire Evening Post*, 1 September 1914, p. 2.

33 *Birmingham Mail*, 19 December 1914, p. 6.

34 http://www.ww1hull.org.uk/index.php/hull-in-ww1/hull-pals-batallion accessed 5 December 2016.

35 L. Milner, *Leeds Pals*, (Barnsley: Pen & Sword Books, [1991] 1998), 1998 edn, p. 42.

36 *Yorkshire Evening Post*, 10 September 1914, p. 3.

37 Ibid., 16 September 1914, p. 3.

38 Ibid., 22 September 1914, p. 3.

39 Ibid., 26 September 1914, p. 3.

40 Milner, *Leeds Pals*, p. 42.

41 Postcard, On Active Service, 4 August 1914, author's collection. The card shows an officer embracing a woman, and was sent to the soldier's wife, in a fashionable part of Eastbourne.

42 Graham, *A Private in the Guards*, p. 192.

43 *Cambria Daily Leader*, 30 May 1916, p. 2.

44 *9th Royal Scots, Diary*, p. 11.

45 *Glamorgan Gazette*, 9 April 1915, p. 3.

46 Vansittart, *John Masefield's Letters*, 3 March 1915, 24 September 1916.

47 E. Blunden, *Undertones of War*, (London: Folio Society, [1928] 1991), 1991 edn, p. 70.

48 Spicer, *Letters from France*, 7 November 1915.

49 Army Club cigarettes advertisement, *The Sketch*, 29 March 1916, p. 23.

50 Hay, *The First Hundred Thousand*, p. 261.

51 Both in Brophy and Partridge, *The Long Trail*.

52 *Daily Express*, 18 June 1918, p. 2.

53 Brophy and Partridge, *Songs and Slang of the British Soldier*, p. 18.

54 *Birmingham Daily Post*, 24 October 1918, p. 4.

55 Unidentified German soldier, quoted in Doyle and Schäfer, *Fritz and Tommy*, p. 107.

56 Cook, *War Diary*, p. 21.

57 Dawson, *A "Temporary Gentleman"*, p. 185.

58 Lord Northcliffe writing in the *Weekly Dispatch*, reported by the *Ballymena Observer*, 17 March 1916, p. 3.

59 *War-Time Tips*, Chapter VI 'The Rules of War', pp. 70, 72.

60 *A War Nurse's Diary*, (1918), p. 59.

61 *The Tatler*, 3 January 1917, p. 23.

62 Osborn, *The Muse in Arms*, p. vii.

63 Pte R. Lawrence, 1 September 1917, quoted in MacDonald, *Voices and Images*, 1991 edn, p. 196.

64 H. O'Neill, *The Royal Fusiliers in the Great War*, (London: Heinemann, 1922), in Doyle, *Kitchener's Mob*, pp. 124, 125.

65 Mottram, *Journey to the Western Front*, p. 23.

66 *Sunderland Daily Echo*, 20 November 1914, p. 1.

67 Douie, *The Weary Road*, p. 117.

68 *Daily Express*, 6 October 1915, p. 5.

69 Chasseaud, *Rats Alley*, p. 135.

70 James Kilpatrick in *Atkins at War*, p. 37, states that 'the British Army, indeed, is an army of sportsmen', meaning betting men.

71 *War Budget*, 3 February 1916, p. 381; 16 March 1916, p. 130; 6 April 1916, p. 228.

72 Tytler, *With Lancashire Lads*, p. 177.

73 Ibid., p. 77.

74 Cpl H. Diffey, quoted in MacDonald, *Voices and Images*, 1991 edn, p. 160.

75 Quoted in ibid., p. 201.

76 *Dublin Daily Express*, 16 August 1916, p. 3.

77 Quoted in MacDonald, *Voices and Images*, 1991 edn, p. 212.

78 Quoted in Holmes, *Tommy*, p. 413.

79 Masefield wrote 'I put up a rabbit in our old lines, & any number of partridges': Vansittart, *John Masefield's Letters*, p. 229, 26 March 1917.

80 Williamson, *The Patriot's Progress*, p. 113.

81 *The Attack* [sound dramatisation].

82 Brophy and Partridge, *The Long Trail*, 1969 edn, p. 108.

83 *The Times*, 18 November 1921, p. 5.

84 *The Athenaeum*, 15 August 1919, p. 759.

85 Brophy and Partridge, *The Long Trail*.

86 *Illustrated London News*, 4 January 1919, p. 6.

87 *Notes and Queries*, November 1918, p. 307.

88 Wood, *In the Line of Battle,* p. 47.

89 Fussell, *The Great War*, 1977 edn, p. 8.

90 Ibid., p. 12.

91 LCpl Abraham, quoted in Arthur, *We Will Remember Them*, p. 19.

92 Partridge, *Slang of the British Soldier*, p. 49.

93 J. Buchan, *Francis and Riversdale Grenfell*, (Thomas Nelson & Sons Ltd, 1920), p. 233.

94 Fussell, *The Great War*, 1977 edn, p. 4.

95 *A Canadian Subaltern – Billy's letters home*, 1917, p. 105.

96 Edmonds, *A Subaltern's War*, pp. 66, 72, 78.

97 Partridge, *Slang of the British Soldier*, p. 49.

98 Quoted in Fussell, *The Great War*, 1977 edn, p. 8.

99 Lighter, *Slang of the AEF*, p. 86.

100 Brophy and Partridge, *The Long Trail*, 1969 edn.

101 Jones, *In Parenthesis*, 1969 edn, p. 42.

102 Fraser and Gibbons.

103 Partridge, *Words! Words! Words!*, p. 207.

104 *Notes and Queries*, December 1918, p. 333.

105 *Manchester Guardian*, 8 June 1917, p. 3; an example of the assessment of change in language as decadence, which was largely reversed by the public interest in and support for new slang during the war.

106 Quoted in *Yorkshire Evening Post*, 17 August 1917, p. 4.

107 *Fifth Gloucester Gazette*, 5 May 1915.

108 Partridge, *Words! Words! Words!*, p. 163.

109 Fraser and Gibbons; Brophy and Partridge, *The Long Trail*.

110 *The Athenaeum*, 1 August 1919, p. 694.

111 Ibid., 29 August 1919, p. 822.

112 *Yorkshire Evening Post*, 16 October 1916, p. 5.

6 Letting Go

1 *Chelmsford Chronicle*, 4 September 1914, p. 2.

2 Quoted in Doyle and Schäfer, *Fritz and Tommy,* p. 53.

3 Spicer, *Letters from France*.

4 *Daily Mirror*, 2 March 1915, p. 7; *Dundee Evening Telegraph*, 9 March 1916, p. 4; *Nottingham Evening Post*, 3 January 1918, p. 3.

5 The *OED* gives 1841 as the first documentation of this sense of 'on' as 'arranged; going to happen or to be carried through to completion'. 'Don't you know there's a war on' was No. 3 on *The Iodine Chronicle*'s list of hackneyed phrases, 20 December 1915 http://eco.canadiana.ca/view/oocihm.8_06748_4/1?r=0&s=1 accessed 17 October 2016.

6 http://www.europeana1914–1918.eu/en/contributions/17242 accessed 7 October 2016.

7 '"They're having a hell of a time", said a Lieutenant, "but they mean to finish the job"' *The Scotsman*, 13 October 1917, p. 7.

8 Letter, 15 September 1918, author's collection.

9 R. H. Mottram, *The Spanish Farm Trilogy*, Vol. 3, p. 690, (London: Chatto & Windus, [1926] 1928).

10 Edmonds, *A Subaltern's War*, p. 113.

11 *The Great War Interviews.*

12 Quoted in Vansittart, *John Masefield's Letters*, p. 148, 24 September 1916.

13 Letter, On Active Service, author's collection.

14 *The Listening Post*, 10 August 1917.

15 Quoted in Arthur, *We Will Remember Them*, p. 56.

16 Todman, *The Great War*, p. 64.

17 Douie, *The Weary Road*, p. 16.

18 Quoted in Arthur, *We Will Remember Them*, pp. 20, 21.

19 Douie, *The Weary Road*, p. 210.

20 *Daily Mirror*, 9 December 1918, p. 7.

21 *Punch*, 4 January 1919, p. 415.

22 *Hartlepool Northern Daily Mail*, Thursday 21 March 1929, p. 5.

23 See http://hansard.millbanksystems.com/written_answers/1921/jun/23/
defence-of-the-realm-act#S5CV0143P0_19210623_CWA_68 accessed 21
October 2016.

24 http://hansard.millbanksystems.com/commons/1931/nov/23/defence-of-
the-realm-act#S5CV0260P0_19311123_HOC_309 accessed 21 October
2016.

25 Fraser and Gibbons.

26 *Auckland Star*, 31 December 1918, p. 5.

27 *Daily Mail*, 4 June 1923, p. 7.

28 *Exeter and Plymouth Gazette*, 1 December 1926, p. 4.

29 *Daily Mail*, 30 November 1932, p. 10.

30 *Illustrated London News*, 7 August 1920, p. 234.

31 *Daily Mail*, 27 April 1925, p. 7.

32 *Derby Daily Telegraph*, 25 September 1939, p. 6.

33 *Manchester Guardian*, 12 November 1915, p. 5; 23 July 1917, p. 3.

34 *Yorkshire Evening Post*, 7 August 1917, p. 2.

35 See Coleman, '"Extraordinary cheeriness and good will"', in Walker and
Declercq, *Languages and the First World War: communicating*, pp. 268–70.

36 *The Bystander*, 1 January 1919, p. 45.

37 'Pop' appeared seldom in the press post-war; its importance to the troops as
a gathering site, out of range of most shells, was never going to be
understood by the Home Front.

38 'Perhaps 200,000 British lads at one time claimed "Plugstreet" as their
wartime home' – *Daily Express*, 15 October 1919, p. 4.

39 *Lancashire Evening Post*, 27 May 1931, p. 3.

40 *Daily Gazette for Middlesbrough*, 28 October 1939, p. 4.

41 *Birmingham Mail*,10 November 1939, p. 8.

42 *Gloucester Citizen*, 30 May 1949, p. 4.

43 *The Times*, 16 November 1962, p. 14, review of Lord Alexander's memoirs.

44 Though reproduced maps in the journal retain the anglicised names of sites like Mousetrap Farm, Paradise Alley, LRB Cottage. *Ypres Times*, April 1922, p. 83.

45 *Ypres Times*, August 1922, p. 23.

46 *Gloucestershire Chronicle*, 4 December 1925, p. 10.

47 Holmes, *A Yankee in the Trenches*, p. 166.

48 Smith, *Four Years on the Western Front*, p. 15.

49 Mottram, *A Personal Record*, p. 99.

50 Partridge, *Slang To-day and Yesterday*, p. 260.

51 *Sunderland Daily Echo*, 15 October 1921, p. 2.

52 Cook, 'Fighting Words', p. 342.

53 In Treves, *Made in the Trenches*, p. 219.

54 D. Lloyd, *Battlefield Tourism*, (Oxford: Oxford University Press, 1998), p. 23.

55 *The Times*, 31 Mar 1915, p. 5.

56 A. Norval, *The Tourist Industry*, (London, 1936), p. 48.

57 W. Ewart, 'Auburs Revisited', *Household Brigade Magazine*, 1921, p. 15, quoted in Lloyd, *Battlefield Tourism*, p. 117.

58 *Sunderland Daily Echo*, 1 October 1914, p. 3.

59 *Dundee Courier*, 24 May 1920, p. 2.

60 *Yorkshire Evening Post*, 15 August 1919, p. 7.

61 *Western Daily Press,* 24 June 1919, p. 6.

62 *Liverpool Daily Post*, 4 November 1915, p. 7.

63 *Aberdeen Evening Express*, 29 July 1916, p. 5.

64 *Dublin Daily Express*, 25 June 1917, p. 8; 28 November 1917, p. 6.

65 *Aberdeen Press and Journal*, 2 August 1918, p. 3.

66 See Lloyd, *Battlefield Tourism*, pp. 24–5.

67 *Daily Record*, 29 April 1916, p. 2.

68 *Leeds Mercury*, 8 September 1916, p. 2.

69 *Hull Daily Mail*, 21 October 1915, p. 4.

70 B. Brice, *Ypres – Outpost of the Channel Ports*, (London: John Murray, 1929), p. 48. A curious comment in *The Story of an Epic Pilgrimage*, p. 98, describes an area where 'so many of our boys fell . . . No wonder wheat and corn grew so luxuriantly.'

71 R. Fielding, *War Letters to a Wife*, (London: Medici Society, 1929), p. 206.

72 *Ypres Times*, October 1921, p. 22.

73 'holy ground' *Illustrated London News*, 21 August 1921, p. 284; *The Story of an Epic Pilgrimage*, title of the book about the 1928 British Legion organised trip; 'Guarding Sacred Ypres', stereoview postcard caption; 'holy ground . . . to be approached with solemn prayer . . . a shrine . . .' *Daily Telegraph*, 9 August 1928, p. 12; 'Pilgrims' Way', *Menin Gate Pilgrimage*, p. 12.

74 *The Story of an Epic Pilgrimage*, p. 40.

75 *The Times*, 5 December 1919, p. 16.

76 *Aberdeen Weekly Journal*, 23 May 1919, p. 2.

77 Brice, *Ypres*, p. 3.

78 *The Story of an Epic Pilgrimage*, p. 39.

79 Lloyd, *Battlefield Tourism*, p. 43.

80 *Illustrated London News*, 14 June 1919, p. 853.

81 Fielding, *War Letters to a Wife*, p. 206.

82 Douie, *The Weary Road*, p. 176.

83 *Manchester Guardian*, 21 May 1920, p. 8.

84 *Daily Telegraph*, 9 August 1928, p. 12.

85 E. Richardson, *Remembrance Wakes*, (London: Heath Cranton, 1934), p. 206.

86 T. Allen, *The Tracks They Trod*, (London: Herbert Joseph, 1932), p. 80.

87 *Manchester Guardian*, 21 May 1920, p. 8.

88 *Daily Express*, 15 October 1919, p. 4.

89 I. Hay, *The Ship of Remembrance*, (London: Hodder & Stoughton, 1926), p. 12.

90 *Northern Whig* (Antrim), 28 April 1927, p. 8.

91 Lloyd, *Battlefield Tourism*, p. 169.

92 *The Story of an Epic Pilgrimage*, p. 97.

93 Mottram, *Journey to the Western Front*, p. 76.

94 *The Story of an Epic Pilgrimage*, p. 150.

95 *Yorkshire Post*, 9 August 1928, p. 9.

96 *The Daily Telegraph*, 9 August 1928, p. 12.

97 *The Story of an Epic Pilgrimage*, p. 133.

98 Ibid., p. 114.

99 Ibid., p. 102.

100 *Gallipoli. Salonika. St. Barnabas, 1926*, 1927, p. 7.

101 *Illustrated London News*, 21 May 1921, p. 696.

102 Letter in the *Sheffield Evening Telegraph*, 18 August 1915, p. 3.

103 Brice, *Ypres*, p. 2.

104 Fielding, *War Letters to a Wife*, p. 208.

105 *Ypres Times*, October 1921, p. 23.

106 Mottram, *Journey to the Western Front*, p. 1.

107 A. Norris, *Mainly for Mother*, (Toronto: The Ryerson Press, 1920), p. 124.

108 From Kipling's poem 'Recessional', first published in 1897.

109 Founded at the end of the war and included in Fraser and Gibbons, an association to support disabled servicemen.

110 Winter, *Sites of Memory*, p. 115.

111 Brophy and Partridge, *Dictionary of Tommies' Songs and Slang*, p. 14.

112 Hamilton, *Gallipoli Diary*, 1920, p. 120.

113 Holmes, *Tommy*, p. 291.

114 *Western Morning News*, 23 July 1928, p. 3.

115 Allen, *The Tracks They Trod*, p. 75.

116 *Aberdeen Press and Journal*, 14 April 1922, p. 4.

117 *Gallipoli. Salonika. St. Barnabas, 1926*, 1927, p. 23.

118 *Surrey Mirror*, 22 July 1921, p. 7, the dedication of the Gatton War Memorial; *Western Gazette*, 16 November 1928, p. 8, Service of Remembrance.

119 Winter, *Sites of Memory*, pp. 97, 113.

120 https://en.wikipedia.org/wiki/Daddy,_what_did_you_do_in_the_Great_War%3F accessed 2 May 2017.

121 D. Athill, *Alive, Alive Oh: and other things that matter*, (London: Granta Books, 2015), p. 170.

122 Graves, *Goodbye to All That*, 1960 edn, p. 83.

123 Wright, *Shattered Glory*, p. 9.

124 Spicer, *Letters from France 1915–18*, 20 December 1915.

125 In Arthur, *We Will Remember Them*, p. 177.

126 H. Miles, *Untold Tales of War-time London: a personal diary*, (London: Cecil Palmer, 1930), p. 29, quoted in Pennell, *A Kingdom United*, p. 122.

127 Wadsworth, *Letters from the Trenches*, p. 116.

128 Ibid., p. 72.

129 Lloyd, *Battlefield Tourism*, p. 103.

130 Quoted in Fussell, *The Great War*, 1977 edn, p. 170.

131 Papers of Cpl J. Bemner, Private collection.

132 Remarque, *All Quiet on the Western Front*, p. 187.

133 Graves, *Goodbye to All That*, 1960, p. 237.

134 Moynihan, *A Place Called Armageddon*, p. 28.

135 Vansittart, *John Masefield's Letters*, 30 March 1917.

136 *Personal Diary of H. H. Cooper*, Private papers held by Imperial War Museum.

137 Paul Nash, letter, On Active Service, 16 November 1917.

138 Langley, *Battery Flashes*, p. 126.

139 In MacDonald, *They Called it Passchendaele*, 1993 edn, p. 127.

140 Remarque, *All Quiet on the Western Front*, p. 183.

141 Southard, *Shellshock*, p. 514.

142 G. Mosse, 'Shell-shock as a social disease', *Journal of Contemporary History*, (London, 2000), Vol. 35, No. 1, p. 101.

143 *The Times*, 2 September 1922, p. 13.

144 W. H. Rivers, *Instinct and the Unconscious: a contribution to a biological theory of the psycho-neuroses*, (Cambridge: Cambridge University Press, 1922), p. 189.

145 P. Leese, *Shell Shock*, (London: Palgrave Macmillan, 2002), p. 123; 'shellshock' was recognised as a lay term 'which will stand to medicine as the term weeds stands to botany', Southard, *Shellshock*, p. 831.

146 *Punch*, 9 April 1919, p. v.

147 Todman, *The Great War*, pp. 20–21.

148 L. Napper, 'Remembrance, re-membering, and recollection: Walter Summers and the British war film of the 1920s', in *British Silent Cinema*, p. 111.

149 Todman, *The Great War*, p. 194.

150 Ibid., p. 195.

151 e.g. Chapter 16, 'We Died in Hell', in *They Called it Passchendaele*, 1993 edn, pp. 185–211.

152 Todman, *The Great War*, p. 202.

153 http://www.qsl.net/gm0fne/diaryt~1.htm accessed 14 December 2016.

154 W. H. Rivers, *The Repression of War Experience*, presented to the Royal School of Medicine, 4 December 1917.

155 Fussell, *The Great War*, 1977 edn, p. 170.

156 Brophy and Partridge, *The Long Trail*, 1969 edn, p. 14.

157 For example, E. O'Neill's essay 'War Words', *The Windsor Magazine*, December 1918–May 1919, pp. 399–403; Edward Cook's essay 'Words and the War', in *Literary Recreations*, pp. 142–75.

158 *The Bodleian Quarterly Record*, 1st Quarter, 1918, pp. 123–5.

159 *Notes and Queries*, November 1918, p. 306.

160 Ibid., December 1918, p. 333.

161 Ibid., March 1919, p. 79.

162 Ibid., June 1919, p. 159.

163 *The Athenaeum*, 23 May 1919, pp. 359–60.

164 Ibid., 11 July 1919, p. 583.

165 Ibid., 25 July 1919, p. 663.

166 Ibid., 26 September 1919, p. 957.

167 Ibid., 7 November 1919, p. 1163.

168 For an investigation of this see J. Walker, in Declercq and Walker, *Languages and the First World War: representation*, pp. 214–36.

169 See J. Coleman, *A History of Cant and Slang Dictionaries*, Vol. 3, (Oxford: Oxford University Press, 2009), p. 247.

170 Ibid., p. 253.

171 'No 9' is one of the more curious survivors from the war, still in use a hundred years later in Bingo calling, as 'Doctor's orders, Number 9'.

172 *Notes and Queries*, 5 November 1921, pp. 378–9.

173 *The Athenaeum*, 18 July 1919, p. 632.

174 'A. H. B.', 1 August 1919, p. 694.

175 Coleman, *A History of Cant*, Vol. 3, 2009, pp. 256–7.

176 Brophy and Partridge, *Songs and Slang of the British Soldier*, p. v.

177 Fraser and Gibbons, p. v.

178 Brophy and Partridge, *Songs and Slang of the British Soldier*, p. 189.

179 Fraser and Gibbons, p. v.

180 Partridge, *Words! Words! Words!*, p. 183.

181 Partridge, *Slang To-day and Yesterday*, p. 260.

182 Collinson, *Contemporary English,* p. 103.

183 H. Hiddeman, *Untersuchungen zum Slang des Englischen Heeres im Weltkrieg*, (Emsdetten: H. & J. Lechte, 1938), p. 135.

184 *The Observer*, 7 November 1965, p. 26.

185 J. Green, *Language!: 500 years of the vulgar tongue*, (London: Atlantic Books, 2014), p. 378.

186 *The Times*, 1 November 2014.

187 J. Brophy, 'After Fifty Years', in Brophy and Partridge, *The Long Trail*, 1969 edn, p. 11.

188 Magazine advertisement, *Home Chats*, 5 September 1914, p. 436; The *Ilford Guardian*, 13 November 1914, p. 3 noted that the names 'The Germanic War', the 'Pan European War' and the 'War of the Allies' had all been tried, but were found to be insufficiently descriptive of the range of combatant nations.

189 Fussell, *The Great War*, 1977 edn, pp. 315–16.

190 Ibid., p. 188.

191 Ibid., p. 187.

192 *Illustrated London News*, 4 October 1914, p. 468.

193 Smith, *Four Years on the Western Front*, p. 23.

194 Graves, *Goodbye to All That*, 1960 edn, p. 105.

195 Moulton, *Papers for Wartime*, No. 31, 1915, p. 5.

196 The *OED* citations for this since 1978 all come from shooting contexts.

197 Quoted in Doyle and Schäfer, *Fritz and Tommy*, p. 191.

198 *The War Illustrated*, 15 January 1916, p. 519.

199 Postcard, On Active Service, 13 February 1915, author's collection.

200 J. Jones, *Diary*, 10 March 1918.

201 The *Derby Daily Telegraph*, 25 September 1939, p. 6, recorded 'as then, so now: "pain", "oeufs", "Coffee-or-lay", "no bon", "tray bon", and "encore", still make up the average soldier's vocabulary'; *What's the Dope?* A slang glossary published after 1939 included 'Bosche', 'heavies', 'strafe' and many more familiar terms, *What's the Dope? An encyclopædia of Army, Navy and Air Force abbreviations, etc.* (Illustrated by Will Owen), London; Bognor Regis: John Crowther, (1944).

202 http://www.bbc.co.uk/news/magazine-29757988 accessed 20 December 2016.

203 Partridge, *Words! Words! Words!*, p. 167.

204 Partridge, *Quarterly Review*, p. 359.

BIBLIOGRAPHY

2/1st Northern Cyclist Battalion, (from 1915), *Northern Mudguard*, Boston; Skegness.

9th Royal Scots (T.F.): B Company on active service; from a private's diary February–May 1915, (1916), Edinburgh: Turnbull & Spears.

Fifth Gloucester Gazette, ([1915–1919], 1993), Gloucestershire: Alan Sutton Publishing.

Agate, J., (1917), *L. of C. (Lines of Communication)*, London: Constable & Company.

Aitchison, J., (1997), *The Language Web*, Cambridge: Cambridge University Press.

Alford, H., (1864), *A Plea for the Queen's English*, London: Strahan.

Allen, T., (1932), *The Tracks They Trod*, London: Herbert Joseph.

'Anzac Slang', (1916), in F. Treves, ed., *Made in the Trenches*, 78–80, London: George Allen & Unwin.

ap Glyn, I., (2016), ' "Dear Mother, I am very sorry I cannot write to you in Welsh . . ."; censorship and the Welsh language in the First World War', in J. Walker and C. Declercq, eds, *Languages and the First World War: communicating in a transnational war*, 128–41, London: Palgrave Macmillan.

Apollinaire, G., (2010), *Letters to Madeleine: tender as memory*, trans. D. Nicholson-Smith, L. Campa, ed., Chicago: Chicago University Press.

Armstrong, E., (1937) *The Crisis of Quebec, 1914–1918*, New York: Columbia University Press.

Army Ordnance Corps, (1916), *The Fuze*, England.

Arthur, M., (2009), *We Will Remember Them*, London: Weidenfeld & Nicholson.

Ashworth, T, (1980), *Trench Warfare 1914–1918: the live and let live system*, London: Macmillan.

Athill, D., (2015), *Alive, Alive Oh, and Other Things That Matter*, London: Granta Books.

Atkin, H., *Diary*, https://davinaatkin.wordpress.com/2014/08/29/28th-july-1914/, accessed 25 April 2017.

Aussie, (1918–1919), Flêtre, France, Australian Imperial Force.

A War Nurse's Diary, ([1918] 2005), Burgess Hill: Diggory Press.

Baggs, T., (1914), *Back from the Front*, London: F. & C. Palmer.

Bagnold, E., (1918), *A Diary Without Dates*, London: Heinemann.

Barker, G., (1931), *Agony's Anguish*, Manchester: Alf Eva.

Barthas, L., trans. E. Strauss, (2014), *Poilu: the World War I notebooks of Corporal Louis Barthas, barrelmaker, 1914–1918*, New Haven: Yale University Press.

Battle of the Somme, The, [film], see under Malins, G. H.

BBC interviews, (1963–4), [BBC television programme], http://www.bbc.co.uk/
iplayer/group/p01tbj6p accessed 25 April 2017

Bean, C., (1983), *The Official History of Australia in the War of 1914–1918*, in
D. Gill and G. Dallas, (1985), *Unknown Army*, London: Verso.

Beck, J., (1923), *A Diary of Armistice Days*, Philadelphia: Printed for private
circulation.

Bergmann, K., (1916), *Wie der Feldgraue Spricht*, Giessen: Töpelmann.

Beyen, M., (2016),'Linguistic syncretism as a mark of ethnic purity? Jeroom
Leuridan on language developments among Flemsih soldiers during the First
World War', in J. Walker and C. Declercq, eds, *Languages and the First World
War: communicating in a transnational war*, 226–40, London: Palgrave
Macmillan.

Bilbrough, E., (2014), *My War Diary 1914–1918*, London: Ebury Press.

Blackie's, (c.1920), *Compact Etymological Dictionary*, Blackie & Son Ltd.

Blackledge, W. J., (1936), *The Legion of Marching Madmen*, London: Sampson
Low, Marston & Co.

Bloch, M., ed., (1997), *Écrits de guerre (1914–1918)*, Paris: Colin.

Blunden, E., ([1928] 1991), *Undertones of War*, London: Folio Society.

Bluett, A., (1919), *With our Army in Palestine*, London: Andrew Melrose.

Bolton W. F. and D. Crystal, eds, ([1940] 1969), *The English Language: essays by
linguists and men of letters 1858–1964*, Vol. 2, Cambridge: Cambridge
University Press.

Boraston, J., ed., (1919), *Sir Douglas Haig's Despatches (December 1915–April
1919)*, London; Toronto: J. M. Dent & Sons.

Bourke, J., (1996), *Dismembering the Male: men's bodies, Britain and the Great
War*, London: Reaktion Books.

Bowd, G., (2016),'From hatred to hybridization: the German language in
occupied France', in J. Walker and C. Declercq, eds, *Languages and the First
World War: communicating in a transnational War*, 190–208, London:
Palgrave Macmillan.

Brice, B., (1929), *Ypres – Outpost of the Channel Ports*, London: John Murray.

Brindle, W., (1919), *France and Flanders*, Saint John: S. K. Smith.

British Legion, The, (1928), *The Story of an Epic Pilgrimage*, England: The British
Legion.

Broadhead, G. W., *Diary*, Private papers held by Imperial War Museum.

Brock, Pte W. C., Private papers held by Imperial War Museum.

Brophy, J., (1929), *The Soldier's War: a prose anthology*, London: Dent.

Brophy, J., and E. Partridge, (1930), *Songs and Slang of the British Soldier:
1914–1918*, London: Eric Partridge Ltd.

Brophy, J., and E. Partridge, ([1965] 1969), *The Long Trail – Soldiers' Songs and
Slang 1914–18*, London: Sphere.

Brophy, J., and E. Partridge, (2008), *The Daily Telegraph Dictionary of Tommies'
Songs and Slang*, Barnsley: Pen & Sword Military.

Bryan, J., (1918), *Ambulance 464*, New York: Macmillan.

Bryant, Percy, (1975), (RFA gunner), Imperial War Museum interview.

Brown, M., (1991), *The Imperial War Museum Book of the Western Front*, London: Guild Publishing.

Buchan, J., (1920), *Francis and Riversdale Grenfell*, Thomas Nelson & Sons Ltd.

Buller, H., (1915), *The Soldiers' English–German Conversation Book*, London: T. Werner Laurie, Ltd.

Burrage, A. M., ([1930] 2010), *War is War*, Barnsley: Pen & Sword Military.

Cable, B., (1916), 'The Blighty Squad', in F. Treves, ed., *Made in the Trenches*, 15–24, London: George Allen & Unwin.

Cable, B., (1919), *The Old Contemptibles*, London: Hodder & Stoughton.

Calwell, C., (1920), *Experiences of a Dug-Out 1914–1918*, Constable & Co.

Canadian Subaltern, A, (1917), London: Constable & Co.

Caseby, A., *Diary*, Private papers held by Imperial War Museum.

Cassell, (1919), *New English Dictionary*, London: Cassell.

Chasseaud, P., (2006), *Rats Alley*, Staplehurst: Spellmount.

Clapham, H., (1930), *Mud and Khaki*, London: Hutchinson & Co.

Clark, A., ([1985] 1988), *Echoes of the Great War: the diary of the Reverend Andrew Clark*, J. Munson, ed., Oxford: Oxford University Press.

Coleman, F., (1916), *With Cavalry in 1915*, London: Sampson Low & Co.

Coleman, J., (2009), *A History of Cant and Slang Dictionaries*, Vol 3, Oxford: Oxford University Press.

Coleman, J., (2016), ' "Extraordinary cheeriness and good will": the uses and documentation of First World War slang', in J. Walker and C. Declercq, eds, *Languages and the First World War: communicating in a transnational war*, 128–41, London: Palgrave Macmillan.

Collinson, W. E., (1927), *Contemporary English: a personal speech record*, Leipzig; Berlin: B. G. Teubner.

Commission instituée en vue de constater les actes commis par l'ennemi en violation du droit des gens, (1915), *German Atrocities in France: a translation of the official report of the French Commission*, London: Daily Chronicle.

Cook, Lt Col E., (1915), *War Diary of the 1st Life Guards. First year, 1914–1915*, England.

Cook, E. T., (1918), *Literary Recreations*, London: Macmillan & Co.

Cook, T., (2013), 'Fighting words: Canadian soldiers' slang and swearing in the Great War', in *War in History*, Vol 20, Issue 3, http://research.gold.ac.uk/11325/1/AngelsofMonspapersocieties-04-00180.pdf accessed 25 April 2017.

Cooper, H. H., *Personal Diary of H. H. Cooper*, Private papers held by Imperial War Museum.

Coppard, G., ([1979] 1986), *With a Machine Gun to Cambrai*, London: Papermac.

Copping, A., (1917), *Souls in Khaki*, London: Hodder & Stoughton.

Cornet-Auquier, A., trans. T. Stanton, (1918), *A Soldier Unafraid*, Boston: Little, Brown, & Co.

'Correspondence Course in Patriotism', (1918), New York: National Security League.

Cowie, Surgeon-Major, (1915), *War Diary of the 1st Life Guards. First year, 1914–1915*, England.

Cowman, K., (2016), ' "The . . . 'parlez' is not going on very well 'avec moi' " ': learning and using "Trench French" on the Western Front', in J. Walker and C. Declercq, eds, *Languages and the First World War: communicating in a transnational war,* 128–41, London: Palgrave Macmillan.

Crofts, J., (1919), *Field Ambulance Sketches,* London: John Lane.

Crouch, L. W., (1917), *Duty and Service: letters from the front by Captain Lionel William Crouch,* London; Aylesbury: Printed for private circulation.

Cude, R., (1922), *Diary,* Private papers held by Imperial War Museum.

Cunliffe, R. J., (c.1920), *Blackie's Compact Etymological Dictionary,* London: Blackies.

Dauzat, A., ([1918] 2007), *L'Argot de la Guerre,* Paris: Armand Colin.

Dawson, A., (1918), *A "Temporary Gentleman" in France,* London: Cassell.

Dawson, C., (1919), *Living Bayonets,* London: John Lane.

De L'Isle, A., (1922), *Leaves from a V.A.D.'s Diary,* London: Elliot Stock.

De Loghe, S., (1917), *The Straits Impregnable,* London: John Murray.

Déchelette, F., (1918), *L'Argot des poilus,* Paris: Jouve & Cie éditeurs.

Declercq, C., and J. Walker, eds, (2016), *Languages and the First World War: representation and memory,* London: Palgrave Macmillan.

Delépine, H., (1914), *What a British Soldier Wants to Say in French,* Wimereux.

Dendooven, D., (2016), ' "Fake Belgium": linguistic issues in the diary of Father Achiel Van Walleghem (1914–1919)', in C. Declercq and J. Walker, eds, *Languages and the First World War: representation and memory,* 43–53, London: Palgrave Macmillan.

Denham, H. M., (1981), *Dardanelles: a midshipman's diary 1915–16,* London: Murray.

Diary of a Nursing Sister on the Western Front, 1914–15, ([1915] 1930), (K. Luard), Edinburgh; London: Willam Blackwood & Sons.

Doughty, R., *Diary of Cpl R D Doughty,* http://www.thekivellfamily.co.nz/military_history/ralphs_diaries/transcribes/diary_five_p3.html, accessed 25 April 2017.

Douie, C., (1929), *The Weary Road,* London: John Murray.

Downing, W., (1919), *Digger Dialects,* Melbourne; Sydney: Lothian Book Publishing Co.

Doyle, P., (2016), *Kitchener's Mob,* Stroud: The History Press.

Doyle, P., and R. Schäfer, (2015), *Fritz and Tommy,* Stroud: The History Press.

Doyle, P., and J. Walker, (2012), *Trench Talk: words of the First World War,* Stroud: The History Press.

Duce, Capt Keith, (c.1975), Imperial War Museum, [sound recording].

Duffin, E., (2014), *The First World War Diaries of Emma Duffin,* (compiled in 1919), T. Parkhill, ed., Dublin: Four Courts Press.

Dunn, J., ([1938] 2004), *The War the Infantry Knew,* London: Abacus.

Easton, J., (1929), 'Broadchalk, a chronicle', in *Three Personal Records of the War,* London: Scholartis.

Edmonds, C., (1929), *A Subaltern's War,* London: Peter Davies.

English–Flemish Military Guide, (1915), Poperinge: Drukk.

Fallon, D., (1918), *The Big Fight,* London: Cassell & Co.

Fielding, R., (1929), *War Letters to a Wife*, London: Medici Society.

Fogarty, R., (2016), 'We did not speak a common language: African soldiers and communication in the French Army, 1914–1918', in J. Walker and C. Declercq, eds, *Languages and the First World War: communicating in a transnational war*, 44–61, London: Palgrave Macmillan.

Foottit, H., (2016), 'Poetry, parables and codes: translating the letters of Indian Soldiers', in J. Walker, and C. Declercq, eds, *Languages and the First World War: communicating in a transnational war*, 115–27, London: Palgrave Macmillan.

Fraser, E., and J. Gibbons, (1925), *Soldier and Sailor Words and Phrases*, London: George Routledge & Sons.

Fussell, P., ([1975] 1977), *The Great War and Modern Memory*, Oxford: Oxford University Press.

Gallipoli. Salonika. St Barnabas, 1926, (1927), London: St Barnabas Hostels.

Gibbs, P., (1916), *The Soul of the War*, London: William Heinemann.

Gibson, S., (2014), *Behind the Front: British soldiers and French civilians, 1914–1918*, Cambridge; New York: Cambridge University Press.

Gill, D., and G. Dallas, (1985), *Unknown Army*, London: Verso.

Goodchild, G., (1916), 'The Sensitive Plant', in F. Treves, ed., *Made in the Trenches*, 49–60, London: George Allen & Unwin.

Graham, S., (1919), *A Private in the Guards*, London: Macmillan.

Graves, R., ([1929] 1960), *Goodbye to All That*, London: Penguin.

Gray, J., (1916), 'A Linesman's Gallipoli', in W. Wood, *In the Line of Battle*, London: Chapman & Hall.

Graystone, J. W., *Diary*, Private papers held by Imperial War Museum.

Green, J., (2014), *Language!: 500 years of the vulgar tongue*, London: Atlantic Books.

Green, J., (2016), *Green's Dictionary of Slang Online*, https://greensdictofslang.com, accessed 25 April 2017

Greenhalgh, E., (2014), *The French Army and the First World War*, Cambridge: Cambridge University Press.

Greenwall, H., (1923), *Scoops*, London: Stanley Paul & Co.

Greifelt, R., (1937), *Der Slang des englischen Soldaten im Weltkrieg 1914–1918*, doctoral dissertation, Marburg.

Grey Brigade, (1915), Dorking.

Grimm, H., trans. J. Bulloch, ([1928] 2014), *Schlump*, London: Vintage Books.

Grimm, J., & W. Grimm, (1922), *Deutsches Wörterbuch*, Leipzig: Verlag von S. Hirzel.

Haasmann, S., (1914), *Deutsch–Englischer Soldaten-Sprachführer*, Leipzig: Verlag Hachmeister & Thal.

Hamilton, Gnl Sir Ian, (1920), *Gallipoli Diary*, London: Edward Arnold.

Harris, W. H., Private papers held by Imperial War Museum.

Har Dayal, (1920), *Forty-four Months in Germany and Turkey, February 1915 to October 1918*, London: P. S. King & Son.

Harmsworth, A., (Lord Northcliffe), (1916), *At the War*, London: Hodder & Stoughton.

Harvey, H., *A Soldier's Sketches under Fire*, London: Sampson, Low, Marston & Co., 1916.

Hay, I., (1916), *The First Hundred Thousand*, Edinburgh; London: William Blackwood & Sons.

Hay, I., (1917), *All In It: K1 carries on*, Toronto: Briggs.

Hay, I., (1917), *Carrying On: after the first hundred thousand*, Edinburgh; London: William Blackwood & Sons.

Hay, I., (1926), *The Ship of Remembrance*, London: Hodder & Stoughton.

Hedin, S., (1915), trans. H. G. de Walterstorff, *With the German Armies in the West*, London: John Lane.

Hepper, E. R., (2011), *Captain E. Raymond Hepper's Great War Diary, 1916–1919*, Kirkby Stephen: Hayloft Pub.

Herbert, A., ([1919] 1930), *Mons, Anzac, and Kut*, London: [Edward Arnold, 1919] Hutchinson & Co., 1930.

Hewett, S., (1918), *A Scholar's Letters from the Front*, London: Longmans, Green & Co.

Hiddeman, H., (1938), *Untersuchungen zum Slang des Englischen Heeres im Weltkrieg*, Emsdetten: H. & J. Lechte.

Hitchcock, F., (1937), *Stand To: a diary of the trenches 1914–1918*, London: Hurst & Blackett.

Hobsbawm, E., ([1990] 1992), *Nations and Nationalism since 1780*, Cambridge: Cambridge University Press.

Hodson, J., (1916), 'The "Sure-To-Be-Hit" Feeling', in F. Treves, ed., *Made in the Trenches*, 180–84, London: George Allen & Unwin.

Holmes, R. D., (1918), *A Yankee in the Trenches*, Boston: Little, Brown & Co.

Holmes, R., (2004), *Tommy*, London: Harper Collins.

Hong Kong Education Department, (1918), *War Stories in English and Chinese*, Hong Kong.

Hotten, J. C., (1865), *The Slang Dictionary; or, the vulgar words, street phrases, and "fast expressions" of high and low society*, London: John Camden Hotten.

Housman, L., (1930), *War Letters of Fallen Englishmen*, London: Victor Gollancz.

Hughes, G., ([1991] 1998), *Swearing*, London: Penguin.

Hulse, E., (1916), *Letters Written from the English Front in France, 1914–15*, privately printed.

Huns Ancient and Modern, (1918), London: Skeffington & Son Ltd.

Hunter-Weston, A., (1918), *Private War Diary*, add. MS 48355–48368, British Library.

In the Hands of the Huns: being the reminiscences of a British civil prisoner of war, 1914–1915, (1916), London: Simpkin, Marshall & Co.

Jenkins, D. F., (2010), *Paul Nash, The Elements*, London: Scala.

John Bull, (1906–1958), London.

Jones, D., ([1937] 1969), *In Parenthesis*, London: Faber & Faber Ltd.

Jones, E., (2006), 'The psychology of killing', *Journal of Contemporary History*, Vol. 41, No.2, London, 244.

Jones, H., (2011), 'Imperial captivities: colonial prisoners of war in Germany and the Ottoman Empire, 1914–1918', in S. Das, ed., *Race, Empire and First World War Writing*, 175–93, Cambridge: Cambridge University Press.

Jones, J., (1998), *The First World War Diary of James Gilbert Jones*, Welshpool: Montgomeryshire Genealogical Society.

Karvalics, L., (2015), 'Crosspoints of information history and Great War', in L. Karvalics, ed., *Information History of the First World War*, 7–28, Paris: L'Harmattan.

Kelley, M. R., (2014), 'But Kultur's Nar-poo in the Trenches', in *Art In America*, June 2014, New York. http://www.artinamericamagazine.com/news-features/magazine/but-kulturs-nar-poo-in-the-trenches/

Kennedy, A., and G. Crabb, (1977), *The Postal History of the British Army in World War One*, Epsom, Surrey: G. Crabb.

Khan, N., (1988), *Women's Poetry of the First World War*, Lexington: The University Press of Kentucky.

Kilpatrick, J., (1914), *Atkins at War, as Told in His Own Letters*, London: Herbert Jenkins.

Kipling, R., (1923), *The Irish Guards in the Great War*, Garden City, New York: Doubleday, Page & Co.

Kipling, R., (2004), T. Pinney, ed., *The Letters of Rudyard Kipling, 1931–36*, Basingstoke: Macmillan.

Knowles, G., (2005), *A Cultural History of the English Language*, London: Arnold.

Koller, C., (2011), 'Representing Otherness: African, Indian, and European soldiers' letters and memoirs', in S. Das, ed., *Race, Empire and First World War Writing*, 127–42, Cambridge: Cambridge University Press.

Lake, H., (1917), *In Salonica with our Army*, London: Andrew Melrose.

Langley, C. W., ('Wagger'), (1916), *Battery Flashes*, London: John Murray.

Laugesen, A., *Glossary of Slang and Peculiar Terms in Use in the A.I.F.* http://andc.anu.edu.au/australian-words/aif-slang/annotated-glossary accessed 25 April 2017.

Le Naour J-Y, 1998. 'Les désillusions de la libération d'après le contrôle postal civile de Lille (octobre 1918–mars 1919)', in *Revue du Nord*, tome LXXX, Vol. 325 (April–June).

Lee, J., (1939), *To-morrow is a New Day*, London: The Cresset Press.

Leese, P., (2002) *Shell Shock*, London: Palgrave Macmillan.

Leroy, O., ([1922] 1924), *A Glossary of French Slang*, London: Harrap & Co.

Lighter, J., ([1972] 1975), 'The slang of the American Expeditionary Forces in Europe, 1917–1919: an historical glossary', in *American Speech*, Vol 47, Tuscaloosa: University of Alabama Press for the American Dialect Society.

Literary Digest, The, (1918), New York: Funk & Wagnalls Co.

Liveing, E., (1918), *Attack: an infantry subaltern's impressions*, New York: The Macmillan Company.

Lloyd, D., (1998), *Battlefield Tourism*, Oxford: Oxford University Press.

Long, R., (1915), *Colours of War*, New York: Charles Scribner's Sons.

Lotterie, P., (1981), *Un village ardennois pendant les deux guerres mondiales*, privately published.

Loyal North Lancashire Regiment, (1916), *Carry On: The Trotters' Journal*, Ashford.

Luard, K., See *Diary of a Nursing Sister*.

MacArthur, C., (1919), *A Bug's-eye View of the War*, United States: privately published.

MacDonald, L., ([1978] 1993), *They Called it Passchendaele*, London: Penguin.

MacDonald, L., ([1980] 1984), *The Roses of No Man's Land*, London: Papermac.

MacDonald, L., ([1988] 1991), *Voices and Images of the Great War*, London: Penguin.

MacDonald, L., (1993), *Somme*, London: Penguin.

MacDonald, M., (1917), *Under the French Flag*, London: Robert Scott.

MacGill, P., (1916), *The Great Push*, London: Herbert Jenkins.

Macmillan, (1922), *A Modern Dictionary of the English Language*, London: Macmillan.

Makepeace, C., (2011), 'Soldiers, masculinity and prostitutes in WW1', in J. Arnold, and S. Brady, eds, *What is Masculinity?*, 413–30, London: Palgrave Macmillan.

Malins, G. H., (1920), *How I Filmed the War*, London: Herbert Jenkins.

Malins, G. H., and J. McDowell, (1916), *The Battle of the Somme* [film], British Topical Committee for War Films.

Manning, F., ([1929–30] 2013), *The Middle Parts of Fortune/Her Privates We*, London: Serpent's Tail.

Manwaring, G. B., (1918), *If We Return*, London; New York: John Lane.

Marlow, J., ed., ([1998] 2005), *The Virago Book of Women and the Great War*, London: Virago Press.

Marwick, A., ([1965] 1991), *The Deluge*, Basingstoke: Macmillan.

Masefield, J., (1984), P. Vansittart, ed. *John Masefield's Letters from the Front 1915–17*, London: Constable & Co.

McBride H., (1918), *The Emma-Gees*, Indianapolis: Bobbs-Merrill Co.

McDonagh, M., (1917), *The Irish on the Somme*, London: Hodder & Stoughton.

McDonald, M., (1989), *'We are not French!': language, culture and identity in Brittany*, London: Routledge.

McNair, D., (2008), *A Pacifist at War: military memoirs of a conscientious objector in Palestine, 1917–1918*, Much Hadham: Anastasia.

Menin Gate Pilgrimage, (1927), London: St Barnabas Society.

Merrill, W., (1918), *A College Man in Khaki*, New York: George H. Doran.

Miles (Killick), H., (1930), *Untold Tales of War-time London: a personal diary*, London: Cecil Palmer.

Miller, D., (2000), *The Illustrated Directory of Tanks of the World*, London: Salamander.

Millman, B., (2016), *Polarity, Patriotism and Dissent in Great War Canada, 1914–19*, Toronto; Buffalo: University of Toronto Press.

Milner, L., ([1991] 1998), *Leeds Pals*, Barnsley: Pen & Sword Books.

Moran, Lord, see under Wilson, C.

Mosse, G., (2000), 'Shell-shock as a social disease', *Journal of Contemporary History*, Vol. 35, No. 1, pp. 101–8, London.

Mottram, R. H., ([1926] 1928), *The Spanish Farm Trilogy*, Vol. 3, London: Chatto & Windus.

Mottram, R. H., (1929), 'A Personal Record', in *Three Personal Records of the War*, London: Scholartis.

Mottram, R. H., (1936), *Journey to the Western Front*, London: G. Bell & Sons.

Moulton, J. H., (1915), *British and German Scholarship* (*Papers for Wartime No. 31*), Oxford: Oxford University Press.

Moynihan, M., ed., (1975), *A Place Called Armageddon*, Newton Abbot: David & Charles.

Mügge, M., (1920), *The War Diary of a Square Peg*, London: George Routledge and Sons Ltd.

Mugglestone, L., (2014), *Words In Wartime*, https://wordsinwartime.wordpress.com accessed 25 April 2017.

Muir, W., (1917), *Observations of an Orderly*, London: Simpkin, Marshall & Co.

Munro, R., (1919), *From Darwinism to Kaiserism*, Glasgow: J. Maclehose & Sons.

Napper L., (2011), 'The Battle of the Somme (1916)', in M. Hammond and M. Williams, eds, *British Silent Cinema and the Great War*, Basingstoke; New York: Palgrave Macmillan.

Napper, L., (2011), 'Remembrance, re-membering, and recollection: Walter Summers and the British war film of the 1920s', in M. Hammond and M. Williams, eds, *British Silent Cinema and The Great War*, Basingstoke; New York: Palgrave Macmillan.

Nevill, B., (1991), *Billie*, London: MacRae.

Newton, William James, (1975), Imperial War Museum interview.

Niceforo, A., (1912), *Le Genie de l'Argot*, Paris.

Nicholson, J., (1889), *The Folk Speech of East Yorkshire*, London: Simpkin, Marshall & Co.

Noakes, V., (2006), *Voices of Silence: the alternative book of First World War poetry*, Stroud: Sutton.

Nobbs, G., (1910), *Englishman, Kamerad!*, London: William Heinemann.

Norris, A., (1920), *Mainly for Mother*, Toronto: The Ryerson Press.

Northcliffe, Lord, see under Harmsworth, A.

Norval, A., (1936), *The Tourist Industry*, London.

O'Neill, E., (1918), *Battles for Peace: the story of the Great War told for children*, London: Hodder & Stoughton.

O'Neill, E., (1919), 'War Words', essay in *The Windsor Magazine*, December 1918–May 1919, pp. 399–403.

O'Neill, H., (1922), *The Royal Fusiliers in the Great War*, London: Heinemann.

O'Toole, T., (1916), *The Way They Have in the Army*, London: John Lane.

Omissi, D., (1999), *Indian Voices of the Great War*, Basingstoke: Macmillan Press.

'One of the Jocks', (1916), *Odd Shots*, London: Hodder & Stoughton.

On the Road to Kut: a soldier's story of the Mesopotamian campaign, (1917), London: Hutchinson & Co.

Osborn, E. B., (1918), *The Muse in Arms*, London: John Murray.

Oxford English Dictionary, online edition, http://www.oed.com, accessed 25 April 2017.

Palmer, S. and S. Wallis, ([2003] 2004), *A War in Words*, London: Pocket Books (imprint of Simon & Schuster).

Parker, Capt F. B., Private papers held by Imperial War Museum.

Parrott, J. E., (1915–1919), *The Children's Story of the War*, London: Thomas Nelson & Sons.

Partridge, E., (1929), 'Frank Honywood, Private', in *Three Personal Records of the War*, London: Scholartis.

Partridge, E., ([1931] 1970), *A Martial Medley*, New York: Books for Libraries Press.

Partridge, E., (1931), *Quarterly Review*, Vol. 256, London: John Murray.

Partridge, E., (1933), *Words! Words! Words!*, London: Methuen.

Partridge, E., ([1933] 1970), *Slang To-day and Yesterday*, London: Routledge & Kegan Paul.

Partridge, E., ([1937] 1974), *A Dictionary of Slang and Unconventional English*, London: Routledge & Kegan Paul.

Partridge, E., ([1945] 1990), *Dictionary of R.A.F. Slang*, London: Pavilion.

Partridge, E., (1936–38), 'Slang of the British Soldier 1914–18', in E. B. Swinton, ed., *Twenty Years After*, Vol. 3, London: Newnes.

Partridge, E., ([1940] 1969), ' "Slang", Society for Pure English", Tract LV, in W. F. Bolton, and D. Crystal, eds, *The English Language: essays by linguists and men of letters 1858–1964*, Vol. 2, Cambridge: Cambridge University Press.

Pennell, C., (2014), *A Kingdom United*, Oxford: Oxford University Press.

Pinfold, J. R., ed., (2006), *A Month at the Front: the diary of an unknown soldier*, Oxford: Bodleian Library.

Ponsonby, A., (1928), *Falsehood in War-time*, London: George Allen & Unwin.

Ponsonby, A., (1916), *The Crank*, (London: Headley).

Poynter, D., (2008), 'A study of the psychological disorders of nurses and female V.A.D.s who served alongside the B.E.F. and Allied Forces during the First World War', doctoral thesis.

Pulvertaft, G., (2014), *Reminiscences of a V.A.D.*, Great Britain: John Brunsdon.

Quigley H, (1928), *Passchendaele and the Somme*, London: Methuen & Co.

Randerson, J. H., (1922), *The Origin of the War Term No Man's Land as Applied to the World War*, Albany: privately published. https://archive.org/stream/originofwartermn00rand accessed 25 April 2017.

Red Cross work with Russian prisoners of war in Germany, (1919), Acount held by Imperial War Museum.

Red Triangle Girl In France, A, (1918), New York: George H. Doran.

Rees, Major A. E., ([1917] 2001), dir., *In the Trenches*, [sound dramatisation], England: 78 rpm disc, No. R2796 B, Columbia; CD41-001, *Oh! It's a Lovely War*, Vol. 1, CD41 Publishing Ltd.

Rees, D., (1906, 1918), *The Briton in France*, London: Leopold B. Hill.

Remarque, E. M., (1929), trans. A. W. Wheen, (1929) *All Quiet on the Western Front*, London: Putnam.

Richardson, E., (1934), *Remembrance Wakes*, London: Heath Cranton.

Rivers, W. H., (1917), *The Repression of War Experience*, presented to the Royal School of Medicine.

Rivers, W. H., (1922), *Instinct and the Unconscious: a contribution to a biological theory of the psycho-neuroses*, Cambridge: Cambridge University Press.

Roberts, F. J., and J. H. Pearson, ([1916–18] 2013), *The Wipers Times, etc*, London: Conway.

Röhl, J., (2014), *Wilhelm II: into the abyss of war and exile 1900–1941*, Cambridge: Cambridge University Press.

Royal Fusiliers (City of London Regiment), (1915–16), *The Pow-Wow/The Gasper*, Salisbury.

Roynette, O., (2016), 'Problems and challenges of a historical approach', in C. Declercq and J. Walker, eds, *Languages and the First World War: representation and memory*, 21–31, London: Palgrave Macmillan.

Russell, M., (2003), *Piltdown Man*, Stroud: Tempus.

Sandes, F., (1927), *Autobiography of a Woman Soldier*, London: H. F. & G. Witherby.

Sarolea, C., (1915), *How Belgium Saved Europe*, London: William Heinemann.

Scheer, T., (2016), 'Habsburg languages at war: "The linguistic confusion at the Tower of Babel couldn't have been much worse"', in J. Walker and C. Declercq, eds, *Languages and the First World War: communicating in a transnational war*, 62–78, London: Palgrave Macmillan.

Seal, G., (2013), *The Soldiers' Press: trench journals in the First World War*, Basingstoke: Palgrave Macmillan.

Shears, E. H., (1919), *Active Service Diary*, Liverpool: Henry Young & Sons Ltd.

Shimazu, N., (1995), 'The racial equality proposal at the 1919 Paris Peace Conference', doctoral thesis, Oxford University.

Shuttleworth, W., *Diary of Walter Shuttleworth*, http://www.klewis.org.uk/Diary/August, accessed 25 April 2017.

Smith, A., (1922), *Four Years on the Western Front*, London: Odhams Press.

Smith, A., (2000), *The Second Battlefield: women, modernism and the First World War*, Manchester: Manchester University Press.

Smith, H (Price E), ([1930] 1988), *Not So Quiet*, London: Virago.

Smith, L., ([1918] 2014), *Lingo of No Man's Land*, London: The British Library.

Southard, E., (1919), N. Fenton, and C. Mills, eds, *Shellshock and Other Neuropsychiatric Problems*, Boston: W. M. Leonard.

Special Constable Smith, ([1915] 2001), [sound dramatisation], (Regal Cat. No. 6842; CD41-003/2, *Oh! It's a Lovely War*, Vol. 2, CD41 Publishing Ltd.

Spencer, W., *War Letters 1914–1918; from a young British Officer at the Western Front during the First World War*, WarLetters.net, 2014.

Spicer, L. D., *Letters from France, 1915–1918*, London: Robert York, 1979.

Spires, C., *Diary of C. B. Spires*, http://www.bertspires.co.uk accessed 25 April 2017.

Stanley, F., *History of the 89th Brigade 1914–1918*, (1919), Liverpool: Daily Post.

Stanley, H., (2007), *Grandad's War*, Cromer: Poppyland Publishing.

Stanley, P., (2011), ' "He was black, he was a White man, and a dinkum Aussie": race and empire in revisiting the Anzac legend', in S. Das, ed., *Race, Empire and First World War Writing*, 213–230, Cambridge: Cambridge University Press.

Stevenson, D., ([2004] 2005), *1914–1918 The History of the First World War*, London: Penguin.

Stewart, H., (1916), *From Mons to Loos*, Edinburgh; London: W. Blackwood & Sons.

Strange, L., ([1933] 1935), *Recollections of an Airman – Diary*, London: John Hamilton.

Stumpf, R., (1967), trans. D. Horn, *War, Mutiny and Revolution in the German Navy*, New Brunswick: Rutgers University Press.

Sunny Subaltern, A, (1916), Toronto: McClelland, Goodchild & Stewart.

Swinton, E. B., ed., (1936–38), *Twenty Years After*, Vol. 3, London: Newnes.

Tarbot, J., (1928), *Jerry Tarbot, the Living Unknown Soldier*, New York: Tyler Publishing Co.

The Athenaeum, (1830–1921), London: J. Lection.

The Attack/The Estaminet, (*Memories of France –*), ([1920s] 2001), [sound dramatisation], England: 78 rpm disc, No. R517, Parlophone; CD41-001, *Oh! It's a Lovely War*, Vol. 1, CD41 Publishing Ltd, 2001.

The Board of Education, (1921), *The Teaching Of English In England*, London: Board of Education.

The Boot and Shoe Retailer and Leather Trades Gazette, (1914), London.

The Champion, (1922–1955), London, England.

The Duke of Cambridge's Own, (1915–1919), *Fall in*, London.

The Ghain Tuffieha Gazette, (1916–17), Ghain Tuffieha: Malta.

The Huns' Handbook, (1915), London: The Echo and Evening Chronicle.

The Ruhleben Camp Magazine, (1916–1917), Berlin: Ruhleben Camp.

The Strafer, (1915), Epsom.

Todman, D., *The Great War*, London: Hambledon, 2005.

Tomlinson, H. M., (1930), *All Our Yesterdays*, London: William Heinemann.

Tommy & Jack: their wit, fun and high spirits, (1916), 'W.S.', ed., London: National Egg Collection for the Wounded.

Trevelyan, G., (1919), *Scenes from Italy's War*, London: T. C. & E. C. Jack.

Treves, F., ed., (1916), *Made in the Trenches*, London: George Allen & Unwin.

Tytler, N. F., (1922), *With Lancashire Lads and Field Guns in France*, Manchester: John Heywood.

Van Emden, R., (2014), *Tommy's War*, London: Bloomsbury.

Van Emden, R. and S. Humphries, (2003), *All Quiet on the Home Front*, London: Headline.

Vansittart, P., see Masefield, J.

Vernède, R., (1917), *Letters To His Wife*, London: W. Collins, Sons & Co.

Vizetelly, F., (1917), *The Soldier's Service Dictionary of English and French Terms*, New York: Funk & Wagnalls Co.

Voigt, F. A., ([1920] 1929), *Combed Out*, London: Jonathan Cape.

Wadsworth, J., (2014), *Letters from the Trenches*, Barnsley: Pen & Sword Military.

Waites, B., (1987), *A Class Society at War*, Leamington Spa: Berg.

Walker, D., (1970), *With the Lost Generation*, Hull: A. Brown & Sons Ltd.

Walker, J., (1844), *A Critical Pronouncing Dictionary and Expositor of the English Language*, Edinburgh: Thomas Nelson & Sons.

Walker, J., (1854), *A Critical Pronouncing Dictionary and Expositor of the English Language*, London: Simms & M'Intyre.

Walker J. and C. Declercq, eds, (2016), *Languages and the First World War: communicating in a transnational war,* London: Palgrave Macmillan.

Walker, J., (2016), 'Wartime citations in Ernest Weekley's *An Etymological Dictionary of Modern English* (1921) and contemporary dictionaries', in C. Declercq and J. Walker, eds, *Languages and the First World War: representation and memory,* 214–36, London: Palgrave Macmillan.

Walker, J., (2016), 'Who owned war slang?', in L. Karvalics, ed., *Information History of the First World War,* 57–86, Paris: L'Harmattan.

Walter, T., 'War grave pilgrimage', (1993), in T. Reader and T. Walter, eds, *Pilgrimage in Popular Culture,* Basingstoke: Macmillan.

War Diary of the 1st Life Guards. First year, 1914–1915, England: British Army.

War-Time Tips for Soldiers and Civilians, (1915), London: C. A. Pearson.

Weekley, E., ([1921] 1967), *An Etymological Dictionary of Modern English,* New York: Dover Publications.

Weekley, E., (1926), *Words Ancient and Modern,* London: John Murray.

West, A., ([1919] 2014), *The Diary of a Dead Officer,* Llandogo, Monmouth: Old Stile Press.

What's the Dope? (1944), London; Bognor Regis: John Crowther.

Wheeler, H., (1918), *Daring Deeds of Merchant Seamen in the Great War,* London: G. G. Harrap & Co.

White Band, The, (1917), Officer Cadet Battalions, Crookham.

Whitworth, G., (1914), *The Child's ABC of the War,* London: George Allen & Unwin.

Williams, G., *Diary,* http://www.europeana1914-1918.eu/en/contributions/17242, accessed 25 April 2017.

Williamson, H., (1930), *The Patriot's Progress,* London: Geoffrey Bles.

Wilson, C., (Lord Moran), *Anatomy of Courage,* ([1945] 1987), London: Constable & Co.

Winter, J., (1988), *The Experience of World War I,* Oxford: Equinox.

Winter, J., ([1995] 1998), *Sites of Memory, Sites of Mourning,* Cambridge: Cambridge University Press.

Winter, J., and B. Baggett, (1996), *1914–18,* London: BBC Books.

Wood, W., (1916), *In the Line of Battle,* London: Chapman & Hall.

Wright, M., (2010), *Shattered Glory: the New Zealand experience at Gallipoli and the Western Front,* Auckland, N.Z.: Penguin.

Wyatt, H., ([1914] 1917), *Malice in Kulturland,* Richmond: The Car Illustrated.

Yerta, G., (1917), *Six Women and the Invasion,* London: Macmillan & Co.

Young, G., *From the Trenches,* (1914), London: T. Fisher Unwin.

Other Reading

Bagnold, E., (1920), *The Happy Foreigner,* London: William Heinemann.

Brittain, V., (1933), *Testament of Youth: an autobiographical study of the years 1900–1925,* London: Victor Gollancz.

Buttenhuis, P., ([1987] 1989), *The Great War of Words,* London: Batsford.

Cholmondeley, A., (Elizabeth von Arnim), (1917), *Christine*, London: Macmillan.

Cummings, E., (1922), *The Enormous Room*, New York: Boni & Liveright.

Doyle, P., (2008), *Tommy's War: British military memorabilia, 1914–1918*, Ramsbury: Crowood.

Doyle, P., and C. Foster, (2013), *Remembering Tommy*, Stroud: The History Press.

Grayzel, S., (2002), *Women and the First World War*, London; New York: Longman/Pearson Education.

King Albert's Book: a tribute to the Belgian King and the people from representative men and women throughout the world, (1914), London: Daily Telegraph.

Kraus, K., trans. A. Gode and S. Wright, ([1922] 1974), *The Last Days of Mankind*, New York: Frederick Ungar Publishing Co.

Kyle, G., ed., (1916), *Soldier Poets: songs of the fighting men*, London: Erskine Macdonald.

Macnaughtan, S., (1915), *A Woman's Diary of the War*, London: T. Nelson & Sons.

Sassoon, S., (1930), *Memoirs of an Infantry Officer*, London: Faber & Faber.

Smith, H., (1931), *Women of the Aftermath*, London: John Long.

Online Resources

British Newspaper Archive http://www.britishnewspaperarchive.co.uk

The Times Digital Archive http://gale.cengage.co.uk/times-digital-archive/times-digital-archive-17852006.aspx

The *Manchester Guardian* and *The Observer* https://www.theguardian.com/info/2012/jul/25/digital-archive-notice

Other websites

http://1914–1918.invisionzone.com/forums/index.php?showtopic=217500 accessed 12 September 2016

http://andc.anu.edu.au/australian-words/aif-slang/annotated-glossary accessed 6 February 2017

http://eco.canadiana.ca/view/oocihm.8_06748_4/1?r=0&s=1 accessed 17 October 2016

http://encyclopedia.1914–1918-online.net/article/censorship accessed 20 December 2016

http://encyclopedia.1914–1918-online.net/article/soldier_newspapers accessed 13 November 2016

http://encyclopedia.1914–1918-online.net/article/warfare_1914–1918_belgium accessed 5 February 2017

http://germanhistorydocs.ghi-dc.org/sub_document.cfm?document_id=755 accessed 17 October 2016

http://hansard.millbanksystems.com/commons/1916/oct/11/statement-by-prime-minister accessed 7 February 2017

http://hansard.millbanksystems.com/commons/1919/dec/17/imperial-war-graves-commission#S5CV0123P0_19191217_HOC_411 accessed 5 December 2016

http://hansard.millbanksystems.com/commons/1931/nov/23/defence-of-the-realm-act#S5CV0260P0_19311123_HOC_309 accessed 21 October 2016

http://hansard.millbanksystems.com/written_answers/1921/jun/23/defence-of-the-realm-act#S5CV0143P0_19210623_CWA_68 accessed 21 October 2016

http://heroletterswww1.blogspot.co.uk/2008/12/ymca-during-wwi-with-photos.html accessed 13 November 2016

http://research.gold.ac.uk/16713/1/Grayson%252c%20R.pdf accessed 2 April 2016

http://www.bbc.co.uk/iplayer/group/p01tbj6p accessed 7 February 2017

http://www.bbc.co.uk/news/magazine-29757988 accessed 20 December 2016

http://www.bertspires.co.uk accessed 14 December 2016

http://www.bobbrookes.co.uk/DiaryCH2.htm accessed 21 December 2016

http://www.bobbrookes.co.uk/DiaryCH2.htm accessed 10 October 2016

http://www.britishnewspaperarchive.co.uk/search/results/1916-01-01/1916-12-31?basicsearch=negro&somesearch=negro&exactsearch=false&sortorder=score&page=0 accessed 29 October 2016

http://www.britishnewspaperarchive.co.uk/search/results/1919-01-01/1919-12-31?basicsearch=blimey&somesearch=blimey&sortorder=score&exactsearch=false&page=2 accessed 2 November 2016

http://www.essexrecordofficeblog.co.uk/the-battle-babies-of-essex/ accessed 19 April 2016

http://blog.nationalarchives.gov.uk/blog/battle-babies/?utm_source=The%20National%20Archives&_utm_medium=email&utm_campaign=6724312_FWW%20update%20February&dm_i=MAN,404IG,AD27MM,EGQQE,1 accessed 19 April 2016

http://www.europeana1914–1918.eu/en/contributions/17242 accessed 7 October 2016

http://www.express.co.uk/news/world-war-1/489831/Charlie-May-s-War-Secret-diary-WWI-officer accessed 27 December 2016

http://www.iwm.org.uk/collections/item/object/17053 accessed 20 December 2016

http://www.klewis.org.uk/Diary/August accessed 12 December 2016

http://www.nancy.cc/2012/06/21/baby-girl-named-zeppelina/ accessed 8 September 2016

http://www.pbenyon.plus.com/Scapa_Diary/Jul_17.html accessed 12 October 2016

http://www.pollingerltd.com/bookshop/martin_body/2nd-devons-somme.pdf accessed 6 February 2017

http://www.pollingerltd.com/bookshop/martin_body/2nd-devons-somme.pdf accessed 20 March 2015

http://www.qsl.net/gm0fne/diaryt~1.htm accessed 14 December 2016

http://www.royalleicestershireregiment.org.uk/archive/journals/green-tiger-
   2015-spring-present/2015-autumn/592921 accessed 19 April 2016
http://www.thekivellfamily.co.nz/military_history/ralphs_diaries/transcribes/
   diary_five_p3.html accessed 14 December 2016
http://www.ww1hull.org.uk/index.php/hull-in-ww1/hull-pals-batallion accessed
   5 December 2016
http://www.wwvets.com/42ndDivision.html accessed 28 October 2016
https://archive.org/stream/defenceofrealmma00grearich/
   defenceofrealmma00grearich_djvu.txt accessed 12 September 2016
https://davinaatkin.wordpress.com/2014/08/29/28th-july-1914/ accessed
   12 December 2016
https://davinaatkin.wordpress.com/2014/08/29/28th-july-1914/ accessed
   6 February 2017
https://wordsinwartime.wordpress.com accessed 25 September 2016
https://wordsinwartime.wordpress.com accessed 26 November 2016
https://www.bl.uk/collection-items/impressions-airship-raids-over-london-scho
   olchildren#sthash.RHecNbj1.dpuf accessed 26 September 2016
https://www.theguardian.com/film/2015/dec/21/chitty-chitty-bang-bang-goes-
   another-ian-fleming-theory accessed 5 February 2017
https://www.theguardian.com/stage/2015/dec/18/chitty-chitty-bang-bangs-not-
   so-pretty-origins accessed 9 May 2017
https://www.theguardian.com/world/2016/aug/11/shakespeare-hut-london-
   first-world-war accessed 20 August 2016

INDEX

seen as degenerating 66–8
spoken by Belgians 31, 39, 242, 244
spoken by French 39
spoken by Germans 23, 41–2
enlisting, sexual pressure towards 231
entertainment 109, 117, 160, 196
'Ersatz' 41, 62, 299
escalation of weapons 131, 135
-ette 235
etymology
    contested 51–2, 54, 170, 288, 289, 291–2
    interest in 47, 49, 51–2, 54, 57, 163, 245, 288–96
evolution of terms 42, 44, 48, 49, 50, 52, 53, 65, 87, 91, 100, 163, 170, 183, 202, 207, 209, 210, 230, 232, 240, 242, 262, 297
executions 140–1
explaining slang 13, 51, 56, 127, 163, 210, 269–70, 292
'eye-wash' 60

familiar, as a theme in slang-naming 129
family relationships 16, 69, 70, 93, 198, 246–8
fatalism 87, 135
father, see Family relationships
fear, soldiers' experience of 6, 64, 78, 124, 140–2, 175, 194, 197, 208, 252, 258, 263
'fed up' 53, 60, 211, 256, 261, 264, 272, 289, 297
fellow-feeling with the enemy, see Compassion
Field Service Postcard 2, 17, 20–3, 28, 44, 75, 79, 149, 185, 282, 297
Flamenpolitik 14, 148
'flapper' 235, 237
Flemish, language 14, 15–16, 28, 32, 35–6, 55, 89, 98, 100, 157, 162
    English slang from 35–6
food and drink 55, 85, 92, 106, 205, 205 n.545, 211

bully-beef 63, 104, 177, 261
eggs 31, 43, 44, 134, 205
hamburgers 67
jam 63, 97, 106, 109, 205, 260, 299
rum 63, 140
tea 183, 213 n.2
football 117, 175, 180, 258–9, 283
foreigners, views of 176, 177, 262
forgetting 278–9
formal writing 254
formulas, in speech and writing 75, 79
France, ethnic tension within 157
Fraser and Gibbons (*Soldier and Sailor Words and Phrases*) 40, 48, 52, 61, 63, 66, 92, 95, 99, 120, 132, 141, 142, 158–9, 163, 169, 170, 175, 178, 189–90, 199, 201, 253, 269, 272, 286, 291, 292, 293, 297
    terms omitted by 168, 224
    terms viewed as journalese by 8, 62, 163, 209, 231, 264
fraternisation 23, 155, 155 n.81
fraud 226
French
    adoptions replacing English words 67, 299
    Anglophones' differing levels of competence in 176
    British soldiers' adaption of (Tommy French) 36, 41, 88–9, 166, 176, 180, 255
    French and English mixed, see code-switching
    French and English used in parallel 36, 37
    spoken by Anglophones 36, 37, 83, 86, 95, 100, 131, 166, 170, 175, 176, 179, 203, 255–6, 261, 269, 278
    terms adopted into English 67, 299
    terms adopted into German 173
    transcribed in English texts 178
    used as a lingua franca 28, 29, 37, 43, 45, 173

exploitation of 152–3, 161–2
and language 147–9, 162
martial races 151
palaeoanthropology 153
supposed characteristics of races
151, 155–6, 160
view of Europe as mixture of races
161
within Europe 153–62
racism 158–60
ranks (*see* temporary gentlemen) 104,
188, 237, 250, 251, 252, 255, 270,
293
'other ranks' 164, 249
'rank and file' 84, 166, 174, 182,
251
ratting, *see* hunting
reading 137
books 12, 61, 136, 144–5, 244, 245
for censorship 70, 71, 80, 107
correspondence 1, 5, 16, 74–5,
78–9, 143, 160, 238, 247, 288
French or Flemish 16, 98, 100
memorials 279
newspapers and magazines 4, 13,
19, 54, 72, 160, 161, 164, 177,
202, 205, 215–19, 226, 243, 262,
270, 285, 291, 292, 295
noise 124
official documents 85
phrasebooks 45, 111
trench journals 17, 26–7, 113, 119,
250
veterans' publications 271
Rees, Major A E 7, 98
refugees 28, 32, 36, 54–5, 222, 226, 242,
243, 252
reinforcing slang 53
rejection of enemy language 66, 67, 68
Remarque, Paul 133, 136, 282, 286
repetition of stories 45, 109 n.291
resentment 52, 104–5, 159, 160, 166,
228, 231, 268, 280, 290
'rest' 12, 56 n.55, 106, 111, 263
retaliation and revenge 86, 102, 130–1,
133, 244, 257

reticence 243, 283–4, 286
rhyming slang 36, 53, 57, 91, 94, 175,
264, 294
rhythm 19, 107, 119, 261
'*Rosalie*' 197, 201, 209, 264
ruins 25, 274
rumour 80, 95, 123, 152, 223, 239, 256,
267
Russian language 28, 29, 44, 149, 238,
291, 295
Russian army, 'steamroller' applied to
189
Russian, slang from 44

'sacred soil' 273–6, 275 n.70, 275 n.73
Salonika 28, 35, 43, 91, 104, 277, 279,
287, 298
sang-froid, *see* understatement
Sassoon, Siegfried 25, 83, 122, 136,
145, 176, 181, 286
satire 17, 21–3, 26, 32, 37, 91, 109, 176,
177, 227, 234
in trench journals 20, 36, 55–6, 62,
103–4
of German culture 207–8, 224–5
'sausages' 65, 123, 205
schoolboy French 29, 37
'*schweinhund*' 53
'scrap of paper' 179, 245
self-control 81, 121, 138, 282, 283,
284–5
sentimental 8, 121, 153, 262, 288
Serbia, name change from Servia 151,
156
sex 60, 72, 193–9, 244
shellshock 145, 196, 233, 251, 284–5,
285 n.145
shells, messages on 19
shells, *see* nicknames
Shibboleth 178
'shirkers' 227–8, 289
silence, veterans' about the war 280–7
'slackers' 228, 231
slang
abandoned post-war 272–3, 285,
287